Washington County, Maryland
MARRIAGES
AN INDEX: 1799-1860

Originally Published in Four Volumes by Traces

Compiled by
Dale Walton Morrow
and
Deborah Jensen Morrow

HERITAGE BOOKS
2008

HERITAGE BOOKS

AN IMPRINT OF HERITAGE BOOKS, INC.

Books, CDs, and more—Worldwide

For our listing of thousands of titles see our website
at
www.HeritageBooks.com

Published 2008 by
HERITAGE BOOKS, INC.
Publishing Division
100 Railroad Ave. #104
Westminster, Maryland 21157

Other books by the authors:
,Distribution of Estates Accounts, Washington County, Maryland, 1778-1835
Wills Of Washington County, 1776-1890
Wills Of Jefferson County, West Virginia, 1801-1899
Wills of Berkeley County, West Virginia 1744-1880

Other books by Dale Walton Morrow:
Washington County Maryland Cemetery Records: Volume 1 through 7

International Standard Book Numbers
Paperbound: 978-1-58549-162-9
Clothbound: 978-0-7884-7121-6

INTRODUCTION

Washington County, Maryland was formed in 1776; however, the earliest marriage indexes begin in 1799. The indexes and marriage records from 1776 to 1798, and the marriage records to the 1870s were destroyed by several courthouse fires. The index, 1799-1860, which is printed in four volumes, recorded the name of the groom, the name of the bride and the date of the license. The four volumes are I (A-E), II (F-K), III (L-R) and IV (S-Z). The marriages are in alphabetical order according to the surname of the male. We have combined these four volumes into one book with a complete index to the brides at the end of this book.

The following abbreviations for given names have been used throughout the book.

Names of males			
		Ph.	Philip, Phillip
		Pt.	Peter
Abr.	Abraham	Rich.	Richard
Al.	Alfred	Rob.	Robert
Alex.	Alexander	Sam.	Samuel
And.	Andrew	Sol.	Solomon
Arch.	Archibald	Tho.	Thomas
Bart.	Bartholomew	Val.	Valentine
Benj.	Benjamin	Wash.	Washington
Chas.	Charles	Wm.	William
Chn.	Christian		
Chr.	Christopher	**Names of Females**	
Dn.	Daniel		
Dv.	David	Am.	Amelia
Ed.	Edward	Barb.	Barbara
Eph.	Ephraim	Cath.	Catherine
Fred.	Frederick	Char.	Charlotte
Geo.	George	Chna.	Christiana
Hez.	Hezekiah, Hezekeah	Chra.	Christina
Hn.	Henry	Eliz.	Elizabeth
Ig.	Ignatius	Han.	Hannah, Hanna
Is.	Isaac	Har.	Harriet
Jc.	Jacob	Hen.	Henrietta
Jer.	Jeremiah	Is.	Isabel, Isabelle
Jm.	James	Isa.	Isabella
Jon.	Jonathan	Mag.	Magdalena
Jos.	Joseph	Mar.	Martha
Lau.	Laurence	Marg.	Margaret
Law.	Lawrence	Na.	Nancy
Leo.	Leonard	Reb.	Rebecca
Mat.	Mathew, Matthew	Ros.	Rosanna
Mich.	Michael	Roz.	Rozanna
Mt.	Martin	So.	Sophia
Nath.	Nathaniel	Sr.	Sarah, Sara
Nich.	Nicholas	Sus.	Susanna, Susannah,
Pat.	Patrick		Suzanna, Suzannah

1. ABEL (ABELL, ABLE, ABILL)
   Sam./Na. Flora 5/18/19
   Wm./Ann Faris 6/13/24
   Lewis V./Mary Burrell 4/17/33
2. ABTAINSELLER
   Hn./Polly Foster 9/23/06
3. ACKER
   Adam./Eliz. Easterday 11/28/48
4. ADAM (ADAMS, ADDAMS)
   And./Cath. Margura 4/24/02
   Abr./Cath. Snyder 5/30/03
   Jc./Mary Lane 8/25/04
   Nath./Reb. Long 5/1/04
   Jm./Marg. Smith 5/24/06
   Hn./Mary Knode 2/5/07
   Jm./Eliz. Farquhar 1/13/08
   John/Cath. Bence 5/10/11
   Elie/Am. Berry 6/22/11
   Wm./Sus. Reeder 7/13/15
   Ph./Barb. Fachler 6/29/16
   Jc./Sr. Barnhiser 6/14/19
   John/Mary Wentlinger 11/19/23
   John Alex./Mary Anna Ritchie 6/23/30
   Geo.M./Malinda M. Helphenstine
     6/4/31
   Adam/Susan Newcomer 1/5/33
   Jc./Eliz. Forry 3/9/36
   Pt. I./Eliz. Butler 3/18/41
   Amos/Cath. Ann Clarke 5/10/41
   Stephen/Mary Rinehart 12/6/45
   Hn./Mary.F. Middlekauff 12/18/46
   John/Eliz. Funk 10/31/48
   Geo. I./Annie Rowland 12/5/48
   Dn./Cath. Kneff 12/20/51
   Stephen/Isa. Miller 1/2/54
   Jc. R./Marg. Newcomer 1/2/54
5. ADLEY
   Chas./Mazey Lee 1/5/22
6. AIKENS
   Dv./Isa. Hansher 4/26/60
7. AINSWORTH (ANESWORTH)
   Hn. H./Mary Julius 3/13/28
   Tho./Char. Muller 12/30/28
   Rob./Eliz. Mullen 9/27/36
   John P./So. Curdy 6/16/37
   Benj./Sr. Marshall 5/31/39
8. AIRES (AIRS)
   John/Sr. Beltzhoover 8/14/00
   Jm./Eliz. Robey 8/21/16
   Geo./Cath. Heller 6/7/44
   Geo./Mary Bombarger 6/18/51
9. AITHER
   Geo./Cath. Wagoner 3/15/53
10. ALBAUGH
    John N./Lydia Deitrick 12/8/49
11. ALBERT (ALBERTS)
    John/Eliz. Winters 5/23/01
    John/Polly Miller 8/26/02

Jc./Barb. Wamb 7/25/03
Adam/Marg. Shrack 8/8/04
Wm./Priscilla Anderson 7/22/05
Geo./Sus. Keyser 4/21/06
Jc./Marg. McDaniel 12/15/06
Mt./Cath. Kline 6/15/11
Hn./Mary Kitzmiller 4/1/24
Tho./Han. Gross 1/15/27
John/Na. Hoover 3/22/27
Geo./Mary Ann Herr 11/24/28
Dv./Eliz. Taulhellum 4/25/31
Geo./Louisa Ann Powles 10/25/37
Geo./Louisa Oldwein 6/13/38
Jc./Mary Powles 9/28/43
Wm. H./Cath. E. Mumma 3/14/47
Ezra/Eliza Ann Ordner 11/27/50
Odelbert/So. Vas 5/6/53
Geo. M./Louisa Dillehunt 5/10/57
Rob. C./Ann R. Gray 10/19/59
Wm. H./Ann Maria Erisman 12/30/57
12. ALBURTIS
    Eph. G./Mary Swartz 12/21/42
    Wm./Ros. E. Foster 2/23/42
13. ALDER
    Marcus/Mary Page 9/20/24
14. ALEXANDER
    Arthur/Lidia Mondonall 2/26/03
    Val./Reb. Burgan 3/23/20
    Val./Eliz. Cross 8/30/24
    Rob./Rozanne Coffman 10/22/28
    John/Eliz. Marteny 10/3/43
    Wm./Eliz. Burke 1/2/51
    John E./M. Kate Reichard 2/23/57
15. ALLABAUGH
    Jc./Eliz. Robinson 8/26/19
16. ALLEN
    Arch./Heziah Boteler 8/28/07
    Rob./Mary Ensminger 7/24/12
    Jm./Char. Ansminger 4/13/35
    Quinby/Eliz. Swingley 3/4/41
17. ALLENDER
    John D./Na. Brown 5/26/07
    Tho./Eliz. Fore 11/3/09
    Wm./Sr. Hammett 12/23/09
    Wm. W./Mary Marker 12/11/21
18. ALLISON
    Sam./Mary Murphy 5/8/15
19. ALLSIP
    Jc./Sus. Norris 4/17/41
    Jos./Eliza Yowler 2/2/42
20. ALTER
    Geo./Cath. Hogmire 9/6/06
    Fred./Eliz. Lefler 3/7/11
    Sam./Mary Brewah 10/16/13
    Sam./Cath. Westenberger 12/22/28
    Jc./Ann Young 1/21/45
    Dv. H./Eliz. Angle 9/29/55
    Geo. W./Emily V. Wachtel 1/25/58

21. ALVEY
    Rich. H./Mary A.M. Wharton 10/18/55
22. AMBROSE
    John/Molly Mundabaugh 10/21/24
    Pt./Sus. Wilt 12/22/30
    Nelson/Wiley Darton 2/23/31
    Dn./Eveline Traverse 10/16/60
23. AMOS (AMESS)
    Jm./Sr. Swingley 8/17/09
    Jm./Ruth Ward 10/9/13
    Geo. B./Barb. E. Swingley 1/31/23
24. AMOY
    Wm./Marg. Fechtig 3/7/12
25. ANDERSON
    Sam./Eliz. Bratter 6/3/24
    Sam./Sr. Yontz 10/30/28
    Rob./Ann Eve Ensminger 3/24/31
    Wm./Alice M. Hupp 8/17/33
    Dv./Mary Speck 9/8/36
    John/Ellen Cain 2/27/38
    J.K./Har. B. Dall 12/11/44
    Jm. H./Eliz. Long 2/9/47
    Jm./Adalaide Dasher 8/6/49
    Chas. W./Elizth Feaster 7/10/50
    Wm./Mary L. Duckett 5/27/54
    Geo. W./Annie M. Winters 9/17/55
    Jos./Ann Priscilla Knepper 12/31/55
26. ANDREW (ANDREWS)
    Wm./Eliz. Hoober 11/3/04
    Chas./Sr. Drury 8/8/07
    Dn./Cath. Glassbrenner 8/15/32
    Wm./Na. Shrodes 8/15/35
    Hn./Mary Kiracofe 12/13/37
    Stephen W./Ann H. Troxell 11/28/46
27. ANDRICK
    Hn./Sr. Fow 4/27/42
28. ANGLE
    Dn./Sus. Fiery 2/7/22
    Harrison/Sr. Jane Byers 10/31/49
29. ANKENEY (ANKONY, ANLCENEY, ANKENY)
    Hn./Na. Kershner 8/17/05
    Hn. Jr./Cath. Miller 10/10/06
    Dv./Eliz. Miller 8/3/08
    Geo./Cath. Troup 3/19/25
    Dv./Eliz. Miller 9/23/30
    Sam./Eliz. Swingly 3/8/31
    John L./Ann Maria Newcomer 6/5/41
    Is./Ellen Jane Ditto 10/13/49
    Dv./Na. A. Clugston 5/9/54
    Calvin/Leah Matilda Shindel 1/8/57
30. ANSPERGER
    Hiram/Mary Ann Weast 3/18/36
31. ARDINGER
    Pt./Sr. Davis 11/30/08
    Chn./Han. Bowers 2/8/12
    Ph./Desia Davis 10/23/15
    John/Manah Smith 2/9/35

Chas./Jane Shook 12/31/36
Ph. D./Jane Edwards 9/24/44
Jm./Eliz. Graves 8/4/47
Benj./Susan Thompson 6/6/54
John/Susan Albert 11/10/57
Chas. H./Ann V. McDonald 2/1/59
Jm. C./Emma J. Nitzell 11/29/60
32. ARISS
    Wm./Reb. Neale 1/8/09
33. ARMSTRONG
    Jer./Sr. Langley 4/2/06
    Alex./Susan Hammond 2/22/32
    Francis/Marg. Grant 1/6/34
    Geo. W./Eliz. Fraley 8/9/42
    Leo./Cath. M. Mullen 11/25/58
34. ARMSWROTHY
    Tho./Sally Nowel 1/30/00
35. ARNDT
    Jc./Ann Maria Kershner 11/23/36
36. ARNOLD
    Jc./Cath. Hoffman 4/5/14
    Jos./Mary Ann Kretzer 3/5/60
37. ARNSBERGER (ARNSPARGER, ARMSBURGER, ANST-
    BERGER, ARNSPERGER)
    Fred./Mary Allabaugh 2/3/08
    Mich./Philbena Poffenbarger 12/12/14
    Hiram/Mary Ann Weast 3/18/36
    Harrison/Eliza Rowland 2/3/40
38. ARTEL
    Geo./Cath. Beichel 8/31/20
39. ARTIS
    Jm./Mary Alabaugh 9/5/18
40. ARTZ (ARTS)
    Hn./Cath. Lowman 4/1/01
    Hn./Na. James 2/23/11
    Dv./Cath. Hammer 3/28/16
    Pt./Eliz. Heartland 11/26/16
    Ph./Har. Lanes 8/24/19
    Dv./Eliz. Aubert 4/11/33
    Wm./Reb. Reynolds 2/13/33
    Pt./Ketturah Cross 6/5/39
    Watkins/Sr. Curtis 7/29/46
    Hn./Eliz. Crisman 2/20/47
    Cornelius/Cath. Young 11/15/48
    Smith/Lydia Long 1/23/49
    Jos./Mar. Show 3/19/50
    Sam./Marg. C. Nigh 4/24/50
    Ph. Vinton/Laura L. Downs 9/20/59
41. ASH
    John/Mary Firey 5/24/00
    John/Matilda Moudy 5/9/33
42. ASHAMON
    Tho./Sr. Dovenbarger 3/25/43
43. ASHBAUGH
    Nimrod/Helen Logan 3/25/40
44. ASHBROOK
    John/Mary Wagoner 6/14/00
45. ASHTON
    Wm./Cath. Westenberger 3/26/31

46. ASKINE
Dn./Na. Zimmerman 12/18/27
47. ASKITTLE
Jm./Eliz. Nesbit 4/6/12
48. ATCHINSON
Wm. Hanson/Susan R. Newman 5/16/21
Wm. H./Eliz. Stonebraker 2/5/52
49. ATHIMON
John/Cath. Warble 2/9/26
50. AUGHINBAUGH
Jm./Cath. Julius 3/29/32
Dv. C./Mary Jane Winters 6/1/53
Dv. C./Mary E. Updegraff 5/7/57
51. AUGUSTINE
Abr./Mary Cloper 9/13/99
Geo./Cath. Clopper 8/6/01
52. AULT (AULD)
Conrad/Eliz. Ann Boswell 9/12/46
Adam/Cath. Bagent 9/12/48
53. AULTER
Jc./Eliza Tice 3/29/28
54. AURIS
Adam/Polly Neal 6/3/09
55. AUSHERMAN
Lawson/Mary Huffmaster 3/6/58
56. AUSHMAN
Hn./Eliz. Malone 1/16/13
57. AUSTIN (AUSTON)
Tho./Mary Shirley 12/13/16
Is./Lydia Keyser 9/14/21
Jos. B./Ann Nourse 4/17/28
Tho./Lavina Lancaster 1/21/33
Alex. P./Susan E. Moffitt 2/28/33
58. AVEY
Jos./Eliz. Hershey 12/24/05
Jc./Sus. Snavely 6/8/07
Chn./Sus. Knode 2/25/09
John/Francy Hershey 6/24/09
And./Eliz. Mondebaugh 4/10/13
Jc./Cath. Palmer 1/5/15
Sam./Eliz. Shook 4/3/16
Chn./Mary Ann Hammond 11/11/16
Dv./Cath. Shupe 10/19/18
Mich./Lydia Moyers 6/8/20
Nath./Ros. Whip 4/16/21
Sam./Sr. Funk 3/11/22
Wm./Na. Glass 11/8/25
Abr./Sr. Powell 10/10/26
Sol./Mary Ann Montabaugh 11/29/31
Geo./Na. Wheeler 4/9/39
Mich./Eliz. Wolf 11/6/39
John W./Eliz. Wilson 12/20/41
Sam. W./Cath. Ecker 11/28/48
Jos./Mary C. Edmonds 3/4/50
Jm./Hen. Meredith 5/21/52
Mt. H./Sr. E. Downs 9/17/57
Jc./Eliz. Marker 2/17/60

59. AVIS
John Jr./Emmagen D. Little 5/15/41
Wm./Ann R. Deaver 6/15/41
60. AXE
Wm./Christiane Keesacre 9/12/03
61. AYERS (AYEARS)
Geo./Mary Tanehill 5/23/18
Jm./Mary Knepper 9/2/36
62. BACHTELL (BAIGHTELL, BEADTCHTEL,
BACHTELE, BAECHTEL)
Jc./Mary Beard 1/26/07
Mt./Eve Springer 3/28/08
Dv./Sus. Keyser 6/13/12
Sam./Eliz. Leckrone 8/5/19
Is. Jr./Sus. Helser 5/8/21
Is. Jr./Har. Snyder 7/17/22
Dn./Betsy Misener 2/7/29
And./Sr. Steffy 11/5/32
Mt./Eliz. Coffman 8/3/33
Geo./Barb. Steffey 8/9/34
Hn./Susan Rynold 4/1/35
John B./Mrs. Hoover 8/26/37
Simon/Mary Middlekauff 1/2/39
Aaron/Eliz. Newfen 12/28/41
Sam. A./Anna Hammaker 1/19/41
Geo. B./Marg. Eliz. Bowers 2/14/44
Dn./Louisa Renner 8/1/46
M.H./Susan Deibert 9/3/51
63. BACUM
Mathias/Eliz. Koon 10/27/10
64. BADEN
John W./Ann C. Mackenheimer 2/11/56
65. BADGER
Dn. C./Mary Coon 5/2/33
Dn. C./Eliz. Huffmaster 9/10/40
66. BAER (BARE, BEAR, BAIR)
John/Na. McCormick 8/7/99
Sam./Cath. Lantz 10/17/15
Pt./Na. Hoffman 11/5/18
Mich./Eliz. Stahl 5/2/21
Is./Ros. Rowland 4/9/22
Geo./Hen. Cox 10/4/25
Geo./Eliz. C. Todd 3/23/26
Is./Anne Donoho 4/20/29
Jc./Sr. Funk 1/17/37
John/Eliz. Maugons 2/11/36
John/Marg. Ann Gelwix 2/27/41
Chn./Cath. Smith 1/1/45
Is./Eliz. Leary 12/31/47
John M./Eliz. Bear 1/1/55
67. BAGFORD
Jm. W.C./Cassandra Barnett 7/21/15
68. BAIGDOLL
Jos./Sr. Crower 5/20/15
69. BAILEY
Sam./Mary M. McDowell 9/2/34

3

70. BAKER
Abr./Mary Barton 4/10/02
Pt./Ros. Otman 3/6/04
Nich./Marg. Webb 2/21/05
Corbas/Eliz. B. Hesselstine 1/27/06
Pt./Cath. Thomas 5/26/06
John/Marg. Shaffner 8/17/07
Alex./Mary Webb 3/1/08
Elias/Na. Zuck 9/8/08
John/Cath. Metz 9/30/09
Pt./Molly Snively 8/14/10
Rich./Ann Webb 7/11/11
Ph./Polly Thomas 3/29/14
Jc./Mary Steel 9/15/17
Pt./Mary Long 11/15/17
John/Mary Sprecher 12/27/19
Jc./Jane Grimes 12/27/24
Nathan C./Mary Ann Roberts 8/2/25
Sam./Mary Leighter 1/16/26
Sam./Eliz. Martin 3/8/26
Maurice/Eliz. Fayman 2/25/30
Geo. S./Cath. Heagle 3/31/31
Jos./Eliz. Yontz 4/16/31
Ezra/Cath. Lyon (Line) 2/24/35
Otho/Susan Stonebraker 9/16/35
Nich./Cath. Mansfield 1/20/38
Sam./Lavenia Thomas 1/13/41
Wm./Lydia Welty 9/17/42
Josiah/Am. E. Knode 1/9/43
Nich. F./Ann Mary Grosh 3/13/43
Hn./Cath. Kolby 12/26/46
Dv./Lydia Sitzler 2/6/47
Jm. H.P./Eliz. Zentmyer 9/26/47
Jc./Julia Ann Hill 11/11/51
Sam./Reb. Crum 7/24/51
I.L.W./Laura Hughes 5/17/53
John/Mary E. Martin 8/2/60
Wm./Eliz. Barlup 12/25/60
71. BALCH
Stephen/Aletha M. Botler 5/14/55
72. BALDWIN
Seth/Cath. Medcalf 7/20/33
73. BALES
Al./Na. Ann Ridenour 3/30/36
74. BALL
Al./Matilda Van Horn 9/5/23
75. BALLARD
Horathio/Sr. Conner 5/17/20
76. BALT
Conrad/Jeluma Mullen 11/30/52
77. BALTHIS
Leo./Am. Grove 5/11/28
78. BALTZ
John/Eliz. Schipper 11/20/50
79. BANDLE
Mich. H./Virginia M. Lushbaugh 10/9/52
80. BANICKDOUL
Hn./Na. Greamer (Gromer) 4/14/04

81. BANKS
Sam./Mary Piper 1/11/02
John/Ann Dillon 10/2/03
And./Barb. Sager 12/30/35
Jesse/Har. Miller 12/22/40
82. BANNON
Eugene/Eliz. Rice 8/15/41
83. BARBER
Allen/Polly Shaw 5/6/11
Ig./Pricilla Row 4/1/15
Rezin/Har. Goldsberry 4/27/16
Ig./Eliz. Duffield 3/15/22
John H./Ellen N. Aniba 1/2/51
Mat. S./Eliz. A. Luchbaugh 3/27/51
Al. F./Josephine A. Oden 11/4/56
Ig./Na. Loudenslager 12/5/57
Geo./Mary Fate 10/7/58
John H./Ann Am. Stouffer 11/25/58
Josias/Na. C. Poffinberger 4/5/60
84. BARGDOLL
Jos./Susan Steffey 10/25/36
Geo./Eliz. Protzman 11/3/38
85. BARGER
Benj./Ann Huffner 6/26/15
Jc./Reb. Jones 7/27/27
John C./Cath. T. Bush 1/12/35
Wm./Sr. Ellen Johnson 2/9/48
86. BARGES
And./Ann Maria Dagenhart 12/4/46
87. BARINGER (BARRINGER)
John/Eliz. Mittoch 10/21/06
John/Eliz. Williams 5/10/42
88. BARKDALE
John/Jean Hable 3/21/07
89. BARKDOLL (BARACKDOLL)
Pt./Mary Mysleman 8/10/99
Jc./Sus. Musselman 4/11/00
Pt./Susan Shank 3/8/41
90. BARKER
Aaron/Isa. I.A. Poe 6/16/13
Jm./Sr. Beerbower 8/20/36
91. BARKMAN (BARCKMAN)
Pt./Eliz. Kepler 8/3/12
Hn./Marg. Biterbenner 3/28/18
Dv./Eliz. Buck 11/19/24
John/Eliz. Lambright 1/15/25
Dv./Reb. Guyton 2/10/27
Wm./Julian E. Hawken 10/11/41
Dv./Mary Malinda Kline 5/4/50
Wm./Cath. Bomberger 6/29/52
Dv./Mary Ann Garner 9/14/53
92. BARKS
Jos./Eliz. Avey 11/29/14
John/Marg. Hovermaile 5/11/16
93. BARNES (BARNS)
John/Amay Tawney 5/12/06
Ezra/Ann Davis 4/24/21
Jm./Eliza Shuwalter 6/15/31

4

93. BARNES (BARNS) (Continued)
Amos/Cath. Mullen 12/24/34
Mich./Marg. Kreglow 1/28/48
Eden H./Cath. L. Beard 10/10/59
Thornton G./Mary Cath. Ripple 11/17/60
94. BARNETT
Hn./Cath. McLaughlin 4/28/01
Jc. Jr./Eliz. Miller 2/27/09
Dv./Ann Snively 6/26/15
John/Am. Moudy 3/21/27
Jc./Ros. Mish 1/26/41
Hn. S./Cath. E. Taney 10/9/45
Dv./M.E. Johnson 5/11/50
Wash./Mary Jane Crow 10/16/54
Dv./Eliz. R.V. Beck 9/6/60
Theophillis/Sr. Jane Murry 6/4/60
95. BARNHART
Pt./Barb. Metz 12/26/00
Jc. H./Cath. Newcomer 5/1/41
Jc./Ann Maria Albert 8/26/56
96. BARNHISER (BARNHYSER, BARNHEISEL)
John/Mary Cohill 4/12/02
Mt./Sr. McDonald 12/30/09
John/Sus. Brown 8/14/28
John/Eliz. Fouts 9/29/35
97. BARR
Dv./Sus. Ridenour 10/2/05
Chr./Barb. Toby 4/13/09
Jc./Mary Miller 5/21/11
John/Betsy Rohrer 1/19/11
Benj./Mary Tutwiler 3/7/16
Chn./Sus. Bachtel 6/3/16
John/Na. Winders 3/8/25
John/Marg. Showman 2/8/26
Jc./Eliz. Kershner 9/7/31
John W./Eliz. Snyder 3/7/33
Jc./Na. Keller 2/2/36
Sam./Sus. Shockey 6/10/41
Jc. H./Susan Reichard 12/18/43
Dv. John/Marg. Emily Ringer 10/14/45
Al./Adaline Protzman 3/9/47
John W./Eliz. Faulders 1/8/52
Dn./Cath. Foster 4/28/53
Geo. A./Mary Areheart 11/23/55
98. BARRETT
Jm. I./Mary Ann O'Donnell 8/17/39
Hn./Marg. Hahn 11/1/51
99. BARRICK
Wm./Mar. E. Hesley (Herlsoy) 7/17/60
100. BARRIER
Geo./Sus. Heavner 10/13/01
101. BARROW (BARROWS)
Jer./Providence Whitekennick
(Withenneck) 12/11/10
102. BARRY (BERRY, BEARRY)
Ed./Cath. Achle 12/20/04
Hn./Phebe Maguire 5/9/10
Wm./Susan Winders 3/16/23

Walter Z./Mary R. Schnebly 5/15/32
John A./Eliz. Blecker 12/6/45
Geo./Ann Maria Suter 12/23/47
Jm. H./Am. Ann Avey 10/3/48
Wash. B./Adelaid H. Fitzhugh 11/21/48
Milton A./Har. Rohrback 2/1/54
Alonzo/Virginia Williams 11/10/58
John/Mary Collins 9/25/60
103. BARTGISS
Titus V./Mary Jane Hedges 11/24/53
104. BARTLESON
Cephas/Marg. Kreps 12/9/30
Hn./Na. Forsyth 6/14/38
105. BARTLETT (BARTLET)
Rich./Mary Newell 2/24/07
Rich./Mary McMechen 2/15/12
John/Eleanor Felker 4/12/17
106. BARTMESS
Jc./So. Rizer 11/14/16
107. BARTON
John/Barb. Stoker 4/28/04
Tho./Eliz. Williams 11/26/05
Stephen/Sus. Charlton 6/14/06
Lloyd H./Frances Bean 3/28/15
Benj. B./Eliz. Miles 11/7/48
108. BASEHORE
Pt./Eliz. Rohrer 6/1/40
109. BASIL
Rich./Mar. Heskett 6/1/11
110. BASLER
Catlip/Mary Sutton 1/30/08
111. BASON
Jc. Sr./Eliz. Morrison 8/16/54
112. BASSETT
Geo./Eliz. Ely 10/6/53
113. BAST
Cornelius/Marg. Hughes 3/22/48
114. BATEMAN
Nath./Cath. Protzman 9/35/15
Arch./Maria Kelly 2/10/20
Wm./Sr. Davis 7/19/25
115. BATT
John/Han. Mangina 11/3/20
Conrad/Salome Mullen 12/23/57
116. BATTORF
And./Polly Heller 12/26/04
117. BAUGH
Geo./Mary Wolgamott 4/7/40
118. BAUGHER
Dn./Eliz. Swope 9/10/30
119. BAUGHMAN
Lewis/Mary Eliz. Schleigh 1/3/46
120. BAUMGART
Caspar/Mary Renner 8/5/45
121. BAUMGARTNER (BAUMGARDNER)
John/Char. Wilks 10/5/26

5

122. BAYER (BAYERS)
Geo./Sus. Kaege 3/1/03
Hn./Mary Steffey 6/4/32
123. BEA
Conrad/Margaretta Crop 3/23/39
124. BEABER
Benj./Har. Kiger 7/27/33
125. BEACHLEY
John/Cath. Linebaugh 9/9/24
126. BEACKLY (BEAKLY, BEAKLEY)
Jonas/Ros. Smith 9/13/43
Hn./Eliz. Ceavier 4/2/29
127. BEAL (BEALE, BEALL)
Fred./Mary Emmerick 5/20/01
Ed./Eliz. Hines 6/22/13
Geo. Ross/Ellen Schnebly 10/8/29
Josephus/Mehetable Gregory 11/15/38
128. BEALER
Jc./Eliz. Miller 7/5/03
129. BEALTUS
Hn. E./Josephine I. Sterrott 1/9/38
130. BEAM (BEAMS)
Dv./Sally Garman 3/29/17
Wm./Anna Morrison 8/5/28
131. BEAMER
Benj./Eliz. Carrel 11/3/06
Hn./Eliz. Shank 2/16/40
132. BEAN
Barton/Barb. Tarlton 10/25/03
Hugh/Ally Howell 12/22/08
Chas./Lucretia Tarlton 8/8/18
Jc./Cath. Ringer 11/11/22
Benj./Minerva Ressley 11/12/37
John/Bridget Gallagher 7/8/41
133. BEARD
Val./Sus. Rineberger 6/19/99
John/Mary Russell 12/27/02
Ph./Eliz. Keyser 12/4/02
Geo./Motlina Moats 11/17/03
Jc./Marg. Bruner 4/19/04
Nich./Magdalena Fink 6/9/04
Geo./Cath. Boyer 6/28/05
John/Sally Harry 9/6/10
Nich./Peggy Beard 9/2/11
Jc./Cath. Foy 12/21/13
Geo./Sarah Gehr 9/4/17
Wm./Cath. Fiery 10/11/17
Adam/Sus. Laverknecht 8/23/20
Dv./Chra. Slice 5/11/22
John/Sus. Sager 12/10/25
Jos./Darcus Raynes 12/13/25
Mich./Eliza Taylor 1/4/25
John Geo./Ann M. Lane 3/13/26
Nich./Eliz. Repp 3/20/30
Nich./Mary Lyday 3/1/31
Sam./So. Sager 12/24/31
Jc./Susan Knode 3/27/32

Wm./Mary Ann Brewer 2/11/32
Geo./Susan Scarberry 7/16/34
And./Sus. Green 3/17/35
John/Susan Sesiar 3/9/36
Dn./Eliz. Colliflower 1/25/37
Louis/Ann E. Kidwell 3/11/37
Mich./Eliza Strause 3/26/38
Jc./Mary E. Byers 4/2/45
Dn. G./Lydia Kessinger 10/24/46
Hiram J./Reb. E. O'Neal 5/11/47
Wm. Hn./Susan Cath. Byers 9/7/48
And. J./Jane McKinney 2/18/51
Dn. G./Isa. S. Harbaugh 1/26/57
Wm. H./Susan Rowland 1/7/57
Benj. F./Han. C. Cromer 8/7/58
Sol./Sr. R. Loudenslager 12/17/58
Oliver J./Julia Ann Houser 1/18/59
Hn. S./Han. E. Heck 9/4/60
Mt. L./Mary E. Feidt 11/22/60
134. BEARSEY
Rich./Eliz. Lowman 1/14/47
135. BEARSHEARS
Tho. H./Mary Ann Keedy 7/11/51
136. BEATTY
Wm. A./Eliz. Miller 4/26/08
Elie/Eliz. C. Derry 12/12/09
Joshua/Marg. Stewart 8/19/11
Sam./Peggy Craft 3/24/14
Wm./Lucy Ann Crown 5/15/18
John/Sr. Mix 1/31/27
Jm./Ann Muir 10/9/28
Ed. W./Maria A. Williams 2/18/34
Elie/Mary D. Yarnall 9/7/42
Lewis S./Mary Ann Snyder 11/26/56
137. BEAVER
John/Ros. Clopper 3/13/51
138. BECK (BECKES, BECKS)
Arthur/Mary Carter 2/22/12
John/Eliz. Kinkle 4/10/27
Geo. H./Mary Ann Householder 9/21/29
Mich./Eliz. Ripley 8/14/33
John/Anna Shoop 3/29/34
Law./Susan Jones 4/15/41
Wm./Eliza Jane Neuman 3/2/48
Wm./Hen. Heffner 6/11/50
John/Eliz. Shafer 11/7/54
Benj. F./So. R. Jones 2/16/55
Ph./Susan Winters 8/25/31
139. BECKENBAUGH
Geo./Mar. V. Leggett 11/28/27
140. BECKETT
Humphrey/Rachel Tyler 9/19/06
141. BECKLY (BECKLEY)
John/Na. Morris 5/20/00
Hn./Na. Bailey 3/15/19
Hn. Jr./Mary Hogmire 3/2/19
John/Na. Boyers 9/1/24

6

141. BECKLY (BECKLEY) (Continued)
Hn./Ann Marie Neff 7/21/27
Sam./Marg. McCoy 5/16/32
Dv./Marg. A. Watkins 2/23/53
John/Emily Louisa Byers 10/24/57
142. BEECHER
Wm./Eliz. Herr 5/12/10
Wm. W./Marie Guthrie 7/26/28
143. BEELER
Jc./Eliz. Shupe 2/14/22
Dv./So. Stonebraker 12/26/27
Sam./Amanda Kalb 7/30/31
Sam./Eliz. Huffer 2/16/33
Dv./Matilda Huffer 5/24/39
144. BEEMER
Geo./Alsenah D. Doudle 4/14/15
145. BEERS
John/Mary O'Brian 5/8/40
146. BEGOLE
Tho./Ann Bowles 11/21/03
Upton/Eliz. Mullin 6/27/07
147. BEHONG
Jc./Ann Cochran 8/2/19 (cross-ref-
erenced as Jacob B. Mong)
148. BELCH
Jm./Sus. Simkins 6/29/08
149. BELL
Pt./Julian Leiter 5/24/17
Wm. D./Susan Harry 11/17/18
John/Cath. Kephart 9/21/19
Dv./Mary Varner 2/26/20
Dv./Eliz. Gearhart 2/27/27
Lancelot/Susan M. Gearhart 11/1/32
Pt./So. McNamee 3/5/34
Dn./Cath. Lyday 2/7/38
Dv./Hen. Naff 3/29/39
Jonas/Cath. Mickley 2/5/39
Lancelot/Eliz. Reitzell 7/31/39
Dn./Mary Mickley 2/3/41
Sam./Eliz. Smith 2/8/43
Jc. E./Na. Hanna 11/29/44
Upton/Mary Ann Bell 10/24/45
Lewis/Ruth S.A. Boteler 2/17/46
Hn./Am. E. Boteler No Date
150. BELLMAN
Hn./Hen. Hyser 9/28/43
151. BELTY
Jos. W./Ruth S. Faulkwell 2/26/49
152. BELTZ
John U./Mary E. South 5/19/47
153. BELTZER
Jc./Mary Barber 1/6/35
154. BELTZHOOVER
Geo./Cath. Golb 12/10/99
155. BENDER
Wm./Sr. Hamilton 2/11/17
Wm./Eliz. Siderstick 9/6/24
Sam./Mary Effinger 9/12/26
Jc./Ros. Domer 8/22/28

John/Barb. Slicer 6/8/30
Sam./Eliz. Domer 9/22/34
John/Mrs. Susan McGoferty 11/20/37
Hn./Reb. Doyle 9/30/47
Dv./Mar. Ann Myers 3/4/56
Hn. D./Lucinda A. Thomas 4/1/56
156. BENFERD
Hn./Sr. Ann Wilcox 6/1/13
157. BENN
Tho./Sally Palmer 3/31/35
158. BENNER
Hn./Eliz. Snowman 2/17/10
John/Eliz. Bowers 12/13/11
Jc./Cath. Raum 12/21/18
Chn./Mary Osborne 11/12/23
Pt./So. Stoner 3/24/26
Jc. C./Har. Athey 10/10/29
John/Har. Koontz 6/8/30
Sam./Mary Reel 5/27/41
Dn./Mary Rye 2/7/48
John/Susan Shay 8/19/48
Jos./Reb. Hine 11/25/48
Sam./Ann Cath. Wilhelm 3/22/53
John/Eliz. Porter 12/23/54
Wm./Eliz. Huyett 12/21/57
Franklin/Am. C. Hime 12/21/59
159. BENNETT
Jm./Eliz. Fisher 7/30/11
Tho./Malinda Crow 8/30/11
John/Barb. Stoner 7/7/21
Amos Dorsey/Louisa Sheckler 9/26/55
J.D./Annie A. Bowman 2/18/58
160. BENTLEY
Geo./Cath. Hoover 7/30/04
161. BENTZ (BENCE)
John/Eliz. Young 2/24/12
Jc./Eliz. Kailer 2/23/14
Sam./Maria Stonebraker 5/24/26
Hn./Chna. Kessinger 12/26/31
162. BERDAN
Chas./Mary W. Meredith 10/7/35
163. BERGESSER
Geo./Eliz. Everhart 12/26/55
164. BERGSHASTER
Adam/Eliz. Bovey 3/25/14
165. BESOR (BESORE, BASORE)
Hn./Reb. Ann Brown 8/9/28
Jer. S./Ann E. Shank 2/5/42
Jos. H./Ann Maria Eyler 9/23/44
166. BESLER
Jos./Mary Ann Grimes 10/22/31
167. BESSY
Ichabod/Mar. Ann Delauney 1/18/49
168. BEST (BESTE)
John/Eliz. Ault 4/2/27
Hn. W./Cath. Lynch 5/3/44
Noah/Ann Eliz. Pierce 7/24/47
John/Rachel Noose 5/9/48

7

169. BESTARD
Wm./Eliz. Warth 12/18/43
170. BETERBRENNER (BITERBENNER,BETEBENNER)
Hn./Cath. Heffley 4/13/05
Sam./Reb. A. Strause 9/27/31
Ezra/Mary E. McKensey 8/13/52
Geo./Lydia Everhand 5/15/32
171. BETTS (BETZ)
Dv./Eliz. Messilli 11/2/14
Jc./Na. Knodle 3/6/15
Fred./Barb. Dagenhart 11/4/16
John/Eliz. Bombarger 6/4/17
Chn./Mar. Williams 1/8/22
Hn./Reb. Leasure 2/6/23
Wm./Mary Bell 11/5/41
Dn. S./Ann Shultz 1/22/44
Hn./Mary Ellen Nunemaker 12/23/47
Luther D./Cath. Yingling 3/24/49
John H./Ann Reb. Hulst 3/27/51
Oliver/Sr. Thomas 9/24/51
172. BETTY
Sam./Mehaly Garnett 2/28/43
173. BEVANS (BIVANS, BEVINS)
Tho./Anna Parsons 12/7/11
Walter/Mary Ann Summers 3/28/17
Jm. H./Eveline L. Bevans 10/24/43
Jos. H./Mary Higgens 1/1/44
Tho./Eliz. Sheriff 2/3/51
174. BIANDS
John/Marg. Boward 1/6/45
175. BIAYS
Hn./So. G. Sharpless 11/15/60
176. BICKLY (BICKLEY)
Jc./Sus. Henneberger 6/7/11
177. BICKNELL
Esair/Sus. Rogers 6/6/07
178. BICSH
Dv./Mary Sholl 4/24/17
179. BIEDAMON
Israel/Angeline Hammond 3/31/40
180. BIEGLER
Wm./Na. Wilson 8/31/11
Geo./Sus. Yost 8/11/12
181. BIEHL
Geo. F./Eliz. Mayer 12/29/46
182. BIERS
John/Sr. Cushwa 2/25/08
183. BIERSHING
Hn./Rachel Steel 9/25/17
Wm./Eliz. Eversole 4/8/19
John Wm./Mary Clopper 1/29/25
Wm./Mary Funk 9/28/41
Geo. W./Sr. Ann Feigley 1/8/46
Wm./Eliz. D. Davis 10/17/46
184. BIGAM (BIGGAM)
Jos./Mary Ann Kershner 5/31/30

185. BIGGERSTAFF
And./Sr. M. Clayton 6/23/18
186. BIGGS
Jm./Mary Gilliland 10/24/16
Augustus A./Marg. Wagoner 6/25/46
187. BIGHAM
Jos./Eliz. Empich 2/21/05
188. BIKLY
Chas. A./Ann Eliz. Houser 12/23/56
189. BILLMYER (BILLMIER, BILLMAR, BILLMIRE)
Gabriel/Peggy Toby 6/14/04
John/Cath. Kreps 4/13/06
Conrod/Mary Martin 2/11/30
Wm. G./Mary Young 10/5/42
Geo./Julia Clark 2/6/45
190. BINKLEY (BINKLY)
Ph./Jane Locke 9/24/06
Jc. Jr./Eliz. Miller 4/4/07
Jon./Esther Simmerman 2/23/18
Jon./Eliz. Kline 10/3/20
Dn./Cath. Weaver 12/26/45
Pt./Eveline Brumbaugh 10/28/46
Wm. H./Mary Jane Tice 2/3/49
John/Cath. Straley 4/26/58
191. BIRD
Tho./Mary Moudy 2/4/32
Isaiah/Han. Myers 6/28/56
192. BIRELY
Ezra/Marg. R. Thompson 2/14/48
193. BISER
Tho./Rosini Betts 6/24/44
194. BISHOP
Elijah/Ann Hoye 5/20/28
195. BITTINGER
Geo. W./Eliz. Melchor 11/26/53
196. BLACK
Sam./Mary West 3/9/18
Geo. W./Cath. Graeff 4/12/25
Sam./Mary Ellen Elifritz 8/8/60
197. BLACKER
John/Barb. Furray 4/6/04
Sam./ Peggy Carver 5/3/11
198. BLACKFORD
Corbin/Jane Jackson 3/30/22
Franklin/Eliz. R. Miller 10/18/36
Wm. I./Ann C. Engle 2/19/49
Wm. M./Fanie M. Robinson 4/12/53
199. BLACKMAN (BLACKMON)
Caleb/Sr. Moore 8/18/03
200. BLACKMEAR
Geo./Eliz. Williams 5/18/08
201. BLACKMORE
Wm./Sr. Ford 7/31/02
202. BLACKSTONE
Jm./Chna. Doyle 1/23/00

8

203. BLACKWELL
Walter/Sr. Ann Brosius 8/11/20
Tho./Sr. Hall 4/19/36
Wm./Isora M. Byers 3/29/54
Geo./Kate King 6/11/56
204. BLAIR
Jesse/Na. Snyder 7/29/28
John/Sr. Richard 12/12/36
Ph. D./Mary E. Blair 1/27/43
205. BLAKE
Benj./Eliz. Aldridge 5/12/02
Simon/Jane Wade 5/28/16
Beizdine/Mazy Simkins 12/14/18
Tho./Ann Morrison 11/29/28
John/Cath. Hammet 3/24/29
206. BLAKENEY
John W./Marion E. Gerrard 6/7/52
207. BLAKLEY
Geo. B./Susan Montgomery 7/16/45
208. BLAND
Hn./Patty Howard 12/31/11
209. BLECHER
Sam./Susan Brantner 7/10/40
Jc./Barb. Shriver 3/11/42
Wm./Eliz. Welty 4/17/44
210. BLECKER
Jc./Tracy Wolf 2/7/32
211. BLENTLINGER
Hn./Lydia Tice 9/27/13
Jc./Eliz. Repp 12/24/16
212. BLESSING
Hn./Han. Zeigler 4/9/18
Chn./Mary Ann Thomas 11/9/22
Hn./Ann Maria Wecknight 12/7/54
Dn. W./Kate F. Unger 1/22/58
213. BLICKENDORFER
Jos./Rosina Recher 6/19/10
214. BLICKENSTAFF
Chn./Cath. Hauver 4/20/09
Dv. W./Mary P. Hoover 1/10/52
215. BLOOM
Enoch/Eve Foutz 11/5/18
Francis M./Eliza Gearhart 5/24/41
John/Lydia N. Harrigan 9/11/58
Geo. D./Caroline A. Shoop 4/7/59
216. BLOOMINGOUR
Chn./Ann Maria Bowers 1/13/51
217. BLOSE
Mich./Eve Grove 11/24/23
218. BLOYER
Jc./So. Neikirk 10/15/57
Mt. L./Mary Cath. Wachtel 9/15/58
219. BLUE
Joshua/Maria Chapman 9/6/31
220. BLY
John/Barb. Bean 12/17/01
221. BLYTH
John/Nellie Fullerton 10/11/99

222. BODMAN
Wm./Susan Kealhofer 6/2/30
223. BOERING
Jessee/Cath. Crecinger 3/16/15
224. BOLINGER (BOLLINGER)
John Jc./Marg. Boword 9/30/30
John/Mary Cronise 4/3/38
Chn./Eliz. Houpt 3/25/52
John/Susan Spong 7/13/54
Geo. W./Marg. S. Staley 10/4/60
225. BOLTON
John/Eve Iseminger 4/12/17
226. BOMBARGER (BOMBURGER, BOMBERGER, BAUMBARGER,
BAUMBERGER, BAUMBURGER, BUMBERGER, BUM-
BERGER, BUMBARGER, BUMBURGER)
John/Cath. Miller 2/9/16
Moses/Cath. Betz 9/2/17
Jc./Ann Betts 11/20/21
John M./Mary M. Snyder 11/8/36
Jc./Sr. Gruber 10/9/41
Jos./Leatha Koontz 8/30/47
Dv./Adaline C. Snyder 4/15/51
Hn./Sally Miller 10/18/53
Emanuel/Alice Jane Angle 7/26/56
Moses B./Annie C. Smith 4/5/58
227. BOMER
John L./Susan Sillhart 11/16/44
228. BONAM
Moses/Anna Marquis 8/21/04
229. BONAR
Jos./Na. Fagan 5/11/33
230. BOND
John/Eliz. Reed 6/24/01
Sam./Han. Reese 5/2/03
Geo./Mar. Johnston 6/16/27
Sam./Eliza Orndorff 11/2/29
Rich. S./Mary E. Fechtig 8/3/46
Geo. W./Mary Myers 3/6/47
Randolph/Angelica Woltz 12/11/43
231. BONNETT
Jm./Marg. Moore 10/3/05
232. BOOBECK
Jos./Na. Yeaneweire 4/16/12
233. BOOCHOUPT
John/Mary Moore 6/18/04
234. BOONE
Mordica/Sus. Shonk 1/5/08
Dn./Mary Arnsberger 10/10/11
Wm./Sr. Heck 11/19/12
Jos./Maria Nichols 6/11/17
Chas. Lewis/Sr. T. Habb 4/7/23
235. BOOSER (BOOZER)
Wm./Lydia Hoffman 8/20/42
Jer./Mary Ellen Poole 1/29/51
236. BOOTH
Wm./Marg. Carr 5/15/17
John/Eliz. M. Schnebly 11/23/41

9

237. BOPP
    Mich./Sr. Ann Secore 12/19/53
238. BOREN (BORIN)
    Wm. C./Sr. Hamilton 3/29/26
    Hn./Eliz. Baker 2/25/35
    Jc./Maria Spessard 9/12/38
239. BORGELT
    John/Caroline Oker 2/23/60
240. BORNAHAN
    Dn./Cath. Black 9/23/33
241. BORTMER
    Hn./Marg. Stotler 7/19/24
242. BOSTATER
    And./Ann Reb. Miller 12/8/58
243. BOSWELL
    Jm./Eliz. Myers 5/28/44
244. BOTELER (BOTELAR)
    Tho./Sr. Claggett 5/23/14
    Ed./Mar. K. Allen 4/9/16
    Elias/Mary Herring 3/20/16
    Hez./Aletha Clagett 12/28/21
    Hez. Jr./Eliz. Easton 1/20/24
    Ed. L./Prudence Chaney 9/1/32
    Bart./Mary Ann Garrett 1/28/35
    Jefferson O./Alice V. Keefer 10/28/57
    R.H.E./Reb.C. Hammond 3/16/57
    Francis M./Mary Ellen Boteler 11/29/59
245. BOTTS
    Wm./Reb. Miller Allen 12/18/21
246. BOUDENHAMER
    Wm./Mary House 3/15/21
247. BOUGHMAN
    And./Juliet Coons 10/8/18
248. BOULER
    Dv./Sr. Ann Weast 4/27/22
249. BOULT
    Tho. A./Sr. B. Harry 12/14/47
250. BOUSE
    John/Cath. Shaffner 3/22/17
251. BOUZIER
    Geo./Sus. Maceswingel 4/28/27
252. BOVEN
    Geo. Jr./Eliz. Bowers 5/10/52
253. BOVEY (BOVY, BOBEY)
    Mich./Eliz. Ankeney 9/15/09
    Dn./Peggy Jones 9/1/10
    Geo./Cath. Rinehart 11/7/14
    Dn./Reb. Reichart 3/27/15
    Jc./Eliz. Burkett 5/20/15
    Adam/Eliz. Rinehart 3/13/20
    Mich./Susan Tice 11/30/24
    Hn./Chna. Varner 10/14/26
    Sol./Mary Ann Biggam 12/29/30
    Dv./Cath. Mauggins 3/20/33
    Jc./Delila Kretzinger 5/5/35
    Chn./Mary Morgan 3/31/17
    Jc./Eliz. Warner 5/10/19

Mich./Ann Troup 7/29/35
Dv./Eliza Newcomer 3/11/37
John/Mary Funk 6/12/38
Sam./Barbary Funk 12/29/38
Simeon/Eliz. Rudasil 4/10/38
Hn./Maria Martin 4/12/44
Dv./Eliz. Stottler 2/18/45
Jc. A./Reb. Bovey 8/12/46
Chas./Mary Lepole 3/31/48 (or Chn.)
Dn. H./Ann Cath. Hammersla 11/8/48
Geo./Han. Knodle 5/21/49
Dn. R./Mary Cost 12/29/51
Hn. A./Mary E. Stine 5/13/57
Sam./Mary S. Besore 3/2/58
254. BOWARD (BOWART, BOWERT, BOWERD)
    Geo./Marg. Burkett 3/5/07
    Jc./Cath. Waggoner 12/26/12
    And./Na. Wolford 10/30/20
    Mich./Cath. Kershner 9/16/26
    Mt. L./Cassandra Young 3/10/52
    Upton/Sr. Bragonier 7/20/52
    Oliver/Mary Ann Grontz 6/26/57
    Wm./Marg. Carns 12/16/60
255. BOWEN
    John/Elisa Ross 10/13/34
256. BOWER (BOWERS)
    Chn./Mary Sibert 6/29/03
    Jc./Esther Coaler 8/12/09
    Jos./Sr. Beard 10/28/11
    Jc./Sr. Miller 8/4/12
    Fred./Marg. Whetstone 2/24/13
    Jc./Eliz. Springer 1/6/13
    Geo./Har. Wilson 12/27/15
    John/Mary Crumback 10/21/15
    Pt./Cath. Bertie 10/14/15
    John/Sr. Coons 4/8/16
    John/Eliz. Hybarger 4/8/16
    Wm./Cath. Hill 10/18/17
    Hn./Eliz. Knave 12/28/18
    Dv./Rachel Hyland 5/5/21
    Jc./Mary Cline 3/17/21
    Moses/Jane Williams 2/15/22
    John/Eliz. Wilkes 11/29/23
    Wm./Susan Nunemacker 1/30/24
    Jm./Marg. Mouser 8/23/25
    Geo./Lavina Zuck 8/12/28
    Geo./Na. Shank 12/15/29
    Hn./Mary Shrouds 9/8/29
    Jos./Cath. Hines 8/8/29
    Geo. D./Marg. Foster 1/7/31
    Jc./Mary Ann Burgessor 1/10/32
    Jos./Sr. A. Iseminger 1/6/34
    Wm./Louisiana Barnett 12/3/34
    Elijah/Marg. Eavey 3/29/36
    Wm./Maria Kepler 5/15/37
    Dn./Mary Pennell 12/2/40
    Levi/Mary McNamee 6/11/40

10

256. BOWER (BOWERS) (Continued)
    Wm./Mahala Porter 2/15/41
    Geo./Patsey Boren 2/3/42
    Mich./Ann Mary Wise 12/5/44
    Sam./Mary C. Leonard 12/20/47
    Chn./Mary Smeltzer 2/11/45
    Jc. C./Layann Stottlemyer 9/4/45
    Jon./Mary Feigley 8/12/45
    Wm./Marg. Ann Early 9/8/46
    Dv./Sr. Ann Knott 3/30/47
    Sam./Rachel Thumb 2/24/47
    Hn./Mary Cath. Koontz 2/5/49
    Jc. C./Susan J. Barber 2/7/49
    Jos./Mary A. Mallin 8/19/50
    Hn./Susann Kline 12/30/51
    John/Mary Spong 12/12/51
    Dv./Marg. Fridinger 4/26/52
    Jos./Ann Cath. Blessing 4/15/52
    Alex. H./Sr. Ann Adams 11/22/53
    Geo./Ann Gaither 5/18/53
    Fomose Morgan/Marg. Ann Stiffler 5/23/55
    Mt. H./Marg. Ann Gruber 12/4/55
    Moses C./Mary Ann Gallagher 1/25/55
    Gotleib/Savilla C. Robinson 6/30/56
    Benj. F./Mary Jane McPherson 1/12/59
    Dv./Mary Cath. Bowman 3/29/59
    Dn./Ann M. Poffenberger 8/7/60
257. BOWERSMITH
    Sam./Mary Ann Stover 1/7/42
258. BOWHAY
    Wm./Cath. Gale 3/28/18
259. BOWIE
    Tho. I.D./Eliz. C. Beatty 11/21/55
260. BOWLAN
    John/Marg. Lynch 1/3/35
261. BOWLES (BOWLAS)
    Jc./Eliz. Barkman 8/31/11
    Jm. H./Na. Johnson 2/2/15
    Rob./Jane Ross 5/25/19
    Geo./Sus. Riley 3/27/20
    Jm. H./Mar. Swope 12/12/21
    John S./Mary Ann Charles 4/18/45
262. BOWLUS
    Abr./Sayann Jacobs 9/19/35
263. BOWMAN
    Jc./Betsy Albregh 6/29/05
    Jc./Eliz. Duple 8/9/06
    Fred./Mary Ridenour 6/15/07
    Hn./Chrz. Broadstone 10/29/07
    Hn./Marg. Stouffer 3/3/12
    John/Mary Ream 6/16/13
    Jos./Sr. Kehler 11/13/13
    Geo./Barb. Davis 3/18/16
    Jc./Sally Hart 6/17/16
    Geo./Cath. Hoover 8/23/19
    Mich./Maryan Barnes 6/1/19
    Geo./Dorothy Stoy 3/11/20

    Geo./Mary Eliz. Feiry 12/29/21
    Geo./So. Tice 10/9/24
    Jc./Lucy McAfee 3/12/27
    Geo./Cath. McAfee 8/2/30
    Sam./Na. Maize 8/22/33
    Jc./Susan Gower 8/5/35
    And./Eliz. Gruber 5/1/37
    Emanuel/Sr. Avey 11/21/37
    Is./Mar. E. Cooper 6/30/37
    John/Julian Forrest 10/27/38
    Sol./Agnes Kensey 3/24/38
    Jos./Ann Eckenbarger 2/22/39
    Jc./Cath. Himes 11/4/40
    Jon./Mary E. Knight 10/20/41
    Sam./Eliz. Ann Maysillis 4/17/41
    John/Reb. Bomberger 10/27/42
    John/Caroline Stottlemyer 2/18/43
    Wm. H./Levinia Iseminger 5/22/44
    Jc./Ruth Young 3/3/47
    Dv. R./Julia A. Poffenberger 12/4/48
    Elie/Ann Maria Folder 2/21/48
    Hn./Sr. C. Rockwell 5/3/51
    Is./Na. Funk 11/9/53
264. BOWSER (BOUSER)
    John/Na. Metz 10/18/16
    Hn./Chna. Drondore 12/14/20
    Jc./Annie Startzman 3/23/30
    Rob./Mary Ann Hoffman 5/20/39
    Adam/Emaline A. McCoy 11/6/44
    Dv. G./Eliz. Ridenour 10/18/45
    Sam./Sr. E. Poffenberger 9/4/47
    Jon./Doratha Judith 2/23/50
265. BOXWELL (BOXELL)
    Rob./Patty McDavid 4/19/19
    Sam. L./Eliz. Boxwell 11/9/48
    Rich. S./Sr. J. Young 3/10/50
266. BOYCE
    Neale/Cath. Hawkins 6/23/13
267. BOYD
    Wm./Peggy McCumsey 2/25/15
    Marmaduke W./Sus. Hogmire 2/12/21
    Hn./Eliz. Harman 10/10/27
    Marmaduke W./Reb. Hogmire 4/10/28
    Sam./Marg. Bender 4/15/28
    John W./Reb. Southwood 2/23/38
    Tho./Matilda Neill 8/21/39
    Benj. R./Mary R. Glenn 5/10/42
    John W./Sr. A. Updegraff 2/1/45
    Wm./Mar. Ann Bowers 5/15/47
    A.G./Cath. A. Hawkens 3/7/49
    John/Sr. Wilkens 3/17/51
    Geo./Ann Eliz. Gehr 12/19/54
    John/Eleanora Suter 10/22/57
    Wm. J./Mary Ellen Taney 10/5/57
    G. Jos./Hetty J. Matthews 11/16/58

11

268. BOYER (BOYERS, BORYERS)
Pt./Mary Bowser 12/20/99
Ph./Eliz. Thomas 3/8/06
John/Eliz. Hines 7/13/27
Wm./Rosina Stickley 3/16/30
Dn./Emily Jackson 4/5/32
John/Reb. Snyder 1/10/33
John/Sr. Wolfersberger 10/27/35
Sol./Sus. Hogmyer 9/2/35
Sam./Minerva McCoy 4/6/50
269. BOYLE (BOYLES)
Pt./Ellen Allison 3/15/53
John S./Jane Hoop 12/13/55
270. BRADLY
Luther/Indiana Chaplin 5/5/35
271. BRADSHAW
John/Mar. Nelson 8/31/08
Geo./Mar. Steel 12/4/16
Jos./Margarette Cassell 2/5/18
Geo./Mary Wotten 10/19/55
272. BRADY (BRADEY)
Joshua/Mary Smith 9/10/04
John/Susan Goulding 8/16/20
Wm./Sus. Kidwell 11/1/24
Tho./Sr. Martin 12/23/26
Barnard/Caroline Sedon 2/10/39
273. BRAGEE
John/Julia Ann Budge 11/20/43
274. BRAGONIER (BRAGUNIER)
Sam./Eliz. Rohrer 5/25/11
Dv./Sally Geiger 12/23/13
Jc./Mary Sleise 10/7/15
Dn./Ros. Houer 4/11/21
John/Sus. Cook 9/25/21
Dv./Maria Long 4/12/53
Mt./Lydia Helser 5/11/57
275. BRAKEY
Wm./Eliz. Bearinger 9/8/10
276. BRALY
Mt./Phebe E. Herbert 1/12/58
277. BRAMBLE
John E./Sr. Ann Thomas 9/5/38
278. BRAMHALL
Jm. W./Marg. Bentz 8/16/32
279. BRANDENBURG
Jc./Sr. Krammer 6/10/15
280. BRANNER
Is./Mary Shreck 7/13/35
281. BRANT
John/Eliz. Doterly 8/25/02
282. BRANTNER (BRANDNER, BRANTER)
Mich./Polly Weast 3/30/11
Geo./Nelly Reeder 5/1/13
Jc./Cath. Arnsberger 12/13/14
Geo./Eliza Shaffner 5/22/20
Jc./Reb. Shriver 1/18/25
Mich./Cath. Allabaugh 11/8/31

Jos./Na. Duble 3/15/45
John/Mary Deitrick 3/27/46
Geo. W./Blanche A. Hedricks 4/5/51
Tho. H./Tabitha C. Leiter 10/17/60
283. BRASHEARS
Van/Na. Lynch 3/8/10
Joshua/Mary Stiffler 3/21/21
Van S./Mary Lynch 8/15/26
Wm./Eliz. Benner 8/17/44
Van/Joanna Renner 12/26/45
284. BREAZLIN
Mich./Cath. Mulherron 11/20/41
285. BREISCH
John J./Sus. Flora 11/10/35
286. BRENDLE
Geo./Eliz. Grave 12/7/99
John/Han. Hahn 10/3/27
Hn. R./Eliz. Cowton 11/22/59
287. BRENEMAN
Dv./Cath. Moyers 9/6/28
288. BRENT
Wm. R./Am. Shrapp 12/5/32
Rob. Jm./Matilda Lawrence 6/16/35
289. BRENTLINGER
Wm./Char. Foutz 3/23/11
290. BRETTELL
Jos. Chas. E./Eliz. Rench Cromwell 10/9/45
291. BREWAH
Jc./Marg. Ankeney 10/2/15
292. BREWER
John/Eliz. Kreps 3/8/06
Jc./Na. Harr 4/26/09
John/Marg. Forsyth 4/10/15
Hn./Sus. Rowland 6/4/16
John/Am. Heller 3/11/19
Jos./Mary Feiry 1/2/19
Adam/Maria Johnston 11/13/20
Dn./Eliz. West 1/18/20
Dv./Sr. Snyder 3/31/20
John/Eliz. Fiery 10/17/20
Emanuel/Cath. Zacharias 3/13/21
Jc. A./Har. Welsh 5/12/21
Jc./Eliz. Bragonier 2/2/22
Dv./Eliz. Gushwa 1/24/25
Pt./Sr. Coss 3/5/27
Geo. J./Eliz. Jacques 3/16/30
Dn./Mary Mish 12/22/31
Hn./Eliz. Reichard 12/11/32
Dn./Mary Heller 1/2/33
John A.K./Leah Hewitt 4/1/35
Pt. S./Anna Smith 1/9/38
Pt. I./Kaskiah Moudy 10/30/40
Jos. G./Hetty Maria Snyder 9/2/41
Geo. I./Marg. Jacques 4/14/47
Jc. H./Rachel Jane Ingle 12/16/49
John C./Mary Ann E. Fiery 5/17/51
John S./Roz. Snively 5/31/52

292. BREWER (Continued
 Hn./Sr. Rowland 12/9/53
 John/Delilah Blair 4/6/53
 Jos. A./Sr. Firey 2/11/58
 Jc. H./Margaretta M. Biays 12/24/59
 Jc. V./Lavinia G. Winder 1/26/59
 Lewis M./Eliz. Miller 3/26/59
293. BRIDGE (BRIDGES)
 John/Mary Bridges 1/25/45
294. BRIDGEMAN
 Wm./Han. Wilson 7/20/05
 Jos./Mary Eversole 10/12/11
 Wm./Alsinda Isa. Dust 10/21/23
295. BRIDGET
 Rob. R./Reb. Lapole 9/6/18
296. BRIDENTHALF
 John/Ellen Beeler 6/8/35
297. BRIEN
 Wm. C./Cath. C. Hughes 10/8/33
298. BRIGHT
 Tho./Louisa Drams 8/25/31
 . Strother/Lucinda Derrer 6/20/43
299. BRIM
 Henesy/Mary Clopper 3/27/05
300. BRINDLE
 Dn. L./Chra. Brewer 10/15/33
301. BRINHAM
 John/Mary Hanna 12/30/07
 Benj./Mary E. Martin 9/4/54
302. BRINING
 Jc./Cath. Spielman 4/23/35
 Fred./Mary Rumler 8/28/45
303. BRININGER
 Dn./Sr. Prince 5/4/05
304. BRINN
 Hn./Cath. Dillon 9/13/60
305. BRISCOE
 Hn.T.M./Eliz. Entler 3/30/30
 Geo. (colored)/Cynthia White 12/22/52
306. BRISH
 Dv./Susan Betterbenner 12/26/44
307. BROADSTONE
 Mt./Cath. Springer 10/23/01
 Leo./Eliz. Zimmerman 3/17/04
308. BROOK (BROOKE, BROOKS)
 Roger/Clotilda Elder 10/10/14
 Wash./Susan C. Henson 7/9/47
309. BROOKHART
 Dv./Teresa Funk 3/22/20
310. BROSI
 Gottleib/Eliz. Keiler 5/12/36
311. BROSIUS
 John/Mary Stale 11/25/08
 Dn./Elenor B. Johnston 2/14/28
 Wm./Susan Hart 10/23/40
 John J./Mary J. Brosius 12/27/45
 Geo./Frances Householder 9/18/48

312. BROTHERTON
 John/Esther Irwin 10/6/08
313. BROUSE
 John/Mary Attom 4/5/03
314. BROWN
 Barton/Linny Neal 10/23/01
 John/Cath. Garman 3/8/02
 John/Cath. Sillhart 12/29/04
 Adam/Keziah Bridgewater 3/9/05
 John/Elley Thomson 10/2/06
 John/Cath. Lewis 12/19/07
 Jos./Ros. Piper 3/16/07 ("d/o Jacob" pencil note)
 Sam./Abigail Jennings 6/23/08
 Sam./Eliz. Cretzer 10/11/08
 Wm./Sr. Protzman 6/25/11
 Dn./Peggy Leary 11/28/12
 Tho. Jr./Ann Carter 12/19/12
 John/Eliz. Smith 11/22/14
 Chn./Sus. Malott 4/11/15
 Dv./Sus. Wright 4/26/15
 Dv./Eliz. Slusser 3/22/17
 Tho./Sus. McAfee 4/9/18
 Alex./Sr. Koons 5/8/19
 Dv./Mary Powell 1/19/20
 Tho./Sr. Hose 12/22/20
 Chester/Delilieh Bennett 8/16/21
 Dn. W./Cath. Johns 1/23/21
 Joel/Mary Jollife 9/20/21
 Wm. M./Mary Bowles 4/29/22
 Dv./Eliz. Barks 9/7/24
 Geo./Cath. Graeff 4/12/25
 John/Eliza Hartman 10/3/25
 Wm. D./Mary Toms 8/1/26
 Benj./Matilda Moudy 2/14/27
 Jm. M./Sr. Howell 6/12/27
 Jm./Lidia Mowry 6/7/28
 John Jr./Han. Brown 12/7/29
 John/Maria Macaba 7/17/30
 Geo. W./Marion Brown 2/9/37
 Wm./Susan Dellinger 11/11/37
 John C./Ann M. Schleigh 7/8/40
 Geo. G./Marg. E. Horn 7/26/41
 Sam./Mary M. Brown 5/23/42
 Tho./Chra. Snavely 8/17/47
 Jm./Savilla Buhrman 5/10/49
 Jos./Diana Buhrman 7/11/49
 Adam/Caroline Hauer 2/18/51
 Hn. J. (negro)/Cath. Craig 2/19/52
 Ezra/Trusilla Smith 12/23/56
 Geo. I./Mary C. Bussard 12/26/57
 Hn. A./Na. Ann Bowers 10/9/60
315. BROWNEIS
 John/Mary Ann Steveson 11/2/33
316. BROWNING
 Sam./Na. Witter 10/18/31
317. BROWNLIE
 John/Ann C. Hill 12/19/55

318. BRUBAKER (BREWBAKER, BREWBECKER)
    Dv./Leah Lineberger 8/6/14
    John/Anna Burgess 3/13/32
    Jc./Priscilla Hanes 5/11/33
    Wm./Na. Boyd 12/19/57
319. BRUCE
    Wm./Cecelia Gorrell 2/19/33
320. BRUFFY
    John C./Ann E. Nichols 1/25/43
    Jason N./Mar. Jane Devier 11/28/50
321. BRUMBAUGH
    Dv./Eve Keesacre 11/2/05
    Geo./Lovice Galewix 4/1/07
    Elias D./Merinda Etta Benner 9/24/36
    And./Susan A. Lynch 9/1/46
    Lewis/Sr. Patton 1/18/48
    Jc. D./Reb. B. Clopper 12/31/55
322. BRUMET
    Mich./Sus. Lysinger 6/5/00
323. BRUNER (BRUNNER)
    John/Cath. Bruner 12/9/09
    Geo./Eliz. Faulkwell 11/25/20
    Pt./Barb. Markin 3/15/28
    Jon./Sr. Middlekauff 5/10/32
    Jon./Mary Middlekauff 10/19/33
324. BRUNSTAKES
    Dn./Cath. Fizer 8/8/01
325. BRUS
    Hn./Eliz. Shindle 2/21/43
326. BRYAN
    Fred./Chna. Sheleburger 2/28/32
327. BRYSON (BRISON)
    Geo./Sr. Ann Thropp 5/30/22
328. BUCHANON (BUCHANAN)
    Jesse/Mary Rock 7/26/06
    John/Maria So. Williams 10/4/08
    John/Na. Welsh 6/17/11
    Jm. A./Elenora Miller 7/25/39
329. BUCHLEY
    Rob./Eliz. Lutz 9/29/25
330. BUCHNER
    Adam/Cath. Schwope 10/1/50
331. BUCK
    Jc./Chna. Shoop 8/26/09
    John/Mary Laub 11/4/15
    Jc./Susan Foutz 3/28/33
    John Jr./Sr. Ann Smith 6/8/38
    Josiah/Mag. Keafauver 2/12/38
    Hiram/Ros. Stine 8/4/47
332. BUCKLES
    Moses/Ruan Benner 8/27/35
333. BUCKSON
    Wm./Clarissa Snider 8/10/41
334. BUCKSTON
    John/Mary C. Heygiss 12/4/50
335. BUCKWALTER (BUCKWESTER)
    Jc./Cath. Stover 12/5/23

    Benj./Cath. Miller 11/3/24
    Kathl/Na. Parrell 11/18/26
336. BUDD
    Sam. W. Jr./Louisa Jane Williams 9/26/40
337. BUGBY (BUGBEY)
    Ed. S./Sr. R. Tritch 10/20/51
338. BUHRMAN (BURHMANN)
    Dn./Mary Lantz 9/7/31
    Geo./Eliz. Bowman 8/21/35
    Sam./Mary Ann Gordon 5/9/36
    Abr./Mary Ann Iler 6/18/38
    Hiram/Elmira Toms 10/9/57
339. BULLMAN
    Sam./Mary Smith 11/26/23
340. BUNEGAN
    Ed./Eliz. Ward 12/29/36
341. BUNESS
    Tho./Mary Webb 8/13/03
342. BUNIER
    John/Betsey Riner 6/18/04
343. BURCH
    John/Jane Wood 6/9/45
344. BURDEN
    Benj./Jane Parther 12/17/14
345. BURDETT
    Jm. H./Rachel M. Christian 4/30/47
346. BURGAN
    John/Sr. Binkley 2/14/21
    Geo./Cath. Hinds 9/2/36
    Nich./Eliz. Choon 2/2/47
    Geo./Har. A. Jamison 7/21/60
347. BURGER
    Sam. W./Maria Fulton 4/23/18
    Dv./Lea Rickson 6/26/27
    Sam./Barb. Zeigler 9/23/41
    John/Ann Wellinger 5/28/60
348. BURGESSER (BURGESSOR)
    Sam./Eliz. Weast 12/20/45
    Sam./Kate Weast 8/9/52
349. BURGOYNE
    Jm./Louisa Redgrave 10/22/39
350. BURK (BURKE)
    Geo./Reb. McCormick 2/1/03
    Geo./Mary Holliday 5/14/05
    Batey T./Har. Jackson 7/22/30
    Wm./Har. Ann Wards 1/19/46
    John/Louisa Stephens 7/8/54
351. BURKETT (BURCKITT)
    Ph./Sr. Creamer 12/16/06
    Jc./Cath. Gole 7/20/11
    Wm./Eliz. Hyatt 8/22/11
    Jc./Mary Lesler 2/11/17
    John/Eliz. Wagoner 1/27/18
    Hn./Eliz. Ennis 1/17/38
    John/Reb. Null 3/12/50

352. BURKHART (BURCKHART)
Geo./Eliz. Ford 1/4/10
Jc./Eliz. Beigler 3/27/19
John D./Matilda Jane Rodgers 9/7/42
Theodore L./Cath. Davis 9/15/48
Lewis H./Mary H. Lushbaugh 5/6/51
353. BURKMAN
Levi/Cornelia Fauss 12/22/53
354. BURLING
Jc./Marg. Sanford 12/1/03
355. BURNER
John/Eliza Stickler 9/17/10
356. BURNETT
John/Sr. Price 8/17/12
357. BURNHAM
Chas. C./So. Kretzer 2/5/31
358. BURNS (BURN)
Tho./Maria Holt 12/4/04
John/Eliz. Seybert 8/15/13
John/Eliz. Moudy 8/19/15
Hn./Matalina Cuhn 5/6/19
John/Na. Sherdon 12/31/33
Geo./Cath. Bellem 4/21/49
Hn./Sarepta A. Bruner 9/16/50
Is. V./Sr. Jemina Southwood 2/20/51
Dn./Cath. Koone 5/28/55
359. BURRAGE
Geo. W./Matilda Molas 4/18/31
360. BURROLL (BURRELL)
Rich./Ruhanmah Wade 6/4/02
Benj./Sus. Weaver 8/29/07
361. BURROW (BURROWS)
John/Cath. Cease 7/26/06
362. BURTNER
Geo. P./Mary E. Eakle 1/23/54
363. BURTON
Bazie A.F./Ann Squires 8/3/43
Benj. B./Eliz. Miles 11/7/49
Al./Sr. E. Fair 10/16/56
364. BURY
Jm. C./Ann Chicester 6/21/37
365. BUSSER
Wm. T./Eliza Wallace 1/11/38
366. BUTLER
Ed./Eliz. Norriss 9/7/02
Hez./Am. Easton 2/20/05
Dn./Marg. Hailler 8/25/07
Jc./Eliz. Burkett 6/4/14
Geo./Theny Green 6/21/20
Chas. T./Virginia T. Van Swearinger
2/9/43
Kennedy H./Mary Ann Ash 8/11/52
Pat./Gertrude Anthony 2/17/60
367. BUTT (BUTTS)
Tho./Barb. Shuck 3/20/05
Ed./Eliz. Basore 9/26/16
John/Eliz. Baumbarger 6/4/17
Zeddock/Julian Sicafuce 8/13/24

Addison/Barb. Coffman 11/13/27
Arch./Mary Ellen Merchant 7/23/31
Wm. H./Han. Snider 9/10/34
368. BUTTERBAUGH
Hn./Cath. Hershey 11/11/44
369. BUZZARD (BUSSERD, BUSSARD)
Dn./Cath. Knode 11/22/03
Sam./Cath. Kuckle 6/22/05
Sam./Mary Delawter 9/9/12
Pt./Sr. Ridenour 4/11/22
John/Char. Ridenour 11/15/25
Jc./Marg. Keplinger 10/19/30
Jc./Susan Wolford 3/19/36
Sam./Tracy Long 10/13/57
370. BYERS (BYER, BUYER)
Jc./Cath. Worley 2/5/03
Sam./Ann Rice 11/6/06
Sol./Mary Young 4/28/06
Chr./Polly Shaffer 10/10/09
John/Eliz. Iantz 8/24/09
Jc./Cath. Snyder 4/15/18
Sam./Na. Bowers 12/26/22
Dv./Mar. Brewer 3/1/24
John/Maria Payne 8/1/26
Jc./Susan Shamel 9/5/27
John/Mary Barr 4/2/27
Wm./Mary Knodle 9/24/27
Frad./Cath. Zeigler 5/20/33
John/Ann. M. Wise 1/24/33
Jos./Eliz. Lefever 1/25/36
Hn./Na. Hoover 6/5/40
Jos./Sr. M. Kline 10/17/50
Tho. H./Laura P. Mallary 2/23/58
Amos/Mar. Jane Springer 9/21/59
Dv./Susan B. Strock 11/1/59
Jc. C./Mary Ann Blecher 2/1/59
Jm./Fedelia Downs 11/12/59
John D./Eliza Jane Leiter 12/5/60
371. BYERLY
Jc./Nully Emarick 2/8/42
372. BYRUM
Elie/Mary Jane Herd 10/10/49

373. CACHILL
Wm./Eliz. Barnhiser 3/1/15
374. CACKEBURGER
Pt./Sus. Wolfe 5/3/16
375. CADE
Tho./Sr. Hoover 8/22/12
376. CADEL
Nelson B./Mary Sanner 12/1/27
377. CAFITZ
Francis/Han. Wakenight 2/12/42
378. CAGARICE
Mich./Esther Hoover 8/11/01
379. CAGE
And./Eliz. Hutchison 9/29/41

15

380. CAHILL
John W./Cath. R. Wells 5/18/41
381. CAIN (CAINS)
Dennis/Levinia Mills 11/6/45
Timothy/Eliza McCoy 12/3/47
John/Marg. Ann Lowrey 9/9/48
Nathan/Fleuretta Desports 4/22/54
382. CALAMAN (CALLMAN, CALAMON, CALAMONS)
Tho./Eliza Patterson 8/5/18
Wm./Peggy Edeman (1821 male index,
1820 female index) 5/5/21 or 20
Wash./Rachel Marshall 5/5/36
Arthur/Eliz. Ainsworth 7/18/38
383. CALBERT
Lingum/Eliza Jackson 3/20/33
384. CALDWELL
Wm./Susan Curfman 2/29/20
Geo. H./Mary Neikirk 5/13/41
Dv./Sr. Ann Creager 8/7/43
385. CALHOUN
John/Mary Cookas 7/23/03
386. CALLAHAN (CALAHAN)
Wm./Sr. McKenney 3/16/11
Wm./Rachel Triggs 10/19/16
John/Bridget McMahan 7/17/37
387. CALLENDER
Sam. N./Eliza Jane Harbine 10/14/48
388. CALVERT
Jm./Mary Ann Calvert 6/27/25
389. CAMERON (CAMMERON)
Dn./Mary Nicelon 10/25/18
John/Mariah McFall 6/5/21
John/Ann McFall 12/4/26
Hn. F./Eliz. Hendrick 4/8/47
Chas. C./Ann M. Wiltshire 1/21/51
390. CAMPBELL (CAMBELL)
Allen H./Esther Robinson 3/26/00
Ja./Reb. Lewis 11/29/02
Dv./Sus. Fausnaught 4/22/05
Jm./Marg. Donaghe 6/3/06
Tho./Eliz. Longanacre 3/25/09
Anthony/Eliz. Dahl 7/21/18
Rob. N./Eliz. Moyer 10/2/22
Copeton/Barb. Jennings 11/1/34
John W./Ary Ann Anderson 7/29/40
Levin H./Mary P. Jones 1/24/55
391. CANDEL
Devalt/Eliz. Boyer 12/31/04
392. CANE
John/Sus. Steel 8/30/02
393. CAN (CANN)
Mark/Mary Jones 10/11/02
Emanuel/Eliz. Shook 8/25/12
Jc./Ruth Poffenberger 6/8/21
394. CANNON
Wm./Sus. White 1/8/13

395. CANTER
John/Mary White 11/27/06
Ed./Eliza Grove 6/1/32
396. CAPERER
Leighman/Marg. Welsh 7/15/20
397. CARBEY
Wm./Reb. Flook 3/2/48
398. CARBURO
Abr./Sus. Hartle 7/28/11
399. CARL
Dv./Susan Spawling 7/28/40
400. CARNEY
Rob./Eliz. Palmer 3/21/01
Jc. V./Ann Reb. Miller 7/20/52
401. CARNICOMB
Sodwick/Kitty Hompart 5/15/99
Jc./Cath. Bower 5/29/10
402. CARNS (CARN)
Sam./Mary Baltes 8/10/12
John/Marg. Brady 6/30/23
403. CARPENTER
Dv./Sr. Swoop 6/6/04
Hn./Eliz. Carpenter 3/14/08
John/Mary Eachus 6/25/18
Stephen/Mary Summers 9/9/24 ("d/o Jacob"
pencil note)
Stephen/Sr. Ann Guyton 3/7/36
404. CARPER
Wm./Cath. Drake 7/1/15
Ph./Esther Hartle 2/19/17
John W./Susan Ophelia Lamar 10/7/59
405. CARR (CARS)
Nich./Eliz. Downey 6/3/11
Ed./Marg. Ann M. Titlow 12/24/50
Wm. F./Rachel Ann Keedy 2/24/52
406. CARRICOE
Levi/Har. Neal 1/8/03
Jos./Am. Butler 11/21/04
407. CARROLL (CARRELL, CARREL)
Jos./Mary Melvin 12/4/00
Wm./Mary Hoes 11/1/06
Wm./Sus. Snyder 4/20/08
Mt./Abigail Glass 7/31/17
Dv./Na. Johnston 2/18/23
408. CARSON
John/Eliz. Neal 2/18/13
Rich./Eliz. Bower 3/25/17
Jm. V./Ros. M. White 1/2/21
Geo./Matilda Hershey 5/11/29
409. CARTEEN
Geo. W./Phebe Gibson 9/24/40
410. CARTER
Noah/Sus. Humerichouse 7/14/20
Sam./Marg. Harvey 7/23/42
Tho. M./Cath. Bridges 3/24/46
Sam./Louisa Beard 3/24/59

16

411. CARTY
    Geo. W./Cath. Ridenour 10/10/35
    Mich./Marg. Donovan 6/15/37
    Jc./Na. Ann Ainsworth 4/9/47
    Geo. W./Am. Ridenour 11/2/47
412. CARVER
    Sam./Marg. Emmerick 4/5/10
    Dv./Am. S. Heaflich 5/6/24
    Hiram/Mary Schnebly 1/30/45
413. CARWELL
    Geo./Eliz. Bowers 11/23/44
414. CASSEL
    Jc./So. Lambert 2/25/23
415. CASSIDY (CASSADY)
    John H./Mary McGeth 4/27/12
    Luke/Cath. Donnelly 7/13/40
    Jm./Louisa Donnelly 6/5/51
416. CASTLE
    Amos/Eliz. Palmer 3/29/26
    John/Eliza Summers 1/5/32
    Hn. L./Mary E. Petre 11/21/39
    Dn./Cath. Zimmerman 3/23/40
    Cornelius/Cath. Blessing 4/16/45
    Hn. L./Naomi E. Ashton 3/1/52
    Wm./Marg. Ann Albaugh 1/10/52
417. CASTLEMAN
    Dv./Anna W. Dellinger 12/28/58
418. CASTOR
    Tho./Cath. Brown 1/20/07
    Fred./Han. Beard 9/13/10
419. CASY (CASEY)
    Tho./Mary Rowe 8/5/33
    Jm. W./Rose Ann Creager 12/13/60
420. CATLETT
    Nathan/Sus. Hendricks 10/25/17
421. CATSENDAFNER
    Wm./Caroline Spohn 10/1/40
422. CAUFFMAN
    Jc./Cath. Slosser 10/17/03
    Jc./Na. Painter 12/23/16
    John/Sus. Cauffman 12/26/16
    Jm./Na. Palmer 3/17/17
    Abr./Eliz. Crow 9/15/19
    Dn./Narrisa Davis 8/21/22
423. CAUSLOWE
    Tho./Ruth Nelson 7/27/05
424. CAUSTEN
    Sam./Hetty Jones 6/8/10
425. CAVAN
    John A./Barb. A. Saunders 3/31/27
    Chas./Roz. Dampsy 7/19/34
426. CAWOOD
    Erasmus/Mary Williams 12/23/99
427. CEARFOSS
    Is./Angeline Lutz 1/18/54
    Simon/Marg. Macguire 1/9/55

428. CHAMBERLANE (CHAMBERLAIN)
    John/Han. Williams 10/14/12
    John/Jemima J. Grantham 11/6/43
429. CHAMBERS
    Vincent/Sr. South 9/2/05
    John/Mary Cook 3/29/06
    John/Han. Taylor 10/29/07
    Vincent/Sr. Coons 5/2/08
    Jc./Anna McMahon 2/1/10
    Otho/Eliz. Garlinger 1/1/17
    Wm./Ann Adamson 9/14/19
    Jm./Mary Hahn 12/24/26
    John/Eliz. Stake 10/9/26
    Jc./Milly Milles 1/3/35
430. CHANY (CHANEY, CHENY, CHENEY)
    Dv./Han. Hammond 4/12/03
    Wm./Eliz. Esminger 7/30/04
    John/Fanny O'Neal 3/21/11
    John/Eliz. Eichelberger 2/12/14
    Dv./Sus. Hammond 3/4/17
    Wm./Na. Newcomer 11/25/20
    Rob./Sr. Newcomer 2/20/27
    Ezekial/Jane Rowe 3/26/36
    Wm. B./Susan F. Beachtel 1/16/50
    Hiram/Lucinda Wise 2/28/55
    Jos. Penn/Maria Van Lear 4/26/60
431. CHAPLIN (CHAPLINE)
    Jm. N./Cath. Hebb 1/21/15
    Chas. J./Mary Ann Bryan 10/24/43
432. CHAPMAN
    Wm./Ann Wallingford 7/28/12
    Geo./Sr. S. Clark 11/2/20
    Pat./Mary Reilley 12/25/32
    Joshua/Mary Hays 9/14/33
    Thornton/Susan Crawford 4/8/41
433. CHARLES
    And./Na. Brunner 3/7/00
    Jos./Chna. Kreps 3/23/47
    Lewis/Susan Kreps 3/13/52
    John J./Mar. Cowton 10/21/54
434. CHARLTON
    John/Sr. Webb 9/13/00
    Tho./Eliz. Mentzer 4/23/01
    Jon./Am. Newson 6/20/16
    John/Susan Pain 11/16/33
    Jon./Mary Nave 9/12/45
    Tho./Jane Eliz. Hetzer 2/3/45
435. CHENOWETH
    John/Philipi Brady 10/26/08
    Jm. B./Rachel Payne 6/19/23
436. CHESTER
    Sam./Eliz. Clum 12/16/05
    John/Mariah Bowles 8/9/06
437. CHESTNUT
    Benj./Phebe Hess 3/16/11
438. CHEW
    Sam. A./Eliz. Lowman 11/28/21

17

439. CHIDLOW
Tho./Sr. E. Goldsborough 7/23/57
440. CHISAM
Wm./Mariah Frozier 7/29/36
441. CHOPPERT
Tho./Eveline Merchant 3/14/54
442. CHOR
Mich./Mag. Thomas 8/24/03
443. CHRISSINGER
Emanuel/Marg. Ridenour 10/15/35
Sam./Susan Wilkinson 9/15/42
Geo. H.L./Sr. Davis 12/18/44
Jc./Emily Boward 11/27/50
444. CHRIST (CHRISTE, CRIST)
Dn./Mary Martin 8/23/99
Abr./Cath. Gearhart 3/15/02
Jc./Am. Snyder 9/6/21
Dv./Eliz. Stoop 7/30/28
Joshua P./Hen. A. Miller 3/1/37
445. CHRISTIAN
Dn./Chna. Arnsberger 5/3/11
Jc./Mary Huffer 4/28/17
Tho. J./Han. E. Chenoweth 4/6/24
John/Bolina Hamilton 2/14/32
446. CHRISTMAN
Mich./Cath. Hicks 5/30/99
Geo./Eliz. Bower 4/7/20
447. CHRISWELL
Jos./Eliz. Geiger 4/3/34
448. CHURCHILL
Israel/Sus. Putman 4/22/15
449. CHURCHY
Israel/Mary Jane Metz 6/28/50
450. CIRCLE
Lewis/Na. Collison 8/2/02
451. CIST
And./Tracy Funk 12/16/50
452. CLABAUGH
Geo. W./Emily Hall 11/14/35
Wm. H./Lucretia L. Brent 1/36/39
Theodore F./Mary E. Schaffer 1/13/48
453. CLAGGETT (CLAGETT)
Dv./Priscilla Boteler 2/12/08
Sam./Eliz. Claggett 2/22/19
Tho./Matilda Claggett 12/28/21
Hez./Eliz. B. Williams 6/6/25
Jm. H./Eliz. Garrett 11/13/29
Grafton A./Caroline M. Stonebraker 8/22/38
Hn./Mary Ann Bean 6/10/39
John Hn./Sus. Lowman 3/4/44
Sam. Jr./Eliz. Shupp 11/29/53
454. CLAIRE
Jm./Cath. Swearinger 6/15/99
455. CLAPPER (CLOPPER, CLOPER)
John/Chna. King 5/4/02

John/Sus. Longman 6/17/20
Jc./Sus. Detrick 12/26/28
Sam./So. Huffer 9/3/29
John/Mary Ann Hanes 12/9/36
Jos./Marg. Ridenour 4/19/36
Josephus L./Marietta Snively 1/25/39
Wm./Lydia Huffer 10/14/44
Hn. A./Marg. E. Petre 10/18/55
Sam. H./Mary E. Beeler 2/24/57
S. Harman/Ann Maria Thomas 7/5/59
Geo. A./Kesiah Holme 7/31/60
456. CLAPPSADDLE
Jc./Eliz. Brook 11/5/12
Jc./Mary Ridenour 2/26/17
457. CLARK (CLARKE)
Sam./Marg. Grubb 5/26/07
Jos./Cath. Shrader 3/9/08
Mat. Jm./Sally Gow 1/11/08
Simon/Cath. Row 9/29/08
John/Na. Swift 1/2/12
John/Sr. Norris 7/22/12
Barney/Mary Figally 9/25/13
Geo. W./Am. I. Hughes 9/26/16
Mat./Reb. Marg. Ridenour 11/13/18
John/Mary Cox 4/14/19
Tho./Mary Morgan 3/28/20
Jm.W./Barb. Iseminger 3/9/23
Sam./Eliz. Reynolds 12/9/24
Mat. J./Frances O. Ferrell 3/27/26
Rob./Aletha Chaney 5/23/36
Pat./Cath. Cuddy 12/11/38
Wm. B./So. Price 2/22/38
Wm./Marg. McClain 8/4/38
Zachariah B./Sr. Ann Anderson 8/19/40
Rob./Ann Eliz. Kuhn 10/22/45
Sam. H./Susan Bitzenburg 8/29/51
Tho./Cath. Maguire 8/27/51
Ed./Barb. Shank 1/26/53
Morgan H./Susan H. Shank 3/15/54
Geo. W./Marg. Bowers 10/30/56
John Dennis/Mrs. Eliz. Burgan 4/15/59
458. CLARKSON
Freeman/Cath. E.S. Balch 7/25/44
R.H./Meliora McPherson 5/7/49
459. CLASSER
Jm./Na. James 3/23/32
460. CLAYBOURN
Tho. S.B./Lucy N. Brooks 12/19/49
461. CLAYCOMB (CLAYCOMP)
Hn./Sus. Holley 4/3/06
462. CLAYTON
Benj./Eliz. Tutterow 8/25/03
Dn./Ros. Myers 1/29/13
Jm./Sr. Boyd 9/2/29
Jos./Louisa Showman 5/12/29
463. CLEAVINGER
John/Bula Ridgeway 1/2/01

18

464. CLELAND
  Tho. W./Malinda Fritz 6/25/53
465. CLEM
  Luke/Susan Myers 7/12/55
466. CLEMENS
  Hez./Jenny Brown (Negro) 11/15/15
467. CLEMMERT
  Pt./Eliz. C. Rosamarin 5/6/53
468. CLENDENAN
  And./Ann Wright 12/11/21
469. CLEVELAND
  Jm. C./Adelia Slosser 3/27/27
470. CLEVERDENCE (CLEVIDENCE)
  Geo./Layer Crior 5/23/01
  Dv./Mary Gantz 9/6/27
  Dn./Eliz. Bond 3/1/28
  Sam./Ann Spencer 8/9/31
  John/Rachel Green 12/2/33
  Geo./Mahala Stottlemyer 10/23/37
  Hn. H./So. E. Middlekauff 1/5/60
  Geo. A./Ellen E. Crissinger 12/26/60
471. CLIMER
  John/Eliz. Yourcus 9/17/07
472. CLINE
  Ph./Cath. Showman 11/27/16
  Geo./Cath. Miller 9/9/24
  Moses/Cath. McCoy 5/29/34
  Dv./Char. Warafelts 12/22/36
  Moses/Rachel Wickers 9/27/37
  Mich./Mary Kurhman 3/25/43
  John M./Sus. Clopper 1/9/44
  Wm. H./Barb. L. Sickman 9/26/54
  Jc./Mar. Ann Swope 12/7/59
473. CLINGAN
  Wm./Sr. Guyton 11/19/25
  Tho./Eliza Lewis 3/2/48
474. CLINKINGBEARD
  Ed./Sus. Ronamus 3/22/06
475. CLONINGER
  John W./Louisa M. Henderson 9/7/50
476. CLOSE
  Conrad/Polly Coss 12/24/10
477. CLOVIS
  Mat./Na. Bear 12/31/08
478. CLUB
  Geo./Caty Artman 11/20/09
479. CLUGSON (CLUGSTON)
  Rob./Na. Boward 9/23/50
  J.C./Mary I. Wolfinger 12/8/59
480. CLUM (CLUMM)
  John/Fanny Eller 6/13/28
481. CLUNK
  Jos./Mary Robinson 8/2/48
482. COAKLEY (COAKERLY)
  Ph. H./Sr. Smith 3/13/28
  Jc. C./Anna E. Schleigh 5/10/58
483. COATS
  Geo. M./Eliz. J. Russell 6/29/54

484. COBAUGH
  Pt./Sr. Shanafeltz 2/15/25
485. COBLENTZ
  Ed. Franklin/Cath. E. Main 11/15/60
486. COCHENOUR
  Dn./Eliza Claggett 7/28/35
487. COCHRAN
  Jc./Sr. McGill 3/29/24
488. COFFIN
  Chas./Cath. Riley 6/17/19
489. COFFMAN
  John H./Barb. Heason 11/1/25
  Hn./Matilda Poffenberger 10/10/26
  John/Eliz. Nighswander 8/25/28
  Hn./Sus. Long 5/22/30
  Jc./Mary Ann Keedy 2/13/32
  Dn./Rhea McNight 6/19/32
  Dv./Lydia Newcomer 3/3/34
  Sam. W./Cath. Downey 11/27/34
  Is./Eliza Shoaff 6/18/35
  Jm. W./Mary Brantner 11/18/36
  John/Ann Artz 6/30/38
  Dv./Caroline Hammond 10/11/48
  Hn. M./Cecilia Jones 10/4/48
  Jm.W./Sr. Ann Norris 5/21/53
  Simon/Sr. Boyd 8/6/56
490. COFFROTH (COFROTH)
  John/Mary Besore 1/2/10
  Wm./Eliz. Wood 7/16/17
491. COLBERT
  Hez./Reb. Jackson 10/11/36
  Clarkson/Eliz. Woland 5/9/39
492. COLBIN
  Tho./Sr. Welsh 2/14/18
493. COLE
  Geo./Cath. Martin 10/28/22
  Hn./Mary Eavey 10/25/22
  Geo. E./Mar. Matheny 2/1/55
  Geo. E./Mary Cath. Drenner 10/5/59
494. COLEHOUSE
  Geo./Cath. Coffman 12/22/59
495. COLEMAN
  Nathan/Eliz. Dempster 9/13/00
  Ph./Ellen Degan 8/4/35
  Wm./Ellen Mahony 9/3/38
496. COLKIESSER
  Dn./Eliz. Keller 11/18/40
  Wm./Ann Am. Oden 2/16/56
  Tho./Cath. Meads 10/18/60
497. COLLETT
  Moses/Reb. Haynes 3/30/05
498. COLLIER
  Wm./Eliz. Hickman 2/9/03
  John/Mary Downey 6/7/09
  Matthias/Reb. Adams 5/26/31

19

499. COLLIFLOWER (COLLEFLOWER)
Pt./Mary Hoover 9/13/11
Geo./Cath. Fishack 6/8/13
Geo./Eliz. Flory 11/24/30
John/Mary Ann H. Webb 6/5/32
Pt./Mary Mackin 1/12/33
Hn./Cardine Houze 5/15/58
500. COLLINS
Wm./Susan Price 11/12/31
Pt./Rosa Syands 9/15/38
Wm. O./Cath. W. Wever 11/2/43
John L./Eliza M. Heck 1/12/49
Noah/Gertrude Ross 10/16/51
501. COLLIS
Nathan/Mary Cath. Weagley 9/13/55
502. COLONY
Mich./Eliz. McCafferty 10/22/38
503. COLP
Ph./Eliz. Cromer 11/11/00
504. COMMER
Sam./Eliz. Smith 7/30/18
505. COMMESKY
Dennis/Sr. Flanagan 5/31/34
506. COMPTON
Stephen/Marg. Compton 10/3/08
Hn./Matilda Drury 4/5/20
John A./Basbar O. Laurence 6/3/56
507. CONFARR (CONFER)
Geo./Cath. Staimel 10/30/30
Geo./Eliz. Bowers 3/19/21
Sam./Mary Baker 11/28/27
508. CONLANCE
Sam./Eliz. Poffenberger 7/23/29
509. CONLEY (CONLY)
Benj./Mar. Burch 2/25/02
John/Eliz. Smith 12/21/05
Hugh/Sus. Burkett 8/5/09
Wm./Eliz. Nowell 10/19/09
Tho. S./Jane E. Hall 12/29/51
Harrison/Rachel E. Friend 2/16/57
510. CONLON
And./Mary Devorem 2/18/38
511. CONNELLY
Elie/Prudence Phears 3/27/33
John/So. Sharp 6/8/39
512. CONNER
Jm. O./Sr. McFaden 7/30/15
Gabriel/Mary Ridenour 1/3/18
Bernard O./Marg. McCaffey 8/31/33
Jc./Susan White 8/3/33
Dv./Helen Artz 6/18/34
Dn./Susan Hunt 11/30/44
513. CONPHER
Pt./Mary Ann Collins 4/2/39
514. CONRAD (CONROD, CONRADT)
John/Sr. Young 1/18/00
Chas./Eliz. Copenhaver 8/10/11

Dn./Eliz. Lowman 10/5/16
Sam./Mary Creager 7/10/22
Chn./Am. Hughes 12/23/23
Chn./Eve Wolf 8/18/23
Geo./Eliz. Young 10/27/30
Is./Eliz. Athey 3/2/39
Jc./Sr. J. Turnbolt 7/19/53
John/Reb. Miller 1/15/53
515. CONRY
Jm./Helinco Ducks 2/15/03
Jm./Cath. Bearn 12/18/40
516. CONWAY
Hugh/Mary Haines 8/19/22
517. CONWELL
Jos./Mary Grantham 8/25/04
Rezin/Na. Garver 3/5/12
518. COOK (COOKE)
John T./Sally Finfrock 9/12/15
Mich./Deborah Robinson 12/28/16
John/Han. Hoffman 11/16/22
Sam./Eliz. Wolf 12/13/26
Roger E./Louisa Ann Hammond 1/9/36
Alex./Mary Mantz 8/9/38
Jc./Cath. McGloughlin 8/29/39
Jm./Mary Davy 12/10/39
Larkin S./Eliza Martin 8/12/40
John/Eleanor Keighn 12/14/41
John/Phebe Ingle 2/3/43
John R./Ann Eliza Laymaster 8/7/43
Cyrus B./Permilia C. Knight 11/18/44
Wm. S./Mary Ann Kessler 9/19/50
Geo./Chna. Warner 2/18/51
Anthony/Marion Gold 7/7/60
519. COOKAS (COOKASS, COOKUS)
Jc./Mary Gordon 11/29/99
Jc./Marg. Michaels 1/29/37
Geo. W./Eliz. Hortensia Baer 2/19/48
520. COOKERLY
Benj./Cath. Hybarger 7/16/31
Benj./Mary Ann Bennett 11/11/43
521. COOKSTON
Elias/Cath. Creager 8/21/37
522. COOMER
Rich./Eliz. Jones 4/16/11
523. COOMS
John/Patience Shirley 7/3/20
524. COON (COONS, COONTZ, CUHN)
John/Marg. Miller 3/28/03
John/Cath. Rhodes 8/28/06
Adam/Polly Lockart 10/26/15
John/Marg. Rare 9/23/15
Geo./Cath. Smith 3/24/17
Jc./Judith Billmyer 4/11/18
John/Patience Shirley 7/3/20
Lewis/Sr. Unger 4/4/23
Jc./Barb. Spitnagle 8/27/24
Mich./Eliz. Moudy 12/21/26
Pt./Mary Miller 9/1/26

524. COON (COONS, COONTZ, CUHN) (Continued)
    Jc./Julian Shroyer 5/16/27
    Jc./Na. Lutz 4/19/30
    Rezin E./Mary E. Harvin 1/18/32
    Jer./Susan Carney 4/8/36
    John W./Clarissa Dennison 4/9/42
    Pt. F./Ann Speck 8/22/48
    Juwayne/Marg. Eliz. Staley 11/8/49
    Abr./Sr. McCoy 12/24/56
    Jm. L./Mary Susan Boyd 2/18/60
525. COOPER
    John/Han. Meeks 3/17/03
    Rob./Scharlotte Geiger 3/28/03
    John W./Hen. Fields 4/3/28
    Jon. G./Eliz. Bowers 2/11/29
    Jm./Eliza S. Dunham 2/22/36
    Wm./Mary Ann Sager 3/4/44
526. COPENHAM
    Mich./Mary E. Coontz 4/20/37
527. COPENHAVER
    Hn./Susan Shanafelt 1/30/30
528. COPES (COAPES)
    Rob./Nelly Burton 2/15/00
    Jc./Han. Shipler 11/20/01
    Wm./Esther Neill 4/21/08
529. COPLEY
    Jefferson I./Ros. Rhode 2/7/33
530. COPP
    Wm./Rachel Powell 4/28/38
531. CORBAN
    _____/Eliz. Fullerton 3/3/35
532. CORBETT
    Tho./Sus. McAllister 11/1/55
533. CORBY (CORBEY)
    Wm./Mary Steffey 2/11/04
    John/Marg. Walker 6/15/26
    Wm./Jane Snyder 11/13/32
    John W.W./Altha Ann Artz 11/4/54
    Geo. W./Helen V. Kershner 11/5/60
534. CORNELIUS
    Geo.W./Marg. M. Gilbert 3/4/48
535. CORNELL
    Sam./Mary Ann Hauver 3/25/50
536. CORROTHERS
    Wm./Adaline R. King 9/18/49
537. CORSON (CORSEN)
    Rob./Chna. Brown Jr. 1/2/28
538. COSGROVE
    Law./Teresa Ann Root 11/14/35
539. COSS
    Geo./Mary Milughley 4/3/04
    Sam./Mary Bowers 4/15/33
    Ezra/Caroline Doub 2/6/39
    Sam./Mary Jane Wilhide 1/30/55
540. COST
    Tho./Sr. Bradshaw 10/3/01
    Wm./Eliz. Cretzinger 4/8/13

    Sam./Barb. A. Keedy 3/21/23
    Sam. W./Sr. Parks 2/16/38
    John/Sr. Boon 3/16/41
    Sam. W./Cath. Stine 8/6/42
    Wm./Mar. A. Beard 1/28/46
    Al. N./Mary Bovey 12/13/51
    Jc. W./Barb. A. Piper 11/5/56
    Aaron/Malinda Stine 11/12/59
541. COTTERMAN
    Sam./Mary Hickman 3/2/02
542. COSTINBEDER
    John P./Marg. Smith 3/22/60
543. COUGH
    Geo./Mary Shurk (or Shush) 8/20/02
544. COURSEY
    Wm. R./Mary Ann Sheets 2/9/36
545. COUSLEY (COUSLY)
    Wm./Tabitha Lucas 4/18/05
546. COW
    Jc./Eliz. Roads 10/26/05
    John/Sus. Cook 4/28/13
    Felty/Mary Smith 2/28/29
547. COWGILL
    Wm./Eliza Coats 9/17/14
548. COWTON
    John/Sr. Harmiston 3/4/25
    John T./Na. Brewer 11/1/51
549. COX
    Jm./Lucy Brokenbrough 11/24/01
    Kelly/So. Todd 12/22/02
    Kelly/Na. Windle 3/8/13
    John/Sus. Springer 2/6/14
    Levi/Ann Hart 7/2/17
    John/Cath. Eakel 3/13/30
    Pt./Eliza Kailor 9/4/37
    John/Mary Boyers 12/14/39
    Jm./Cath. McFadon 9/24/40
    Hn./Susan Hoover 11/12/45
    Moses/Ann Lorshbaugh 2/1/48
    And./Eliz. Hoover 10/10/49
    Geo. W./Jane Wike 6/9/53
    Pt./Mary Ann Kuhn 2/22/53
    Sol./Sr. E. Horner 10/15/53
    Wm. Is./Ann Cath. Otto 11/29/59
550. COXEN
    Jos. C./Ellen McCormack 10/6/32
551. COYLE
    John N./Julia E. O'Banon 9/15/35
    Ed. B./Mary Ann Winsigler 2/20/37
    Jm. W./Marg. M. Elliott 5/11/46
552. COYSIL
    Elizur/Ann Cath. Baer 1/2/26
553. CRADDOCK
    John/Marg. Mong 6/8/30
    John/Am. Mong 1/7/39
554. CRACOLING
    John/Sr. Wolford 8/7/13

21

555. CRAIG
Sam./Sr. Ann Hogg 12/30/24
556. CRALEY
Sam./Har. Cline 11/8/36
557. CRAMER (CREAMER, CRAMMER, CRAUMER, CREMMER)
Pt./Eliz. Keller 12/6/08
Sam./Hetty Harman 11/20/22
Sam./Mary Ann Spillman 7/14/26
Lau./Mary Schriver 6/9/36
Dv./Han. Faulders 10/23/39
Rob. I./Ellen Entler 6/4/42
Dn./Marg. Bowers 5/18/49
Jm./Han. Roux 8/22/50
Mt. Oliver/Delia Myers 5/17/59
558. CRAMPTON
John/Eliz. Clopper 6/24/01
Geo./Mary Byrd 12/21/09
Moses/Sus. Lorshbaugh 3/18/11
Elie/Maria Rohrer 6/8/30
Tho. H./Ann Maria Kellar 8/28/30
John/Eliza Ann Bartgiss 6/22/31
Jos./Sus. Fasnaught 11/21/43
John/Mary A.R. Gray 11/1/52
559. CRANWELL
Chas. A./Ann Jane Williard 9/11/50
560. CRAVEN
John/Mary Heiskell 8/30/24
561. CRAVER
John/Mary Muck 12/27/02
John/Ann Grimes 11/13/09
562. CRAWFORD
Jm./Eliz. Van Lear 7/22/11
John/Ann Whitney 3/10/12
Is./Mary Richardson 8/2/33
Joshua/Sr. South 3/19/36
Joshua/Ann South 8/7/44
Sam./Jane Conner 4/6/45
Wm./Mary McClay 3/12/45
Sam./Sr. Gantz 5/14/59
563. CREAGER (CREEGER)
John/Eliz. Conrod 4/10/06
Harry/Cath. McDonald 6/20/12
Pt./Sus. Daily 6/28/15
Sam./Sr. Wagoner 8/17/15
Dn./Mary Bower 2/17/16
Hn./Sr. Bowerd 4/07/17
John/Na. McCall 7/28/19
Abr./Sr. Zentmyer 12/21/30
Wm./Cath. Shiess 2/22/43
John/Mary Ann Pretzman 7/16/46
Wm./Isa. Harry 5/17/52
John T./Susan Moats 11/30/59
Hn./Mary Johnson 2/9/60

564. CREEK
Pt./Peggy Yerk 7/23/00
Nich./Juliet Bowles 3/19/03
Jc./Sr. Fisher 6/22/05
John A./Rachel E. Norris 4/20/48
565. CREPNER
Geo./Eliz. Dorenberger 1/29/56
566. CRESSUP
Mich./Sr. Ann Hobletzell 2/24/37
567. CRETZER
John/Mary Pattoon 12/26/06
Geo./Cath. Iler 12/5/07
Dn./Mary Ann Miller 5/25/26
John/Ellen McCoy 1/30/30 (may be
Cretzinger)
568. CRETZINGER
John/Sr. Rhinehart 3/21/27
Jos./Reb. McCrey 12/19/29
John/Ellen McCoy 1/30/30 (may be Cretzer)
569. CRIDER
John/Eliza Seibert 10/14/33
570. CRINER
John/Eliz. Smith 12/12/01
571. CRISE
Jc./Eliz. Myers 10/11/26
572. CRISMAN (CRISEMAN)
Mich./Har. Davis 2/5/22
573. CRISSINGER
Wm./Mary B. Hammersla 5/11/53
Mt. L./Caroline Hellane 3/5/60
574. CRISWELL (CRESWELL)
Jos./Marg. Gibson 12/26/07
John/Dolly Gragen 8/29/09
And./Mary Jane Lefever 3/23/40
575. CROFFORD
Dv./Ann Maria Hess 12/27/58
576. CROFT
Conrad/Sus. Baker 4/7/10
577. CROM
Abr./Cath. Lum 10/30/50
578. CROMER
Jer. D./Mary M. Keller 10/24/55
579. CROMWELL
Oliver/Na. Reeder 1/13/02
Rich./Sus. McLaughlin 11/15/02
Nath./Mary Zeller 2/13/09
Jos./Marg. Zeller 4/8/19
Philemon A./Mary Ann Montgomery 3/11/34
John H./Sr. Cath. Binkley 9/9/58
580. CRONIGH
Dv./Barb. Wright 5/4/20
581. CRONIN
Pat./Mary Blair 7/20/53
582. CRONISE
Geo./Eliz. Beeler 6/17/06
John/Cath. Nichodemus 5/1/33
Wm. M./Sr. Watson 4/6/50
Chas. E./Sr. Cath. Naff 11/22/60

22

583. CROON
　　Jean D./Margaretta Delkour 3/27/56
584. CROSS
　　Jos./Sr. Reeder 3/13/21
　　Rob./Sus. Hamilton 5/9/25
　　Benj./Mary Lafever 4/1/28
　　John/Sus. Northcraft 2/2/29
　　John W./Eliz. Myers 8/22/35
　　John W./Mrs. Matilda Clelin 12/8/36
　　Jon./Mary Himes 10/18/39
　　Rob./Reb. Mungan 4/8/41
　　Rezin/Ann Parmelia Cassell 2/19/56
　　John H./Eliz. Itnire 12/30/59
585. CROSSLEY
　　Tho./Ann Wilkins 8/31/01
586. CROULEY
　　Bernard/Marg. Lane 9/9/39
587. CROUYN
　　Wm. B./Eliz. L. Blood 10/11/52
588. CROW
　　Jc./Dorothy Foutz 9/13/02
　　Ph./Eliz. Cruthers 9/5/04
　　Benj./Eliz. Lefever 9/1/19
　　Jc./Sr. Tice 4/17/20
　　John/Matilda Barger 3/31/31
　　Wm./Eliza Edwards 4/9/37
　　Corbin/Mary Ann Fritts 11/19/39
　　Nathan/Har. Edwards 8/1/39
589. CROWN
　　Tho./Hepsey Emberson 3/2/16
590. CROWL
　　Jos./Mary Ann Dillahunt 12/31/17
　　John/Ann Steinmetz 2/19/21
591. CROY
　　John/Mary Nave 4/3/06
592. CRUM
　　Abr./Mary McDonald 2/6/19
593. CRUMBAUGH (CRUMBACH)
　　Sam./Clarissa Briscoe 3/2/16
　　Wm./Eliz. Coon 9/28/22
594. CRUSH
　　And./Mary Hammer 4/4/01
595. CRUTZINGER
　　Sam./Na. Spessard 7/31/34
596. CRUZER
　　Rich. R./Am. W. North 12/4/25
597. CUBBAGE
　　Arch./Eliz. Jenkins 10/8/39
598. CULLEN
　　Jm./Mary Hamia 5/19/54
599. CULLENBAR
　　Hn./Eliz. G. Cromwell 12/26/23
600. CULLER
　　John Harman/Lucinda C. Kefauver 3/1/60
601. CUNNING
　　John/Mary Peters 3/26/22
602. CUNNINGHAM
　　Jos./Na. Troll 4/28/01
　　John/Marg. Rhodes 7/17/02

　　Jon./Marg. Rutter 1/21/07
　　Ph./Matty Davis 6/10/08
　　Walter/Na. McCraft 9/28/16
　　Jos./Sus. Bealch 10/18/21
　　Wm./Ros. Warner 2/28/22
　　Sam./Mary Ann Wilson 1/20/23
　　Sam./Eliz. Machin 8/9/26
　　Tho./Mary Ann Bowerd 12/14/33
　　Sam. S./Eliza Ann Yontz 2/9/35
　　John/Marg. Hobert 11/28/40
　　Sam./Eliz. Boyd 3/17/48
　　Chas. E./Eliz. A. Jones 3/7/49
　　Wm./Louisa Bowers 1/26/54
　　John/Jane Little 9/6/60
603. CULP
　　Fred./Cath. Coaler 6/3/06
604. CUPBREAST
　　Augustus/Barb. Lantz 6/25/04
605. CURAIN
　　Tho./Ann Rawlings 6/13/29
606. CURFMAN
　　Wm./Eliz. Long 12/15/46
607. CURLING
　　Fred. H./Mary Spielman 10/8/39
608. CURRY
　　Abr./Eliz. Shaw 4/20/11
　　John/Sr. Kreps 10/9/16
609. CURTIS
　　Wm./Mary Zuck 7/22/07
　　Josiah/Ester Arnsberger 4/14/20
　　Josiah/Na. Malott 7/5/36
　　Rob. W./Jane M. Newcomer 1/25/54
610. CURUTHERS (CURRUTHERS)
　　Geo./Julianna Evans 8/25/12
　　Hn./Mary Seibert 10/17/18
611. CUSACK
　　Nich./Judy Carroll 2/7/34
612. CUSHING
　　Rob./Cath. Houser 5/27/23
　　Rob./Eliz. Brown 5/7/27
613. CUSHION (CUSHEN)
　　Rob./Eliza Bussard 4/12/55
　　Rob. Howard/Susan Eliz. Garver 1/22/56
614. CUSHWA
　　Dv./Cath. Ressler 4/28/01
　　Benj./Maria Berry 11/25/08
　　John S./Reb. Martin 2/5/44
　　Wm./Ann Eliz. Prather 11/15/45
　　Jm. R./Sr. L. Kroh 1/9/54
　　Victor J./Mary A.J. Kreigh 3/31/58
615. CUSTIN
　　Jc./Mary Cini 5/15/14
616. CUTSHAW (CUTSHALL, CUTTSHAUL)
　　Sam./Na. Combs 6/3/06
617. CYESTER (CEYESTER)
　　Dn./Sr. Ann Moudy 8/3/19
　　John/Eliz. Weisell 4/2/29
　　Sam./Eve Wolf 2/3/29
618. CYRIS
　　Nath./Eliz. Owens 5/21/16

619. DAGENHART (DAGANHART)
    Chn./Esther Easterday 3/4/15
    Conrad/Eliz. Honenecht 8/20/21
    Sam./Mary Painter 9/23/22
    Conrad/Mary Hoffmaster 12/8/27
    Emanuel/Lucy Rogers 10/21/39
    John/Eliz. Norris 10/10/48
620. DAHLMAN
    Jc./Mary Johnson 3/27/10
621. DAILY (DALY)
    Sam./Mar. Melong 12/20/03
    Anthony/Cath. Mulholland 5/16/36
    John/Kesia Rowland 10/2/39
    John M./Is. V. McQuilken 11/2/54
    Pat./Marg. McMannus 8/21/58
622. DALRYMPLE
    Wm. P./Eleanora Claggett 11/7/16
    Tho./Sus. Steffey 4/24/17
623. DANIEL (DANIELS)
    Rob./Mar. Hackney 11/10/08
    Wm./Eliz. Powell 8/2/11
    Rob. G./Han. Daniels 4/12/37
    Wm. F.A./Mary Ann Grim 1/21/45
    D.M./Ann R. Flanagan 5/24/52
624. DANNEL
    Wm. F./Na. Flory 12/20/30
625. DANNER
    Jos./Ellen Dagenhart 8/17/44
    And./Rhuan Joy 12/4/47
626. DANNISON
    Aaron/Peggy Pipers 8/23/10
627. DARBY
    Hn./Han. Gilbert 5/21/99
    Dv./Matilda Culbertson 9/9/57
    Francis M./Louisa K. Price 12/20/59
628. DARFER
    Hn. O./Eliz. Hammond 5/2/17
629. DARK
    John/Han. Pickerin 11/19/21
630. DARLINGTON
    Tho./Isa. Henderson 3/3/01
631. DARNELL
    Emanuel/Eliza Hyett 8/1/23
632. DASHER
    Dv./Chna. Glassbrenner 12/12/26
633. DAUBEL
    Hn./Barb. Killerin 2/7/22
634. DAUGHERTY (DOUGHERTY)
    Sam./Cath. Embigh 5/2/07
    Tho./Mary Holman 2/11/08
    Chas./Marg. Trimbles 12/14/12
    Alex./Eliz. F. Mackey 2/21/16
    Jm./Susan Palmer 7/24/45
    Jm./Marg. Palmer 12/6/51
635. DAVENPORT (DEVENPORT)
    Wm./Na. Catlett 11/24/08
    Benj./Eliz. Cramer 11/9/26

636. DAVID
    John/Cath. Hose 12/1/21
637. DAVIDSON (DAVISON)
    John/Mary Gearhart 7/19/10
    Rob./Latitia Kinner 2/14/14
    John/Rachel Moss 12/29/37
638. DAVIN
    Wm./Mary Ann Daniel 3/10/34
639. DAVIS
    Stephen/Rachel Peddicord 7/16/00
    Francis/Ephla Carey 7/28/03
    Jm./Na. Panott 7/21/03
    Sam. H./Mary Slimmer 2/10/03
    Tho./Mary Snyder 4/9/03
    And./Eleanor Jones 2/20/04
    Eph./Eliz. Brantner 11/22/08
    Dn./Mary Bowles 9/4/09
    Jc./Mary Tice 11/16/10
    And./Betsy Vansant 6/24/11
    Nathan/Matilda Hayes 10/24/12
    John/Mary Betts 8/5/13
    Ezekiel/Sr. McKinney 5/8/15
    John/Eliz. Bowles 5/5/18
    Vincent/Sus. Hammond 2/1/18
    Jese F./Eliz. Stine 3/14/20
    John/Matilda Arnold 4/8/20
    Rich./Eliza Downs 3/28/20
    Ed./Na. Smith 4/26/21
    Elias/Am. Seybert 12/23/22
    Jc./Sr. Potter 5/29/22
    Wm./Cath. Blentlinger 4/6/22
    Jesse/So. Grim 3/28/23
    Tho./Mary Haynes 11/29/23
    Hn./Jenny Shirley 9/27/26
    Sol./Mary Zuck 10/10/26
    Jm./Mary Ann Murry 9/11/27
    Wm./Clara R.C. Linkhorn 2/20/27
    Wm./Eliz. Clayton 3/15/27
    Zachariah/Eve Haller 5/19/28
    John/Hester McNet 12/14/31
    Ed./Rachel Neill 5/11/33
    Gilbert/Ann Mary Barr 1/2/34
    John A./Mary Ann Shirley 6/3/34
    Rich./Eliz. Wolcott 1/17/34
    Wm./Mary A. Knodle 9/1/34
    Cornelius/Lavania Barks 6/3/37
    Ed./Mary McFarland 9/18/38
    John S./Reb. E. Neff 4/6/38
    John/Maria Artz 2/18/40
    Rich. W./Susan A. Tilghman 12/3/40
    Denton/Am. Middlekauff 1/21/41
    Wm./Amanda E. Gelwicks 6/1/41
    Geo./Barb. Craiglow 8/5/42
    John/Ann Maria Shriver 4/3/43
    Nathan/Ellen Denure 16/25/45
    Wm./Marg. E. Rohrer 2/18/45
    Sol./Reb. E. Fletcher 8/5/48

639. DAVIS (Continued)
     John/Delana Kretzer 3/3/49
     John/Sus. Buhrman 3/30/50
     Elias/Marg. A. Strause 11/8/51
     Jonas/Mary Roher 9/22/51
     Mt. J./Mary Rohr 9/22/51
     Rich. L./Ann Am. Hammer 12/8/52
     Jon./Mary Lookensland 2/14/53
     John/Mary Gruber 8/15/54
     Elias Jr./Matilda Barber 3/12/56
     F.M./Maria M. Bender 9/8/56
     Wm. D./Louisa Stiffler 5/5/56
     Jm. A./Ruey Chrisman 3/16/58
     Rich./Maria Hawthorn 12/29/60
640. DAWSON
     Lewis/Amanda Wigginton 4/27/41
641. DAYHOFF (DAYHOOF, DEHOFF)
     Joshua/Marg. Preadt 4/1/28
     John/Sr. Prett 12/16/36
     Hn./Mary R. Houser 10/10/49
642. DEAL (DEALE, DEEL)
     Jc./Cath. Ridenour 4/21/07
     Tho./Eliz. McCoy 8/29/11
     Francis M./Mary A. Crouse 1/12/50
643. DEAN
     Geo./Mary Snider 5/3/24
     John/Caroline Boersth 11/1/25
644. DEANER (DEENER)
     Wm./Eliz. Grimm 1/20/19
     Conrad/Mary Doll 3/25/20
     Chn./Eliz. Shrouder 10/9/24
     Chn./Eliz. Geeting 12/20/28
     Chn./Eliz. Detwiler 3/27/32
     Jonas S./Ann M. Baker 10/28/48
645. DEAVER (DEAVERS, DEEVERS, DEVERS)
     Josiah B./Am. Shanabarger 4/29/28
     Geo. W./Kate Cordelia Bowers 4/5/56
646. DEBRING
     Francis/Lucy M. Grosh 1/25/60
647. DECK
     Dv./Lethy Prather 4/3/38
648. DECKER
     Wm./Marg. Hall 2/23/29
649. DECROON
     Jean/Margaretta Delkour 3/27/56
650. DEEDS
     Mich./Sr. Spielman 1/28/30
651. DEEHART
     Pt. S./Mary Hany 12/16/19
652. DEGNAN
     Mich./Eliz. Deacon 6/17/38
653. DEGRAFT
     Abr./Am. Beckley 10/24/12

654. DEIBERT (DIBERT)
     Jc./Eliz. Warner 3/21/08
     John/Eliz. Cretzinger 5/19/08
     Hamilton V./Mary Jane Flora 7/21/60
655. DEIFFENBAUGHEN
     Geo./Cath. Justice 12/29/51
656. DEIHL (DIEHL)
     Hn./Cath. Shank 5/5/10
     Geo./Elizth Powles 7/16/50
657. DEITER (DIETER)
     John/Mary Pencil 3/7/08
     Geo./Cath. Stover 8/26/22
658. DEITRICK (DEITRICH)
     John/Mary Ann Dinkle 3/28/33
     Hn./Eliza Ann Hicks 11/30/38
     Sam./Susan Haines 5/11/44
     Dn./Ann Bevans 4/2/53
     Lewis/Rose Ann Moats 2/22/54
659. DELAUGHTER (DELAWTER, DELAUTER)
     Dv./Cath. Harshman 5/26/12
     Geo./Eliz. Bussard 1/10/14
     Dv./Eliz. Harshman 9/19/15
     Jon./Eliz. Witmer 8/9/28
     Hn./Am. Bowman 11/15/43
     Geo. Adam/Mahala M. Boyer 8/29/46
     Geo. W./Isa. Brown 3/27/55
660. DELCOUR
     John/Mary Walder 11/18/52
661. DELLEN
     Aaron/Eliz. Havener 6/5/13
662. DELLINGER (DELINGER)
     Hn./Cath. Cromley 1/25/05
     Fred./Eliz. Wyant 11/20/09
     Wm./Mary Lefever 1/6/31
     John F./Sr. Lefever 2/1/32
     Hn. W./Mary M. Snider 4/28/34
     Chas./Susan Roby 11/30/35
     Lewis H./Eliz. J. McClain 12/8/41
     Wm./Ann A. Reynolds 12/26/43
     John F./Ann Cath. Steinmetz 8/19/45
     John F./Ann E. Johnson 10/26/57
663. DELOTZER
     Ig./Sus. Nicholson 10/29/05
664. DENCER
     Wm./Lena Goody 3/7/38
665. DENER
     Sam./Chra. Wyne 3/22/24
666. DENIUS
     Sol. K./Mary Ann Shafer 2/18/30
667. DENNY (DENEY, DENNEY)
     Neale/Mary Eichelberger 2/25/10
     Jos./Har. Burrows 6/26/12
668. DENOON (DENOONS)
     Elias/Eliz. Howard 12/31/16
     Emanuel/Rachel Malott 8/31/28
669. DENTLER
     John H./Dorothy A. McGinley 10/16/56

670. DERNLY
Mark/Adeline M.L. Zwisher 1/25/31
671 DERR
Geo. W./Ellen Eliz. Shaw 4/28/43
672. DESPOES
Leon/Berthilde Levy 11/8/54
673. DETER
Wm. S./Cath. Clevidence 4/6/58
674. DETERLY
I.L./Frances Taylor 6/25/35
675. DETRICK (DIETRICK, DEITRICH)
Geo./Barb. Houser 3/7/05
Fred./Eve Gilbert 3/14/09
Pt./Cath. Keyser 7/20/13
John/Na. Avey 3/21/15
Jc./Sus. Waltmerry 3/18/16
Jc./Sr. Startzman 9/3/17
Sam./Eliz. Reitz 12/22/24
676. DETLOW
Hn./Susan Grove 10/2/37
677. DETRO
Joshua/Sr. Ann Barkman 4/30/46
678. DETTLEBAUGH
S.L./Miriam Arnold 9/20/51
679. DETWILER
Elijah/Cath. Geeting 11/8/41
680. DEVENNY
Dv. C./Mary Light 7/8/24
681. DEVLIN
John/Mary McGonagle 7/15/28
682. DIAMOND
John/Mary A. Clevidence 10/23/37
683. DICK (DICKE, DICKES, DICKS)
Hn./Eliz. Baryman 8/1/07
Dv./Na. Leiser 10/5/09
Geo./Eliz. Bowman 7/27/23
Alex./Bridget Causgrove 2/12/33
Hn./Barb. Beechler 8/31/39
Dv./Rachel Kline 11/28/53
684. DICKENSON
Jm. G./Susan O. Throp 1/25/43
685. DICKERHOOF
Geo./Mary Brewer 9/15/44
Sol./Maria Dugan 12/10/49
686. DICKEY
John/Lucretia Athey 4/25/32
687. DIFFENBACHER
Mt./Na. Sweitzer 6/8/26
688. DIFFENBAUGH
John M. Jr./Barb. Charles 5/7/14
689. DIGGINS
Tho./Esther Casson 9/4/02
690. DIGGS
Is./Reb. Holmes 6/2/49
Perry/Char. Gay 5/19/49
Is. M./Gennett Piper 5/22/60

691. DIL
Jm./Sr. Gouff 4/3/47
692. DILALTER
Fred./Marg. Rone 9/30/41
693. DILGOUR
Jos./Marg. Smouder 5/29/52
694. DILLAHUNT (DILAHUNT, DILLEHUNT)
Wm./Cath. Creigh 5/27/05
Jm./Cath. Leckroon 10/18/17
Wm./Sr. Ann Hennebreger 5/17/32
Dv./So. Lemon 9/17/39
Alex. M./Han. Malong 5/16/40
695. DILLMAN
Ph./Na. Springer 11/9/04
696. DILLON
Tho./Polly Stultz 6/21/03
Ig./Sr. Hammett 3/9/11
John/Eliz. Rilblitt 2/25/25
697. DILLY
Jm./Sr. Burkhart 6/17/18
698. DIMICK
Alphuis/Maria T. Carr 11/5/18
699. DISHONG
Hn./Mary Groombaugh 8/22/00
700. DITCH
Hn./Eliz. Jones 4/13/05
701. DITMER
John/Mary Stultz 5/21/05
702. DITTO
Abr./Mary Berry 10/22/07
Wm./Caroline Kershner 11/29/23
Jm. B./Eliz. Sibert 2/25/35
Abr./Ann Strite 12/7/52
Nelson J./Mar. B. Keller 6/16/53
Wm. J./Charity Hitchcock 10/5/54
703. DIVELBISS (DEVALBISS, DEVILBIST,
DIVILBEST)
Geo./Mary O'Ferrel 2/14/06
Jm. W./Ann Mary Hookes 5/7/49
Adolphus/Sr. J. Weast 6/9/58
704. DIVINE
Mich./So. May 11/16/39
705. DIXON
Hez./Marg. Bowman 4/20/30
Hn. F./Annie E. Brown 1/6/35
Jm./Susan Kidwiler 11/29/47
Wm./Ellen Kitzmiller 12/4/48
706. DOCHERTY
Pat./Ellen Ryan 12/28/33
707. DOCTOR
John/Mahala Scary 12/4/27
708. DODD
Sam./Cath. Speck 10/9/17
709. DOLEN
Chas./Cath. Crow 10/4/27
710. DOLING
Sam./Eliz. Devore 4/4/16

711. DOLL
John R./Meliora Buchanan 2/23/19
712. DOMER
John/Sr. Majers 8/14/26
Jc./Rachel Dennison 5/10/30
Raleigh/Susan Hill 10/30/47
Hn./Mary Eliz. Netts 12/20/53
713. DONALDSON
Tho./Mary Snyder 2/7/01
Hez./Sr. Willis 4/14/18
John/Reb. Mallory 6/24/24
714. DONHELM
Chas./Malinda Tracy 4/2/44
715. DONNELLY (DONNALLY)
Dn./Sr. Mohler 5/26/19
Dn./Eliz. Mohler 8/1/22
Owen/Mary Manion 11/29/32
Hugh/Mrs. Garraghty 7/5/37
Ed./Mary McHann 1/7/51
Ed./Mary Kail 2/12/55
716. DONOHOE
Sam./Mary Jane Morris 12/30/58
717. DONOVAN (DONAVAN)
Cornelius/Marg. Barret 10/9/33
Timothy/Mary Lane 2/18/24
718. DOOBLE (DOOPLE, DUBEL, DUPLE, DUBBLE,
DUBBEL, DUBAL, DOUBBLE)
Jc./Sus. Avey 6/25/10
Jon./Cath. Palmer 10/6/10
Hn./Susan McDill 3/24/19
And./Susan Glooze 3/7/22
Jon./Marg. Boward 9/26/33
Jos./Marg. Wolf 3/11/53
Mt./Amanda Thomas 1/24/53
Elias/Cath. Schlusser 10/10/55
719. DORENTZ
Jm./Mary Kershner 12/14/31
720. DORSEY
Benj./Cath. Porin 4/5/03
Fred./Sr. Clagett 1/25/03
Francis/Sr. Forbus 11/18/06
Francis/Eliza Crow 7/20/24
John Clagett/Louisa Ann Hughes 4/1/25
Wm. H./Marg. C. Martin 1/8/52
Benj./Eliz. Ardinger 6/11/56
721. DORSIN
Fred./Eliz. M. Davis 7/25/57
722. DOTTERER
Fred./Eliz. Wolf 4/1/15
723. DOUB
Sam./Lydia Stouffer 2/11/32
Jon./Cath. Rinehart 3/4/38
Jon./Eliz. Spessard 2/21/40
Ph. R./Cornelia Witmer 2/22/54
Simon/Ann Maria Leckrone 1/17/55
724. DOUGLAS (DOUGLASS)
Otho/Han. Gillis 5/25/11
Is. R./Marg. G. Stephenson 3/11/29

Rob./Mary Robertson 9/19/36
Dv./Ann M. Clark 5/24/51
725. DOUMM
John/Eliz. Meely 6/9/29
726. DOUP
Joel/Mary Schlosser 3/5/27
727. DOVENBERGER
John/Mary Eakel 9/13/13
Chn./Eliz. Butterbaugh 2/2/46
728. DOWELL
John/Juliet Hamilton 11/28/21
729. DOWERMAN
Jc./Mary Ann Barkdoll 12/23/47
730. DOWLER
Jm. C./Sr. Mills 10/23/16
Jm./Phebe Robertson 10/28/19
Jm. W./Mary Shank 11/20/60
731. DOWNEY
Jm./Cath. Wishard 12/2/05
Basil/Matilda Jones 3/26/06
Rob./Barb. Bealer 2/22/12
John/Anna Deal 9/13/15
Sam. I./Ann Maria Conradt 4/9/27
Pt./Mary McDade 12/5/32
Louis/Dassy Brown 8/26/34
Wm. Harrison/Eveline Curry 5/10/42
Tho. E./Hen. Clarke 10/20/49
732. DOWNIN
Jc. I./Mary Jane Kreigh 2/16/39
Sam. S./Mar. Fichter 9/19/54
Dv./Sr. Ellen Stine 11/10/55
Dn./Cath. Bridge 9/14/57
733. DOWNING
Timothy/Chra. Bowser 12/29/02
Timothy/Cath. Sonsall 7/5/06
John/Abigail White 2/17/07
Dv./Celinda Rothrauff 2/26/25
734. DOWNS (DOWNES)
Wm./Hen. Downs 12/22/13
Benj./Eliz. P. Downs 1/18/14
Chas. G./Sr. Esminger 3/19/20
Elxious/Mary Ann Stiffler 3/5/27
Chr./Ann Reb. Kurfman 1/29/50
Lewis/Maria Downey 12/17/56
735. DOYLE
Barnett/Na. Bivens 4/14/06
Wm./Marg. Byers 4/17/28
Pat./Na. Frill 8/10/33
Jm./Eliz. Dugan 1/18/41
John/Bridget Horn 10/8/50
736. DRAGESSER
Tho./Marg. Hartman 9/29/38
737. DRANE
Rich./Mar. E. Watson 11/26/50
738. DRAPER
Geo./Mary Ryan 10/15/36
Is./Lenora Hover 8/23/37

27

738. DRAPER (Continued)
Wm./Char. Hurley 4/3/38
Jm./Ann E. Brewer 2/3/40
John/Eliza Kline 6/5/47
739. DRENNEN
John W./Susan Stine 1/30/44
740. DRENNER (DRENNERS)
Hn./Sus. Miller 1/15/19
Jer./Susan M. Fluck 2/14/37
Jos./Hen. Taylor 11/20/44
Jc./Mary Jane Duke 2/28/47
John W./So. Keefauver 4/11/53
Jon./Mary Neikirk 4/12/54
Geo./Malinda C. Hager 12/20/54
John W./Helen Eliz. Myers 12/8/56
Silas/Eliz. Carr 9/10/57
741. DRESCOLL (DRISKELL)
Pat. O./Mary Byers 4/9/35
Mich./Caroline Lauer 11/21/37
742. DRESLER
Jc./Barb. Fare 4/4/05
743. DREW
Dn./Julian O'Boyle 6/6/28
744. DREXLER
Fred./Caroline Bowser 6/10/47
745. DRILL
John/Eliz. Protzmann 3/3/30
John Hn./Lay Ann Wice 6/27/56
746. DRUBY
Jc./Mary Welty 11/8/17
747. DRUM
John/Marg. Hess 8/18/04
748. DUCKETT
Tho. B./Eliza C. Gabby 3/13/39
749. DUDLEY
Wm. Guilford/Na. Rankin 6/29/10
750. DUFF
John/Mary Barks 6/6/32
751. DUFFIELD
Rich./Eliz. Dark 9/2/06
752. DUFFIN
Mich./Elleanora Davis 3/3/41
753. DUFFY
Wm./Eliz. M. Dusing 9/15/38
Wm. S./Eliza F. Stake 2/14/54
754. DUGAN (DOUGAN)
Wm./Mary Billings 5/2/09
Francis R./Lucretia McCardell 8/21/27
Anthony/Mary Smith (or South) 10/15/36
Cumberland/Har. Buchanan 9/16/56
John/Mary Davis 6/7/15
755. DUKE
John/Mary Link 8/22/11
Wm./Eleanora Smith 4/18/39
756. DULANY
Mich./Mary Newman 2/3/38

757. DULAPLAIN
John/Jane Breathed 12/16/35
758. DUMISON
And./Sus. Wyant 3/18/03
759. DUNBAUGH
Jc./Barb. Wilds 10/3/37
760. DUNCAMON
Ed. M./Cath. Kearon 1/13/34
761. DUNCAN (DUNKIN)
Burnard/Mariah McGary 7/18/35
Rob./Hen. Byers 7/27/44
John G./Louisa Laypole 12/4/50
762. DUNIMERICAN
Fred. H.R./Mary C. Long 8/18/39
763. DUNKLE
Dv./Sus. Schartzer 8/29/10
764. DUNLAP
Jm./Eliz. Britten 4/11/07
765. DUNN
John/Mary Kershner 8/18/04
John/Na. Schnebly 5/16/10
Jc./Ros. Kershner 8/3/11
John/Eliz. Baldwin 10/6/11
Rob./Mary Ann Forsythe 8/22/26
Owen/Mary Wheling 4/5/36
Wm./Bridget Fitzgerald 1/20/36
Allen/Sr. Troxall 3/23/37
Sam./Elleatta Susan Howard 3/7/38
Dn./Eliz. Shindle 12/12/39
Jm./Hen. Poe 5/11/41
766. DUPY
John/Mary Smith 4/29/23
767. DURANBERGER
Jc./Cath. Holler 2/9/36
768. DURBAN
Wm./Ann Faulders 5/22/30
769. DURBORAW
Absalum/Ann Staphey 4/14/35
770. DURFF
Otho/Marg. Kearney 2/25/31
771. DURNBAUGH
Jc./Sr. Lambert 3/7/46
772. DURNEND
Ed./Cath. Munday 6/17/33
773. DUSING
Sam./Mary Ann Clarke 7/3/24
Hn./Mary Ann Rutter 2/25/30
Pt./Na. Wilkinson 8/30/38
Jc./Malinda Morrison 12/22/53
Elias C./Savilla Smith 1/23/58
774. DUSINGER
Is./Cath. Eliz. Leggett 2/3/43
775. DUTROW (DUTARO, DUTTEROW)
John/Mary Fulton 11/17/06
Geo./Sus. Miller 3/25/06
Jc./Eliz. Weast 2/13/15
776. DWYER
Mich./Cath. Clarke 4/9/32

777. DYE
Joshua/Sr. Ann Lopp 5/26/58
778. EACH
Tho./Mary Button 6/18/25
779. EACHUS
Phineas/Sr. Gaff 1/12/13
And./Char. Springer 12/18/55
780. EAGAN (EAGON)
Wm./Sr. Louise Meritt 5/8/34
Pt./Cath. Eagan 6/17/36
Hugh/Frances Terry 4/21/54
781. EAGLETON
John/Peggy Branson 11/10/20
782. EAKEL (EAKLE)
Wm./Eliz. Colleflower 9/3/07
Hn. Sr./Francy Funk 10/9/10
Jc./Eliz. Fink 5/5/12
John/Sr. Line 3/12/18
Jos./Cath. Kauffman 3/26/22
Abr./Na. Ott 4/7/28
Geo. Colliflower/Susan Dundore 10/3/29
Hez./Marg. A. Varvel 3/6/32
John D./Mary Thomas 2/26/33
Amos/Mary Eakle 8/8/36
John D./Eliz. Yessler 9/15/36
John P./Ann C. Wheritt 9/29/38
Mt./Cath. Schnebly 11/27/38
Absolum/Arnslia Grim 1/7/39
Elias/Leathia Reynolds 4/19/42
Elias/Eveline Ambrose 3/7/43
Tho./Anna Norris 12/21/44
Wash. H./Rea Ruth Fogler 3/20/44
Jc./Cath. Wagoner 6/3/47
Caleb F./Sr. C. Bear 3/2/52
Geo. W./Mary A. Hammond 5/26/52
Hn./Caroline Doub 2/17/52
Absalom/Amanda Cath. Stone 10/16/60
783. EARHART
John W./Susan C. O'Neal 8/9/45
784. EARICK
Jc./Cath. Nickless 3/1/47
John Hn./Am. Creager 11/27/48
785. EARLEY
Jm. A./Mary Ann Moore 7/20/41
786. EARLOUGHER
Mich./Marg. Smith 10/10/40
787. EASTERDAY
Mich./Motlena Daganhart 9/28/02
Geo./Susan Smith 9/9/26
Jc./Francy Nafe 4/13/29
Sam./Lavinia Shecter 3/26/30
Jc./Eliz. Marteny 2/24/37
John/Marg. Leiser 6/16/56
788. EASTON
Wm./Sr. Butler 10/30/04
Elisha/Mar. Allen 8/27/11

Wm. B./Mary Molendore 10/27/29
Wm./Reb. Blecher 11/18/35
Elisha/Eliz. Norris 5/16/44
Hez./Mary Ann Reynolds 4/23/44
Levi/Mary B. Kealhofer 1/9/50
789. EAVEY (EVEY, EAVY)
Sam./So. Nighswander 4/12/20
Is. D./Caroline T. Hammond 5/29/37
John/Marg. C. Knode 3/5/38
Jc. D./Marg. Weast 1/20/47
Sol./Cath. Beard 3/4/52
Hn. S./Sr. C. Hoffman 2/15/53
790. EBAUGH
John S./Eliza Ann Kreps 9/15/18
791. EBB
Edwin/Cath. Spahn (Spong) 11/25/37
792. ECKERT (ECARD, ECKER)
John/Eliz. Snively 9/10/01
Pt./Cath. Ambrose 4/11/11
John/Mrs. Cath. Boone 2/10/38
Elhanan/Anna S. Keedy 12/21/53
John/Eliz. Fisher 5/15/58
793. ECKMON (ECKMAN)
Geo./Marg. Davis 8/24/59
794. ECTON
Wm. A./Mary Jane Himes 2/1/48
795. EDDINGER
Jos. S./Mary Eversole 12/18/41
796. EDELER
Chas./Eliz. Ridenour 4/9/29
797. EDMONDS
Elias/Na. Strode 8/19/09
Benj./Sr. Cable 11/12/25
Joel/Sr. Houser 5/7/27
Alex./Mary Rulett 1/1/30
Benj. Alex./Marg. Wolf 12/20/42
John Wm./Sr. Morgan Thomburg 11/25/47
798. EDWARDS
John/Mary Combs 4/25/99
Pat./Teresa Smith 4/12/00
Benj./Elenor Perin 10/26/03
Rob./Jane Anderson 11/13/06
Geo./Cath. Harman 4/17/09
Owen/Maria Sterrett 2/29/13
Dn./Eliz. Borauff 6/1/16
Pt./Cath. Unger 12/28/22
Tho. O./Marg. M. Boerstler 4/30/32
Emory/Han. P.B. Grim 3/7/36
Geo./Letitia Nicholas 12/6/37
799. EICHELBERGER
Pt./Sr. Kershner 7/18/15
Jos./Mahala Snider 7/30/38
Dr. P.I./Mary Ann Fockler 3/16/41
Geo./Eliz. Mouse 10/7/44
Elie H./Ann Virginia Roulette 4/12/51
John/Ann Mills 5/24/53
Jon. D./Sr. C. Wildt 2/23/53

800. EIDSON
   Hn./Marg. Baylor 6/3/34
801. EIKELBARNER
   John L./Ellen Ault 9/18/56
802. EILER
   Geo./Ann Myers 1/9/08
803. ELDRIDGE
   Clarke/Eliz. Jane Stephens 9/5/36
804. ELIFRITZ (ELIFRITS)
   Geo./Eliz. Boward 8/20/40
805. ELLICOTT
   Ed. T./Ann Cath. Swope 5/26/42
806. ELLIOTT
   Geo./Eliza Dilahunt 1/12/19
   Jm. B./Eliz. Marshall 11/24/29
   John/Mary Ann McAhan 11/3/41
   Rob./Eliz. Emiline Hartman 2/2/42
   Wm./Mary Ellen Snyder 4/15/52
807. ELLIS
   Jc./Han. Ogelsby 3/29/10
   Abr./Sr. Couchman 7/30/17
   John/Eliza Jacques 3/12/34
   Jm./Eliz. McCoy 3/2/38
   Dv. H./Susan E. Small 2/15/45
808. EMBIGH (EMPICH, EMBICH, EMPICK)
   Ph./Marg. Stuckey 6/27/05
   Jc./Marg. Woldwine 4/26/08
809. EMERSON (EMARSON, EMMERSON)
   Jos./Eliz. Hershberger 8/1/06
   Tho./Rachel Stoner 1/18/20
   John/Marg. Bridgeman 2/10/27
   John/Marg. French 11/29/54
810. EMLEY
   Tho./Hetty Burr 5/26/03
811. EMMERICK
   John/Eliz. Smelser 9/18/06
812. EMMERT
   Mich./Na. Moyer 10/5/19
   Jos./Eliz. Reynolds 2/24/24
   John/Eliz. Forny 11/20/26
   Dn./Sr. Stouffer 3/29/27
   Dn./Reb. Eavey 2/4/29
   Jc./Mary Newcomer 12/15/30
   Sam./Mary Newcomer 2/2/30
   John/Mary Newcomer 4/22/34
   Mich./Mary Wolf 2/10/38
   Leo./Sr. Newcomer 2/1/40
   John/Ann Hershey 10/28/43
   John/Louisa M. Burchart 10/14/46
   Mt. L./Ann Russell 9/4/49
   Jc. P./Cath. Dubbel 2/26/50
   And./Sus. Hoffer 8/28/52
   Jc./Mag. Welty 11/7/53
   Leo./Sr. Webster 3/5/53
   Benj./Elmira Crampton 1/31/55
   Leo./Sr. Warvel 12/10/55
   Hn. F./Urilla Winder 1/8/56

813. EMMONS
   Tho./Sr. Rogers 7/21/20
814. ENDERS
   Sam./Sus. Parrott 9/27/22
815. ENDEY
   John/Mary Cath. Dinges 4/27/44
816. ENGLAND
   Sam./Mary Worley 7/23/31
817. ENGLE
   Mt./Stasha Robey 8/27/03
   Edwin C./Na. Snyder 2/29/36
   Ph./Sr. Ann Strider 3/8/36
   Bennett W./Mary E. Lee 11/2/40
818. ENGLEBRIGHT
   I.W./Eliz. C. Mish 4/29/34
   Wm. F./Mary Cath. Reid 4/14/57
819. ENGLISH
   John M./Ann Maria Martin 1/5/32
820. ENNIS
   Jos./Juliann Miller 3/5/46
821. ENSMINGER (ESMINGER)
   Ludwick/Polly Wyant 2/16/00
   John/Cath. Wiant 3/3/01
   Geo./Marg. Albert 6/6/08
   Ph./Eliz. Stamm 9/16/12
   Mt./Marg. Smith 11/28/21
   Wm./Eliz. Little 1/4/53
822. ENSTEIN (EINSTEIN)
   Myer/Miriam Levi 6/17/56
823. ENSWILER
   Jc./Eliz. Newby 6/1/26
824. ENSWORTH (ENDSWORTH)
   Tho./Sr. Ann Himes 11/3/47
825. ENT
   Geo. W./Marg. Woltz 9/30/06
826. ENTLER
   Jos./Mary Rickert 9/12/17
   Geo./Cath. E. Lakins 9/1/27
   Mt. L./Lizzie B. Herr 6/3/59
827. EPPREIGHT
   Hn./Mary Moyer 4/3/09
828. ERNEST
   John G./Julianna Gardnour 9/16/34
829. ERNST
   John M./Cath. Entler 11/16/37
830. ERRICK
   Jc./Marg. Chernutt 8/5/05
831. ERRICKSON
   Jm./Reb. Malone 5/20/01
832. ERVIN
   John/Molly Bomgardner 8/29/01
833. ETNIRE (ETNYRE, ETTENERE, ETTENIRE)
   Hn./Sally Bealer 3/31/10
   John/Eliz. Piper 1/31/17
   Joshua/Susan Rhodes 9/16/43
   Sam./Cath. Doubble 1/30/47
834. ETTINGER
   John A./Barb. Neikirk 5/12/46

835. EVANS
     Tho./Clarissa Thomas 3/14/03
     Jm./Eliz. Tagore 4/1/07
     Wm. W./Sr. Chapline 2/4/08
     Geo./Mary Turner 3/14/15
     Evan/Mary Bruce 4/4/16
     Jos./Han. Lincoln 5/19/17
     Timothy/Eliz. McCain 6/19/19
     Wm./Fanny Lambert 3/17/23
836. EVERETT
     Benj. H./Mary I. Gilmer
     Amos/Sr. Blair 8/17/55

     Amos/Marg. Bowman 11/25/57
837. EVERHART
     John/Julianna Harbaugh 12/26/22
     Dn./Mary Dutrow 10/19/47
     Romanus/Eliz. Thombson 2/28/50
838. EVERSOLE (EBERSOLE)
     Emanuel/Ann Miller 4/19/08
839. EYLER
     Hn./Mary Jane Morrison 5/12/51
840. EYERLY
     Wm./Malinda Eakle 12/5/49
     Dn. H./Emily I. Winders 12/10/57
     Franklin/Mary Mathews 1/26/58

1. FACHENCOTH
   Geo./Eliz. Fritz 3/8/14
2. FAGAN
   Rich./Phebe O'Brian 5/7/44
3. FAGUE
   Geo. Jr./Na. Jurden 6/1/13
   Mich./Ros. Liser 6/6/15
   John/Cath. Boone 1/24/39
4. FAHAY
   Rich./Polly Elliott 8/5/33
5. FAHNESTOCK
   Pt./Caroline Yeakel 7/23/33
6. FAHRNY (FAHERNEY, FAHRNEY)
   Sam./Barb. Gantz 9/30/17
   Jc./Cath. Welty 11/20/22
   Pt. Jr./Eliz. Emmert 2/24/29
   Dn./Amey Welty 11/8/39
   Dv./Barb. Bowser 6/22/42
   And./Sr. Rice 3/12/45
   Nich./Mary Gray 11/19/47
   Pt./Tracy Hanna 9/9/48
   Sam./Han. Wyles 1/1/49
   And./Eliz. Funk 3/14/51
   Jc./Mary Cath. Rohrer 4/29/51
   Josias/Lydia Ellen Drenner 9/27/51
   John/Marg. Foulder 7/9/53
   Jc./Mary L. Middlekauff 11/14/55
   Benj./Lucy A. Tice 2/8/59
   Dn. P./Susan M. Middlekauff 1/9/60
7. FALE
   John/Sr. Nowell 3/9/05
8. FALEY
   Tho./Jane O'Donnell 5/2/35
9. FALKLER
   Jc./Cath. Fishauk 2/7/18
   Geo./Reb. Wilson 6/27/43
10. FALIS
    Wm./Diana Freaney 6/12/32
11. FANGWELL
    Geo./Reb. Friend 1/14/23
12. FARBER (FAUBER)
    Adam/Cath. Wagoner 2/14/04
    Sebastian/Mary Jones 8/29/08
13. FARE
    Mich./Eliz. Blickenstaff 11/8/03
14. FARMER
    Dn./Mary Gray 5/2/09
    And. M./Cath. Esminger 4/8/28
15. FARNSWORTH
    John/Jane Messen 6/10/99
16. FARQUHAR
    Geo./Eliz. Springer 5/10/14
17. FARR
    Levi/Mary Ann Saunders 4/9/20
18. FARRAN (FARREN, FARRON)
    Geo./Mary Ribble 4/4/16

19. FARRELL (FARREL)
    John/Alice Sharkey 7/20/14
    John O./Eliza Humerichouse (probably John
      O'Ferrell) 10/22/22
    Wm./Bridgett Farrell 10/26/33
    Jm./Susan Murry 2/11/34
    Jm./Mrs. Lee 2/2/37
20. FARROW
    John/Peggy McCall 12/29/27
    John/Sr. E. Brengle 11/25/51
    Jos. H./Mary Susan Nitzell 9/3/53
21. FARSON
    Nathan/Mary McCall 4/16/24
22. FARST
    Jc./Sr. Hogan 2/16/24
    Sam./Malinda Wolf 8/10/40
23. FASNAUGHT (FAUSNACH, FAUSNAUGHT, FOSNAUGHT)
    Bernard/Eliz. Wolf 4/30/99
    John/Barb. Wornick 8/6/04
    John/Ros. Wallich 8/31/12
    Wendal/Eliz. Wallich 5/3/13
    Jc./Betsy Snyder 12/23/15
    Abr./Barb. Nighwander 2/8/28
    Jos./Caroline Orrick 2/26/33
    Hn./Marg. Carls 5/1/37
    Hn./Lydia Ross 11/4/47
    Urias/Loretta Adams 12/9/54
24. FAUGHT
    John/Drusilla Bright 2/3/30
25. FAULDERS (FALDER, FALDERS, FAULDER)
    Wm./Mary Ann Faulders 5/21/17
    Tho./Na. Rohrer 9/3/22
    Sam./Marg. Coon 8/18/29
    Dn./Eliz. Foutz 4/5/36
    Pt./Malinda Moser 9/15/46
    Dv./Eliz. Snyder 2/23/53
    Tho./Leah Hildebrand 1/3/57
    Jm./Ann Am. Snyder 2/10/58
26. FAULKWELL
    Wesley Wm./Marg. M. Kershner 3/14/43
27. FAUST (FOUST)
    Ph./Eliz. Cash 5/9/11
    Hn./Polly Fogwell 4/22/23
28. FAUVER
    Hn./Sabra A. Stottlemyer 8/25/48
29. FAY
    Levy/Mary McCoy 12/19/14
    John/Marg. Morgan 12/21/30
30. FAYALT
    Bart./Mary E. Paull 1/2/41
31. FEBRIC
    Geo./Marg. Hotz 4/11/49
32. FECHRY
    Baylis/Jane Templeman 1/17/54
33. FECHTIG
    Francis Sr./Eliz. Moudy 3/23/18
    John/Sr. Beecher 3/14/22

33. FECHTIG (Continued)
    Geo./Mary E. Yoe 4/17/23
    Jm. I./Cath. J. Emmert 5/6/46
    Chn. C./Sr. O.A. Carver 6/4/46
    Louis R./Mary Ann Oden 10/19/47
    Benj. Yoe/Sophronia A. Morris 9/27/58
34. FEIDT
    John Jr./Cath. Jacques 3/12/33
    John H./Helen Zellers 12/15/57
35. FEIGLEY
    Wm./Mary C. Wiles 4/27/52
    Wm. H./Ann Marg. Stine 3/6/54
    Ed./Eliza Renner 4/18/60
36. FELAY
    John/Mary Jane Moore 11/19/38
37. FELKER
    John/Ann E. Brewer 1/11/50
38. FELLER
    Jos./Na. Finck 6/9/34
39. FELLHEIMER
    Hn./Hen. Enstein 12/14/59
40. FELLINGAURE
    Benj./Ann Hughes 2/10/20
41. FELLINGER
    Fred./Rosaly Weismiller 12/25/37
42. FELTZ
    J. Warren/Susan L. Stonebraker 12/16/54
43. FEMOICK
    Albin/Eliz. Pryer 10/1/99
44. FENBY
    Wm. M./Mar. E. Wade 2/21/17
45. FENN
    Horatio/Hen. Hughes 10/9/32
46. FENTON
    And./Frances Funk 7/21/49
47. FERGUSON (FURGUSON)
    Jos./Na. Jones 12/24/12
    Wm./Na. Hoover 9/21/20
48. FERNSNER
    Lewis/Mar. S. Silver 4/1/52
49. FESSLER
    Dv./Mary Ann Snyder 11/21/49
    John/Susan Macguire 2/25/51
50. FICK (FICH)
    Jm./Sus. Dalong 8/1/07
51. FIELDS
    Isaiah/Esther Stonebraker 8/5/15
    Wm./Eliz. Hause 5/23/25
52. FIELON
    Wm. D./Evanah Hull 6/4/22
53. FIERY (FEIRY, FIREY)
    Jos./Cath. Roach 2/18/12
    Jc./Mary Houser 4/26/15
    Hn./Mar. Miller 10/31/21
    Jc./Barb. Hershey 3/13/28
    John/Ann Mary Brewer 1/21/31
    Jos./Maria Newcomer 11/1/38
    Wm./Eliz. Tice 2/12/40
    Sol./Ann Maria Shindle 1/14/43

    Jos./Cath. Saner 1/17/43
    Benj. F./Ann S. Beckley 2/4/45
    Benj. F./Amanda H. Emmert 12/8/53
    Jos. O./Almira Burckhart 1/25/57
    Jos. H./Mary C. Ridenour 5/18/58
    John H./Caroline E. Shindel 5/16/60
54. FIGALLY (FIGELY, FIGLEY)
    John/Marg. Bowart 11/11/03
    Wm./Sus. Bomgardner 10/13/03
    Jc./Mary Wright 4/8/05
    Pt./Eliz. Coon 5/20/05
    Pt./Na. Moyer 11/30/07
    Hn./Polly Ridenour 3/15/11
    John/Sr. Zimmerman 3/26/31
    John/Sr. Ann Lovier 11/19/35
    Geo./Urilla Night 6/15/44
    Is./Eliz. Redman 9/30/44
55. FIGHT
    Pt./Eliz. Brewer 12/24/03
    Geo./So. Ankeney 4/19/24
56. FILES
    John/Marg. Sylar 2/1/23
57. FILLONEY
    John/Ann Bombarger 12/1/19
58. FILSON
    John/Cath. Swisher 9/13/10
    Wm./Susan Clowser 9/17/29
59. FINFLINCH
    Dn./Ros. Middlekauff 1/13/20
60. FINFROCK (FINAFOUCK, FINEFRUCK)
    John/Marg. Beatty 10/19/26
    John/Louisa V. Betts 10/24/49
    Elias/Sr. Wolf 2/4/50
61. FINK (FINCK)
    Sebastian/Mary McClure 9/2/09
    Geo. F./Mary Dugan 11/21/26
    John Mich./Reb. Bachtell 9/5/29
    And./Na. Blair 4/6/53
62. FINLEY (FINLY)
    Mich. A./Eliza Van Lear 10/3/09
    John M./Mary Van Lear 1/12/15
    Wm./Han. Hope 11/24/18
63. FINNEGAN
    Jm./Har. A.B. Householder 11/26/49
    John H./Mary A. Crouse 2/15/53
    Jm. Wesley/Cath. Grontz 12/23/58
64. FIRESTONE
    Mich./Sus. Russell 1/28/12
65. FIRTH
    Rob. Mawson/Ann Arnold Hibert 1/8/31
66. FISH
    Wm./Mary Ann Brantner 5/1/38
67. FISHAUCK (FISHAUCK, FISHAUGH, FISHUH, FISCHAUCK)
    Hn./Marg. Febry 3/23/22
    Sam./Mary Branstater 1/30/27
    John/Reb. Protzman 10/30/30
    Hn./Polly Gray 3/12/33
    Jc./Eliz. Selser 1/31/35

68. FISHER
    Price/Mary Youngert 6/30/00
    Jc./Ros. From 4/14/20
    John/Eliza Conway 11/27/21
    John D./Sr. South 11/7/26
    Geo./Sr. Fausnaught 1/12/28
    Wm./Delila Stanton 1/2/34
    Geo. I./Is. Johnston 2/9/35
    Chas./Marg. Barber 2/9/41
    Tho./Reb. Jones 5/1/44
    Jm./Julia Ann Burgesser 9/10/45
    Geo./Ellen Smith 3/23/53
    John W./Hellen E. Himes 2/8/59
69. FISSELL
    Geo./Mary Kurfman 12/8/47
70. FITCH
    Dv./Cath. Palmer 11/26/42
    Dv./Mary Poffenberger 1/21/45
71. FITZ (FITZE)
    Fred./Marg. Bevans 1/4/19
    Ulery/Marg. Bridges (Budges) 10/21/37
    Sam./Mary Howard 3/15/42
72. FITZGERALD
    Donald/Maria Estell 9/16/33
73. FITZHUGH
    Wm. Jr./So. Claggett 3/15/09
    Wm. H./Mariah A. Hughes 2/28/18
    Sam. T./Eliza M. Fitzhugh 1/16/23
    Peregrine/Sr. Marg. Pottenger
       9/24/33
    Benj. G./Am. Ragan 3/2/38
    Frank/Ann C. Dorsey 11/23/59
74. FITZPATRICK
    Anthony/Ann Riley 1/16/41
75. FLAGG
    Josiah D./Caroline E. Burckhart
       5/5/35
76. FLAGING
    Fred./Cath. Shilling 5/9/55
77. FLANAGIN (FLANNIGAN)
    Jm./Cath. Wherrett 5/2/26
    Wm./Cath. Holler 10/2/34
    Mich./Maria Farrell 12/19/40
78. FLAUGHER
    John/Marg. Webb 9/15/36
    Wm./Caroline Nichols 3/13/55
79. FLAUTT
    Wm. M./Mary Ann Allender 8/30/27
80. FLEMMING
    Rob./Eliz. Stembaugh 9/21/09
    John/Mary Harrison 8/4/24
    Jm./Am. McCoy 12/24/40
    John A./Mary Susan Wolf 6/9/60
81. FLETCHER
    Azol/Fiscey Dizards 9/9/02
    Lewis/Reb. O'Neal 11/21/17
    Louis/Deliah Shafer 1/5/25
    Chas. A./Eliz Geigler 3/21/29
    Leander/Paten Scriner 12/28/37
    Wm. J./Eliza Neff 5/7/44
    John I./Ann E. Taylor 1/30/51

82. FLINN (FLYNN)
    Chas. H./Marg. Locke 10/8/19
    Mich./Sarah Grove 8/12/34
    Elias C./Sr. M. Foutz 3/19/57
    Jm./Mary Drennen 6/15/59
83. FLOOK (FLUCK)
    Dn. I./Caroline Eliz. Birely 10/7/42
    Dn. B./Eliz. Susan Mumma 11/18/43
84. FLORA
    John/Na. Liday 8/25/01
    Chr./Eliz. Oswald 2/15/04
    John Jr./Sus. Hunt 9/5/07
    John/Ann McKesick 2/20/27
    Adam/Eliz. Unger 4/2/28
    Dv./Eliz. Bignoll 12/16/28 ("of Peter"
       pencil note)
85. FLORY
    Jc./Isa. Liter 10/2/32
    John C./Reb. Bachtel 8/6/36
    Sol./Mary A. Grant 6/2/51
    Berlin H./Barb. Ann Swope 7/28/60
86. FOCKLER
    John/Sus. Westeberger 4/23/10
    Pt./Sus. Yakle 8/6/23
    Geo. T./Marg. Morgan 10/4/37
    Wm./Sus. Schryock 4/25/39
    Benj./Louisa Colleflower 3/3/51
    Wm. F./Mary Ellen Shafer 9/2/59
87. FOGLE
    John/Sus. Beard 9/1/07
88. FOGLER
    John/Cath. Misener 8/24/26
    Curtis/Sr. Geiser 12/10/55
89. FOGLESONG
    Geo./Cath. Snavely 11/9/05
90. FOLK (FOULK, FOUKE, FULK)
    Gasper/Caty Dingler 6/8/99
    Wm./Cath. Wilks 8/12/06
    Geo. J./Eliz. Negley 11/22/32
    Rob. P./Marg. Hessey 9/28/40
    G.F./Mary J. Dorsey 11/18/51
    Geo. F./Ann Wintermyer 3/17/57
    Tho. Van/Calanthia Jane Huyett 12/30/57
    Wm./Lucretia O. Fowler 3/22/58
91. FOLTZ (FULTZ)
    Hn./Eliz. Roseberry 6/28/08
    John/Cath. Gray 1/27/17
    Hn./Ann Goldsberry 6/24/18
    Geo./Mary Smith 8/11/24
    Hn./Na. Rowland 4/29/33
    Jc./Na. Petry 5/19/34
    John/Mary Forrest 3/7/40
    John/Cath. Limebaugh 12/31/41
    Hn./Hen. Fishack 12/22/43
    Geo./Eliz. Betz 12/6/45
    John/Caroline Sager 11/27/47
    John H./Na. Emmert 9/21/58
92. FOOHY
    John/Mrs. Relive 5/27/36

34

93. FORBES
    Tho./Cath. Selser 6/15/00
    A.C./Ann Reb. Rush 1/7/48
94. FORCE
    Wm./Mary Ann Newman 11/15/43
95. FORD
    Jm./Chna. Renner 5/12/06
    Tho./Mary Winters 2/1/20
    John/Mary Fry 7/12/26
    Tho./Julian Alsop 7/28/29
    Price/Mary Itnire 4/2/32
    Jarret B./Cath. Albert 9/25/33
    Joshua/Peggy Smice 3/6/33
    Wm./Marg. Ann Gelwicks 4/17/34
    Wm./Maria Matheny 10/17/42
    John/Cath. Burchart 10/21/47
    Tho./Ann So. Easterday 1/15/49
    Tho./Marg. J. Grosh 10/14/50
    John/Louisa Herd 9/9/52
96. FOREMAN (FORMAN)
    Fred./Marg. Burkett 2/21/09
    Abr./Mary Rowland 12/3/12
    Jos./Juliana Iseminger 3/20/15
    Jc./Eliza Lock 7/20/25
    Jm./Ann Brewner 10/21/31
97. FORGUSON
    John/Rachel Williamson 3/29/05
98. FORNESSER (FOMESSER)
    Hn./Sus. McKenney 6/2/06
    Casper/Mary Price 4/26/09
    Hn./Polly Gower 10/4/17
99. FORREST
    Pt./Rachel Stephens 1/24/03
    Pt./Cath. Martin 1/1/13
    Owen/Eliz. Stottlemeyer 9/2/19
100. FORRESTER
    Chas./Mary Rourke 12/20/36
101. FORRETT
    Sol./Eliz. Wolf 11/22/17
102. FORRY
    John/Cath. Miller 4/11/05
103. FORSYTHE
    John/Sus. Briesh 4/21/52
    Dv./Susan Maria Murray 11/5/59
104. FORTNEY
    Sam./Ann Moffitt 3/11/50
    Tho./Mary Munday 9/12/54
105. FOSTER
    Geo./Sr. Ridenour 3/13/06
    Jer./Mary Webb 12/22/07
    Dv./Sus. Gardner 10/4/28
106. FOUBLE
    Tho./Eliza Beeler 3/14/35
107. FOUCH
    Dv./Louisa Grim 6/9/45
    Dv./Matilda Norris 9/27/48

108. FOUTZ (FOUTS)
    Jc./Eliz. Storm 1/2/06
    Wm./Eliza Eversole 1/10/16
    Hn./Sr. Grosh 6/23/28
    Dv. Jr./Magdalon Emmert 2/22/30
    Greenbury/Ann Eliza Post 2/18/39
    Jackson/Mary Ackerson 3/4/39
    Geo. W./Caroline Wolf 4/6/59
109. FOW
    Jos./Esther Silver 3/22/09
110. FOWLER
    John/Cath. Lutz 11/19/11
    Jm./Mary Inglebrote 12/10/18
    Rob./Susan Keedy 7/23/34
111. FOX
    Hn./Mary Stonebraker 4/11/01
    Casper/Eliz. Wilson 4/8/07
    Abr./Rachel Foreman 4/10/15
    Geo./Mary Gowger 10/20/15
    Ph./Cath. Moggins 11/28/21
    Geo. P./So. Busserd 1/1/22
    Jc./Cath. Buhrman 1/31/34
    Pat./Mary Adlum 3/29/34
    Hn./Cath. Bragonier 3/5/39
    Fred./Cath. Dusing 3/30/43
    Geo. W./Sr. Ann Stayley 7/3/47
112. FOY
    John/Eliz. Hughes 11/2/15
    Mich./Eliz. Gilbert 11/9/19
    Mich./Juliann Wayman 1/2/36
113. FOYLE (FOYLES)
    John A./Sr. Ann Vanmeter 5/15/51
114. FRANCAURY
    Jos./Na. Ray 5/20/03
115. FRANCIS
    Wm. F./Sr. Palmer 7/20/41
116. FRANCISCUS
    Geo./Eliz. Myers 8/26/34
117. FRANKENBERGER
    Conrad/Nelly Boyd 7/21/00
118. FRANKENBERRY
    Sam./Mary South 3/29/15
    Sam./Eliza Redgraves 5/6/23
    Wm./Susan Sigler 2/23/47
119. FRANKHOUSER
    Hn./Mary Bowman 9/3/32
120. FRANTZ
    Fred./Barb. Palmer 4/8/09
    Emanuel/Mary A. Dorrance 4/16/56
    N.W./Mary Warner 9/24/60
121. FRAVER
    Elie/Mary Caffelt 8/31/35
122. FRAZIER
    Lloyd/Mary Jones 6/4/31
    John/Susan McBride 3/15/49
    Wm. R./Har. Eyerly 4/27/55
123. FREAGER
    Geo./Barb. Sarver 6/28/06

35

124. FREANOR (FREANER)
John/Mary Baker 12/31/05
Pat./Mary Burke 9/11/35
Vincent H./Mary C. Weast 1/7/56
125. FREDERICK(FREDRICK)
John/Mary Gortie 8/2/03
Sam./Mrs. Cath. Mott 12/3/37
Conrad/Ann Sisler 2/2/48
126. FREE
Nich./So. Frye 3/20/22
127. FREEMAN
Geo. W./Chna. Startzman 12/30/43
Elias/Mary Null 4/6/48
128. FREESE (FRIESE)
Jc./Har. Babb 11/8/21
And. B./Susan Colliflower 7/12/36
Jc./Lucinda A. Thomas 8/30/55
129. FREIETT
Benj./Molly Snyder 7/20/16
130. FRELAND
Geo./Mrs. Clarine S. Blood 10/23/38
131. FRENCH
Hn./Mary Lefever 6/8/05
John/Na. Wolfensberger 4/21/10
Dv./Mar. Anderson 10/16/11
Geo./Maria Booth 5/24/14
Anthony/Eveline Piles 5/17/28
Geo./Na. Bargett 2/17/41
Andra/Ann Ridenour 1/22/49
Geo./Eliz. R. Hollingsworth 4/6/58
132. FRESH
Jc./Cath. Myers 3/30/40
133. FREY
Jos./Mary M. Beard 6/29/24
Jc./Cath. Shutzen 3/19/35
Enoch/Cath. Kline 10/27/42
134. FRICK
Chas./Mar. Elliott 3/8/26
John/Louisa Stoner 10/23/49
135. FRIDINGER (FREIDINGER)
Chas./Chna. Treiber 4/7/42
John/Isa. Feigley 1/24/49
Hn./Mary A. Easterday 9/15/52
Hn./Frances Coon 10/12/58
136. FRIEDLY
John/Na. Hoover 3/9/24
137. FRIEGLEY
John/Eliz. Sheller 10/7/44
138. FRIEND
Rob. T./Na. Porter 4/17/01
Jc./Cynthia Porter 12/29/18
Kennedy T./Seville S. Shaffner 9/28/26
Hn./Na. Watts 9/8/31
Ed. H./Char. E. Albert 6/18/60
139. FRIENDLY
Jc./Frany Newcomer 1/20/45
140. FRISHCON
John/Barb. Montz 3/14/55

141. FRISKEY
John/Mary E. Hughes 2/23/57
142. FRITZ
Jc./Cath. Cook 12/26/22
John/Cath. Shriver 9/28/27
Wm./Marg. Goodinting 9/1/49
143. FRONK
John/Barb. Shupe 10/24/07
144. FROTT
Nath./Eliz. Linn 4/20/20
145. FRY (FRYE)
Geo./Eliz. Harker 6/5/02
John/Eliz. Miller 3/25/02
Geo./Eliz. Jordan 9/13/08
Mich./Sus. Thomas 10/24/11
Pt./Mary Hayes 2/3/18
Aaron/Cath. Pockley 12/12/32
Dv./Sus. Ridenour 7/27/41
Israel/Sr. Myers 6/30/42
Jos./Emily Rice 1/28/43
Dn./Eliza M. Delaughney 9/8/54
Enoch/Hen. Long 6/5/58
146. FRYER
Moses/Mary Ann Petter 8/2/32
147. FRYMAN (FRIMAN)
Geo./Julian Iseminger 3/10/07
Jc./Eliz. Broadstone 8/29/07
Geo./Maria Shaffer 6/8/11
148. FRYMIER
Jc./Rachel Swann 5/21/05
149. FUCHMAN
John/Eliz. Grim 9/6/38
150. FUGITT
John R./Frances Carper 12/29/53
151. FULL
John/Barb. Shafer 9/29/08
152. FULLER
Francis/Sus. Boyer 11/17/12
153. FULLERTON
Humphrey/Eleano Davidson 3/20/27
154. FULTON
Geo./Marg. Keiffer 2/19/33
Jm./Eve Marg. Bowers 3/20/33
Wm. D./Mar. Forman 8/13/39
155. FUNK (FUNCK)
Dv./Cath. Line 4/19/06
Hn./Eliz. Good 2/24/06
Is./Judith Scott 6/27/07
Is./Ann Newcomer 8/24/07
Dv./Mary Funk 5/15/11
John/Cath. Newcomer 3/16/15
Tobias/Mary Shelly 11/23/16
Mich./Amey Chaney 7/4/17
Sam./Barb. Newcomer 9/21/19
Dn./Maria Seigler 8/24/22
Jos./Mary Seiderstick 8/26/22
Hn./Har. Motes 8/23/23
Hn./Sus. Miller 3/13/24

36

155. FUNK (FUNCK) (Continued)
    Jc./Sus. Myers 3/9/24
    Dv./Lydia Grim 1/7/25
    Jc./Lavina Ingram 11/20/26
    John/Anna Shank 3/28/33
    John/Reb. Hoffman 1/23/34
    Sam./Eliza Ann Arnsperger 2/7/35
    Mt./Susan Sailer 4/9/36
    Geo./Mary Welty 5/9/38
    Jos./Marg. Householder 11/13/38
    And./Cath. Doub 2/20/41
    Jc. H./Marg. E. Nicholas 8/6/42
    Sam./Mary L. Wagoner 2/8/48
    Jc. L./Caroline Adams 4/7/51
    Eph. W./Reb. S. Knode 2/21/53
    John W./Mary A. Fahrney 1/2/56
    Elias D./Na. C. Winters 2/14/58
    Mich./Barb. Hershey 12/13/58
    Geo./Mary Caldwell 8/4/59
    Sam./Susan Rowland 2/14/59
    Sol./Kate Rowland 1/1/59
156. FUNKHOUSER
    Jos. E./Eliz. Hellen Beeler 5/14/60
157. FUNSTEN
    Oliver/Marg. McKee 7/12/00
158. FURMAN
    Jm./Mary Swearinger 7/18/00
159. FURRELL
    Abr./Cath. Lesler 12/31/02
    Is./Marg. Freeze 9/18/20
160. FURRY (FURRAY)
    Mt./Ros. Myers 5/5/20
    Sam./Susan Siderstick 5/5/30
    John/Leah McCoy 11/19/31
    Wm./Na. Hayden 3/29/34
    Dv./Lavinia Long 11/6/38
    John Ed./Eliza Ann Fraver 3/3/58
    Wm./Am. Flemming 4/1/58
161. FURTNEY
    Dv./Eliz. Young 2/16/36
162. FUSS
    Elie/Louisa Slagle 10/6/41
    Fred./Mary Holmes 11/23/57

163. GABRIEL
    Wm./Cath. Trainer 3/1/00
    Josiah/Cath. Felker 12/31/21
164. GAFF
    John/Barb. Kefauver 11/5/17
165. GAINER
    Tho./Ann Tingary 4/30/35
166. GAITHER
    Zachariah/Eliz. Garver 1/11/15
    Hn. H./Cath. R. Williams 8/4/24
167. GALBRAITH
    John/Susan Morrison 4/16/39
168. GALE
    Wm./Cath. Malott 3/21/05

169. GALL
    John G./Barb. Kendal 5/14/18
170. GALLAGHER
    Rob./Eliz. Kilotz 10/8/06
    Hn./Susan Hammaker 8/15/25
    Eli/Cath. Ditcher 4/25/26
    Hugh L./Eliz. Bowen 4/19/37
    Francis/Ann Murray 5/23/38
    John W./Mary McKee 8/27/40
    John/Eliza Bartman 12/23/51
171. GALLION
    Aaron W./Cath. Ann Sellers 10/10/56
172. GALLOWAY
    Jos./Mary Rideout 1/31/39
173. GALOR
    Pt./Drucilla F. Coy 12/19/49
    John/Mahala Rohrer 1/20/52
174. GALVIN
    Jm./Eliz. Cochlan 2/11/34
    Jm./Mary Burns 2/15/36
175. GANSON
    Gideon/Eliza Kindel 9/11/33
176. GANSWYK
    Herman J.T.Z./Mary A. Carr 10/20/49
177. GANTZ
    Jc./Mary Rowland 8/27/05
    Sam./Mary Lenn 7/28/10
    John/Eliz. Landis 2/20/28
    Emanuel/Marg. A. Slifer 3/7/49
    Hn./Cath. Shoop 12/13/49
    Mt./Mary E. Bomberger 9/1/51
178. GARBAUGH
    Hn./Ann Maria Kershner 4/27/11
179. GARBER
    Jc./Na. Hogens 12/6/08
    Abr./Eliz. Rice 6/1/10
    John/Eliz. Smith 3/11/13
    Sam./Mary Long 11/9/44
180. GARDENOUR
    Jc./Mar. Ann Dickson 4/2/50
181. GARDNER
    Francis/Polly Quantrill 3/24/01
    Jm./Mary Agleston 2/28/05
    Francis/Sr. Keys 6/12/27
    Wm./Rachel Ann Rigney 8/21/36
    Geo./Mary Ann Fetter 1/12/43
    Rob./Mary Mullen 12/22/47
    Wm./Eliz. Hershey 2/24/49
    Geo. Hn./Cath. Masters 8/22/57
182. GARLING
    Dn./Mary Ann Bovey 1/24/35
    Sam./Mary Ann West 2/12/44
183. GARLINGER
    Jc./Reb. Renner 8/15/18
    Jc./Rachel McNitby 4/26/24
    Horatio/Reb. Deibert 8/5/46
184. GARLOCK
    Hn./Polly Harmason 3/22/28

185. GARMONS
    John W./So. Dubble 8/24/55
186. GARNEND
    Joel/Mary Ann Ludy 10/23/38
187. GARNETT
    Bennett/Julian Frazier 10/20/40
188. GARNHART
    Hn./Sr. Hare 9/9/18
189. GARRAGHTY
    Jm./Cath. Hart 10/14/46
190. GARRETT (GARROTT)
    Ed./Mary Ann Claggett 5/4/07
    John D./Matilda Garrett 11/13/29
    Warren/Eliz. Susan Hawkins 5/17/45
    Warren/Priscilla Hardy 10/1/51
191. GARRISH
    Jos./Cath. Albert 5/1/30
192. GARVER
    John/Eliz. Weldy 5/13/01
    Is./Ann Snavely 1/29/02
    Wm./Mary Lambert 2/10/12
    Jos./Mary Hallam 8/29/28
    Benj./Eliz. Martin 11/22/30
    Jc./Mary Mentzer 11/30/35
    Abr. H./Rosinda Staley 1/27/38
    Jc./Eliz. Smith 6/4/38
    Benj./Barb. Burgher 5/15/38
    Jos./Eliz. Huntsberry 2/11/40
    Abr. H./Eliz. Spessard 11/1/41
    Is./Fanny Newcomer 2/1/43
    Wm./Sr. A. Leggitt 11/13/50
193. GARVIN
    John/Eliz. Hartman 2/19/16
    Hn./Reb. Staley 7/23/49
194. GASSAWAY
    John H./Cath. A. Armstrong 3/15/55
195. GASSMAN
    Wm./Sr. Ann Thomas 4/7/58
196. GATER
    Sam./Cath. Cunningham 11/29/38
197. GATRELL (GATIELL)
    John H./Mar. J. Seaman 5/17/55
198. GATTEN
    Zachariah/Ellen Jane Murry 2/7/37
199. GAUGER
    Geo. W./Sr. E. Myers 8/4/57
200. GAULK
    John S./Sr. Kiser 2/21/25
201. GAUMER
    Ed./Marg. Creswell 8/9/30
202. GAUNTZ
    Sam./Ann R. Hemsworth 9/8/38
203. GAVER
    John/Ellenora Kershner 4/27/36
204. GAY
    Hn./Eliza Miller 5/20/48
205. GAYLORD
    Amos/Eliz. Shaneburger 3/25/13

206. GEARHART (GIERHART)
    Hn./Mary Steece 2/18/00
    Dv./Eve Lambert 6/13/01
    Jc./Marg. Albright 1/24/01
    Dn./Na. Hannah 6/12/05
    John/Polly Carpenter 11/14/11
    Dn./Eliz. Mong 2/21/20
    E.V./Eliza Rickenbaugh 1/3/43
207. GEARING
    Chr./Marg. Slice 10/20/10
208. GEARINGER
    Dv./Mary Collier 3/9/03
209. GEARY
    Rich./Marg. White 5/13/09
    Tho./Eliz. Virginia Irwin 7/4/45
210. GEDDINGER
    Sam./Sr. Gantz 10/13/29
211. GEEDING (GEETING)
    Hn./Marg. Himes 11/15/05
    John/Cath. Miller 10/17/14
    John/Ros. Snyder 11/5/27
    Dv./Elisa Toby 1/7/29
    Geo./Na. Wagoner 6/11/30
    Jos./Mary Marg. Shoren 3/11/44
    Sam./Julian Thomas 8/19/44
    Wm./So. Baker 5/20/46
212. GEESE
    Chn./Barb. Green 11/23/11
213. GEHR (GIER)
    Geo./Sr. Fisher 11/10/11
    Dn. Jr./Polly Funk 4/14/12
    And./Mary Ann Hoover 8/21/14
    Dn./Marg. French 8/15/15
    Sam./Na. Hoover 8/9/16
    Sam./Eliz. Miller 12/20/25
    Wm./So. Kinsel 10/25/36
    Is./Cecelia Harriett 8/18/43
214. GEHRET
    Jc./Eliz. Deal 8/20/14
215. GEIGER
    Je./Eliza Geiger 11/3/21
    Geo./Marg. Beerbower 11/13/33
216. GEIGHT
    John/Cath. M. Suter 5/11/58
217. GEISBERT
    Chas. E./Sr. E. Kemp 2/21/56
218. GEISER
    John/Mary Senger 2/13/13
    Dn./Na. Newcomer 12/27/48
    Dn./Na. Hoover 10/27/54
    Mt./Ellen R. Brinham 12/4/55
    Pt./Mary Hoover 4/18/55
    Dv./Ann Lavina Brown 6/23/58
219. GELNEY
    Hn./Mary Johnson 4/18/12

38

220. GELTMACHER (GELTMACHEN, GELTMAKER, GELTMOCKER)
John/Eliz. Jones 3/3/23
Hn./Eliza Buck 3/23/49
Tho. J./Lydia A. Slifer 11/9/58
221. GELTNER
John/Eliz. Potter 3/16/40
222. GELWICKS (GELWIX)
John/Marg. Gushwa 8/22/09
Wm. T./Char. Householder 1/11/41
223. GENTMYER
Geo./Na. Boyer 5/4/30
224. GEORGE
Jm./Mary Huston 12/9/05
John Jr./Eliz. Slenker 9/11/28
225. GESSFORD
Jm./Mary Potts 12/15/59
226. GEST
Jos. Groff/Mary Ann Harbine 8/14/38
227. GESY (Gray in cross-index)
Jc./Sus. Leatherman 5/17/09
228. GETTLE
Dn./Sr. Ann Binkley 9/8/47
229. GETZ
Chn./Mary Brown 1/11/17
Jos./Barb. Reckley 6/4/42
230. GETZENDANNER
Hn./Cath. Lowry 4/20/25
231. GEYSINGER (GISINGER)
Sam. L./Eliz. Julius 6/2/29
Jefferson/Rachel Ann Ward 11/27/41
232. GIBBONS
John L./Eliz. Spotts 4/22/52
233. GIBBONEY
John/Sus. Wachtell 2/7/12
234. GIBBONS
John L./Ellen Carr 2/22/25
235. GIBBS
Chas./Lydia R. North 7/10/07
Wm./Marg. Ann Leopard 9/16/43
236. GIBSON
Rob./Mary Martin 11/26/09
Rob. H./Sr. Wishart 3/27/09
Tho. H./Isa. C. Neill 2/27/36
Wm. M./Mary Y. Hollingsworth 10/18/36
237. GICE
Jos. A./Mary C. Hiatt 5/11/54
238. GIESSELMAN
Geo./Fanny Cook 5/26/46
239. GIFT
Adam/Mary Ann Mullen 7/30/59
240. GIGOUS
Geo./Reb. Boyer 9/18/33
241. GILBERT
Sam./Peggy Mentzer 4/16/11
Reuben/Maria Norris 3/19/18
Dv./Sr. Young 10/16/20
Jc./Eliz. Ritter 6/4/22

Jos./Eliza Perry 3/2/47
Eph./Cath. V. Webb 5/25/49
242. GILES
Mark/Har. Reulitt 3/23/26
Dn./Har. McCoy 1/8/31
243. GILL
Wm./Bridget Higgins 4/18/35
244. GILLAN (GILLIN)
Jm./Eliza Jane Heanson 6/29/29
Pat./Winna Malloy 2/2/37
245. GILLIS
John/Eliz. Board 3/12/22
246. GILLMYER (GILMYER)
Geo. S./Mary Eliz. Macguire 1/26/47
247. GIMPLE
Is./Marg. Ann Bowers 8/5/57
248. GISE
John/Mary Ann Bear 6/25/46
249. GITTINGER
Theopolis/ Mary Carter 10/11/54
250. GLACE
Wm. L./Mary Kneedy (Keedy) 10/20/40
251. GLADHILL
Dn./Mary Bowers 3/20/41
252. GLANDERS
Wm./Mag. Peacock 8/16/11
253. GLASS
John/Lydia Stiffler 8/31/26
John/Marg. Seibert 8/20/29
Val./Sr. Tritch 9/26/44
Pt./Delana Moore 5/9/54
John Thornton/Lucinda Jane Wilkins 3/6/55
254. GLAZE
Dv./Eliz. Furry 4/21/21
Mt./Maria Stine 12/29/25
Geo./Lucinda Ann Rogers 3/28/29
255. GLECKNER
Jc./Eliz. Wise 8/6/18
256. GLENN
Jm./Sr. Shoafstall 8/18/03
Rob./Eve Shank 1/25/44
257. GLOSE
Dn./Sr. A. Smith 11/10/46
258. GLOSS
Wm./Eliz. Smith 11/28/31
Simon/Sr. Potter 9/8/51
Dv./Anna T. Jackson 9/20/59
259. GLOSSBRENNER
Pt./Chra. Shane 12/8/07
Abr./Eliz. Lambert 4/6/08
Adam/Eliz. Miller 8/12/12
260. GLOSSER
Jc./Eliz. Bealer 11/8/20
261. GODDARD (GODDERD)
Elias/Maria Kellar 2/26/30
Rich./Mary Barry 10/30/40
John W./Mary C. Wolf 5/2/53

262. GODE (GODI)
    Earnest/Elis. Hammel 12/9/11
    Earnest/Mary Miller 7/11/17
263. GODHELP
    Chas. Fesler/Barb. Creek 2/14/07
264. GOINES
    Luke/Han. Reader 1/16/37
265. GOFF (GOUFF, GAUFF)
    Adam/Cath. Blacker 1/4/01
    Jc./Cath. Bowers 12/16/15
    Hn./Han. Seigler 12/9/24
    Geo./Na. Wisewenkle 9/26/25
    Isaiah/Mary Downes 10/19/44
    Jos./Na. Snyder 5/3/45
    Sam./Sus. Garner 4/23/47
    Josiah/Mary Cath. Potter 2/8/59
    Adam/Char. Cretzinger 12/19/27
266. GOLD
    John/Chna. Shafer 11/7/33
267. GOLDEN
    Geo. Boestler/Na. Miller 1/20/45
268. GOLDER
    Geo./Betsy Rommel 11/2/15
269. GOLDSBOROUGH
    Wm./Sr. Norris 9/22/10
270. GOLL (GOLE, ZOLL)
    Chn. F./Mary Stull 3/26/11
    Jc./Eliz. Shafer 3/28/34
    Dv./Eliz. Smise 10/1/39
271. GOLLADAY
    Is./Eliz. Shall 11/13/09
272. GONDER
    Conrad/Reb. Cobler 8/31/09
    John/Maria Hamacker 11/26/27
    Dn./Na. Kendle 12/27/34
273. GONTZ
    Jc./Sus. Longanacre 8/23/99
274. GONSONARFFER
    Geo. W./Marg. F. Waters 2/27/55
275. GOOD
    John/Marg. Summer 10/3/18
    Jc./Sr. Stover 3/20/22
    Hn./Mary Welty 12/6/39
    Levi/Eliza Downey 6/18/42
    Dn. F./Susan Mickle 10/4/47
    Cam. M./Mary D. Seibert 9/25/57
276. GOODIS
    John/Reb. Davis 8/15/07
277. GOODRICK (GOODRICH)
    Tho./Cath. Dellinger 10/21/44
    Caleb/Eliz. Corbey 7/21/46
278. GOODWIN
    Tho. E./Eliz. E. Swope 12/8/47
279. GOODYCOOTY
    Geo./Mary Beaver 9/4/00
280. GORDON
    Pat./Jane Baldwin 6/16/02
    Hn./Eliza Smith 10/24/08
    Geo./Na. Gordon 1/2/12
    Sam./Matilda Summerville 8/21/16
    Hn./Matilda Bowman 4/3/28
    Rob./Eliza Brosius 8/12/33
    Josiah W./Kate E. Umbaugh 8/13/49
281. GORGORY
    Rob./Na. Stephens 2/24/07
282. GORISE
    Geo./Margaretta A. Stickle 10/1/57
283. GORMAN
    Terence/Lethy Ann Hooper 12/14/33
    John/Julia Ann Denny 6/14/38
284. GORREL (GORRELL)
    Wm./Na. Van Meter 12/13/10
    Jos. C./Mary A. Turner 7/24/51
285. GOSHNER
    Hn./Eliz. A. Kensley 3/27/29
286. GOSLIN
    Mich./Char. Mossbury 8/15/18
287. GOSNELL
    Herod/Mary Ellen Harne 1/8/40
288. GOSS
    John/Ellen Deal 10/5/30
289. GOSSART
    Jc./Eliz. Mensor 5/7/01
290. GOTFRIED
    Karl/Anna C.M. Laiss 9/20/58
291. GOTH
    Baltzer G./Mercy S. Beall 11/27/10
292. GOUKER (GOWKER)
    Dn. W./Eliz. Hartman 7/31/40
    John/Ellen Hartman 11/17/40
    Dv./So. Cyester 5/5/41
    Sam./Eliza Allsip 7/19/60
    Jos. Wm./Mary Kate Gouker 8/7/60
293. GOULDING
    Tho./Reb. Price 4/26/20
294. GOWER
    Adam/Eliz. Beard 1/31/04
    Adam/Matty Winders 6/16/06
    Jc./Polly Swope 10/30/15
    Dn./Marg. Dick 8/16/19
    Hn./Eliz. Kelly 11/17/21
    Geo./Mary Ann Bond 4/1/26
    Hn./Mary Cushwa 4/1/40
    Mich./Louisa Row 2/24/51
    Jc./Sr. Louderslager 7/16/52
295. GRAFF
    Jos./Sr. Kausler 11/3/07
    John/Reb. King 3/10/31
    Is./Marg. Kontz 11/4/54
296. GRAHAM (GRAYHAM)
    And./Jane Young 11/5/07
    John/Mary Curtis 10/26/18
    Sam./Ann McDonald 5/3/14
    Tho./Mary Troup 10/9/44
    Wm. W./Sus. Wolfersberger 12/22/46

297. GRAHL
John M./Eliz. Maysilles 11/19/53
298. GRAMKE
Hn./Eliz. Niernam 8/23/38
299. GRANDSTAFF
Jon./Sr. Leggett 12/5/27
300. GRANT
Hn./Mariah Wickham 1/22/19
Sam./Mary Ann Brainhall 6/20/21
301. GRANTHAM (GRANTHAMS)
John/Na. Hodge 5/30/05
Jos. T./Lydia Ann Watson 8/29/52
302. GRAVES
Jos./Cath. Brosius 1/9/17
Augustus W./Eliz. Beton 4/23/31
Silas/Eliza Hart 6/25/41
Geo./Am. E. Murray 11/24/48
John T./Lucinda Rowland 9/18/48
Denton T./Sr. E. Shipley 2/18/52
Chas. E./Mary R. Ridenour 10/11/57
303. GRAY (GREY)
Geo./Polly Gaff 6/22/09
Jc./Sus. Leatherman 5/17/09 (Jc.
Gesy in cross-index)
Rob./Eliz. Claggett 1/12/18
John/Mary Clam 12/17/25
Jos. G./Mary Mummert 10/1/31
Pt./Eliz. Lester 4/7/32
John/Na. Grooms 12/6/34
_____/Rachel Ann Ray 8/1/40
John F./Mary A. Claggett 7/20/44
Tho./Eliz. Sisserler 9/21/44
Wm. H./Mary Jane Logan 7/17/44
Tho./Mary Jane Balt 12/20/51
Benj. F./Cath. T. Gilmyer 9/22/56
Geo. W./Marg. E. Albert 2/17/59
304. GRAYBILL (GRABILL)
Mich./Esther Lambert 2/4/08
Jos./Mary Cox 7/15/13
John M./Anna Prather 11/1/58
305. GREATHEAD
John/Almira V. Dellinger 9/22/60
306. GREEN (GREENE)
Wm./Eliz. Henry 8/9/00
Jos./Matilda Holly 11/15/14
Jos./So. Davis 3/28/20
Geo./Sr. Ann Wilson 11/26/32
Wm./Eliz. Price 5/13/33
Mathias/Barb. Ann Easterday 3/17/36
Rich./Bridget Smith 9/16/37
Wm./Eliza Bennett 5/20/47
Dn./Mar. Brown 5/11/48
Hn. F./Alice G. Lawrence 10/15/53
307. GREENFIELD
John/Eliza Bender 12/22/48
John/Ellen Gastor 7/27/52

308. GREENWALT (GREENAWALT)
Mt./Ros. Oats 6/27/13
Jc./Reb. Myers 3/2/24
Jos./Eliz. Jackson 1/24/37
Jos./Hester Hoops 1/12/38
309. GREER
Jm./Hen. M. Powles 5/26/58
310. GREGG
John/Marg. Guthing 3/9/38
311. GREGORY
Richmond/Ann Louisa Snively 5/20/47
Wm. H./Char. Wolverton 8/20/60
312. GRESINGER
Geo./Eliz. Ernst 8/15/12
313. GRIDER
Alex./Ann Bear 2/9/02
314. GRIEVES
Jm./Maria Melton 5/2/40
315. GRIFFIN
John/Marg. Dugan 3/26/39
316. GRIFFIS
Elias/Mary Ann Ainsworth 1/8/42
317. GRIFFITH
Sylvanus/Eleanor Keepers 2/22/06
Dn./Sr. Swope 1/7/08
Silvanus/Eliz. Scaggs 7/31/09
Tho./Cath. Carty 8/16/38
Elias/Caroline Hays 6/9/48
F.E./Cath. Peltz 3/2/49
Lewis A.B./Amanda C. Knode 5/10/49
H.C./R.C. Remley 7/31/50
318. GRIFFY
Tho./Mary Ann Mertz 10/18/54
319. GRIM (GRIMM)
Dv./Cath. Dinger 12/15/04
Dv./Eliz. Mourer 11/21/19
John/Agnes Martin 6/21/22
Chn./Mary Hammond 9/3/24
Benj./Cath. Rohrback 6/15/25
John/Sus. Rohrer 7/25/26
Jc./Marg. Kealtmocker 4/14/27
Fred. A./Eliz. Geltmocker 10/2/30
Alex./Susan Long 9/27/34
Tho./Eliz. A. Hains 5/20/35
Jos. S./Sr. Huffer 11/21/36
John J./Mary Thomas 9/19/37
Dn. B./Mar. Keedy 12/29/40
Dv. H./Eliz. Myers 1/28/51
Sam./Eliz. Lambert 3/18/51
Dn./Ann Staubs 11/6/56
Josephus/Marg. F. Cline 8/20/59
320. GRIMES
Jm./Cath. Colliflower 12/26/99
Jm./Marg. Stude 11/6/11
John/Reb. Lynch 8/9/15
Joshua/Louisa Ware 6/21/15
Joshua/Mary Bence 2/25/19

41

320. GRIMES (Continued)
    Jm./Cath. McCauley 3/8/25
    Wm. H./Susan Harbin 10/6/29
    Joshua/Lucy Ann Orrick 12/1/32
    Jm./Frances Foster 9/14/43
    John A./Ann Eliz. Claggett 10/29/44
    Wm./Mary Ebert 2/23/44
    Wm. H./Sally Rentch 5/14/55
    Wm. H./Ann Maria Grove 9/21/57
321. GRIPPEN
    Hn./Eliz. Green 1/27/21
322. GRISER
    Mt./Ellen R. Brinham 12/4/55
323. GROER
    Wm./Maria McAtee 7/27/20
324. GROFF
    Dn./Ann E. Boeman 6/4/57
325. GROFT
    Jos./Rose Ann Monigan 3/18/58
326. GROMES
    Joshua/Mary Bentz 2/15/19
327. GRONTZ
    John/Sus. Miller 2/17/07
328. GROOMS (GROOMES)
    John/Sus. Ainsworth 11/28/40
    Dv./Har. Shuff 12/14/46
    Dv./Eliz. Mullen 5/6/50
    Wm./Cath. Morrison 2/22/51
329. GROSH (GROSCH)
    Hn./Prudence Leggett 9/23/21
    Fred./Eliz. Grimmer 6/27/29
    Lewis A./Eliz. Betz 4/1/37
    Benj. F./Matilda Householder 11/11/45
    John/Mary Ann Buckley 11/22/47
330. GROSHING (GROSHONG)
    John Jr./Eliz. Baugher 4/17/15
331. GROSINGER
    John/Peggy Tare 11/30/14
332. GROSS (GROCE)
    Jc./Barb. Miller 8/15/01
    Jc./Leonora Baunering 8/1/40
    Lawson/Marg. Rohrer 1/30/49
    Mich./Cath. Fultz 8/26/51
    Urias/Sr. Poffenberger 4/15/54
    Dv./Lucretia A. Morrison 4/26/59
333. GROSSNICKLE
    Pt./Han. Gross 8/2/02
    John A./Mary J. Tracy 10/4/54
    Lawson P./Barb. Ellen Grove 12/23/54
334. GROUND
    John/Mary Huffman 8/5/06
    Jos./Barb. Reel 9/16/29
    Josephus/Mary C. Zeigler 8/9/56
335. GROVE (GROVES)
    Ph./Cath. Hess 3/8/00
    Hn./Sabina Boyer 9/1/02

    Geo./Ros. Cousler 2/21/03
    John/Barb. Foltz 5/14/08
    Mich./Sus. Cramer 4/5/09
    Dv./Mary Grove 6/19/15
    Dv./Mary Eakle 10/25/15
    Ph./Sus. Hess 3/9/16
    Wm./Wettimince Corsen 5/30/18
    Jm./Cath. Albaugh 11/24/19
    Paul/Char. Smith 8/10/19
    John/Patsy Burgan 11/2/26
    Sam./Ann Stephenson 9/18/27
    Elias/Mary Ann Smith 12/27/28
    Sam./Lavinia Houser 4/7/29
    Mich./Eliza Young 3/1/31
    Lemon/Lydia Stevenson 2/22/31
    John/Mary Kindel 8/23/31
    Jm./Mary D. Colliflower 12/31/35
    John D./Eliz. P. Hays 3/5/35
    Jos./Susan Houser 1/28/36
    Geo./Louisa C. Horn 4/6/37
    Abr./Har. McFerran 5/17/38
    Ph./Marg. Morgan 12/28/40
    Dv./Sally Miller 5/11/46
    Stephen P./Maria Robinson 2/26/50
    Lewis/Lavinia Himes 3/13/51
    Wm. F./Josephine Snyder 8/5/51
    Jm. M./Cath. Peltz 2/19/52
    Is./Fanny Shank 10/20/53
    Sam./Marietta Williams 9/6/54
    Jm. A./Har. Hays 9/15/
    Jm. H./Br. L. Perry 6/1/58
336. GRUB (GRUBB)
    Smith/Atty Romine 7/25/14
337. GRUBER
    Jc./Dorothy Grove 2/21/32
    Sam./Susan Miller 3/20/33
    Dv./Susan Bombarger 3/16/41
    Geo./Ann Malinda Hu____ 2/28/44
    Mt. M./Ann Lavely 12/22/57
    Is./Sr. Jane Cowton 11/4/58
338. GRUMFINE
    J.A./Lavinia Michael 9/20/55
339. GRUSH
    Mich./Mary Kistler 3/19/12
340. GUCK
    Hn./Esther Higgs 4/27/03
    Jc./Mary Slencker 3/25/13
    Jc. H./Marg. Lewis 2/3/59
341. GUGLER
    Hn./Sr. Smith 4/4/32
342. GUIGOUS
    John/Eliza Ann Heck 2/6/32
343. GUINN
    John/Eliz. Cramer 4/10/47
344. GUMMERT
    Chn. P./Han. M. Eaty 2/7/29

42

345. GUYER (GEYER)
    Wm./Matilda Snyder 3/24/31
    Hn. Allen/Kate M. Yeakel 11/13/60
346. GUYTON
    Hn./Sr. Simpkins 12/25/05
    Benj./Reb. Ditto 6/23/06

347. HABBELL
    Ed./Margaretta Snyder 3/1/41
348. HABER
    John/Eliz. Graham 12/12/17
349. HABERT
    Adam/Marg. Benker 7/16/40
350. HACKINS
    Benj./Mary Griffith 4/27/18
351. HADAWAY
    Wm./Ruth Combs 10/15/06
352. HADDEN
    Jc./Cath. Herring 7/21/04
353. HADE
    Emanuel/Mary Binkley 1/19/25
    Dn./Louisa Wever 12/23/53
354. HADLEY
    Rich./Sus. Bryan 9/12/08
355. HADSON
    Tho./Lydia Mantle 4/13/15
356. HAFFER
    Sol./Maria Eckert 11/30/47
357. HAGAN
    Wm. H./Hester Am. Lemen 6/12/47
358. HAGANBARGER (HAGANBERGER)
    John/Mary B. Aniba 2/14/40
359. HAGER (HAGERR)
    Chn./Eliz. Dunn 2/3/00
    Levin/Mildred Forrester 12/26/00
        (listed as Levin Hayes w/ Hayes
        crossed out, Hager put in)
    Dv./Marg. Cellers 6/7/03
    Mich./Sus. Carter 9/12/07
    Jon./Cath. Hogmire 4/20/16
    And. H./Sr. Ensminger 8/14/48
360. HAGERMAN
    Adn./Juliann Hershberger 8/29/50
    Fred./Anna Monce 3/11/56
361. HAHN
    Hn./Mary Warner 8/20/08
    Jc./Reb. Russell 4/19/19
    Geo./Eliza Homes 8/6/36
    Benj. F./Mary E. Smith 4/13/54
362. HAIL
    Albert/Caroline Bloominour 6/1/52
363. HAINES (HAINS,HANES, HAYNES)
    John/Barb. Bovie 12/1/04
    Dv./Na. Ankeney 10/19/07
    John Jr./Rachel Jones 3/11/08
    Geo./Cath. Shupe 11/11/09
    Dv./Na. Armsley 12/12/11
    Stephen/Sr. Roulette 10/4/14

Adam/Sus. Brewer 5/19/15
Jc./Fanny Hersh 12/9/17
Adam/Sr. Tice 6/16/18
Pt./Cath. Haines 1/16/18
Jc./Han. Crow 11/13/24
J.F./Har. Fry 9/12/26
Jc./Sr. Marmaduke 9/11/28
John C./Eliza Ann Crutzwell 4/29/35
Josiah/Marg. Grim 11/11/37
Jm./Susan Grim 5/25/39
John/Mary Williams 2/26/40
John C./Eliz. Wealck 10/7/40
Wm./Mary Buck 4/15/40
Mat./Eliz. Rinehart 12/7/44
Tho./So. Goff 11/16/50
Alex./Chna. C. Anders 7/17/52
John B./Marg. Ingram 1/26/55
Lineum C./So. Norris 8/2/55
364. HAINTON
    Tho./Matilda Brent 8/25/17
365. HAKMAN
    Chn./Chna. Stockes 1/18/44
366. HALBACK
    John F./Prudence Bartly 7/25/15
367. HALBAUGH
    Tho./Sus. Heller 12/7/33
368. HALBERT
    John/Na. Mouse 8/29/18
    Arch./Cath. McLaughlin 4/7/21
369. HALE
    Jm./Mary Teach 1/21/19
    Tho./Mary Fritz 3/11/19
    Wm./Eliz. Kershner 1/24/49
370. HALL
    Nich./Jane Ferguson 6/10/05
    John/Har. Miller 2/8/09
    Dv./Sr. Faulkisell 6/15/20
    John/Mary McKee 1/29/22
    John H./Ann Russell 11/18/33
    Dn./Mary Stiffler 5/29/39
    Sam. M./Mary A. Shafer 8/13/50
371. HALLER (HAILLER)
    Chas./Abagail Havitt 1/26/19
    Wm./Sr. Haverstick 3/16/30
    Chas. Miner/Eliz. Neikirk 3/31/46
372. HAMBURGER
    Conrad/Marg. Nichols 6/25/21
373. HAMES
    Jm. W./Ann Maria Stine 11/30/53
374. HAMILL (HAMMEL)
    John/Mary Curnicum 10/26/99
    Sam./Sr. Coon 1/19/04
    Ed. B./Irene Huhges 11/21/53
375. HAMILTON (HAMELTON)
    Alex./Jane Craig 10/14/05
    John/Mary Spong 11/26/12
    Hn./Mary Ann Hess 10/28/19

375. HAMILTON (HAMELTON) (Continued)
John/Reb. Ridenour 8/30/20
Geo. C./Am. Iseminger 9/23/21
Geo./Lydia Betzer 3/23/24
John/Han. McCauley 6/13/25
Sam./Mary Funk 5/14/29
Geo. C./Eliz. Miller 11/11/35
Francis/Abigail Jane Holler 8/5/45
Sam./Eliz. Show 9/1/51
Josiah/Ann Eliz. Wachtel 1/19/55
Hn. F./Susan Rohrer 10/2/55
Chas. T./Kate A. Stonebraker 2/25/57
376. HAMM
Geo./Polly Reel 3/11/06
John/Mary Deibert 3/5/14
Jos./Polly Light 12/4/19
377. HAMMAKER (HAMMACHER, HAMACHER, HAMAKER)
Pt./Eliz. Crouse 10/20/17
Sam./Eliz. Robinson 5/20/24
Dn. S./Susan Bender 6/24/30
Eph./Sus. Shank 2/8/43
Sol./Cath. Newcomer 10/4/49
Dn./Isa. Colliflower 2/15/53
378. HAMMER
Pt./Cath. Brendle 1/27/25
John/Eliza Witmer 2/14/32
379. HAMMERSLA
Jos. A./Marg. Ann Decker 6/16/53
380. HAMMETT (HAMMET)
Dv./Ann Funk 2/8/00
Wm./Eliz. Eakel 3/28/05
Jm./Na. Foster 4/4/12
Sam./Narcissia Boult 6/12/17
Wilford/Mary Nesbitt 4/4/31
John I./Marg. Martin 4/7/32
381. HAMMOND (HAMMON, HAMON)
Ph./Na. Musselman 2/4/01
Hn./Rachel Williams 5/27/05
John/Sr. Bridge 10/14/05
Mich./Cath. Rohrer 11/25/05
Larkin/So. Carr 8/15/11
Wm./Nelly Friend 5/18/12
Jc./Eliz. Riley 8/5/13
Jc./Mary Bealer 4/22/14
Nich./Esther Rutledge 6/9/14
Wm./Mary Tilghman 3/21/14
Simpson/Mary Berier 7/24/15
John/Salome Myers 1/13/17
Mich./Leannah Thomas 12/24/17 ("2d wife" pencil note)
Otho/Eleanor Friend 5/25/22
Dv./Ann Newcomer 3/12/29
Rob./Mary McCrane 3/30/30
Wm./Louisa Santmann 8/13/31
John/Sr. Allabaugh 1/5/32
John/Eliz. O'Neill 12/28/33
Josiah/Du Ann Hoff 3/11/37
Edwin/Mary Knode 9/1/42

Wm./Eliza J. Reid 3/8/42
Josiah/Lilay Lampert 4/11/45
Dv. C./Cath. Hoffman 12/22/46
Wm. Jr./Eliza Mitchell 2/7/49
Josiah/Matilda J. Davis 8/25/51
Abr./Eliz. Doub 2/15/54
Josiah/Marg. Ann Blecher 2/24/55
John/Marg. Saylor 1/7/57
And. J./Cath. Bangly 3/21/59
382. HANENKAMPF
Arnold/Marg. Humerichouse 4/12/00
383. HANEY (HANY, HANIE)
John/Eliz. Mourer 5/30/11
John/Barb. Oderfer 3/26/16
384. HANLEY
Jm./Elisa I. Dixon 5/3/34
385. HANNA (HANNAH)
John/Eliz. Gray 1/8/00
Jm./So. Gearhart 1/25/03
Wm./Sr. Wolf 1/12/22
Is./Na. Funk 2/23/20
Geo./Reb. Allen 6/24/23
Rob./Cath. Billmyer 9/27/26
Is./Sally Young 11/19/31
Rob./Mary Miller 4/9/38
Hn./Mar. McCrea 12/7/39
Jm./Mary Slagle 9/3/40
Gabriel/Eliza Ann Furley 2/15/48
386. HANNER
Wm. H./Ellen Paden 6/22/40
Hn. J./Marg. Springer 5/26/56
387. HANNING
Wesley/Mary Sager 3/24/29
388. HANSHER
John/Ann C. Rorick 1/30/27
389. HANSON
Geo./Eliz. Ridenour 2/7/16
Alex./Mary Ann Ridenour 3/30/48
390. HANT
Wm./Mary Lutz 4/24/30
391. HANTER
Wm./Lavinia Shertz 6/19/38
392. HARBAUGH
Yost/Eliz. Mong 3/30/02
Elias/Cath. Pencer 1/1/18
Jon./Mary Sheets 5/11/18
Sam./Cath. Bentz 9/26/23
Jon./Eliz. Steffy 2/21/29
Lewis M./Cath. M. Beard 9/26/40
Wash./Mary Jane Boteler 12/13/47
And./Savilla Buhrman 12/30/51
Jc./America Brigham 2/28/54
Mt./Susan Barkdoll 12/23/54
Milton A./Ann M. Buhrman 12/5/59
393. HARBINE
Jer./Eliz. Thompson 6/22/22
John/Hetty Herr 7/30/27
Tho./Cath. Aloisa Smith 4/19/47

44

394. HARDEN
Sam./Sus. Felix 4/7/09
395. HARDING
Chas. Albert/Reb. Murray 12/12/49
396. HARDY
Geo. I./Editha Edwards 9/8/26
Geo. Wm./Mary Marg. Johnson 2/15/47
Hiram/Susan Best 5/1/48
Benj. B./Eliz. J. Gainer 9/20/56
397. HARE
Dv./Maria Root 11/3/04
Mich./Mary Roner 1/12/33
398. HARGER
Wm./Eliz. Hartman 5/15/17
399. HARLEMAN
Conrad/So. Bramhall 3/27/20
400. HARLEY (HARLY)
John/Eliz. Stanton 7/13/19
Nathan/Sus. Stottlemyer 3/27/21
Wm./Ann Eliza Lowe 2/10/24
Wm. M./Isa. K. Lowe 8/3/57
401. HARLING
John/Fanny Rench 4/20/08
402. HARMAN
Jc./Cath. Amen 11/10/07
Jc./Eliz. T. Harn 10/7/22
John/Na. Beackley 2/1/23
John Jc./Reb. Gutman 4/1/24
Geo./Eliz. Hoover 9/4/34
Nich./Mary Ann Becks 6/5/41
Dominic/Judith Dougherty 7/20/43
John/Ellen Reid 6/15/42
Jesse/Lydia Virginia Snyder 12/29/56
Jc./Har. D. Snyder 12/14/57
403. HARMISON
Wm./Frances E. Hawkins 9/27/34
Jos./Mary Ann Prather 10/7/39
404. HARNE (HARN)
Hovedore/Sus. Forrest 2/7/07
Horatio N./Ann Maria Webb 12/7/31
And. J./Mag. Bear 11/25/54
Geo. W./Lydia Winders 12/24/56
F.T.L./Mary F. Meredith 3/6/60
405. HARNER
Jc. W./Marg. A. Cox 11/15/50
406. HARNISH
Geo./Mag. Hershey 3/7/48
407. HARP
Van/Eliz. A. Richard 9/16/40
Joshua/Mag. Wolf 12/8/47
John L./Ann Eliz. Doub 12/20/59
408. HARPER
Jc./Mary Fisher 7/24/02
Jm./Sr. Bean 12/22/08
Jm./Eliz. Smith 6/7/10
Abr./Char. K. Pennell 2/17/25
Jm./Reb. Youtz 1/26/27

Jc. F./Eliz. Leggett 11/7/35
Jm./Ellen Harper 1/24/39
Chas. N./Cath. Shaneberger 3/12/59
409. HARR
Sam./Sus. Leigh 8/27/01
410. HARRIS
Wm./Char. Myers 2/23/04
Jos./Sus. Hite 2/18/07
Wm./Mary Casper 11/22/17
Jm./Mary Melvin 5/29/20
Benj./Eliza Cook 8/29/38
Josiah/Mag. Zeigler 5/26/41
Wm./Eliz. Morris 6/1/42
Albert/Jane Remley 5/28/47
411. HARRISON
Jm./Uscilla Porton 2/6/04
John S./Holland Stull 6/3/05
Jm./Eliz. Hudzell 7/22/06
John/Mary Biroad 11/21/10
Jm./Sus. McNeal 1/17/14
John/Deborah Kendle 4/27/16
Sam./Eliz. Friend 2/5/20
Sam./Lucretia Levy 3/27/37
Jos./Mary Ann Snyder 3/10/49
Wm. H./Na. Paxton 10/23/51
Ed./Virginia Gelwicks 8/21/55
Jos./Mahala Eichelberger 5/28/56
412. HARRY
Wm./Rachel Lowman 4/11/00
Dv. Jr./Peggy Startzman 3/10/10
Geo. I./Am. Knode 5/21/11
Wm./Mary Wolford 11/28/13
John/Mary Ashberry 3/13/15
Geo. I./Sus. Bell 6/15/19
Otho/Cath. Shell 9/13/32
Jc. K./Cath. A. Kausler 11/18/40
413. HARSH
Dv./Eliz. Sheller 5/5/23
Hn./Cath. Summers 10/23/23
And. J./Ann Victoria Buchanan 10/11/58
414. HARSHMAN
Ph./Fany Dombaugh 4/14/04
Jon./Mary Ann Rouzahn 11/16/50
415. HART
Miles/Mar. Scott 3/9/05
Mich./Sus. Stockes 1/25/14
Jc./Eliz. Tysher 4/22/17
John D./Eliz. Swope 1/27/17
Edwin/Eliza J. Anderson 3/5/25
John/Susan Dixon 6/22/25
Wm./Eliz. Tolhelm 9/3/35
Mich./Ann Roe 11/23/37
John/Sus. Kretzer 2/28/43
416. HARTER (HARDER)
Jc./Polly Marker 4/19/06
Dv./Mary Lantz 15/15/43
Dv./Cath. Bussard 11/11/52
Josiah/Marion S. Suter 4/13/59

45

417. HARTLE (HARDLE, HERDLE)
Sebastian/Sus. Moyer 11/21/08
Geo./Barb. Swope 10/25/14
John/Maria Leckrone 3/17/21
Rich./Mary Ann Shriner 12/10/23
Jc./Na. Coon 4/24/24
John/Cath. Wallace 10/10/29
John/Ann Norford 2/5/42
Jc./Am. Creager 2/19/45
Eph./Ann Eliz. Poe 1/5/47
Sol./Mary Wagoner 12/22/59
418. HARTMAN
Jos./Eliz. Quarters 1/29/03
Jc./Eliz. Rohrer 10/13/08
Benj./Judith Leighter 4/6/11
Geo./Cath. Miller 3/24/18
Jos./Anna Mar. Keelsman 10/30/42
419. HARTSOCK
John/Cath. Fox 4/11/01
420. HARVEY
Wm. M./Eliz. Brown 6/7/21
M. Wm./Mary E. Holliday 12/4/24
Wm./Eliz. M. Rice 12/19/29
421. HASSETT
Tho./Ellen Silvers 2/12/49
422. HASWELL
John/Ann Bidamon 10/21/30
423. HATFIELD
Abr./Reb. Longanacre 4/1/10
Wm./Mary Ann Edmonds 9/14/33
Rob./Marg. Cramer 7/11/35
424. HATHAWAY
Joshua F./Lucinda Beterbenner 6/27/40
425. HATHERDLY
Jos./Sr. Hayes 2/7/14
426. HATHRALLERS (HATHRALLES)
John/Han. Emmerson 1/1/18
427. HATSENBILLER
John/Marg. Gamble 3/20/21
428. HATTER
Jc./Mariah Butler 5/17/17
Dv./Eliz. Kuntz 12/7/25
429. HATZELL
John/Eliz. Zittle 5/27/34
Jc./Lavinia Warble 7/23/49
Dn./Chna. Young 3/2/55
430. HAUBER
Dn./Eliz. Brown 4/6/15
Jc./Eliz. Poorman 10/19/18
431. HAUGH
Chr./Mary Fisher 8/12/12
432. HAULEN
Geo./Sus. Kepler 3/9/13
433. HAUPT
I.N.D./Amanda M. Glessner 4/13/58
434. HAUSE (HAUS)
Geo./Cath. Sheitz 4/18/25

Wm./Mary Liffich 4/14/25
Sam./Eliza Sheitz 1/14/32
John/Mag. Maugins 12/18/35
435. HAUVER (HAVER)
Geo./Elisa Swope 5/16/37
Luther C./Ann Eliz. Sprecher 3/2/55
436. HAVERSTICK
Dv./Marg. Harrison 11/14/29
John/Eliz. Holly 3/2/33
437. HAWBAKER (HAWBECKER)
Dn./Char. Nisswaner 12/8/54
Chn./Mary Richard 10/20/55
438. HAWK (HAUCK)
Jc./Elisa Thurston 4/15/34
John M./Cath. B. Miller 2/27/45
439. HAWKEN (HAWKIN, HAWKENS, HAWKINS)
Jm. L./Eliz. Claggett 10/14/02
Sam./Ros. Oster 9/19/15
Wm./Cath. Stake 4/4/20
Wm./Leah Cramer 7/17/21
Jc./Cath. Allison 3/30/22
Rhesa/Eliza Crabill 9/25/37
Jc. M./Eliz. Leonard 4/29/40
Geo. T./Sr. Grimes 9/22/47
Wilford E./Mary E. Long 10/21/47
Jm. E./Mary Susan Mendenhall 7/3/60
Wm. H./Han. Eliz. St. Clair 12/19/60
440. HAWKEY
Geo./Marg. Kreps 7/1/09
441. HAWLEY
Sam./So. Ripple 10/6/12
442. HAWN
John/Eve Miller 10/3/01
Dv./Agnes Barnett 8/4/27
443. HAWHTORNE (HAWTHORN)
Wm./Marg. Hilliard 9/20/25
Dv./Mary Chany 3/26/29
Wm./Marg. Hammett 4/4/43
Wm./So. E. Preston 10/10/44
Jon./Louisa Brooke 2/5/53
444. HAYBARGER
John/Mary McGowan 5/7/11
445. HAYES (HAYS, HAISE)
Levin/Mildren Forrester 12/26/00 (Hayes
crossed out, Hager substituted)
Ed./Prudence Hayes 9/20/04
Wilson/Mary Hatherdly 12/20/10
Rob./Sr. Richardson 3/6/13
Levin/Marg. Eichelberger 1/9/18
Wm./Jane Lynn 10/21/18
Adam/Eliz. P. Alexander 4/19/20
John J./So. B. Pottinger 11/29/21
Abner/Polly Leiter 8/11/25
John/Cath. Eakel 1/3/25
Jos. C./Lavenia Grove 12/12/25
Hiram/Sr. Cadel 8/27/27
Wm./Mary Ann Chambers 5/18/31

46

445. HAYES (HAYS, HAISE) (Continued)
Hn./Sr. Eakle 1/23/32
Geo. W./Am. Ann Albert 3/25/34
Jos. C./Mary Fales 9/28/35
Tho./Frances Hiestand 1/26/36
Denton C./Mary Grossnickel 9/2/39
Jm. D./Juliann Shaffner 6/15/41
Ed./Chna. Hershberger 11/3/42
John W./Cath. Westonhaver 5/31/47
Wm./Caroline Miller 8/29/51
446. HAYDEN
Wm. I./Har. Spittler 3/5/39
447. HAYET (HAYETT)
Pt. Lewis/Cath. E. Stonebraker 5/21/33
Jer./Susan Coler 3/27/37
448. HAYGIS
Geo. Hn./Barb. Sperr 2/3/55
449. HAYWARD
Dv./Marg. B. Kain 12/6/25
450. HAYWOOD
Tho./Eliz. Gray 3/8/21
451. HAZELET
Rob./Sr. Green 1/6/46
452. HEAFER
John Jr./Na. Ann Whitington 3/22/43
453. HEAFLICH
Jc./Cath. Mong 4/13/18
454. HEASTER
Pt./Cath. Adams 9/17/14
455. HEATH
Wm./Eliz. Sager 11/28/13
456. HEBB
John/Cath. Gower 7/31/19
Wm./Eliz. Smith 6/27/29
Edwin/Cath. Spahn 11/25/37
Jos./Mary Florence Webb 9/20/59
457. HEBER
Geo./Eliz. Sweney 7/2/11
458. HECK
Pt./Eliz. Baker 7/23/07
Pt./Reb. Green 10/9/15
Chn./Eliz. Greenawalt 9/28/19
Hn./Drusila Chany 5/5/27
Jc./Mary Ann Harmon 10/13/32
Ruben/Eliza Maria Russell 10/24/42
John/Ann Zeigler 1/29/47
459. HECKMAN
And./Betsey Dyce 9/25/03
460. HECKROTTE
Wm./Eveline Smith 10/21/47
461. HEDDER
Geo./Eliz. Himes 1/12/33
462. HEDDINGER
Jos./Har. Lynn 2/7/54
463. HEDGES
Baily/Eliza Meixsel 10/9/41

464. HEDRICK
Geo./Peggy Tyson 10/7/09
Jos./Sr. Knode 12/18/13
John/Sally Hahn 4/30/14
Benj. T./Ann Maria Shryack 10/19/41
Dv./Barb. Ann Rohrback 11/7/43
Elie/Matilda Tedrick 5/26/45
John/Mary Miller 3/11/45
John/Sr. Ann Martz 4/14/47
465. HEFFLEBOWER (HAFFLEBOWER)
John/Hulda Arnold 3/3/23
John/Violetta Mullendore 6/17/57
466. HEFFNER
Dv./Marg. Potts 6/17/43
467. HEGERT
Hn./Cath. Zekel 11/27/39
468. HEIGLE
Mich./Mary Mittaugh 12/31/23
469. HEIRRONIMUS
Wm. F./Cornelia M. Herbert 1/26/57
470. HEIST
Wm. H./Pauline Benner 11/8/59
471. HEISTAND
Hn./Eliz. Newcomer 3/18/30
472. HEISTER
Sol./Marg. Winsborow 1/23/21
473. HELDT
John/Eliz. Neikirk 1/3/20
474. HELEFINGER
Jc. S./Cath. Line 2/17/41
475. HELFESTAY
John/Mar. Ann Creager 5/28/55
476. HELLANE (HELEINE)
John/Marg. Roots 3/3/47
John/Virginia Fox 12/7/58
477. HELLER
Jc./Isa. McKinsey 4/23/01
Dn./Dorothy Barkman 9/4/07
Sam./Eliz. Kershner 10/31/16
Dn./Mary McClain 2/15/32
Dv./Mary Painter 10/30/39
Elie/Mary Ann Kreps 3/15/48
478. HELM (HELMS)
Meredith/Eliz. Orondorff 10/17/25
Ezra/Margaretta Russell 10/28/43
479. HELPTAY
Chas. Luther/Reb. Ann Peltz 12/10/56
480. HEISER
Dv. P./Ann C. Martin 11/2/54
481. HELSEY
Emanuel/Maria Reynolds 4/27/20
482. HEISINGER
Jc./Ann Slaen 4/16/36
483. HEISLEY
Francis/Ann Shuber 6/12/48
484. HELVERSTONE
Hiram/Na. B. Caldwell 4/13/19

485. HEMPHILL
    Wm./Eliz. Glass 8/15/57
486. HENDERSON
    Sam./Mary Allison 7/30/28
    Amistead M./Maria Louisa Foster
      12/5/39
487. HENDRICKS
    Nath./Sr. Martin 8/10/31
    Al. M./Eliz. Smith 2/8/41
    John B./Sr. Eliz. Bane 9/10/53
488. HENDRICKSON
    Jm./Ellen M. Woodbury 9/20/43
489. HENECY (HENESY)
    Tho./Mary Sullivan 9/2/33
    Pt./Ellen Doland 9/20/56
490. HENNEBERGER
    Geo. W./Ann Reb. Brozier 12/2/46
491. HENRY
    Dn./Esther Tice 8/1/01
    John/Nelly Nimmey 7/23/04
    Wm. L./Sus. Price 11/27/18
    John O./Polly Fotherill 11/16/19
    Dn./Mary M. Dillehart 11/24/42
492. HENSON
    Chas. H./Eveline Newman 3/18/56
493. HEPLEIGH
    Pt./Cath. Stover 2/7/04
494. HERBERT
    John/Rachel Sackett 5/12/17
    Stewart/Reb. Doyle 1/1/18
    John/Sr. Ann Mealy 5/13/22
    Chas./Caroline Wakenight 2/25/45
    F. Dorsey/Marg. Ann Wise 8/16/47
495. HERBST
    John E./Annie E. Artz 7/20/58
496. HERD (HEARD)
    Wm. V./Hen. Warfield 8/3/18
    Wm. V./Sr. A. Grosuch 8/13/46
    Franklin Anderson/Mary A.C. Mobley
      2/5/50
    Nimrod/Lucinda Horine 7/21/58
497. HERR
    John/Cath. Borehoff 8/28/10
    Jos./Cath. Moudy 10/14/12
    Conrad/Cath. Beagler 3/28/18
    Abr./Na. Herr 2/9/24
    Hn./Eliz. Brewer 4/6/25
    Emanuel/Cath. Petre 8/26/30
    John/Clarissa Chaney 10/28/33
    Jos./Eliz. Herr 12/27/36
    Sam./So. Smith 2/27/36
    Jos./Eliz. Herr 12/27/36
    Rudolph Jr./Eliz. Diffenbaugh 10/24/42
498. HERRING
    Dn. C./Eliza A. Thomas 8/3/46
499. HERRON
    Alex. G./Eliza Donaldson 3/31/25
500. HERSH
    Geo./Sr. Burkhart 4/13/20

501. HERSHBERGER (HARSHBERGER)
    Sam./Sr. Brewah 2/26/16
    Jc./Eliz. Kenney 5/15/18
    John/Marg. Rothrauff 7/5/24
502. HERSHEY
    Jc./Mary Young 12/6/03
    Jos./Barb. Hershey 2/22/06
    John/Barb. Hershey 2/1/08
    Jos./So. King 7/3/21
    Dv./Mag. Hershey 12/14/22
    Is. S./Emeline S. Lee 9/17/32
    Jos. M./Maria Witter 6/17/33
    Is./Susan Long 11/17/38
    A.M./Eliz. I. Lee 9/12/39
    John J./Chna. Bair 3/15/43
    Dn./Reb. J. Garns 4/19/53
    John I./Ros. Watkins 3/24/59
503. HESS
    John/Sus. Locker 3/16/01
    Dv./Ann Sharrick 4/21/09
    Geo./Han. Wolgomot 7/30/12
    Abr./Sr. Shank 2/21/32
    Sam./Marg. Unkel 11/4/34
    Jm./Frances Eliz. Fisher 8/21/48
504. HESSER
    Sam. L./Ann Maria Slagle 9/12/26
505. HESSLEY (HESLEIGH)
    Jc./Na. Betts 5/18/01
    Sol./Louisa Reynolds 7/17/04
506. HETZELL
    Gottleib/Chna. Ridenour 2/27/40
507. HETZER
    John/Eliz. Neitzell 12/23/11
    John/Caroline Hetzer 6/11/49
508. HEUBER
    Hn. S./Priscilla I. McCurdy 3/30/41
509. HEWITT
    John/Eliz. Mock 3/16/16
    Jc./Eliz. Ingram 1/20/20
    Dn./Mar. Gaither 1/27/34
    Wm./Cath. Ingram 4/13/39
    Theodore D./Sr. Felker 3/5/53
510. HEYSER
    Wm. Jr./Sr. Artz 1/2/13
    Geo. F./Cath. Artz 12/24/39
    John H./Susan F. Fechtig 9/6/43
    Wm./Mag. Barr 1/17/44
511. HICHSON
    Wm./Jane Craigwell 6/29/06
512. HICKEY
    John/Rachel Van Meter 12/3/28
513. HICKLE
    Jos./Eliz. Hoffman 9/23/20
514. HICKMAN
    Wm. T./Sr. Etnire 9/19/38
515. HICKS
    Geo./Mary Branner 6/13/18
    Geo. W./Eliz. W. Metcalf 2/25/60

516. HIETT (HYETT)
And./Marg. Wimmer 10/3/18
Elias/Cath. Jones 6/6/29
A.J./Mary M. Boyd 12/10/56
517. HIEVEL
John/Ann Hornberger 11/28/01
518. HIGGENS (HIGGINS)
Rob./Lavina Wherrott 10/1/18
Geo. W./Sr. Miller 2/24/34
Chas./Sr. Friend 1/11/43
Josiah/Marg. R. Mohler 10/19/47
Tho./Marg. Gingery 2/21/54
519. HIGGS (HIGS)
Tho./Am. Duvall 4/17/05
Jm./Cynthia Ann Seaman 6/30/18
Jm./Cath. Householder 7/9/53
520. HIGHBARGER (HIGHBERGER)
Abr./Reb. Morstetter 3/19/32
Jos./Eliz. Naff 3/26/38
Geo./Na. Ambrose 11/2/39
Dn./Cath. Long 8/9/44
Adam/Rhuanna Spong 1/19/46
Jos./Cath. Avey 6/1/53
John/Eliz. Stiffler 6/26/54
Nathan/Eliz. Agnes Webb 5/5/56
Jc./Cath. A. Light 9/29/57
Abner/Mag. Emmert 3/16/58
521. HILDEBRAND (HELDEBRAND, HILDEBRANDE)
John/Eliz. Liser 5/26/11
Is./Eliz. Wolfensberger 12/4/22
Adam C./Barbary Oswald 6/23/51
Simon/Ann Am. Gantz 12/18/52
Frisby/Marg. Funk 1/16/54
522. HILL
Wm./Cath. McNamee 12/24/01
Sam./Mary Eakel 5/15/09
Jon./Mar. May Farquhar 6/1/14
Mich./Maria Deevers 11/27/15
Pt./Mary Ann Eifert 4/29/15
John/Eliz. Smith 4/17/24
Ira/Lydia Wilson 1/5/28
Dv./Cath. Householder 12/9/34
John/Ros. Kingery 5/31/36
Rob./Cath. Norris 1/2/37
Umphre/Ann E. Doyle 10/2/38
Dn./Mary Stiffler 5/29/39
Cornelius/Eliz. Neikirk 2/12/48
Wm./Hen. Spong 3/3/49
Hn. Zephania/Fame Ellen Ridenour
4/1/51
Dv./Mary Ann Thomas 1/9/58
523. HILLARY
Wm. J.I.G./Joanna Am. Fechtig 6/25/44
524. HILLEN
John/Mary Ann Luckett 12/20/31
525. HILLERD
Chr./Maria Mittig 3/6/32
526. HILLIARD
John/Eliza Brown 9/5/40

527. HILLING
John/Eliz. Shepherd 9/13/13
528. HILTBILE
John/Jane Hamilton 8/7/15
529. HIMES (HYMES)
Matthias/Eliz. Longman 8/4/12
John/Sr. Shroyer 5/13/26
Hn./Amy Downs 9/9/29
Jc./Eliz. Yerty 12/4/29
Mich./Mary Beichel 5/10/32
Elias/Mary Fridinger 9/5/36
Jos./Eliz. Fridinger 5/8/37
Dv./So. Yerty 5/16/48
Geo./Am. Fraker 9/3/52
Mt./Jane McCoy 10/22/53
Dn./Mary F. Zimmerman 4/5/58
I.P./Mary E. Smith 12/28/59
530. HINDS
Mich./Eliz. Scholls 10/18/25
John/Mary Sultzer 1/26/40
531. HINEMAN
Jm./Ruth Crunkleton 6/23/12
532. HINES (HINE)
John/Mary Cretzer 3/28/09
Geo./Betsey Poffenberger 1/26/11
Dv./Sally Yearty 12/4/28
Jc./Eliz. Yerty 12/4/29
Jc./Sr. Mose 1/2/36
John/Mary Longman 11/1/38
John/Mary Williams 2/26/40
Jc. F./Cath. Eichelberger 3/11/41
Urias/Eliz. Miller 8/5/46
Enoch/Eliz. A. Siess 7/27/47
John/Eliz. Miller 8/8/48
Silas W./Eliz. Snyder 9/1/52
533. HINKLE
Sam./Na. Ricklird 2/11/28
Chn./Sus. Funk 8/3/33
534. HINTON
Chas./Maria Taylor 12/21/19
John/Cath. Raney 12/23/52
Tho. Hn./Mary Ann Adley 5/12/58
535. HIPP
Jos./Ellen Meyre 7/10/36
536. HITCHCOCK
Chas. B./Mary Ditto 11/13/22
537. HITEMAN
John/Mary Losebaugh 7/6/07
538. HITESHAW
Chas./Na. Gehr 2/19/57
Wm. H./Ann R. Graves 12/28/58
539. HITT
Sam./Barb. Hershey 4/20/23
540. HIX
John/Mary Beasley 9/13/36
John Jr./Eliz. Speck 1/22/40
541. HOARBAUGH
Pt./Eliz. Bracher 7/10/09

49

542. HOBBS (HOB)
    Sam. P./Mary E. Hobbs 6/4/27
543. HOBLETZELL
    John F./Eliz. Brosius 11/23/43
544. HOBSON
    And./Eliz. Mays 5/9/29
545. HOEY
    Rob./Alice Farlton 6/10/05
546. HOFF
    Owen/Hetty McCraff 12/18/32
    Jc./Susan Spielman 2/2/36
    John/Emily Gunder 9/16/57
547. HOFFER
    Jos./Cath. Miller 8/29/01
    Abr./Eve Speelman 8/26/08
    Abr./Esther Foltz 3/3/12 ("d/o John"
      pencil note)
    Jc./Marg. Domer 2/8/21
    John/Cath. Mullendore 3/27/22
    Sam./Eliz. Welty 12/3/24
    John/Larah Blecher 5/21/29
    Sam./Cath. Swope 10/27/29
    Jc./Sr. Beeler 5/1/33
    Dn./Mary Ann Thomas 5/21/46
    Sol./Maria Eckert 11/30/47
    Geo./Eliz. Clopper 12/20/52
    Al. C./Sr. Ann Toms 12/2/59
    Jo. B./Sr. N. Snyder 9/13/59
    Silas/Barb. A. Keedy 11/12/59
    Abr./Barb. Tice 10/15/60
548. HOFFHINE
    Jc./Ann E. Winters 12/31/57
549. HOFFMAN (HUFFMAN)
    John/Cath. Eakel 10/18/00
    John/Cath. Caw 10/24/01
    Fred./Eliz. Peters 12/14/03
    Dv./Peggy Wolf 3/20/09
    John/Eliz. Horine 9/12/10
    Jc./Eliz. Wade 1/21/14
    Adam/Mary Ann Clarke 5/13/15
    Chn./Ann Newcomer 9/1/15
    Hn./Sus. Garver 10/26/16
    Hn./Cath. Painter 5/10/20
    Jc./Polly Bowser 8/17/20
    John/Barb. Deedy 7/29/20
    Jc./Mag. Stoufer 2/19/22
    Jc./Chna. Hoffman 3/8/23
    John/Mary Winebrenner 2/5/23
    John/Susan Byers 10/7/23
    Joshua/Eliz. Kretzer 11/17/27
    John/Sus. Thomas 4/5/32
    Francis/Eliz. Smith 3/30/33
    John/Reb. E. Dust 3/10/35
    Wm./Caroline B. Shafer 9/20/36
    Jos./Eliz. Hoover 12/2/43
    John/Mar. Keedy 2/29/44
    John/Sr. Bramhill 9/2/53

    Francis/Eliz. Socks 7/18/54
    Matthias/Lucinda Beaver 11/13/55
    J. Calvin/Clara J. Knode 11/18/56
    Lewis/Eliz. Bowman 12/5/57
    Is./Eliza Shafer 3/21/60
    Jos. T./Mary McCaulley 1/16/60
    Sam./Barbary Bowman 1/31/60
550. HOFFMASTER
    Geo./Eliz. Eakel 8/14/26
    Jc./Marg. Eakel 1/21/28
    Chr./Eliz. Norris 11/9/31
    Geo./Eliz. Negley 11/22/32
    Sam./Sr. Hill 5/6/33
    John/Eliza West 1/21/36
    Geo./Eliz. Stoner 8/27/49
551. HOFFMEIER
    John Wm./Eliz. C. Campbell 11/1/43
552. HOFINS
    John Hn./Marg. Harry 4/9/07
553. HOGAN
    Garrett/Cath. Duple 9/20/40
554. HOGG
    John/Reb. Stoops 2/15/09
    John/Jemimah Woodward 7/3/18
555. HOGMIRE (HOGMYRE)
    Dn./Marg. Hewitt 5/7/02
    Sam./Eliz. Raun 1/30/08
    Dn./Am. Grosh 9/27/22
    Hn. H./Isa. Binkley 7/19/26
    Dn./Hen. Waugh 10/17/36
556. HOKENSTEIN
    Lienhard/Marg. Fayettin 9/8/41
557. HOLBERT
    Dn./Sr. Bryroun 3/30/07
558. HOLBRUNNER
    Jc./Mary Small 5/22/38
559. HOLINGER
    Dn./Eliz. Burkett 5/29/04
560. HOLL
    Hn./Chna. Bachtell 4/12/14
561. HOLLAND
    Sam./Han. Chapman 5/27/07
    Zachariah/Laura S. Williams 12/28/37
    John/Ann Mary Miller 11/11/39
    John W./Ann E. Moore 9/14/47
562. HOLLAR (HOLLER)
    John/Cath. Rodes 10/16/30
    Phineas B./Clara S. Pretzman 11/19/58
563. HOLLENBERGER
    Dv. S./Eliz. A. Bigham 2/23/46
    Wm. H./Almyra Myers 11/29/53
    Geo./Malinda Bell 4/17/60
564. HOLLIDAY (HOLLYDAY)
    Wm./Ann B. Tilghman 8/31/30
    Rich./Susan Ragan 11/6/37
    Wm./Louisa Lamar Tilghman 9/12/37

565. HOLLINGSWORTH
John/Eveline Gardner 4/6/46
Is./Han. Perkins 10/1/99
566. HOLLMAN
Dv. S./Maria Herr 5/30/37
Benj. F./M. Caroline Foster 11/12/40
567. HOLLOWAY
Levy/Ann Clarke 5/26/12
568. HOLLY
John/Ann Gregory 8/24/03
569. HOLMAN (HOLLMAN)
Jos./Cath. Steffey 6/21/13
570. HOLMES (HOLME, HOLM, HOMES)
Hn./Char. Sword 12/24/05
Wm./Reb. Campbell 10/9/05
Geo./Barb. Roback 10/15/30
Jc./Sr. Bottell 3/9/32
Hez. A./Mary E. Carlisle 11/29/45
Sam./Ann E. Long 2/20/50
Pt./Mary Long 11/1/56
571. HOLSINGER
Dv./Eliz. Bostater 11/29/54
572. HOLT
Jesse/Mary Cox 9/5/05
573. HOMELL
Francis/Julia Ann Hofecker 7/23/38
574. HOMMER
Lewis/Mary Ann Smith 2/21/38
Tho./Mary Smith 10/20/51
575. HOOF
Mich./Mary Bennett 10/31/07
576. HOOPER
Abr./Mary Stewart 8/3/20
John W./Sr. M. Burkett 4/23/41
577. HOOSE
Geo./Cath. Wiles 8/20/03
578. HOOTZELL
Jc./Susan Itnire 4/21/35
579. HOOVER
Jc./Cath. Aley 10/29/99
Adam/Hetty Doner 8/7/02
Jon./Eliz. Kellenberger 1/18/09
Chn./Eliz. Welty 5/27/12
Chn./Eliz. Statter 10/24/14
Geo./Eliz. Deal 4/6/18
Able/Char. Emlick 2/11/19
Abr./Sr. Ream 8/25/20
John/Na. Shank 11/8/24
John/Cath. Steffey 3/28/25
Jc./Na. Stouffer 10/30/27
Pt./Polly Wolford 4/7/28
Benj./Emily Harrison 11/6/32
Jc./Mary Ann Orner 5/27/34
Chn./Eliz. Haines 10/15/36
John (of Jc.)/Cath. Macken 4/2/39
John/Isa. Weagly 11/12/39

Sam./Cath. Spessard 2/8/40
John W./Chna. Warner 3/8/41
Gideon/Eliz. Ramsburgh 3/27/41
Dv./Jane Eliz. Ray 2/3/45
Ezra/Roanna Warvel 2/7/46
Joel/Mary Ann Potter 4/1/46
Dn./Har. Douple 1/25/50
Dv./Eliz. Stephey 12/14/50
Mt./Maria Stotler 1/29/53
John/Eliz. C. Krouse 2/6/55
580. HOPLETS
Wm./Mary Ridenour 3/28/15
581. HOFWOOD
Ed./Rachel Williams 1/2/33
582. HORANG (HORRING)
Adam/Cath. Whitmire 8/18/00
583. HORINE
John/Barb. Shrader 10/4/06
Conrad/Na. Schrader 3/22/16
John/Fannie Chany 5/19/30
Hn. A./Maria Kreps 3/1/32
John/Na. Smith 9/29/36
Hn. A./Eliz. McCauley 9/23/48
Mich./Ellen Doyle 3/16/50
584. HORN
Jos./Eliz. Mentzer 12/16/13
Geo./Lida Kreps 12/25/19
John/Hen. Hetenhouser 11/23/44
John/Sus. Stough 8/30/47
585. HORNBAKER
Aaron O./Anna V. Small 6/26/56
586. HORNER
John/Lydia Faucet 1/16/02
Dawson/Ann Eliz. Payn 11/29/47
587. HOSE
Geo./Na. Holmes 5/6/99
Ph./Marg. Whoy 10/18/06
Pt./Sus. Moyer 7/3/13
Jc./Eliz. Fauckler 2/7/18
Asa Harvey/Reb. McP. Lupton 4/21/30
Hertman/Eliz. Knodle 1/9/37
Hn./Mary Burkhart 3/17/53
Sol./Mary Ann Forest 3/11/57
John/Mary Cornelia Miller 3/2/59
588. HOSFORD
Othniel/Ann Hunter 1/1/20
589. HOSKINS
John/Cath. Rohrback 12/22/29
590. HOSS
Jc./Sr. Goll 2/13/15
591. HOSSELTON
Chn./Eve Rohrer 6/28/16
592. HOSTATER
John/Eliz. Yakel 4/19/31
593. HOSTETTER
John/Lucretia Wolf 12/30/47

51

594. HOUCK (HOUK, HOUCKE, HOUKE)
Sam./Jane McGowan 12/31/06
Matthias/Ros. Emmerick 3/28/07
Mich./Cath. Smith 11/9/11
Adam/Julian Mahugh 4/12/19
Jc./Mary Hershey 5/19/24
Geo./Cath. Harrison 9/10/25
Wm./Susan Turner 10/9/30
Sam./_____ Weller 6/11/51

595. HOULETTE
Francis/Mary Miller 3/8/28

596. HOUP (HOUT, HOUTS)
Jos./Mary Rohrback 3/8/30
Wm. G./Eliza Taylor 11/27/33
Wm./Mahala Gow 3/22/45
Wm./Reb. C. Ringer 5/4/59

597. HOUSE
John/Eliz. Nesbitt 1/28/09
John/Ann Maria Betz 4/19/34
Wm. C./Marg. Strider 12/12/37
John/Mary Zeigler 9/4/49

598. HOUSEHOLDER
Fred./Cath. Lefever 10/19/99
Adam/Chna. Zemft 3/26/01
Dv./Mary Thompson 4/30/14
Leo./Ellen Baker 3/29/30
Elie/Sr. Startzman 10/30/34
Sam./Mary Shouts 1/23/34
Wm./Mary E. Gelwick 11/25/45

599. HOUSEMAN
John/Cath. Weaver 1/16/23

600. HOUSER (HOWSER)
Sam./Sus. Leighter 4/18/01
Chn./Ros. Geedy 6/20/05
Jc./Cath. Leighter 11/11/06
Is. Jr./Barb. Mumma 12/2/07
Chn./Eliz. Mumma 11/27/09
John/Ann Patterson 9/28/09
Conrad/Molly Newman 5/3/14
Jc./Eliz. Nighswander 8/9/24
John/Reb. Yeakle 7/29/28
Sam./Magdalen Huffer 4/5/30
Elias/Eliza Malott 11/11/33
Jos./Sr. Norris 1/14/34
Abr./Sr. B. Lynch 3/27/34
Chn./Ann M. Brown 1/30/41
John H./Susan F. Fechtig 9/6/43
Abr./Eliz. Boyers 4/6/46
Barney/Mary Jane McWilliams 4/3/46
Jc./Har. Grove 2/22/51
Sam./Caroline C. Burckhart 5/7/57

601. HOUSLEY (HOUSELY)
Levi/Mary Lowman 1/6/14
Dn./Eliz. Shanefelt 3/7/26

602. HOUSWORTH
John W./Mary A.E. Curtis 9/26/55

603. HOVE
John B./Marg. V. Hill 6/9/56

604. HOVERMALE (HOVERMAILE)
John/Reb. Youtz 11/4/16
Pt./Mariah Gardenour 6/15/22

605. HOWARD
Jm./Mary Kerfort 4/17/01
Ig./Mary Barnes 1/27/14
Geo./Cath. Hunt 4/14/15
John D./Eliz. Cullerson 1/12/19
Jon./Lydia Castle 9/10/19
Wm./Mary Christman 2/11/23
And./Frances Cath. Palmer 9/25/60

606. HOWELL
Dv./Marg. Roberts 4/29/37
Tho./Mar. Eaton 9/30/47

607. HOWER
John/Mary Bovey 3/13/12
Dn./Eliz. Spiegler 4/15/15
Jon./Lizzie M. Moore 2/12/58

608. HOWIATY
Owen/Mary McCohe 4/4/39

609. HOWLSINGER
Wm./Sus. Raum 6/21/06

610. HOWSER
John/Sr. Drill 4/30/36

611. HUBBARD
Dv./Marg. Shriver 10/24/25

612. HUBERT
Joshua/Mary Ann Cushwa 3/8/43

613. HUBLEY
Wm./Eliz. Shaw 8/8/29

614. HUDDLE
John/Eliz. Swadz 4/13/03

615. HUDGELL (HUDZELL, HUTZELL)
Mich./Marianna Floyer 2/19/03
Tho./Na. Hile 6/4/07
Adam/Marietta Line 1/11/48
Jc./Marg. Unklesbee 8/8/49
Dn./Chna. Young 3/14/54

616. HUDSON
Abr./Easter Keller 6/2/00
Tho./Sr. Walker 8/15/00
Josiah/Sr. Cross 8/4/28
Sam./Reb. Bean 2/26/34

617. HUDWOHL
Sam./Marg. Kable 10/13/17

618. HUFFERD
Hn./Eliza Jane Myers 12/22/60

619. HUFFMAN
Mich./Mary Coy 11/19/03
Hn./Reb. Roberts 11/29/06

620. HUGHES
Dv./Ann Elliott 12/30/06
Dv./Marg. Mong 11/19/27
John/Eliz. D. Meredith 11/12/31
John/Mary Dutro 12/13/31
John/Susan Conner 5/21/32

620. HUGHES (Continued)
   Jm./Mary Duffy 8/18/34
   Hugh R./Cath. Betz 4/1/37
   Ed./Eliz. Lambert 6/3/39
   Hugh R./Sr. Ann Hanna 5/3/42
   Sam./Levinia S.M. Knight 9/3/46
   John/Mary Ann Gorman 10/1/49
621. HULL
   Tho./Sr. Strosnyder 9/29/03
622. HULLENBERGER
   Wm. H./Almira Myers 11/29/53
623. HULSMAN
   Hez./Mary Ann Fulton 3/7/57
624. HUMRICHOUSE (HUMERICKHOUSE)
   Pt./Sr. Shuman 3/1/08
   Albert/Eliz. Weis 3/26/11
   Fred./Han. Harry 11/17/14
   Ed. P./Am. M. Knode 12/21/59
625. HUNT (HUNTT)
   Wm./Mary Nackey 8/31/13
   Dv./Milley Myers 4/6/41
   Hn./Ann Eve Myers 2/14/56
626. HUNTER
   Jm./Sr. Shriner 5/7/18
   Wm./Eveline C. Kownslar 8/31/35
627. HUNTSBERRY (HUNTSBERY)
   Hn./Cath. Rohrer 5/24/16
   John/Ann C. McCollister 11/19/52
   Aaron/Ann Nyman 1/31/53
   Hillary/Susan A. Nicodemus 3/21/60
628. HUNTSDIRE
   Mich./Cath. Slifer 11/29/39
629. HUPPER
   John/Cath. Butt 10/19/18
630. HURLEY
   Jm./Maria Thomas 12/12/29
   John/Eliz. Stouffer 5/1/32
   Jm./So. Smith 10/29/33
   Dn./Maria Ann Cross 7/27/40
   Hez. W./Cath. E. Welty 5/10/53
   Rich./Ellen Desmond 5/13/58
631. HURST
   Tho. N.G./Georgeanna O'Bannon 10/5/48
632. HUTCHEL
   Jc./Ann Lydia House 9/29/31
633. HUTTLE
   Geo./Cath. Oxx 11/1/99
634. HUTTON
   Arthur/Sus. Coon 5/17/17
635. HUYETT (HUYETTE)
   Pt./Eliz. Ann Clagett 2/10/40
   Dn./Margaretta Brinham 1/7/43
   Hn./Mary E. Winder 2/25/46
   Hn./Sr. Huyett 12/22/46
   Jc. S./Lucretia Hildebrand 1/31/49
   Dn. Gaither/Emma Merrick 11/29/60

636. HYBARGER (HIGHBARGER, HAYBARGER)
   Dv./Rachel Barnes 6/20/17
   Dv./Leah Eakel 9/16/18
   Jc./Marg. Bowers 6/9/20
   Jc./Cath. Smith 3/10/29
637. HYEL
   Chr./Cath. Hogmire 5/30/12
638. HYLAND
   John/Char. Talbott 11/2/03
639. IGEL
   Geo./Kunigunde Seyfert 12/7/46
640. ILER
   Dv./Mary Harman 11/12/07
   John/Eliz. Myers 10/28/35
641. IMMEL (IMMELL)
   John/Eliz. Barnett 1/21/01
   Jc./Sus. Barnett 5/6/11
642. INBODY
   John/Mary Reynolds 4/21/12
643. INESLINE
   Hn./Nanie Binderin (Bimlerin) 3/22/41
644. INGLE (INGLES)
   Mich./Eliz. Cook 9/21/01
   Beverly/Manerva McNight 12/14/30 or
      12/19/38 (2 dates given)
645. INGRAM
   Wm./Mary Johnson 12/23/00
   John/Anna Moore 5/25/08
   Francis/Marg. A. Jackson 9/26/40
   Ed./Mar. Ann Huyett 10/20/45
   Jos./Cath. Strippy 11/22/53
646. IRACK (IRRICK)
   Geo./Sus. Shilling 8/9/10
   John R./Reb. Ridenour 5/1/29
647. IRELY
   Josiah/Mary Virginia Michael 11/30/54
648. IRVING
   Tho. P./Bridget Philburn 12/30/16
649. IRWIN (IRVIN)
   Jm./Eliz. Barnes 7/28/03
   Geo./Mary Herr 8/4/06
   And./Sr. Dillon 6/17/07
   John/Lydia Lawson 6/26/16
   John/Lea Irvin 8/9/17
   John/Marg. Troup 8/7/17
   Allen/Anebel Thum 10/30/23
   And./Ann Farren 11/11/29
   Sam./Mary So. Hawn 2/14/32
   John/Sr. Sloan 8/8/33
   Wm./Maria Wolf 10/3/33
   Jc./Lavina Bowers 10/16/38
   Fomose H./Eliz. Rickard 7/29/59
650. ISBSON
   Wm./Han. Lynch 6/19/05
651. ISEMAN
   Wm./Mary Ann Thomas 7/27/19

53

652. ISEMINGER (ISAMINGER, ICAMINGER,
     ISENMINGER)
     Mich./Cath. Smith 9/6/00
     Geo./Sus. Adams 1/9/19
     Hn./Mary A. Springer 2/17/34
     Mich. Jr./Sus. Robinette 12/22/41
     Mich. Jr./Cath. Gimple 6/13/51
     Dv. Luther/Ann So. Furry 6/9/59
     Mich. Jr./Rose Ann Karnes 2/18/59
653. ISENBARGER
     Gabriel/Sr. Sensel 4/22/15
     Nich./Jane Rocksbury 9/29/18
654. ISRAEL
     Jc./Reb. Turner 8/26/02
     Marx/Adelia Kohn 6/1/50
655. ITNYER (ITINIRE, ITNIRE, ITTENIRE,
     ITENEYER, ITNOIRE, ITNYRE)
     Hn./Ann Nikerk 2/16/06
     John/Cath. Christine 8/22/07
     Geo./Eliz. Bealer 3/7/12
     Dn./Cath. Weast 12/30/19
     Emanuel/Eliz. Frederick 4/1/35
     Dn./Susan Duterow 8/15/37
     Wm./Cath. Leiter 9/5/37
     Sam./Mahala Gardenour 5/2/39
     Jonas/Sr. Wallick 12/21/57
     Jc./Cath. Wilkins 3/16/58

656. JACK
     Wm./Na. Williams 1/6/01
     Jer./Eliz. Otto 2/18/17
     John/Na. Dugan 6/17/20
     And./Eliz. Harry 9/8/38
657. JACKSON
     Jc./Mary Tracey 9/30/12
     Abr./Jane Wright 4/2/17
     John C.W./Eliz. McClain 8/29/18
     John/Han. Carothers 5/22/27
     Arch./Eliz. Colbert 8/1/35
     Benj./Drucilla Bidamon 6/5/35
     Tho./Eliz. Wilson 4/6/39
     Josiah/Cath. Twig 5/22/40
     John/Eliz. Coleman 11/19/44
     Ed./Han. M. Shepherd 9/9/47
     John/Elmira McCoy 6/12/47
     Geo. W./Ann Maria Haines 10/25/49
     Tho./Ann Divine Colbert 5/26/58
658. JACOBS
     Emanuel/Ellen Rowe 4/18/32
     Sam./Eliz. Coffman 2/27/34
     Wm./So. Lighter 3/19/45
     Wm. Tho./Ann Maria Davis 12/9/56
     Geo. W./Helen R. Monigan 12/22/59
659. JACQUES
     Arthur/Sr. Lowe 3/7/12
     Lancelot Jr./Mary Bowman 6/2/12
     Lancelot/Juliann Gehr 3/18/46
660. JAMES
     Geo./Mar. Hughes 3/9/01
     Geo./Polly McCoy 10/20/03

Wm./Sally Riley 7/29/09
Rhesa/Han. Davis 4/7/16
Wm./Eliza Mahany 8/8/16
Ed./Chna. Snort 12/24/17
Abr./Sr. Stiffler 1/22/20
Watkins Jr./Louisa Baker 6/3/31
Walter/Susan Ault 2/14/32
Watkins/Maria Davis 3/3/35
John/Har. Wilson 4/16/39
John/Mary Downs 2/20/39
Walter/Polly Taylor 5/25/40
Watkins/Maria Reynolds 7/27/40
Wm./Jane Friend 9/28/53
Elias/Ann Creek 10/30/54
Wm./Eliz. Dubble 10/25/54
John W./Mar. A. Smith 2/28/57
661. JAMISON
     Wm./Chna. Ford 5/17/08
     Ph./Eliz. Tucker 6/24/41
     Jm./Cath. Stoner 10/4/44
     Alex./Doleana Summers 3/3/58
     Jm./Mary E. Crampton 7/21/60
662. JEANNES
     Amos/Har. Moudy 3/9/40
663. JENETH
     Arch./Mary Roads 3/18/11
664. JENKINS (KINKINS)
     Wm./Sr. Myers 8/8/48
     Tho. A./Jane Fry 9/5/51
     Asa/Ann Cath. Dodd 1/15/57
     Sol./Hellen M. Beard 7/4/59
665. JENNINGS (JENNING)
     Mahlon/Mary Collins 12/4/26
     Joshua/Eliz. Kratzer 2/6/33
     Sam./So. Nicholl 12/18/37
     Wm./Sr. Houser 3/23/37
666. JESSOP
     Ed./Susan S. Wolf 10/22/46
667. JIMISON
     John/Jane Taneyhill 8/18/31
     Sam./Maria Fridinger 1/17/45
668. JOBE
     Wm./Lucinda Farnesworth 5/16/36
669. JOHN (JOHNS)
     Hn./Cath. Bovey 3/14/10
     Leo. H./Hen. Geiger 8/4/26
670. JOHNSON
     Tho./Cath. Nichols 6/12/00
     Arthur/Sr. Slye 1/25/04
     Francis/Mary Cleaton 5/31/06
     Rob./Eleanor Sheckler 10/12/07
     Tho./Mary McGeeghan 8/8/07
     Geo./Cath. Morehead 4/23/10
     Wm./Barb. Piper 3/24/12
     Jm./Jane Gabby 11/10/29
     Richard/Ann Yerty 7/11/38
     Sam./Am. Stump 11/22/42
     Aaron H./Marietta Boone 3/27/43
     Dr. James/Ann R. Locher 7/1/46
     Rob./Cath. J. Matthew 4/28/46

54

670. JOHNSON (Continued)
    Aaron/Cath. Hicks 10/7/48
    John E./Susan P. Kershner 2/20/51
    Dr. J./Mary E. Reynolds 10/6/52
    D. Clinton/Eliz. B. Dall 9/16/56
    Rob./Louisa Jacques 1/2/57
    John H./Susan Stottlemyer 12/27/58
671. JOHNSTON
    John/Sus. Fisher 4/19/13
    Jc./Mag. Wertebecker 9/18/17
    Ed./Eliz. Gray 7/21/22
    Tobias/Ruth Mason 5/11/26
    John/Esabella Day 9/25/27
    Jc./Eliza Schnebly 6/5/30
    Jm./Ludy McCabe 10/25/34
    John/Sr. Hains 5/14/40
    John H./Am. Eliz. Milton 6/3/42
    Arthur/Susan Rudisell 1/6/43
    Hn./Eliz. McCoy 8/17/44
    Geo. W./Mary E. Hendricks 5/19/51
    Rev. Wm./S. Eliz. Coup 10/21/51
672. JOIN
    Mich./Mary Keough 1/14/37
673. JONES
    Dn./Nelly Talbot 3/1/00
    Enoch/Mary Neal 3/7/00
    John/Eliz. Davis 1/24/00
    Noah/Mary Wells 12/29/00
    Dn./Am. Wells 8/10/02
    Denny/Eliz. Hinch 10/15/02
    John/Barb. Rouch 1/7/05
    Absalom/Magdalene Dibert 8/30/08
    Jos./Sally W. McCoy 8/5/09
    Sam./Am. Jones 4/29/09
    Jc./Cath. Ankeney 9/3/10
    Ludwick/Char. Belt 12/27/11
    Noah/Hen. Bayly 3/29/13
    John/Eliz. Rutter 9/3/14
    Jos./Eliz. Keadle 8/8/17
    Leventon/Eliz. Denoon 12/29/18
    John/Eliz. Massey 6/14/21
    Wm./Peggy Adams 1/6/21
    Wm./Sr. Ann South 3/20/27
    Levin/Sr. Hunt 2/23/29
    Jc./Sr. Ann Winters 3/18/30
    Jon./Eliz. Bovey 4/12/33
    Joshua/Mary Greenwell 4/27/33
    John/Eliz. A. Foils 5/6/35
    Mich./Cath. Kinney 8/8/36
    Sam./Sr. Morgan 10/12/36
    Ezra/Eliza Blessing 1/24/39
    Isaiah/Ann Maria McCartney 11/26/39
    John W./Eliz. W. Chipley 12/22/41
    Hn./Ann Stanton 8/19/44
    Wm. Harrison/Rachel A. Haynes 11/16/47
    Jos. W./Har. Moore 6/12/49
    Leo./Marietta Rohrer 4/2/50
    Dv. S./Ann M. Sprecker 12/13/51

    Tho. A./Jane Fry 9/5/51
    M.C./A.C. Younkins 2/28/55
    Wm. Hn./Susan Hill 11/8/59
674. JORDAN
    John/Eliz. Breaker 9/13/08
    Thornton G./Reb. H. Mullenix 6/19/23
    Tho./Cath. Kreps 8/3/38
675. JOY
    John/Ruanna Weast 8/17/44
    Jm./Am. Seigler 7/24/52
676. JULIUS
    Geo./Mary Cottingham 3/30/54
677. JURETON
    Wm./Han. French 1/22/13
678. JUSTICE
    And./Maza Russell 4/14/17

679. KAGERIES (KAGEREIS)
    Jc./Barb. Burger 2/5/11
    Mich./Na. Troup 9/18/20
680. KAHL
    Jc./Cath. Myers 10/18/49
681. KAHN
    Aaron/Rosa Goldsmith 8/20/53
682. KAIL
    Wm./Betsy Nelson 2/9/25
683. KATLER (KALLER)
    Jc./Sr. Dennison 12/5/29
    Dv./Reb. Bowers 4/11/32
    And./Polly Bowers 1/28/40
684. KALBE
    Elijah/Reb. Tenant 3/18/29
685. KALSER
    Jc./Mary Myers 1/22/20
686. KANAVEL
    John/Cath. Forsythe 8/8/39
687. KANE
    Jm./Mary McMannus 2/5/38
688. KAPP
    Mich./Mary Lorshbaugh 8/24/08
    Jc./Barb. Keller 5/12/28
    Fred. G./Har. E. Martin 1/5/32
689. KARNES
    Hn./Marg. Lutz 11/14/40
    Chas./Cath. Moudy 4/15/47
690. KARRELLS (KARROL)
    Moses/Mary Ward 12/11/12
    Dv./Polly Miles 7/9/44
691. KAUFFMAN
    John/Eliz. Kaufman 10/21/13
    Leo./Mary Kerbaugh 8/17/13
    Abr./Sus. Herr 5/10/19
    Sam./Cordelia James 12/11/27
    Jc./Maria Malott 9/24/52
    Smith H./Marg. A. Fouble 11/22/59

692. KAUSLER
Jc./Cath. Shale 6/18/08
Jos./Mary E. Baechtell 12/12/49
Geo. S./Har. H. Snyder 7/29/50
John H./Prudence Cheney 2/16/50
693. KAY
I.W./S. Jannette McDuell 2/13/59
694. KEADLE
Abr. L./Eliz. Clevidence 10/22/32
John A./Mariah Sholl 4/28/32
Geo./Chra. Emerson 7/10/57
John G./Helen Ford 2/25/58
695. KEAF
Jm./Mary Patterson 12/25/19
696. KEALHOFFER (KEALHOFER)
Jc./Am. Ridenour 2/27/07
Geo./Mary E. Hannankamp 5/17/38
697. KEAN
Joel Tho./Han. C. Chapman 9/4/52
698. KEE
Arthur/Sr. Files 1/13/16
699. KEEBER (KOEBER)
John F./Mary Horning 6/14/21
700. KEEDY
Hn./Na. Nighwander 8/30/06
John/Eliz. Snively 5/25/18 ("s/o
Daniel" pencil note)
Jc./Susan Messely 10/23/19
John D./Eliz. Schnebly 4/27/22
Adam/Eliz. Leaser 10/1/24
John/Mary Ann Middlekauff 4/11/26
Dn./So. Miller 12/20/27
Hn./Leah Clopper 12/20/27
Dv. H./Eliz. Hanna 4/16/28
Hn./Susan Shutt 11/2/30
Sam./Susan Middlekauff 4/11/31
Dn. G./Malinda Funk 4/1/37
Dv. H./Jelis McCoy 1/14/40
Jc./Maria Stine 2/19/40
Chn./Mary E. Carr 11/7/49 (Chn.
Reedy in cross-index)
Alford/Eliz. Stine 10/21/50
Jos./So. Clapper 12/23/51
John D./Mary Ann Zittle 10/16/52
Ed./Eliz. Blecker 9/12/53
John S./Marg. N. Nicodemus 8/5/58
701. KEEFAUVER (KEFAVER, KEFUVER, KEVAUVER)
John/Mag. Miller 12/18/07
John/Cath. Young 7/9/34
John/Mary Ann Snavely 12/31/39
Fred./Marg. Huntsberry 1/23/41
Geo. W./Ann Stotler 3/13/47
John/Eliz. Young 11/30/47
702. KEEFER (KEAFER, KEFER, KEIFFER, KIEFER)
Mt./Mary Varner 1/7/00
Wm./Eliz. King 3/15/00
Jc./Mary Gross 8/29/01
Mt./Marg. Blocher 1/16/04

Chr./Mary Shank 3/11/07
Geo./Cath. Armestrout 3/22/09
Jc. J./Jane M. Hebberd 6/10/19
John Dn./Eliz. Schmuts 5/31/23
Geo./Sus. Fogwell 12/16/26
Jc./Mrs. Anna Funk 12/31/36
Theobald/Rosina Barb. Leipold 2/23/47
703. KEEPERS
Israel/Eliz. Harper 7/8/07
704. KEERL
Chas. F./Lydia Ann Barr 10/13/35
705. KEESECKER (KEESACRE, KESAKER, KEISECKER)
Conrad/Na. Parker 3/26/07
Jc./Eliz. Criswell 9/12/25
Aaron/Marg. Rightstine 11/22/27
Dv. C./Annetta Lewis 10/23/50
Jc./Eliza Davis 5/25/59
706. KEESEY
Conrad/Mary Burget 3/20/13
707. KEETH
Mich./Fanny Hoover 11/2/05
708. KEEVE (KEEVES)
John/Mary Ann Stewart 1/22/43
709. KEIRNAN (KIERNAN)
Pt./Mary Flora 6/24/03
710. KEISLE
Wm./Ellenor Douglass 3/19/32
711. KELAS
Jm./Eleanor Usher 6/23/07
712. KELL
Fred./Maria May 11/28/56
713. KELLER (KELLAR)
Jos. C./Eliz. Crampton 3/27/09
Dv./Han. Bassaw 3/27/10
Pt./Mary Trovinger 2/27/16
Hn./Mar. M. Ford 5/28/19
Israel/Marg. Schnebly 5/6/19
Pt./Reb. Cobert 8/5/20
Hn./Mary Leckrone 3/14/27
Lewis/Marg. Leckrone 3/14/27
Tho./Eliza Jane Martin 5/1/27
John/Sr. Bryson 4/19/28
John/Eliz. Newcomer 4/24/28
Adam/Mary Beckenbaugh 8/1/30
Geo./Sr. Brewer 5/3/31
Al./Susan Blecher 6/11/38
Wm./Rachel Steele 3/29/39
Sol./Cath. Maysille 11/2/40
Jc./Marg. McCall 5/29/45
Wm. N./Sr. Winders 2/13/51
714. KELLEY (KELLY)
Jc./Sus. Ervin 6/20/01
Wm./Eliz. Ripple 10/2/06
Aaron/Sus. Oldfield 6/8/15
Ed./Lydia A. Stonebraker 3/27/26
Hn. A./Marg. McGonagle 4/16/27
Ed./Eleanor Brown 12/29/29
Tho./Maria Kennedy 7/1/33

714. KELLEY (KELLY) (Continued)
    Jos./Cath. Dick 2/1/34
    Tho./Jane E. Pockins 4/20/37
    Wm./Mary Smith 2/16/38
    Pat./Sr. Mooney 1/5/39
    Jos./Eliz. Lampkin 9/21/48
    Wm./Marg. Jane Malott 11/21/49
    Jm./Ruanna Johnson 2/20/51
715. KELSEY
    Dv./Jane E. Cronise 12/29/42
716. KELSO
    J./Mary Jane Randall 10/3/56
717. KELTMAKER
    John/Eliz. Rohrer 7/29/06
718. KEMP
    Ezra L./Eleanor Bealer 3/3/19
    Geo./Maria McCoy 6/2/31
719. KEMPER
    Jc./Lydia Oswald 5/16/30
720. KENDLE (KENDELL, KENDAL, KENDALL, KINDLE)
    Hn./Eve Smith 4/20/10
    Elie/Han. Engleman 2/18/15
    Jos./Peggy Rice 10/21/18
    Wm./Ros. Bowers 9/7/18
    Jm./Marg. Wherrett 12/9/20
    John/Cath. Hays 8/8/21
    Wm./Eliz. Burrell 1/24/24
    Jm./Cath. Gearhart 11/1/26
    Geo./Eliz. Sprecker 1/8/31
    John Hn./Eliz. Myers 6/17/37
    John/Susan Deal 3/16/42
    Dv./Eliza Rice 8/29/49
    John E./Eliz. Armstrong 3/14/57
    Geo. C./Caroline Gouff 6/9/57
    Jc. S./Sr. Ann Getter 9/9/57
    John/Reb. Syester 10/30/58
    B.F./Adelaide E. Davis 7/11/60
721. KENESTRICK (KNESTRICK)
    John/Sr. Kevener 4/23/08
    Wm./Polly Younce 1/22/11
722. KENNAN
    Elie/Mary Rinker 10/13/29
723. KENNEDY
    Ed./Sus. Gordon 4/16/01
    Jos./Adriana Brill 10/13/02
    John/Marg. Wagner 12/25/04
    Jabez/Milkey Windel 11/4/13
    Alex./Susan S. Booth 5/15/22
    Rob./Jane Lang 8/20/29
    John/Eliza Jane Brown 3/30/35
    R.F./Susan Hershey 3/12/41
    Jm. H./Lydia E. Hollingsworth 5/23/43
    Wm. B./Eliz. M. Zeller 2/22/55
724. KENNELLY
    Dv./Jane Shanon 5/26/03
725. KENNER
    Alex./Maria Burgan 1/30/46

726. KENNEY (KENNY, KINNEY)
    Sam./Marg. Hanna 10/12/00
    Barney/Mag. Goble 7/23/07
    John/Mary Myers 11/2/19
    Jon./Mary Ann Chambers 11/20/33
    Geo./Cath. Clevidence 12/19/38
    Arthur/Bridget Hennesy 8/9/51
727. KENTNER
    John/Sr. Dooble 6/30/18
728. KEPHART
    Jc./Delilah Peters 9/25/27
    Levi/Cath. Ensworth 7/26/39
729. KEPLER (KEPPLER)
    Nath./Cath. Springer 6/27/21
    Wm. McK./Emily E. Steffey 10/30/37
730. KEPLINGER
    Jc./Eliz. Highshoe 8/4/00
    John/Mary Smith 4/20/11
    Adam/Mag. Smutz 9/7/12
    Mich./Am. Kenney 2/18/37
    Dv./Cath. Snider 3/12/38
    Jon./Ann Maria Kinney 2/21/39
    Elias/Mar. Ann Joy 1/26/46
    Nich./So. Karn 3/2/46
731. KERCHAVEL
    Jos. K./Ann M. Karrington 8/1/49
    Walter/Leah Mallen 1/18/51
732. KERFOOT
    Geo. W./Mary Seifert 12/21/21
    Sam. H./Ann W. Lawrence 9/14/47
    Wm./Reb. Kemp 5/26/47
    Rich. D./An Eliza Flemming 12/24/51
    Jm. M./Cath. R. Jones 3/25/52
733. KERLIN
    Sam./Barb. Reynolds 9/3/57
734. KERN
    Nich./Mary Carrell 2/18/01
735. KERNEY
    Uriah B./Maria C. Hunsaker 5/22/50
736. KERRON (KERRIN)
    Tho./Ann Gray 11/9/07
    John O./Ann McEvoy 11/5/37
737. KERSH
    Jc./Susan Weis 3/26/19
738. KERSHNER
    Geo. Jr./Marg. Flenner 11/23/99
    Sol./Marg. Kershner 12/11/00
    Jc./Eliz. Ridenour 2/9/03
    Mt./Mag. Ankeney 1/19/04
    Pt./Cath. Ankeney 1/19/04
    Israel/Eva Startzman 2/22/05
    Benj./Eliz. Ankeney 11/9/07
    Jc./Mag. Wachtel 6/23/08 ("s/o John"
      pencil note)
    Jc./Mary Kershner 5/10/09
    Sam./Mary Waughtele 6/2/11
    And./Eliz. Moudy 12/26/12

738. KERSHNER (Continued)
Abr./Sr. Morgendall 1/21/13
Dn./Mag. Weld 8/7/13
Sol./Eliz. Cole 8/8/18
Jc./Cath. Slice 6/13/20
Jon./Cath. Miller 4/25/20
Dn./Na. Westerberger 12/8/23
Jc./Cath. Albert 4/8/26
Josiah/Sus. Snyder 8/31/26
Jc./Sr. Verble 2/27/27
Josiah/Cath. Stine 10/20/29
Nath./Maria Deal 10/4/30
Gustavus/Ann Brewer 3/19/36
Dv./Eliz. Lung 4/8/40
Cyrus/Na. Ellen Smith 6/1/46
Benj. F./Reb. Freaner 5/8/51
Dv./Eliz. Trovinger 3/25/51
Van L./Mary L. Ringer 2/22/58
Mt./Susan Miller 11/28/60
739. KESSEL
John G./Eliz. Zilhart 8/9/41
740. KESSINGER (KIESLINGER, KISINGER,
KYSINGER)
Chas./Eliz. Eakel 2/25/04
Jc./Cath. Conn 4/16/05
Jc./Mag. Genawein 4/9/07
Geo./Barb. Roach 8/13/10
Jc./Marg. Beard 10/2/16
John Jr./Sr. Ann Watts 3/17/31
Geo./Cath. Shank 12/21/43
741. KESSLER
Dv./Sus. Nigh 4/2/02
John/Mary Ann Rhodes 3/23/47
Hn. Nelson/Mary A. Keifer 4/7/49
Wm. E./Ann C. McClain 1/7/53
742. KEY (KEYS)
John R./Virginia Ringgold 9/25/34
Pt./Frances Criswell 10/8/36
743. KEYSER (KEISER, KIESER)
Ph./Eliz. Kannon 8/19/06
Mt./Eliz. Marker 5/20/07
John/Chna. Bowert 11/19/11
Hn./Sr. McClanahan 2/7/32
744. KICKORN
Ph./Cath. Highbarger 11/13/23
745. KIDWILER
Jc./Mary Lambright 4/24/35
Chas./Marg. Nichols 12/23/42
Mich./Juan Pennell 4/12/43
746. KIFER
Hn./Lydia Ann Kreps 3/25/45
747. KIHL
Geo./Eliz. Wolfersberger 5/4/25
748. KILLIN
Jm./Na. Hering 8/7/02
749. KIMBALL
Rob./Sr. Boteler 2/6/34

750. KIMES
Wm./Emily Hooper 7/9/47
751. KING
John/Mary Baker 3/3/01
John/Elly Shryock 10/8/01
Chn./Marg. Raip 3/15/10
Dn./Cath. Young 10/5/20
Mt./Marg. Pifer 3/25/24
Pat./Bridget McLaughlin 2/17/24
John W./Susan G. Haines 11/20/29
Sam./Mary Start 4/8/31
Sam. L./Eliza Lane 10/15/33
John/Ellen Miller 6/28/37
Tho./Cath. Keeting 10/5/37
John/Cath. Neikirk 1/30/43
Owen/Ellen Heslehan 11/22/51
Franklin L./Ellen Jane Ruth 2/12/55
Jerome E./Rachel Ann Shook 11/10/57
752. KINGAN
Jm./Cath. Gan 8/18/17
753. KINGERY (KINGARY, KINGRY)
Jc./Mary Myers 2/27/06
Chn./Eliz. Hovermaile 3/25/20
Jc./Sr. Watson 2/4/22
754. KINKLE
Adam/Cath. Eichelberger 10/31/16
Jc./Polly Williams 11/1/23
John/Ann Maria Shaffner 12/22/24
Adam/Mary Thurston 7/22/52
755. KINSELL
Fred. B.O./Mary Mag. Young 12/22/15
Enoch B./Han. Dillman 10/28/17
756. KIRBY (KERBY)
Meshack/Mary Chambers 9/14/19
Wm./Eliz. Murry 12/26/23
Wm./Mary Engle 2/21/28
757. KIRKHAM
And./Cath. Cronise 5/28/31
758. KIRKPATRICK
John/Susan Cath. Byers 9/7/48
759. KISSEL (KISSELL)
John/Ann Martin 3/10/36
Jc./Ros. Bell 5/3/41
760. KITCHEN
Geo./Maria Gantt 4/9/30
761. KITER
Benj./Caroline E. White 12/27/50
762. KITZMILLER
John/Eliz. Wolford 9/1/00 ("buried near
Forreston, IL" pencil note)
John/Marg. Robinson 5/17/24
Jc./Reb. Syers 12/22/30
Sam./Mary Palmer 8/16/30
Wm. H./Cath. M. Crayton 9/27/30
John/Ruanna Iler 12/22/32
Sam./Rachel Drurenburgh 2/1/32
Adam/Mrs. Lydia House 6/3/36
Hn./Sr. Sullens 2/24/36

762. KITZMILLER (Continued)
Dv./Mary Mag. Rohrer 11/28/46
Wash./Susan Ambrose 2/17/46
Dn./Mary Keyser 6/14/56
Frisby/Rose Ann Miller 7/26/59
Jc./Eliz. Itnire 12/22/59
763. KLIM
Dv./Na. Shade 5/1/32
764. KLINE
John/Marg. Cooke 4/9/03
Hn./Polly Bobst 2/13/10
Hn./Peggy McGinness 11/20/10
Geo./Marg. Myers 1/9/13
Sam./Mariah Senseman 12/13/23
Jc. A./Eliza South 3/4/24
Jos./Am. South 1/22/29
Jc./Mary Farrow 3/23/30
John D./Jane Fleming 7/16/35
Geo./Cath. Elliott 9/27/47
Jm./Mary Marker 3/1/52
Geo. H./Sus. Mundebaugh 1/3/55
Geo. Adam/Susan Ann Frey 12/13/56
John/Susan Lum 3/12/57
Levi/Cath. E. Bruner 1/21/58
Is./Susan Lucretia Miller 12/21/60
765. KLINK
Mich./Eliz. Brannon 5/4/31
766. KNABEL (KANBLE)
Leo./Julianna Lyser 1/4/05
Geo./Sus. Stoltz 11/28/08
767. KNADLER
Pt./So. Cretzer 5/26/32
768. KNAVE (KNAVES)
Mich./Eleanor O'Hare 3/7/08
Jc./Ann Matilda Akey 7/25/44
769. KNEEDY (KNEADY)
Geo./Eliz. Guy 9/30/03
770. KNEISS
Adolph Lepold/Marg. Emilie Finger
8/14/50
771. KNEPPER
John/Sus. Davis 8/4/16
772. KNEXTERDT
Theodore/Mary A. Riffsnyder 4/16/53
773. KNIGHT
Lloyd/Helen R. Kealhofer 10/8/45
Aaron Dv./Cath. Ann Feigley 7/19/56
774. KNIPE
Chr./Jane Farquhar 3/27/26
775. KNODE (KANODE)
John/Na. Eakle 7/24/01
Conrad/Sus. Duple 7/9/02
Jc./Eliz. Hammond 12/4/02
John/Reb. Ironheum 11/25/05
Hn./Mary Warner 6/16/07
Hn./Maria Hewett 1/23/09
Jc./Sus. Rohrer 2/23/13
Jc./Marg. Bentz 12/20/13
Jc./Cath. Piper 10/23/13

Sam./Sr. Smith 6/5/19
Jonas/Mary Donaldson 1/23/23
Jc. Jr./Mary Chaney 2/3/25
Wm. H./Susan Landis 6/3/34
Hez./Ruth Hinds 5/27/35
Sam./Cath. Herr 8/3/35
Urias/Mary Cox 4/15/35
Dn. T./Na. Hoover 9/18/37
Simon/Louisa Humrickhouse 9/11/38
Wm./So. Ross 3/17/38
John E./Hester Ann Stonebraker 3/25/39
Augustus/Cath. Gigler 4/28/41
Oliver/Mary Nyman 4/17/44
Frisby/Cath. Shriver 5/5/45
Elias U./Eliza M. Pretzman 1/29/51
Arch./Amanda C. Yerty 1/29/53
Frisby/Mary Marker 10/4/55
John G./Ann E. Wantz 10/11/55
Arch. P./Lavinia Rohrback 6/17/57
Josiah/Manscella Welty 9/14/58
Cyrus/Marg. E. Evans 11/17/59
Urias/Cath. Cox 3/21/59
776. KNODLE
John/Barb. Long 11/12/03
Sam./Jane Cutshall 6/3/06
John/Sus. Woolford 12/7/07
Wm./Sr. Cutshall 6/2/07
Jon./Barb. King 7/20/19
Pt./Sus. Moats 10/17/25
Wm./Rachel Coffman 9/22/28
John/Chna. Yeakle 11/13/34
Geo./Marg. Spielman 10/17/38
Jon. S./Marg. Slusman 8/15/38
Jc. J./Maria Snider 3/2/41
Jon./Naomi Robinett 5/31/42
Josiah/Har. Miller 4/6/42
Sam. Jr./Ellen Dick 1/12/43
Wm./Mary Ann Beck 1/10/44
Elias/Susan Slussman 12/18/47
Hiram/Mary Beecraft 2/21/48
777. KNOTT
Jm./Char. Snyder 2/7/12 (listed as Knox,
crossed out, replaced with Knott)
Sam./Marg. Saunders 2/23/22 (listed as
Knox, crossed out, replaced with Knott)
Wm./Lydia Sanner 9/9/30
Hn./Malinda Hutzell 11/20/52
778. KNOUFF
Geo. W./Hetty Hartle 12/22/49
779. KNOX
Jm./Char. Snyder 2/7/12 (listed as Knox,
crossed out, replaced with Knott)
Wm./Sus. Renn 12/12/15
Sam./Marg. Saunders 2/23/22 (listed as
Knox, crossed out, replaced with Knott)
Jos./Na. McCoy 11/12/40
Rich./Ellen King 5/18/59
780. KOENIG
Bernard/Eliz. Christopher 5/2/40

59

781. KOHLER (KEHLER, KOLER)
John/Han. Wendling 4/29/15
Jonas/Sus. Broutzman 4/6/41
782. KOOFY
Hn./Reb. Young 9/5/01
783. KOOGLE
Adam/Cath. Miller 9/4/30
784. KOON (KOONS, KOONTZ, KUNTZ)
Pt./Polly Pierce 9/2/05
Jc./Eliz. Zacharias 10/24/10
John/Mary Panning 9/9/15
John/Susan Bowman 1/1/25
Hiram/Ann Runimus 4/10/32
John/Louisa James 12/29/35
Is./Na. Harman 6/3/39
Landon/Na. Funk 12/28/41
Eph./Angelina Stonebraker 3/13/45
Columbus/Sus. Fahrney 12/6/51
Jc./Mary Farrow 10/16/51
Silas A./Na. Stouffer 3/31/51
Elie/Louisa French 3/7/55
Wm. C./Eliz. A. Emmert 8/6/58
785. KOPPISH
Fred./Lydia Brown 11/1/27
786. KORO
Fred./Eliz. Wills 2/12/05
787. KOROCK
Benj./Sus. Shupe 1/1/00
788. KOROSELLOR
Remington B./Mary Chenewith 5/17/43
789. KOST
Jc. S./Cath. Snavely 11/18/28
790. KOUTZ
Pt./Cath. Pfouts 3/27/21
791. KRANTZ
John D./Cath. Arter 4/20/15
792. KRATZ
Ph. Nich./Barb. Fischer 12/23/36
793. KREAGER
Leo./Han. Perry 6/30/04
794. KREBS
Hn./Kate Titus 12/2/57
795. KREIGH
Ph./Mary Cline 2/11/01
Wm./Marg. McCleary 3/12/30
Ph./Sr. Hammer 6/22/30
Elie/Mary Ann Willyard 10/29/33
796. KREPS
John/Frances Herr 1/7/16
Wm./Mary Russel 10/25/16
Geo./Cath. Osterdock 11/29/17
Geo. F./Eliza Orondorff 10/12/19
Mich./Polly Hoffman 5/25/20
Mich./Ann Scott 7/22/24
Jc./Sr. Newcomer 8/9/26
Geo./Na. Baughman 4/30/28
Al./Marg. Staley 4/26/30

Mich. H./Ellen Creamer 3/27/49
Emanuel/Mag. Palmer 3/22/51
Hn./Mar. Miley 12/15/53
Rudolph/Eliz. Kuhn 12/21/58
Sam./Susan C. Feidt 10/1/59
797. KRETZER
Dn./Cath. Beall 8/9/99
Jc./Susan Hines 3/13/30
Jc./Mary Show 8/8/36
Adam/Cath. McCoy 6/8/40
Noah/Eliza Hamilton 11/15/47
Sol./Susan Lambert 3/10/51
Franklin/Hen. Grim 9/16/53
Sam./Sr. A. Johnson 9/15/54
Wm./Maria Double 2/4/54
Sam./Ann Eliz. Bender 11/5/55
Jos./Mary Crisvile 11/17/60
798. KRETZINGER
Geo./Dolly Eckenbarger 7/2/03
Is./Mary Deitrich 10/25/36
Sam./Cath. Stotler 1/5/39
Geo./Anna Stotler 7/29/40
799. KRICK
Jc./Ann Goulding 7/30/19
And./Am. Castle 5/4/24
800. KRIDER
Hn./Marg. Harbaugh 11/10/60
801. KRINER
Dn./Mary C. Marks 9/15/53
802. KRISE
John/Mary Ridenour 5/1/51
803. KROM
I.I./Sr. Young 1/13/46
804. KROTZER
John M./Sr. Winders 8/24/36
805. KROUSE (KRAUS)
Pt./Sus. Winters 8/11/23
John/Delilah Widdis 1/7/53
John G.P./Iaretta L. Burckhart 12/17/53
Jos. D./Mary Stonebraker 2/19/56
Bernard I./Maria A. Brehm 2/7/40
806. KUHN
John Hn./Han. C. Pryer 11/10/55
Wm./Eva Kuhn 4/17/58
807. KURFFMAN
Wm./Roz. Foutz 12/4/55
808. KURTZ
Benj./Ann Barnett 9/1/18
809. KYNE
Matthias C./Cath. White 8/13/50

60

1. LAHEY
   Dn./Cath. Haley 12/24/33
2. LAKIN
   Wm. F./Am. Adams 8/20/41
3. LALEY
   John/Mary Campbell 9/19/15
4. LAMAR (LAMARR)
   Arch./Sus. Brown 5/12/30
   Benj. F./Han. M.L. Hall 8/29/48
5. LAMBERT
   Jc./Eliz. Gearhart 1/1/02
   Geo./Jane Johnson 12/5/03
   John/Sus. Wolfensberger 9/14/11
   Jonas/Cath. Russell 3/1/15
   Abr./Reb. Artz 2/16/18
   Jos./So. Smith 12/21/25
   Wm./Mary Longman 6/10/27
   John/Barb. Poe 12/30/45
   Elias/Ellen Moore 4/11/57
6. LAMBIA
   John/Ann Eliza Kreps 6/5/34
7. LAMBRIGHT
   Geo./Anne Ault 12/22/38
   Mich./Mary Kidwiler 10/17/38
8. LANAGAN
   Rich./Ann Corogan 5/25/33
9. LANCASTER
   Chas./Marg. Hamilton 9/23/12
   Benj./Mary Ann Myers 3/4/33
   St. Clair A./Marg. A. Miller 6/4/57
10. LAND
    Mich./Julia O'Brian 9/20/40
11. LANDEGER
    Gideon/Rachel Grabill 9/2/29
12. LANDIS (LANDES, LANDS)
    Chn./Mary McCoy 3/20/19
    Hn./Lavinia Middlekauff 11/16/30
    Chr./Ellen Adams 3/15/59
13. LANDUKIN
    Pat./Marg. Winters 10/4/27
14. LANE (LANES)
    Geo./Cath. Maloy 6/27/12
    Timothy/Mary Lane 2/18/24
    Chas. G./Maria F. Kirkpatrick 12/4/28
    Wash. W./Matilda Brown 1/31/35
    John C./Eliz. Horine 4/3/38
15. LANTHORN
    Geo./Mary Stripton 9Shipton) 9/5/06
16. LANTZ
    Chn. Jr./Esther Musselman 8/7/04
    Geo./Cath. Wolgomot 8/22/09
    Hn./Polly Schwartz 9/4/10
    John/Cath. Reads 9/5/26
    Jc./Mary Weltzheimer 7/18/33
    Geo. W./Mary B. Drill 3/12/34
    Chn./Hen. Shiess 3/17/36
    Ezra/Sus. Finfrock 2/10/40

    Jc./Cath. Smith 3/22/42
    John/Juliann Burhmann 9/26/44
    Dv./Ellen Banks 4/26/53
    John Nelson/Mary C. Hoffman 9/24/57
    Ezra/Sr. L. Gigous 11/15/59
    John F./Ann Eliz. Hartman 3/23/60
17. LAPOLE (LAYPOLE)
    Fred./Mary Dornbaugh 3/4/24
    Godfrey/Cath. Holmes 12/8/37
    John/Mary Hutzel 3/5/39
    Ph./Mary Ann Stone 7/10/47
    John H. (or M.)/Mary M. Reeder 9/6/60
18. LAPPON
    Alex. H./Ann M. Colliflower 11/15/33
19. LARKINS
    John/Na. Bell McCoy 3/28/12
    Joshua/Eleanor Lawneyhill 2/20/17
20. LARNEY
    John/Cath. Horgan 1/18/34
21. LASHER
    Chn./Cath. Glossbrenner 5/2/40
22. LASKINS
    Ed./Sr. Robison 7/4/43
23. LATCHSHOWER
    Geo./Eliz. Branstater 6/10/06
24. LAUB
    John/Sr. Mourer 8/12/20
25. LAUCHBAUM
    Sam./Sr. Davis 2/21/57
26. LAUVER
    John/Mary Stake 7/16/11
    Jc./Barb. Rohrer 1/12/18
    Elliott J./Mary A. Smith 9/18/48
27. LAWRENCE (LAURENCE)
    Upton/Eliz. Hager 2/1/03
    Ed./Eliz. Rieseler 4/18/07
    John/Reb. Long 6/3/07
    John/Anna Rankin 4/11/15
28. LAWSON
    John/Isa. McCardell 1/29/51
29. LAYTON
    Jos./Mary Ann Tritt 7/22/28
30. LEAKINGS
    Jc./Amanda Porter 9/27/52
31. LEAMON (LEAMAN)
    John/Cath. Dellinger 11/12/08
    Jc. Kelb/Maria Legett 2/10/19
32. LEANY
    Hugh/Na. Bear 4/18/33
33. LEAR
    Jc./Fanny Blair 9/29/01
34. LEARY
    John/Mary Burns 5/5/35
35. LEASURE (LEISURE)
    Elijah/Sus. Miller 10/5/11
    Hn./So. Shane 12/14/24

36. LEATHERMAN
Fred./Mary A.E. Ridenour 10/15/56
Jc./Mary E. Brown 11/23/59
37. LECKRON (LECKRONE, LECKROON, LECH-
RONE, LACKROON)
Simon/Sr. Liday 7/31/02
Jc./Ann Rohrer 2/21/14
John/Cath. Wolfelsburger 4/29/15
John/Cath. Mowing 5/6/17
Dn./Eliza Quantrill 2/12/31
Jon./Cath. Bigham 3/31/34
Jc./Sus. Spessard 1/14/37
Jonas/Na. Dugan 8/12/37
Simon/Ann E. Middlekauff 8/19/43
38. LEE
Chas. H./Eliz. Harvey 7/21/10
John/Cath. Garrity 4/19/24
Lewis L./Cath. Winder 4/21/30
Rob./Cecilia Wats 9/9/38
John/Julia Salmon 10/29/57
39. LEEP (LUP?)
Nich./Eliz. Robinson 10/16/19
40. LEESE
Hn./Lydia Cadwalder 4/30/11
John/Maria Bell 1/14/32
41. LEFEVER (LEFEVRE)
Is./Ann Martin 12/13/30
Hn./Reb. Seyester 12/27/32
Hn./Cath. Starling 1/1/34
Dn./Eliz. Lowman 1/29/42
Sam./Ann Herr 5/31/54
Geo./Eliz. Lushbaugh 11/6/58
42. LEGERE
Sam. W./Mary Eliza Smith 7/30/31
43. LEGGETT(LEGETT)
Rob./Sr. Brook 2/8/00
Jer./Mary Easterday 8/21/21
Geo./Holly Davis 4/21/24
Jos./Mahala Harris 3/27/33
Rob./Ros. Smith 3/20/33
Rob./Reb. Myers 12/28/41
John/Eliza Wolfkill 1/1/45
Jer./Levinia Shafer 6/16/51
Jos./Julia Rice 10/20/58
44. LEHMAN (LAHMAN, LAYMAN)
John/Selma Russia 7/2/38
Sam./Mag. Foutz 10/5/46
Hn. F./Sr. W. Stewart 3/6/54
John F./Lizzie A. Middlekauff 12/26/60
44A. LEIGHTY (LICHTY)
Hn./Mary Wallick 8/10/07
Jc./Mary Ann Gray 11/9/47
45. LEISTER
Ph./Eliz. Weaver 11/13/15
Nich./Sr. Gehr 12/20/41
Levi/Lydia Ann Oswald 6/13/45
46. LEITER
Ezra K./Susan Thomas 1/2/53

Jos./Roseann Masters 10/18/53
John W./Sr. E. Lantz 11/8/56
Geo. A./Lizzie M. Lyday 11/28/59
47. LEMLY
Geo. A./Frances Wolf 5/8/34
48. LEMMISON
Rich./Mary Ann Cook 12/24/30
49. LEMON (LEMEN, LEMMONDS, LEMMEN)
John Vance/Louisa Flagg 3/13/24
Chn./Eliz. Emmert 3/4/31
Wiloughby/Hester Billmyer 2/14/32
Wm. W./Marg. El Rutherford 5/26/49
Law. V./Maria L. Wagoner 12/20/55
50. LENTMORE
John/Cath. Welch 12/13/04
51. LEONARD
Tho./Eliz. Dunn 4/5/09
Jc./Sr. Kreps 12/20/10
Hn. A./Mariane Duckett 6/29/29
Sam./Har. Am. Watts 10/5/47
52. LEOPARD
Mich./Susan O'Burn 3/18/43
53. LEPPO
Sam./Eliz. Welsh 10/23/32
54. LESCHEA (LESCHEN)
Augustus/Cath. Spigler 2/2/29
55. LESHER
And./Mag. Shank 8/12/34
Wm./Marg. Martin 6/7/53
Abr./Ann E. Tice 12/24/60
56. LEVES
Chas. E./Rosamond C. Blake 12/25/50
57. LEVI (LEVIS)
Lee/Susan Colliman 6/30/19
Chas./Mary Kellar 4/7/25
Abr./Paulina Arnold 2/5/51
58. LEWIS
John/Anna Marg. Horn 4/19/02
Hn./Mary Hager 5/20/02
John/Na. Grove 4/7/10
Wm./Sus. Miller 6/5/21
Jc./Sr. Thompson 1/26/24
Mich./Lydia Baumbarger 10/20/24
Anthony/Na. Hawkins 3/31/25
Tho./Mar. Hodson 12/27/28
Wm./Eliza Brosius 10/4/30
Hn./Louisa Miller 4/10/33
Rob./Mary Shervan 5/12/34
Anthony W./Mrs. Sr. Chaney 7/30/35
Wesley/Ann McPherson 7/3/39
Levi/Sr. Kries 9/11/49
Jos./Marg. Ann Wolf 1/19/53
Rob./Isa. Shafer 5/28/59
59. LIAS
John/Barb. Forthman 8/29/60
60. LICE
Geo./Marg. Stinemetz 4/6/33

62

61. LICKLIDER (LECKLIDER)
   Hn./Mariah Moler 2/28/21
   Sam./Mary Ellen Bowers 1/28/39
62. LIGHT (LEIGHT)
   Benj./Cath. Downey 8/27/01
   Jc./Na. Austin 4/8/19
   Jc./Na. Feery 2/21/23
   Jc./Mary Wolf 9/17/30
63. LIGHTER (LEIGHTER)
   Abr./Mary Houser 3/21/01
   Sam./Cath. Myers 1/29/11
   John/Cath. Leighter 3/16/12
   Jos./Ann Zeigler 4/26/28
64. LIKENS
   J.H./Mary Eliz. Harry 10/13/41
65. LILBY
   Wm./Jane Flemming 3/6/26
66. LIMAN
   Dn./Chna. Downey 10/2/05
67. LIMBARGER
   Jos./Chna. Siber 4/16/35
68. LIMPKIN
   Anthony/Reb. Redman 11/2/48
69. LINCOLN
   John S./Hester Ann Burnside 3/18/31
70. LINDEN (LINDON)
   Joshua/Cath. Sleigh 10/5/11
   Tho./Sr. Crofford 10/25/31
71. LINDSAY (LINDSEY)
   Abr./Abigail Stuart 2/6/03
   Jm./Susan Isler 5/30/21
   John/Marg. Coon 12/31/34
72. LINE (LYON, LYONS)
   Tho./Sr. Ann Staley 7/29/11
   Geo./Mary Foltz 11/11/15
   John/Mag. Foltz 8/27/22
   Jc./Leah Nichodemus 1/7/23
   Mt./So. Thomas 12/22/40
   Geo./Eliz. A. Poffenberger 3/4/56
   Reuben H./Reb. Toms 12/30/56
   Jc. S./Louisa Emmert 2/7/59
73. LINEBAUGH
   Jos./Barb. Creager 4/29/00
74. LINEINGER
   Conrad/Barb. Fink 3/20/02
75. LING
   Ph./Cath. Fritz 10/1/24
76. LINK
   Geo./Matilda Link 1/3/09
   Ph./Char. Bayly 5/8/13
   Wm./Eliz. Swageler 3/25/14
   Chn./Ann M. Berkeley 7/10/52
77. LINTHICUM
   Harman R./Mary Cath. Hill 10/14/54
78. LINTON
   Alex./Louisa Rife 6/23/51
79. LINTZ
   Geo. P./Eve E. Binkley 5/3/38

80. LINUS
   Joshua/Eliz. Dunn 9/7/15
81. LISER
   Jon./Judith Keyser 4/9/17
82. LISLES
   Rich./Rachel Thomas 2/9/29
83. LITTER
   Jm./Sr. Blair 10/2/17
84. LITTLE (LYTLE)
   Chas./Eliz. Watson 11/22/15
   Dv./Mary Prankard 12/10/16
   Elias/Mary Barnhiser 6/25/21
   Nathan B./Mary Ann Fouke 2/21/26
   Freeman/Mary Ann Yeakle 5/21/27
   Sam. H./Ann M. Fields 4/3/28
   Dn. F./Eliz. Saylor 3/27/33
   John/Sr. Summers 6/19/33
   Pt. H./Cath. Hutzell 9/24/33
   Jos. Sr./Cath. Carother 11/21/37
   Pat./Isa. Dugan 8/22/43
   Tho./Eliza Davis 10/31/48
   Jm. R./Ann Eliz. Hocken 6/4/50
   Jos./Cecelia Ridenour 1/4/55
   Jm./Sr. Myers 10/24/55
85. LITTON
   Caleb/Sr. Snyder 8/6/25
86. LIZER
   Geo./Mary Stottlemyer 7/24/22
   Geo./Anna Sultzer 8/14/38
   Wesley/Mary Eliz. Gouker 8/31/48
   John/Sr. Gowker 9/27/59
87. LOCK
   John/Drusilla Shurman 11/14/35
   John W./Han. O. Farnsworth 9/4/51
   John/Matilda C. Mercer 4/8/58
88. LOCKARD (LOCHART)
   Chas./Ann Senaile 11/24/03
89. LOCKER (LOCHER)
   Hn./Reb. Brannon 3/16/04
   Harry/Phillis Braford 2/1/08
   Geo./Eliz. Shafer 2/4/19
   Jc./Mary Grove 3/1/22
90. LOGAN
   John/Polly Whettis 4/17/15
   Jm./Eliz. Jones 8/27/17
   Wm./Marg. Oyler 9/15/48
   Dv. H./Mollie C. Proctor 12/23/57
91. LOGUE
   John/Ann Martin 9/10/99
92. LOHR (LOAR)
   And./Eliz. South 8/14/02
   Chr./Jane Patton 1/6/14
93. LOMAN
   John P./Sr. E. Hessey 9/14/48
94. LONG
   Jc./Mary Miller 11/7/05
   Jm./Eve Eversole 8/11/07
   Ellis/Barb. Currell 8/3/09

94. LONG (Continued)
    Sam./Isa. McKey 9/2/13
    Adam/Mar. Beck 4/6/16
    John/Eliz. Sensel 1/15/18
    John/Jane Weaver 3/9/19
    Pt./Ros. Moudy 1/25/19
    Dv./Mary Gletner 3/16/20
    John/Am. Lynch 8/15/33
    Jc./Polly Keyfauger 4/11/36
    Dv./Sr. Wochtell 9/24/38
    Dv./Mary Reichard 10/25/41
    Benj./Sr. Eakle 10/20/42
    Dn./Susan Wolfe 11/8/43
    Is./Cath. Highbarger 10/28/43
    Jc./Ann Reb. Keedy 9/12/48
    John/Mary Eliza Woltz 1/9/49
    Emanuel/Barb. Miller 3/3/52
    Simon/Hadassah Downey 8/13/53
    John/Louisa Garrish 7/15/54
    Pt./Matilda A. Dovenberger 2/4/54
    Franklin W./Lucinda Thomas 11/25/56
    John W./Char. E. Culler 4/6/58
    Pt./Mar. Dovenberger 12/18/60
95. LONGANACRE
    Dn./Sr. Mock 6/29/99
    Jc./Na. Rineberger 11/24/01
96. LONGBREAK
    John/Caroline Baylis 5/15/29
97. LONGMAN
    Jc./Sus. Werdebecker 3/25/16
    Jos./Mary Ann Keefauver 2/10/19
98. LOOP (LOP, LOPP)
    Jc./Sus. Cretzinger 8/14/26
    Jc./Cath. Seibert 3/21/35
    John/Eliz. Lambert 10/30/49
99. LOOSE
    Jon./Ann Maria McClain 2/27/43
    Jos. B./Hen. B. Baechtel 4/10/44
100. LORA
    John/Eliz. Norris 8/12/09
    Hn./Cath. Sterr 4/15/13
101. LORSHBAUGH (LOSEBAUGH, LOOSHBAUGH)
    Jc./Mary Bowser 8/6/18
    Geo./Cath. Albert 8/15/22
    Geo./Maria Renner 1/15/26
    Geo./Fanny McIntire 11/4/47
102. LOSE
    Jc./Eliz. Zacharias 9/17/20
103. LOUD
    Geo./Am. Bloomingour 10/12/46
104. LOUDENSLAGER
    Hn./Cath. Cross 3/27/10
    John/Na. Gruber 7/30/29
    Everhart/Eliz. Fie 4/22/50
    Sol./Mary Gantz 2/12/55
    Sam. G./Hellen L. Faugher 1/7/60

105. LOUGHRIDGE
    Geo./Eliz. Funk 4/29/36
    Wm./Rachel Eavey 3/24/36
106. LOUNDS
    John/Mar. Palmer 8/27/03
107. LOVE
    Rev. Wm./Susan B. Harry 10/13/46
108. LOVEALE
    Tebulon/Peggy Keefer 4/27/15
109. LOVIER
    Rich. M./Hen. Creager 8/23/34
110. LOW (LOWE)
    Jos./Na. Wiggins 4/14/04
    John/Eve Glass 4/1/19
    Overton G./Mary Ridenour 8/14/27
    Overton G./Mary Page 5/19/39
    Wm./Eliz. Power 5/17/42
    Overton G./Ellen S. McKinley 10/8/49
    Stephen B./Mar. Durff 5/7/52
111. LOWER
    Sol./Juliana Nunamaker 6/15/11
112. LOWMAN (LOOMAN)
    John/Mary Tom 11/25/02
    Rich./Sr. Conler 4/16/03
    Mich./Sr. Nelson 4/4/05
    Geo./Mary Welsh 4/19/06
    Jm./Barb. Welsh 9/2/06
    John/Mary Bush 7/30/11
    Paul/Regina Holtzapple 1/8/11
    Abr./Deborah Marrett 10/26/13
    Jm./Sr. Stevebaugh 3/16/19
    Hn./Mary Poffenberger 1/5/21
    Dv./Eliz. Robinson 8/20/25
    John/Mary Smith 3/5/33
    John/Marg. Flocher 12/8/38
    Geo./Orinda Slifer 1/11/48
    Hn. Jc./Ann Cath. Artz 11/4/56
    Jos. Wesley/Mary Eliz. Rager 8/24/58
113. LOWRY (LOURY, LOWERY)
    Tho./Eliz. Heffley 11/20/28
    Harrison/Edith Allen 10/8/34
    Fred./Eliz. Filler 5/10/42
    Benj. H./Sr. A.C. Heck 12/27/53
    Jm. M./Cath. Hoover 4/11/53
    Wm. D./Susan Gonder 11/24/57
    Pt./Lavinia Morrison 12/15/60
114. LOY
    Mt./Chna. Sellers 4/24/00
    Josephus/Eliz. Brewer 1/19/59
115. LOYSTER
    John/Han. Camerer 6/18/07
116. LUCAS
    Ed./Eliza Hendricks 5/14/35
117. LUCIUS
    Chas./Mary Stoner 9/22/41
118. LUCKETT
    Hez./Eliz. Kuhn 9/23/40
    Jm./Ann Chambers 9/18/44

119. LUDY (LUDEY)
    Jc./Mary Protzman 4/2/16
    John/Sus. Moggins 2/22/20
    Dv./Mary Brewer 3/22/31
    Jc./Mary Warenfels 3/31/31
    Dn./Mag. Wyonfelts 4/8/37
120. LUM (LUMB)
    Rob./Mary Beard 7/25/15
    Geo./Cath. Coons 8/17/16
    Geo./Mary Flora 4/3/50
    John F./Marg. A. Starr 1/28/53
    Sol. S./Jennie Bergonier 9/22/55
    Hn./Lavinia Forrest 10/27/57
121. LUNDRAGON
    Chas./Mary Wallis 9/4/33
122. LUPTON
    Is./Mary Compton 4/13/16
    Benj./Mary Ann Piles 11/30/19
    John/Marg. Smith 1/7/28
123. LUTHER
    Jc./Reb. Stover 10/8/39
124. LUTZ
    Chr./Sus. Lowman 6/13/14
    Hn./Fanny Moudy 9/21/26
    Is. C./Matilda Calvert 6/27/26
    Abr./Ann Maria Hunt 2/10/35
    Benj./Anna Mickley 12/26/38
    And./Jackson/Ann Cecelia Smith 12/31/55
    Augustus/Mary Most 5/29/55
    John/Saville Wolford 3/20/55
125. LYDAY (LYDEY, LEIDAY, LIDAY)
    Hn./Delilah Hayes 8/6/02
    Jos./Ann Ludy 5/29/21
    Hn./Eliz. Ridenour 10/15/22
    Sam./Eliz. Beard 11/24/30
    Geo. W./Eliz. Stockslager 1/24/34
    Hn./Mary Evans 2/29/40
126. LYNCH
    John B./Pamela Watts 5/21/25
    Tho./Mary Ann Ivy 6/1/39
    Pat./Bridget Connelly 9/18/41
    Tho. I./Na. McCoy 9/20/44
    Wm./Ann Reb. Grove 4/7/45
    Simon Pt./Mary Ann Kitzmiller 10/7/47
    John B./Ann E. Aniba 9/8/48
    Blackstone/Elizth C. Keisecker 2/14/53
127. LYNN
    Elijah/Sr. Otto 2/2/29
128. LYSON
    Jos./Cath. Suven 9/1/29

129. McAFEE
    Wm./Ann Maria Creager 3/12/31
130. McALLISTER
    Geo. Wash./Sus. Wertz 8/26/48
131. McANDLY
    Wm./Julian Fausnaught 1/16/22
132. McANLEY
    Wm./Cath. Stouffer 11/19/39

133. McATEE
    Wm. B./Ann A. Boyd 10/2/27
134. McAULY
    Milton/Maria Newcomer 3/29/54
135. McBRIDE
    Ph./Har. Lock 5/20/33
    Anthony/Cath. Thomas 5/31/36
    Wm. J./Susan Snyder 6/6/54
136. McCABE
    Wm./Jane Brannigan 4/11/33
137. McCAFFERTY
    John/Susan Funk 7/5/34
    Rob./Ann Cornelia Hesletin 4/16/44
138. McCAFFREY
    John/Na. Knode 4/26/52
139. McCALL
    Dv./Mary Nottingape 7/20/48
140. McCALLEY
    Hugh/Cath. Houser 6/11/10
    Wm./Eliz. Grey 4/14/10
141. McCALLISTER
    John/Mary Seibert 11/15/38
    John/Lavinia Greenawalt 11/23/53
142. McCAMMON
    Tho./Mary Jane Hawthorne 10/30/55
    Tho./Amanda Worley 2/17/59
143. McCAIN
    Wm./Marg. Warner 6/23/18
144. McCANN
    John/Ann Quinn 7/30/38
    Chilas/Mary Fealy 8/1/40
145. McCARDELL (McCARDLE)
    Tho./Anne Nogle 9/22/00
    Wm./Marg. Powles 11/4/13
    Ulton F./Ann E. Morin 12/25/51
    Chas./Cath. Wolf 7/19/60
146. McCARLEY
    Owen/Ally Rice 11/30/15
147. McCARTER
    Jos./Mary Albert 3/7/33
    Albert/Cath. Ridenour 9/26/55
148. McCARTIN
    Ed./Cath. McLaughlin 3/2/31
    Wm./Ann Maria Needy 5/8/56
149. McCARTY
    Arch./Maria Cath. Lum 11/13/59
150. McCAULEY (McCAULLEY)
    Wm./Jane Cadders 12/10/01
    Geo./Mary McDonald 2/5/05
    Tho./Marg. Hartman 6/25/18
    Arch./Na. Arnold 2/5/18
    Sam./Barb. Landes 9/30/20
    Sam./Ann Stonebraker 6/7/28
    Chas./Eliz. Roach 12/29/29
    Sam./Eliz. McCoy 1/17/32
    John/Cath. Gorman 4/12/41
    Chas./Anna Black 12/20/43
    Chas./Ellen Hammond 12/22/51
    Hn./Cath. A. Troup 2/18/52
    Jm./Lena Rowland 1/6/58

151. McCLAIN
   Jm. Jr./Marg. Brown 6/26/02
   John/Eliz. Kirk 7/26/03
   Tho./Reb. Carlin 1/14/05
   Dn./Ros. Lowman 12/11/10
   Elias/Betsy Kerron 12/27/10
   Pt./Eliz. Harbaugh 4/13/20
   Eli/Eliz. Barnett 5/2/23
   John/Mary Smith 5/28/24
   Josiah/Eliza Coss 5/18/24
   John/Sus. Harbaugh 12/18/28
   Wm. B./Ann Meredith 10/5/31
   Lewis/Matilda West 5/21/34
   Otho G./Margaretta Shercky 6/16/34
   Ulton/Susan Ann Wolf 11/28/43
   Jm. A./Clarissa C. Middclaf 2/1/47
152. McCLANNAHAN (McCLANAGAN, McCLANAHAN,
   McLANAHAN)
   Alex./Na. Vicars 3/15/03
   Sam./Reb. Long 10/19/07
   Mat./Mary Newson 9/4/17
   Mat./Eliza Byers 4/2/25
   And. G./Eliz. A. Doyle 9/25/37
   John M./Cath. S. Davis 3/10/45
153. McCLARY
   John H./Cath. R. Ward 4/11/60
154. McCLEARY
   John/Na. McGlassen 4/7/04
   John/Eleanor Hooper 12/9/15
155. McCLUNG
 * Wm./Eliz. Ridenour 9/10/08
160. McCLURE
   John/Mary Bell 10/25/24
   Hn./Eve Cath. Painter 9/29/32
   Sam./So. Barkman 3/24/59
161. McCOMAS
   Zachias/Sus. Fechtig 3/7/16
   Fred./Cath. Angle 9/5/40
   John E./Eliz. Murray 3/3/51
   Lewis F./Mary A. Culbertson 9/14/53
162. McCON
   John/Ros. Shervin (Shewin) 11/3/45
163. McCONNELL (McCONEL)
   Dn./Mary Courtney 8/31/07
   John B./Providence Boren 12/22/18
   John/Ann Has 11/18/37
164. McCOOL (McCOOLE)
   Gabriel/Eliz. Thomas 8/18/04
165. McCORMICK
   Otway/Sr. Ann Alexander 10/1/29
   Pat./Marg. Flannagan 11/20/32
   John/Mary McIntire 7/6/33
   Wm./Reb. Falder 9/16/34
   Wm./Emily I.T. Higgins 6/19/38
166. McCOSKER
   Hugh/Mrs. Marg. _____ 10/7/37
167. McCOUSH
   Jm./Sus. Ditch 11/13/10

168. McCOY
   Arch. Jr./Ann Gower 5/31/06
   Dn./Cath. R. Jacques 7/28/10
   Jm./Eliz. Avey 3/18/11
   Jer./Mary Westeberger 6/1/18
   Singleton/Mary McClure 5/17/19
   And./Massey Roads 8/3/20
   Mich./Mary Johnston 1/26/20
   Wm./Eliz. Taylor 5/25/24
   John/Sr. Bond 11/21/25
   Jm./Mary Withnay 3/23/26
   Wm./Mary Sheeler 9/13/27
   John/Ann Connelly 1/10/30
   Geo./Sr. Ann Heck 4/19/34
   Arch./Rachel Watts 1/12/35
   John/Polly Myers 1/23/37
   Denton I./Susan Miller 10/3/38
   Wash./Susan Smith 1/24/38
   And./Susan Kemp 7/31/41
   Jer./Louisa Gegler 2/17/41
   Walter B./Mary A. Huyett 1/11/43
   Ed./Caroline Cook 12/24/51
   Hn./Har. Mose 12/20/54
   Arch./Mar. Furry 4/7/59
169. McCRAFT
   Benj./Marg. Boyd 8/22/21
170. McCREY (McCREA, McCRAY)
   John/Kitty Fenceler 10/13/06
   Adam/Eliz. Brewer 12/14/38
   Mich./Eliz. Smith 3/8/41
171. McCRURE
   Tho./Marg. Kper 11/16/34
172. McCUBBINS
   Tho. F./Ann Rye 9/23/40
173. McCULLOGH (McCULLOCH)
   Jm./Marg. White 1/3/09
   Jm./Marg. Matzebaugh 10/18/14
   Wm./Ann Sterrett 12/21/16
174. McCURDER
   John/Nelly McCool 9/29/06
175. McCURDY
   John/Rachel McCleland 3/19/18
176. McDADE (McDAID)
   Wm./Reb. Brooke 6/29/07
   Walter/Mary Wolford 11/10/19
   Wm./Cath. Barnes 2/25/26
   Pat./Susan O'Donnell 12/24/37
   Chas./Ann Line 12/8/47
177. McDANIEL
   Wm./Reb. Burnes 12/5/08
   Chas./Letitia Fox 1/11/31
178. McDERMOT (McDERMOTH, McDERMOTT)
   Tho./Julian Sanders 8/16/23
   Tho./Feaby Herbert 10/9/33
   M.F./Mary E. Albert 5/14/34
179. McDONALD
   John/Alice Farquhar 5/10/14
   Ph. T./Eliz. Gyer 8/22/54

* Nos. 156-159 not used

180. McDONNELL
  Pat./Mary Sharer 12/26/40
  Mich./Laura Chrissinger 10/1/49
181. McDONOUGH
  Pat./Mary A. Wentlinger 11/21/16
182. McDOWELL
  Nathan/Emily Gabby 1/8/34
  Nathan/Lucretia Post 6/4/55
183. McELRAD
  Jm./Mary Morris 4/5/21
184. McELVOY (MvELROY)
  Jos./Sr. McClanahan 5/3/38
  Wm./Mary Ann Grove 7/4/44
185. McFADDEN
  Jm./Cath. Coy 11/14/32
186. McFADGEN
  Hn./Han. Stevemats 2/16/27
187. McFARLAND
  Jos./Eliz. Stiffler 9/16/13
  John/Cath. Eberly 3/16/16
  Sam./Na. Carroll 3/6/20
  John/Maria L. Rockenbaugh 9/19/22
188. McFEE
  Dn./Cath. Brown 6/7/26
189. McFELLIN
  Wm./Ellen Chaney 2/1/47
190. McGARVEY
  Ed./Cath. Myers 7/10/08
191. McGEE
  John B.F./Eliz. Kershner 7/11/12
  Hugh/Maria Miller 11/17/17
  Jm./Mary Ann Flemming 7/27/23
  Dn./Cath. Staunton 11/19/25
192. McGINNESS
  John/Mary Doople 10/26/05
  Rob./Am. Schleigh 10/2/44
193. McGONAGLE (McGONIGAL, McGONNAGEL)
  Jm./Susan McLaughlin 11/5/29
  Cornelius/Bridget McIntire 10/16/34
194. McGOWAN
  Wm./Cath. McMahan 3/23/11
  Geo./Mary Albert 11/8/17
195. McGOODWIN
  Terrance/Mary McElvoy 2/27/38
196. McGRANE
  Pat./Cath. McQuaid 2/18/38
197. McGRATH
  Dn./Jane Moore 12/23/48
198. McGRAW
  Sam./Eliz. Hill 10/6/57
199. McGRAY
  Wm./Cath. Wilson 8/17/33
200. McGREGOR
  Wm./Eliz. Alice Hughes 12/26/39
201. McGROW
  Jm./Eliz. Dant 9/9/41

202. McGRUDER (MAGRUDER)
  Sam. E./Cath. Oden 8/10/35
  J.S.G./Adelaide So. Craley 6/23/59
203. McGUIN
  Tunis/Mary Duginer 1/18/20
204. McGUIRE
  Wm./Na. Downey 11/25/37
205. McGUNN
  Sam./Eliz. Cooper 4/11/06
206. McGURK
  Wm./Sr. Reed 7/8/38
207. McILHENNY
  Jos./Eliza Newcomer 2/25/06
  John/Na. Newcomer 12/11/10
  Mich./Mary Ann Munahan 10/19/20
208. McINSTRY
  Wm./Mary McKinley 12/24/99
209. McINTIRE
  Jc./Sr. Turner 8/22/06
210. McKAIN
  John/Eliz. Flora 12/6/06
  Tho./Sr. Ann Fox 11/24/32
211. McKALL
  Preston R./Mary Bopp 12/19/51
212. McKEAN
  Rob./Ros. Gustard 4/22/00
213. McKEBEE
  Gassaway/Marg. Isenberger 12/30/10
214. McKEE (McKEY)
  And./Eliz. Cole 5/17/04
  Jos./Mary Pierson 9/10/13
  Rob./Han. Thompson 11/24/20
  Jm. B./Ann Mary C. Bender 5/1/32
  Rob./Eliza Schryock 5/10/38
  Wm./Reb. Stinemetz 9/8/42
  Allen/Urilla Hanna 1/15/51
  Leander/A.M.P. McDowell 12/31/57
  Tho./Eliz. Fahrney 10/30/58
  Gideon G./Lydia Ann Purcell 10/28/59
215. McKELVIN
  Wm./Polly Godwin 1/10/01
216. McKENNEY (MACKENNEY)
  Rob./Cath. Baker 2/9/32
  Tolly/Mary Ann Lindsay 10/17/40
217. McKENSRON
  Dr. M.J./Am. Jane Shindel 5/5/57
218. McKIM
  John Wm./Margaretta F. Prettyman 6/30/53
219. McKIMIE (McKIMMEY)
  Sam./Sr. Wilkinson 12/29/10
  Wm./Sr. Row 12/16/54
220. McKINLEY
  John/Eliz. Hughes 6/4/00
  John/Raney Lett 8/19/00
  Stephen/Sr. W. Bowles 5/9/31
  Arthur/Amy Rowland 2/5/36
  Nelson/Mary Ann Hart 7/31/49

221. McKINNAN
Francis/Cath. Smith 1/25/17
Wm./Shartelle Miller 1/23/39
John/Eliza Kershner 2/1/57
222. McKINSTRY
Wm. D./Marg. Schnebly 8/10/36
223. McLAUGHLIN (McGLAUGHLIN, McLOCHLEN)
Sam./Cath. Docharty 5/1/01
Hn./Cath. Barnett 10/25/02
Barnett/Ruth Bagford 12/24/03
Geo./Grace Hark 12/9/18
Mich./Jane Toland 6/19/24
Jm./Am. Newcomer 4/21/28
Hn./Cath. Cushwa 10/26/35
Mt./Bridget Hopkins 10/4/37
Jm. R./Kate B. Doyle 8/17/54
John/Chna. Frey 6/25/56
224. McLEAN
Wm. Francis/M.T.A. Windsor 7/7/57
225. McLELAND
Dv./Jane Brandt 12/3/32
226. McLEARY
Jos./Marinda Hess 9/15/42
227. McMACHEN
Pt./Susan Clarke 1/2/38
228. McMAHON
Pat./Cath. A.S. McDermot 10/24/31
229. McMULLIN (McMULLINS, McMULLEN)
Wm./Sus. Spessard 6/5/15
John/Cath. Dixon 8/21/49
Wash./Mary Funk 8/25/59
230. McNAME (McNAMEE, McNEMEY)
Geo./Marg. Springer 7/22/01
Job/Peggy Bragonier 3/11/29
Pat./Na. Mundy 12/18/35
Dv./Mary Ritter 8/27/39
Geo./Sr. Davis 1/28/39
231. McNAMEL
Moses/Mary Miller 7/23/08
232. McNEAL
Arthur/Eliz. Boyer 1/18/08
233. McNEILL
Arch./Marg. E.B. O'Neall 11/1/47
234. McNETT
Bart./Am. Knodle 8/29/40
235. McNIGHT
Moses/Mary McDaniel 3/19/31
236. McNILL
John/Priscilla Cahill 8/15/01
237. McNITTY
Sam./Rachel McClaire 2/27/19
238. McNULTY
Hn./Marg. Whalen 9/10/34
239. McPHERSON
Jonas/Marg. James 8/19/06
Ed. B.N./Ann Tolbert 5/15/21

Horatio/Mary S. Buchanan 12/10/23
Dr. Wm. S./Har. A. McPherson 9/18/48
John/Cornelia Ann Fitz 2/2/57
Geo./Marg. Kitzmiller 5/4/60
Jos. H./Mary Ann Stone 2/25/60
240. McQILTON
Jm./Sr. Strite 8/14/00
241. McSHANE
John/Mary Pope 5/16/18
242. McWILLIAMS
Rob. P./Sr. Ground 8/10/24
Rob./Ann Hebb 6/27/29
Cyrus/Magdalene J. Baker 6/9/30
243. McWINN
Jos./Cath. Moose 12/4/48

244. MACE (MASE)
Jc./Sr. Hoover 9/16/25
Geo./Marg. Parks 6/1/36
Geo. W./Eliz. R. Wilson 4/29/57
245. MACEY
Davis/Mary Smith 5/17/28
246. MACGILL
Chas./Mary Ragan 4/16/29
247. MACK
Gotleib/Eliz. Ogle 2/8/30
248. MACKAFEE
Arch./Mag. Gouker 2/12/28
249. MACKALL
Walter/Reb. C. Bayly 1/18/04
Preston R./Mary Popp 12/19/51
250. MACKIN
Hn./Ann Eliza Danner 3/2/48
251. MACKLE
John D./Na. Robinson 3/10/21
252. MACKY (MACKEY)
Jm./Eliz. Flemming 4/30/22
253. MADCAP
Mapam/Eliz. Lynch 6/24/34
254. MADISON (MADDISON)
Wm./Julian Ray 5/30/20
Jonas/Tracy A.C. Boyer 4/17/45
Jm. W./Ann Maria French 7/12/48
255. MAGAN (MAGGEN, MAGGENS)
Dv./Cath. Blickenstaff 12/2/06
Pat./Mary Brown 10/7/38
256. MAHAFFEY
Wm./Udolphus Emerson 7/5/48
257. MAHANNAN
John/Mary Ann Hysinger 6/12/00
258. MAHERR
Pat./Chna. Shoop 5/28/18
259. MAHON
John/Eliza Kennedy 5/21/35
Darby/Ann Smith 2/7/37
John/Emily Reid 4/27/43

260. MAHONEY
    Wm./Ellen Forey 2/8/34
    Dn./Mrs. Char. McClelland 5/14/35
261. MAIDEN
    Spencer/Mar. St. Clair 12/23/17
262. MAIDS
    Ph./Eliza Thomas 1/16/38
263. MAIN (MANE)
    Geo./Mary Miller 4/21/18
    Wm. H./Marg. E. Martin 5/3/58
264. MAISACK
    Leo./So. Forthman 3/8/60
265. MAKAR
    John/Ann McCormack 2/2/33
266. MALEY
    John/Hen. Bowers 12/21/50
267. MALLON
    John/Bridget Philip 2/23/41
268. MALONE
    Dn./Biddy Miles 6/17/03
    Dn./Ros. Murray 4/5/06
    Jm./Mary Reynolds 4/21/12
    Jm./Sus. Albert 8/12/12
    Wm./Cath. Bowers 11/15/14
    Lemuel/Susan Wade 6/5/19
    John/Mary Neitzell 4/11/21
    John/Chna. Hoffman 3/13/22
    John K./Sr. Grosh 11/19/50
269. MALOTT (MELOTT, MELLOTT)
    Dn./Sus. Blew 2/2/04
    Tho./Mary Albert 3/27/07
    Pt./Sus. Isenberger 12/25/10
    John/Reb. Howell 5/23/12
    Mich./Cath. Tritch 3/11/13
    Dn./Sr. Esminger 4/19/14
    Theodore/Mary Bartlett 6/17/23
    Wm./Matilda Donnelly 2/13/23
    Is./Eliz. Booser 5/7/51
    Is./Mary Sisler 9/27/55
    Denton/Mary E. Welsh 3/7/60
    John S./Marg. Ann Reeder 8/8/60
270. MALTZ
    Jc./Eliz. Turnbull 3/16/19
271. MALVANY (MULVANEY)
    Jm./Na. Norris 5/16/07
272. MANER
    Caleb/Eliz. Shard 12/1/27
273. MANFORD
    Wm./Mary J. Lickains 8/31/41
274. MANN
    Sam./Susan Withers 12/9/28
    Jon./Mary Ann Brosius 3/9/35
275. MANNING
    Jm./Sr. Owens 7/15/36
276. MANNON
    Tho./Marg. Gourt 1/14/37
277. MANSBERGER
    Dn./Han. Jones 10/19/05

278. NANTZ
    Chas./Mary Grove 4/9/34
    John A./Elisa Ann Showman 4/14/34
279. MANUEL
    Thornton J./Agnes F. Robbins 5/27/51
280. MARCAN
    Sam./Marg. Brunner 3/12/22
281. MARKER
    John/Eliz. Wertebecker 5/29/10
    Jos./Sr. Barringer 11/8/17
    Wm./Mary Ann Sheets 5/20/19
    Geo./Mary Moats 11/8/24
    Paul/Mary Esminger 6/12/30
    Jm./Am. Naff 4/11/32
    Paul/Amy E. Douglass 1/17/37
    Paul/Isa. West 7/13/39
    John L./Susan Hartle 12/31/56
    Wm./Mary F. Highbarger 1/19/59
282. MARKIN
    Jc./Reb. Garnand 3/25/30
283. MARKS
    Jc./Ann Eliz. Chrike 7/11/48
    Alex./Ros. Booker 1/5/53
284. MARKWOOD
    Jc./Arbelin R. Rodefer 3/23/46
285. MARLOTT
    Jos./Maria Morgan 6/24/30
286. MARMADUKE
    Reuben W./Mar. Ellen Beckley 4/14/51
    Jm./Eliz. Stefler 1/3/55
287. MARR
    John/Anna Shell 2/9/32
    Mich./Abigail Jennings 6/5/33
    And./Eliz. Bomburger 11/6/39
    Wm./Roz. Suter 11/12/44
288. MARSHALL
    Tho./Chna. Maukeman 11/26/08
    Rob./Eliz. Moats 10/26/15
    Jm./Mar. E. Eves 10/6/31
    Wm. M./Eliz. M. Leeds 11/30/31
    Ed./Mary Ann Carty 2/4/36
    Tho./Ros. Butts 6/25/36
289. MARSTELLER
    Asa C./Sr. Ann Eustis 4/9/34
    Dennis/Reb. Benner 12/1/35
290. MARSTETTER
    Geo./Mary Wilders 5/7/18
291. MART (MARTS)
    John P./Mary Shrader 4/16/10
292. MARTELL
    Wm./Mary Ann Griffith 11/28/43
293. MARTENY (MARTENEY)
    John/So. Shugart 4/29/15
    Geo./Mary Cox 1/10/18
    Geo./Cath. Lider 7/10/24
    Geo./Eliz. Miller 1/13/34
    Geo./Louisa Farrow 12/20/34
    Wm./Mary Creager 4/3/56

294. MARTIN
Stephen/Barb. Good 12/9/06
Geo./Sus. Long 8/26/08
Hn./Lucy Beall 6/1/09
Tho./Sus. Karnes 6/1/10
Hn./Mary Hamm 7/29/11
Tho./So. W. Helm 9/5/15
Wm./Jemimah Long 10/1/16
Jc./Eliz. McClure 10/12/18
Dn./Mary B. Hamilton 10/13/31
Jm. A./Susan Endres 4/16/35
Rob. S./Sr. Stall 3/22/36
Chas./Eliz. Wright 5/22/37
Francis/Johanna Hohfacker 10/14/38
Sam./Sus. Boone 3/9/38
Augustus/Eliza Herr 9/3/39
Dv. C./Prucilla Ann Watts 2/14/40
Hn./Louisa Hemsworth 6/15/41
John/Ann Clarke 3/11/41
John G./Cath. McLaughlin 5/17/41
Jc. R./Susan Avey 4/17/43
Dv. G./Eliz. Zeigler 5/20/44
Sam. F./Susan R. Barr 5/29/44
Adam/Susan Oswald 3/21/49
John Hn./Lucy Moore 2/27/51
Dv./Isa. Mouse 3/29/52
Geo. W./Sr. A. Yeakel 5/7/54
295. MARTZ
Dn./Mar. Dusing 10/13/40
Jon./Sr. Newcomer 11/3/43
Dv./Mahala Reeder 1/20/47
Jc./Eliz. Lopp 4/13/54
John N./Eliza Ann Smith 1/24/53
Dn./Barb. Ellen Kennedy 11/6/56
Elias/Anna Bomberger 12/22/57
Pt./Reb. _____ 12/24/40
296. MARVEL
Ed./Sr. Reed 10/21/11
297. MASLIN
Wm./Na. Myers 4/20/04
298. MASON
Jer./Nanny Jacques 4/26/27
Jer./Sr. Prather 6/19/32
John/Rose McMullen 4/12/34
Sam./Eliz. Bair 12/18/41
Jer./Ann Reb. Reitzell 11/12/49
Pt./Caroline Harden 7/20/49
John Tho./Cath. Starliper 4/1/51
299. MASTERS
Hn./Sr. Brewer 1/16/22
John/Sr. Blackmore 7/3/24
John/Susan Stultz 11/30/30
Jm./Cath. Starch 9/6/34
John D./Emily McCollister 8/23/51
300. MASTETLER
John/Mary B. Kercheval 7/29/29

301. MATHEWS
Nich./Marg. Hall 2/11/34
Pat./Ellen Colvin 7/26/43
Hn. C./Susan Monghine 6/18/51
Chas. J./So. Body 2/28/56
302. MATTOX
Aquilla/Barb. Steffy 8/20/14
Lorenzo D./Ann Caroline Young 7/31/44
303. MATZEBAUGH
Dn./Barb. Zimmerman 11/28/12
304. MAUGANS (MAUGINS)
Dn. Mag. Leatherman 3/10/25
John/Amy Moser 3/22/33
Dn./Mary Craver 10/20/34
Sam./Mary Geiser 3/23/54
305. MAUGHLER
Chn./Cath. Crow 11/10/01
306. MAUGHLET
Sam./Na. Adams 9/5/40
307. MAUGHT
Tho./Savilla Wolf 10/22/46
308. MAUTHER (MAUTER)
Hn./Eliz. Beckenbaugh 9/11/13
309. MAX
Jos./Eliz. Conrad 10/6/14
310. MAXWELL
Jm./Eliz. Grove 10/16/47
Ed. W./Rosa E. Alburtis 5/20/50
Rob./Ann R. Swartz 1/20/52
Rob. E./Mary Jane Cather 10/11/59
311. MAY (MAYS)
And./Sus. McGuin 4/24/04
Dn./Reb. Grubb 10/5/13
John/Maria S.W. Kendle 5/13/22
312. MAYBERRY
Wm./Cath. Bealer 1/2/15
313. MAYER (MAYHER)
John/Philipine Markel 7/19/06
314. MAYHUGH (MAYHEW, MAHUGH, MAYHU)
John/Viney Bell 12/2/01
Jm./Reb. Jackson 4/1/16
Benj. F./Jane E. Bridgement 7/26/39
Jm. P./Han. Deitrick 8/17/59
315. MAYSILLES (MASELL, MERCILLIS)
Nich./Mary Ann Hoover 5/26/11
Hn./Am. Parks 11/28/18
John/Cath. Mowry 11/20/29
Sam./Barb. Rice 1/3/31
Jc./Na. Bowman 11/8/33
John/Cath. Eakle 8/27/34
Hn./Ruan Bowman 1/21/47
316. MEADS (MEADES, MEDES)
Benj./Eliz. Hayes 9/29/09
Jer./Marg. McCoskar 6/22/33
Benedict/Rachel Hopwood 2/6/43
Benj./Am. Ann McClain 1/28/57

317. MEALY (MEALEY, MEELEY)
    Ed./Sr. Nowell 6/18/16
    John W./Reb. Gearhart 3/20/22
    Lewis H./Frances A. Miller 12/7/52
318. MECKINS
    Clarence W./Sr. Bealer 1/26/21
319. MEDLEY
    Wm./Har. Ann Yong 7/11/32
320. MEISSNER
    John Tho./Cath. Hoffman 8/30/50
321. MEIXSELL
    Jos. H./Mary A. McLaughlin 11/30/43
    Pharis/Cath. Electa Gehr 4/29/43
    Hn./Sr. Ann Mace 10/16/56
322. MELLINGER
    John E./Eliz. Phoutz 12/26/48
323. MELVIN
    Jos./Jane Butler 3/30/22
    Dv. D./Cath. R. Snyder 5/12/51
324. MENAPENNY
    Sam./Sr. Ann Gouff 9/20/34
325. MENCER
    Wm./Ellis Roach 2/9/15
326. MENDENALL
    Jc./Bersheba Silver 10/3/03
327. MENDINGHALL
    Sam./Eliza Mooney 9/15/08
328. MENGHINS
    Jos./Iorda E.A. Flagg 5/27/26
    Sensoney/Eliz. Gardner 5/29/28
329. MENS
    Geo./Cath. May 9/1/51
330. MENTZER (MAINTZER)
    Conrad/Barb. Pinkly 9/15/13
    Sam./Har. Hoover 6/2/29
    Sam. H./Julia A. Hartman 11/13/43
    Geo./Eliz. Newcomer 11/24/46
    John W./Esther Hoffman 11/9/53
    Lewis L./Reb. T. Bell 10/16/57
    Chn./Mary Matilda Bayard 1/3/60
    Chn./Cath. Newcomer 2/3/51
331. MERCHANT (MERCHANTS)
    Eden/Eliz. Merchant 5/22/09
    Tho./Ann A. Anderson 3/19/50
332. MEREDITH
    Sam./Cath. Eckert 1/5/33
333. MERRICK
    Jos. I./Mary Ann Hughes 6/10/17
    Jos./So. B. Hays 4/20/31
334. MERTZ
    John N./Eliz. Rudy 9/5/57
335. METZ
    John/Eliz. Beck 6/1/13
    Jc. Albert/Eliz. Good 3/18/52
336. MICHAEL (MICHAELS)
    Adam/Na. Reel 7/30/17
    Wm./Marg. Lambright 1/8/25

    Sam./Reb. Ann Pirkey 11/8/32
    John Chr./Mary Ann Beaver 3/9/50
    Dn./Ellen Carney 2/24/52
    Wm. H./Lanah Summers 5/19/59
    John Gotleib/Cath. Lineman 5/29/55
337. MICHELIUS
    Goethey/Mary Trayer 2/15/16
338. MIDDCALF (MIDCALF)
    Wm. Ed./Sr. Ann Hammersla 11/13/54
339. MIDDLEKAUFF
    Dn./Mary Sailor 10/1/02
    Dv./Han. Sailor 12/27/06
    Jc./Eliz. Stonebraker 5/11/12
    Jc./Eliz. Poffenberger 11/13/16
    Dv./Cath. Hefflebower 3/22/23
    Jonas/Na. Zuck 8/6/23
    Sam./Eliz. Charles 5/15/23
    Dn./Theresa Newcomer 3/19/28
    John/Eliz. Neikirk 12/26/28
    Leo./Mary Bragonier 2/23/31
    Pt./Eliz. Wolf 1/19/31
    John A./Mary M. Chambers 5/1/32
    Dn. M./Mary Sailor 2/7/33
    Dn./Esther Middlekauff 12/28/35
    Pt./Cath. Petre 3/4/35
    Dv./Mary Ann Swope 3/18/37
    Sam./Cath. Barr 3/27/37
    John D./Mag. Kuntz 12/19/38
    Benj./Mary Snyder 5/27/39
    Elias/Eliz. Ridenour 1/17/39
    Jon./Ann Maria Schindle 12/29/45
    Dn./Sr. Wolfersberger 10/31/46
    Jc./Barb. Rohrer 8/18/46
    Pt./Susan Shindle 3/3/46
    Jc./Mary A.S. Boggs 12/5/47
    John H./Mary Butterbaugh 11/11/47
    Emanuel/Eliz. Susan Doud 6/28/48
    Sol./Mary Miller 3/23/48
    Jos./Mary Eliza Firey 11/24/52
    Hn. C./Sr. A. Coffman 12/21/53
    Simon/Joannah Nunemaker 3/1/53
    Jc. Simon/Ann Cecelia Adams 1/17/54
    Benj. T./Mary Jane Davis 11/10/56
    Jc. M./Marg. A. Snively 11/22/58
    John Calvin/Rachel A. Jones 9/13/58
    Jos./Sr. Ann Ford 3/24/58
    Dn. E./Eliz. Jones 1/13/59
    Hirem E./Ann E. Rohrer 10/18/59
    Jos. M./Anna P. Horine 10/28/59
340. MIDDLETON
    Hugh/Mary Sillhart 1/11/00
    Tho./Cath. Thompson 12/31/08
    Rob. White/Ann Eliz. Shreiner 7/26/28
341. MILES
    Elijah/Eliz. Cox 4/9/04
    John/Sus. Maloney 9/9/13
    Wm./Cath. Emmert 1/29/16

341. MILES (Continued)
Stanislaus F./Cath. Clarke 3/28/18
Israel/Mary Crowl 12/6/36
Wm./Maria Young 11/27/40
Jc./Sabina Mack 10/30/50
Chas. P./Sr. Myman 7/25/59
Elisha/Na. Bachtell 3/8/59
342. MILEY (MYLEY)
Abr./Eliz. Myers 4/24/20
Mt./Adaline E. Schindel 1/10/48
343. MILLBURN
John/Marg. Randell 4/3/05
Jm./Han. Bishop 10/2/14
344. MILLER
Dn. Jr./Cath. Rench 5/5/00
Hn./Eliz. Soister 10/14/00
John/Mary Robey 4/12/00
Chn./Cath. Crist 8/3/01
Hn./Cath. Snyder 11/27/01
Dn./Mary Jones 5/16/02
Geo./Na. Thompson 4/2/02
Jc./Cath. Weaver 8/3/02
John D./Eliz. Gibbs 12/31/02
John/Eliz. Shane 1/5/05
Sam./Mary Ankeney 1/25/06
Adam/Eliz. Bear 5/26/06
John/Mary Poffenberger 6/20/07
Abr./Mary Zeller 4/26/08
Hn./Eliz. Reader 2/6/08
Jos./Marg. Everly 4/14/08
Pt./Peggy Mong 12/23/09
Geo./Peggy Wyant 8/28/10
Jc./Cath. Rench 10/3/11
Rob./Cath. Roush 4/15/11
John/Eliz. Snyder 3/27/12
John/Marg. Hawken 12/12/12
Dn./Eliz. Snyder 3/11/13
Hn./Eliz. Leckrone 3/27/13
Jc./Barb. Freet 4/9/13
John/Cath. Powlas 12/4/13
John/Mary Knode 1/9/13
John/Sus. Kreps 5/13/13
Sam./Mary Mumma 3/17/13
Dv./Peggy Brenner 2/16/14
Jc./Sus. Artz 3/25/14
Jc./Eliz. Johnston 4/19/14
John/Sus. Smith 2/15/14
John/Mar. Kindle 6/1/15
Rob./Am. Mosher 2/18/15
Dn./Eliz. Newcomer 11/14/16
Elish B./Sr. Newcomer 12/20/16
John/Eliz. Gillis 2/30/16
John W./Mary Shugart 3/30/16
Sam./Mary Fiery 3/2/16
Sol./Peggy Cook 11/27/16
Dn./Eliz. Shelletto 4/18/18
Fred./Barb. Miller 1/9/18

Jc./Judith Hovermaile 11/26/18
John/Cath. Cramer 2/12/18
John/Eliz. Bentz 10/16/18
John/Mary Halfestine 3/3/18
John/Sr. Hale 2/16/19
John M./Har. H. Patton 1/29/19
Balzer/Reb. Schriver 4/8/20
Jc./Na. Strite 3/15/20
Pt./Eliz. Brumbaugh 4/20/20
Dv./Cath. Dick 6/9/21
Hn./Eliz. Hoffman 1/11/21
Hn./Na. Spitsnogle 2/19/21
Is./Eliz. Kline 7/20/21
John I./Mary Smith 3/27/21
Dv./Rachel Houser 2/23/22
John/Mary Runner 1/8/22
Wm./Eliz. Bell 6/13/22
Wm. H./Mary M. Parks 11/19/23
Arwine/Jane Williams 3/17/24
Sam./Sr. Ann Price 4/7/24
Otho/Marg. Rummell 11/30/24
Hn./Cath. Glaze 12/3/25
Jc./Mary Hoffer 12/28/25
John/Eliza Knead 2/1/25
Is./Eliza Fisher 5/25/26
John/Susan Ankeney 4/26/26
John/Dorethy Leckrone 8/3/26
Tho./Lucinda Brimet 4/16/27
Geo./Marg. Ielar 12/5/27
John/Sus. Hovermaile 10/17/28
John G./Cath. Newcomer 1/30/28
Hn./Cath. Byers 5/5/29
Jc./Eliz. Snively 5/19/29
John/Chna. Hertzel 10/16/29
John/Na. Cretzinger 8/18/29
Dn./Jane Reed 10/21/30
Geo./Gertrude Kenney 9/23/30
Hn./Mary Leckrone 10/16/30
Wm./Cath. W. Mempin 7/4/31
Wm./Susan Hoffman 5/28/31
Hn./Barb. Silvers 1/6/32
And. N./Sr. Cuppenhouse 2/18/33
Dn./Mary Watts 2/4/33
Jc. F./Ann Martin 12/20/33
Jm./Matilda Piper 8/24/33
Dv./Marg. S. Cridler 10/31/34
John H./Ann Roberts 3/31/34
Alburtis A./Har. Davis 3/11/37
Pt./Hulda Heflebower 10/31/37
Jc. A./Mary A. Knode 4/21/40
Wm. B./Eliza A. Bowen 9/23/40
Abr./Cath. Long 1/27/41
Jc./Eliz. Houser 4/10/41
John/Sr. Tare 1/16/41
John A./Lacy Ann Hower 4/22/41
Fred./Eliz. Weisner 10/18/42
Mich./Eliz. Neikirk 11/21/43

344. MILLER (Continued)
    Hn. T./Sr. A. Humrichouse 12/11/44
    Jc. F./Na. Zittle 6/1/44
    John W./Sr. Ann Dellinger 12/9/44
    Geo./Barb. Camerer 8/18/45
    Israel R./Sr. Ann Myers 1/6/45
    Sam. S./Mary A. Baker 1/3/45
    Dv./Cath. Miley 11/24/46
    Dv. R./Marg. B. Pottenger 4/1/46
    John/Cordelia Curffman 2/9/46
    Wm./Reb. Clopper 2/24/46
    Dv./Leana Sager 12/8/47
    Jc./Eliz. Palmer 3/27/47
    Pt./Eleanora Wolfersberger 11/13/47
    Nelson F./Eliz. K. Syester 5/10/48
    Sam./Eliz. Aulum 6/9/48
    Dn./Mary Lampert 10/13/49
    John McClelland/Marg. Highbarger
      2/13/49
    Upton/Maria L. Davis 4/21/49
    And. B./Hester Ann Smith 7/25/50
    Benj./Marg. Patton 11/30/50
    Francis/Prudence Miller 12/9/50
    Oliver J./Eliza Milligan 4/30/50
    Pt./Julia Ann Seabright 7/6/50
    Sam./Cath. Miller 3/25/50
    Baltzer B./Marg. A. Stover 1/14/51
    Chn D./Ann M. Hartle 4/12/51
    Jc. P./Mrs. Susan Long 2/12/51
    John Luther/Mary Eliz. Neall 10/11/51
    John S./Mary Ann Snyder 11/22/51
    Jos./Ruana Newcomer 10/28/51
    Alex./Louisa Davis 11/17/52
    Dn. R./Mary Rench 10/29/52
    Hn. S./Ann Nitzel 5/18/52
    John/Leah Hoffman 6/3/52
    Mich./Chna. Schindel 3/8/52
    Wm./Mar. Knode 9/15/52
    Elias/Ann Maria Zittle 7/23/53
    Pt./Mary Ann Deener 3/4/53
    Sam. H./Sr. Hufford 12/31/53
    Simon/Cath. Sager 3/12/53
    Levi S./Sr. Ann Brandner 10/21/54
    W.H.H./Virginia Hammett 11/16/54
    Dv. H./Susan Winders 10/30/55
    Jc. N./Mary E. Neibert 1/31/55
    John/Cath. Hartle 3/21/55
    John S./Eliz. A. Snyder 12/6/55
    John S./Sr. Long 5/8/55
    Hn. C./Matilda Rodney 5/9/56
    Jc./Eliza Rush 1/29/56
    Sam. H./Leath Ann Moyer 10/11/56
    Geo. S./Louisa Freaner 11/18/57
    M.V.B./Eliz. Creek 10/8/57
    Benj./Matilda Ecker 3/30/58
    Joshua C./Amanda E. Shiffler
      11/16/58
    Dv. Z./Mar. J. Monninger 11/30/59

    Jm. Weley/Amanda Embrey 12/10/59
    Dv. R./Mary Ann Reitzell 2/6/60
    Geo. W./Jane Ulhum 3/5/60
    John/Eliz. Jane Dellinger 2/21/60
    Sam. F./Eliz. Sager 12/18/60

345. MILLS
    Abr./Eliz. Toncray 12/19/05
    Jc./So. Wells 1/28/23
    Levi/Esther Blair 3/17/35
    Rob./Mar. Nicholson 8/3/39
    Otho O./Mary Bowman 10/9/47
    Abr./Eliz. Whetstone 11/1/53

346. MINER
    John/Phebe Burkhart 12/28/12

347. MINICKE (MINICH)
    John/Cath. Gow 8/17/03
    Jos./Cath. A. Springer 8/19/54

348. MINSHELLE
    Jon./Ellender Watson 10/21/02

349. MISH
    Geo./Sr. A. Winders 5/19/58

350. MISINGER
    Jc./Mary M. Gouker 7/4/40

351. MITCHELL
    Alex./Am. L. Caw 6/22/22
    Geo. W./Cornelia D. Baldwin 11/29/33
    Wm. H./Cindarella Hychew 10/12/40
    F. Dorsey/Mary Yost 9/23/50

352. MIX
    Is./Eliz. French 8/26/26

353. MOATS (MOATES)
    Jos./Han. James 10/30/17
    Jc. Jr./Sr. Beckly 4/14/20
    Jc./Cath. Kline 12/17/22
    Sam./Sally Domer 9/22/30
    Dn./Mary Zellers 11/17/31
    Elias/Reb. Morseburg 4/23/31
    Dn./Eliz. Hays 3/26/35
    Wm./Eliz. Brantner 1/15/40
    John H./Marg. Bloom 10/26/43
    Sam./Helen Hammond 4/3/44
    John H./Ann Bloom 6/8/49
    Sam./Helen Hammond 4/3/44
    John H./Ann Bloom 6/8/49
    Hn./Eliz. Gross 11/11/53
    John W./Leah Longman 3/25/57

354. MOBLEY
    Ed. M./Ellen C. Carver 10/27/43

355. MOCK
    John/Reb. Smith 11/4/03
    Fred./Marg. Fryman 10/26/05
    Godfrey/Marg. Barlip 9/25/60

356. MOFFETT
    Wm./Eliz. Showman 9/7/13
    John/Eddy Taylor 8/20/14

357. MOGART
    Bolsar/Edna Roby 4/21/40

358. MOHLER (MOLER)
Hn./Har. Mohler 4/19/23
Adam/Eliz. Bean 11/17/24
Chas./Jane Lancaster 9/19/36
Lemuel/Matilda Chaney 1/5/36
John/Eliza Huffman 4/20/41
Hn./Isa. Higgins 12/30/50
Jc./Eveline Downey 10/13/52
359. MONAHAN (MONOHAN)
Terrence/Bridget Ayerly 5/31/33
Byrne/Mary Calens 10/17/37
360. MONDEBAUGH (MONDERBAUGH, MONTEBAUGH, MUNDABAUGH)
Wm./Eliz. Bealer 11/11/05
John/Sus. Powlas 10/30/10
Hn./Cath. Kretzer 12/18/32
Jc./Eliza Snider 3/1/41
John/Sr. Orrick 9/28/53
361. MONDELL
John Ivy/Ann E. Binkly 5/4/46
362. MONEGAN
Jos./Sally Miller 2/9/43
363. MONG
Pt./Sus. Funk 12/18/04
Jc./Marg. McMilon 2/1/09
Val./Reb. Lower 11/17/08
Jc. B./Ann Cochrane 8/2/19 (Jc. Behong in cross-index)
Jos. P./Eliz. Newcomer 11/10/35
364. MONGAN
John/Sr. Shilling 1/1/47
Dennis/Eliz. Jones 7/21/49
Wm. Hn./Marg. E. Boyers 3/29/58
365. MONNINGER
John/Eve Pence 9/18/02 ("Bentz" penciled after "Pence")
Chn./Roz. Miller 12/3/34
Hn./Eliz. Cunningham 9/16/39
Jon./Eliz. Davis 11/23/46
Wm./Levinia Knodle 2/25/45
Jon./Ruann Thompson 9/25/52
366. MONROE
Jm. W./Maria Nyman 11/15/49
367. MONSON
Lewis/Eliz. Swope 3/5/33
368. MONTGOMERY
Tho./Cath. Hawn 11/2/09
369. MONTLE
Jer./Mary Kendle 8/22/01
370. MOODY
I.P./Emily Virginia Fryer 8/9/55
Jos. H./Kate Culbertson 4/26/55
371. MOORE
Benedict/Mary Neal 12/21/01
Dn./Anna Hyett 2/7/01
Alex./Mar. Mains 1/28/04
John/Marg. Maloy 9/10/05

Jos./Cath. Renner 1/8/08
Alex./Eliz. Bevans 6/8/13
Rich./Mary Beckley 1/24/18
Jm. D./Mary Saunders 3/14/20
Geo./Ann Bryan 4/2/21
Jessee/Mary Ann Boteler 10/29/29
John/Eliza King 3/10/31
Dv./Marg. Palmer 12/29/35
Hamilton/Chna. Fink 4/29/36
Leo./Cath. Mattingly 2/19/41
Dn./Mary Porter 6/6/42
Sam./Ann Spong 8/24/42
Upton/Mary Ann Sprecher 12/26/42
Jm./Mar. Ellen Haines 12/30/43
Jm./Sr. Ann Burd 4/24/43
Jm. B./Mary Jane Logan 11/2/46
John S./Mary Ann Feidt 9/30/46
Dv./Reb. Hanna 3/3/47
Ulton/Eliz. Myers 8/27/47
Sam. S./Mary D. Hurst 2/18/52
Is./Matilda Mills 1/24/53
John/Mary Cath. Jackson 8/29/53
Stephen A.J./Jeanette Bower 4/15/54
Jm./Angeline Myers 1/18/56
Tho. Hn./Mary Ann Mouse 1/30/58
Joshua W./Hen. E. Knode 2/6/60
Wm. Perry/Eliz. Ann Hill 7/31/60
372. MORETENA
Jc./Adeline M. Reed 11/8/54
373. MORGAN
Ed./Addrilla Allender 8/19/02
Rich./Mary Stipp 11/22/02
Dennis/Mary Poffenberger 9/26/09
Wm./Jane Keene 12/16/22
Morgan/Eliz. Reel 2/19/19
Jm./Na. Keller 4/20/37
Sam./Mrs. Sus. Kindle 8/14/37
Dn./Eliz. Blickenstaff 9/24/40
Dennis/Eliz. Jones 7/21/52
Abr./Sally S. Waugh 3/29/52
Morgan Jr./Mary A. Silver 12/4/52
Jos./Barbary Ann Boyers 12/1/53
Sam. C./Susan Snyder 2/9/54
Wm. C./Cath. Hageline 9/9/58
Geo./Eliz. Boyers 8/6/59
374. MORGENTHAL (MORGENCHAL, MORGANSAULL)
John/Na. Frederick 7/15/15
Geo. W./Lydia Ellen Shipp 8/16/60
375. MORIN
Blair/Eve Startman 3/20/15
Dv./Susan Spielman 11/17/48
376. MORRIS
Arch./Mary Holbert 7/15/19
Wm./Sus. Leiser 3/15/20
Evan/Mary Kinkle 6/3/33
Wm./Marg. Boward 10/26/36
John C./Hen. Stiewalt 11/16/57

74

377. MORRISON
Alex./Ann Marstiller 4/4/17
Jm./Na. Corse 10/16/20
Dv./Am. Dillman 1/11/23
Emanuel/Mary Baker 5/8/23
Lloyd/Priscilla Butler 2/24/23
Manby/Mary Ann Donaldson 4/6/24
John H./Isa. W. Dickey 2/10/25
Wm./Susan Hine 10/3/35
Ed./Eliz. McCoy 1/2/36
John/Reb. Myers 11/9/38
Dv./Ann Eliz. Cookey 1/6/39
Jesse/Cath. Marg. Martin 9/21/44
Dv./Cath. Cost 4/1/52
Simon P./Caroline Netz 11/16/59
378. MORROW
Chas./Francis Paten Christian
4/3/23
Pt./Eleanor Spong 1/4/26
379. MORTEY
Francis A./Eliz. Middlekauff 1/21/32
380. MOSE
Hn./Cath. Santman 12/12/09
Hn./Mary Hamilton 9/4/30
Wm./Mary Bender 1/10/32
Geo./Mary MoCoy 5/28/36
John/Mary Jane Grim 12/18/51
Benj. A./Arabella Fraker 8/29/54
381. MOSEY
John/Cath. Renner 11/1/36
382. MOSS
Pt./Jane Corbert 11/20/19
Gabriel/Sr. Bender 12/20/25
Jm./Na. Shirety 6/2/51
383. MOTTER
Abr./Am. James 6/6/37
Reuben/Maria Blessing 2/25/40
Wm./Mary Ann Bell 10/29/45
Jerome/Lucinda Eagle 12/10/49
Geo. Hn./Ruan Huffer 11/2/50
John S./Mar. M. Rudisill 4/1/56
Hiram W./Maria So. Chambers 9/23/57
384. MOTZ
Jc./Mary Ann Clark 3/21/39
385. MOUDY
Mich./Sus. Swingley 6/8/07
Geo./Eve Holtzman 2/23/16
Geo./Marg. Brewer 3/23/20
Pt./Na. McClain 11/29/23
Fred./Polly Snyder 3/22/25
John/Susan Morgan 9/25/50
Mt. L./Mary Eliz. Fortney 11/8/54
Fred./Ruey Artz 3/15/56
386. MOURY
John/Eliz. Shiffler 6/25/05
387. MOUSE
Pt./Mary Moore 8/2/55
Tho./Mary Bear 3/17/56

388. MOUSER
Dv./Eliz. Hanes 9/6/21
Jc./Marg. Markwould 11/10/29
389. MOUVER
Mich./Eliz. Hill 6/17/25
390. MOWEN
John/Lucy Ann Willis 11/20/46
Mark/Eliz. Bloyer 3/6/54
Dn./Barb. Snakeaburger 12/3/60
391. MOWER
Mich./Mary Manley 10/14/13
392. MOWRY
Wm./Marg. Ensminger 12/10/23
Geo. W./Eliza Jane Gamble 3/6/36
Dn./Na. Newcomer 11/14/43
Jon./Ellen Norris 3/9/49
393. MOYER (MOYERS)
Mich./Mary Maloy 8/14/04
Dn./Marg. Kailer 10/6/10
Pt./Eliz. Slice 12/26/16
Chn./Sus. Spigler 10/12/19
Lewis/Sus. Bergman 9/16/24
John/Mary Tice 3/19/28
394. MOYLE
John/Reb. Faulkwell 4/4/49
395. MUCK
Conrad/Cath. Sager 11/3/18
Jc./Sr. Traver 6/11/19
Tho./Eliz. Barber 12/24/51
John/Eliz. Arnold 10/14/57
396. MUIR
Jm./Marg. Locke 5/22/06
397. MUISE
John R./Na. Morris 6/19/32
398. MULL
John/Maria Kindle 8/31/39
399. MULLENDORE (MULLINDORE)
Jc./Cath. Blecker 4/8/23
Dn./So. Knode 4/15/33
Jc. H./Elizth M. Gloss 10/22/50
400. MULLER
Neill/Biddy Bradly 2/8/34
401. MULLIGAN
John/Marg. Kelly 8/9/39
402. MULLINS (MULLENS, MULLEN)
John/Barb. Lorshbaugh 10/21/26
Hn./Eliz. Shemel 12/29/43
403. MULNSON
Ezra/Cath. Lavinia Castor 1/10/34
404. MUMMA
John/Eliz. Shafer 3/26/08
Hn./Adelius Staups 4/18/10
Jos./Marg. Beckley 5/20/16
Jc./Eliza Gehr 6/23/19
John/Mary Schnebly 6/13/21
Jos./Eliz. Shafer 2/24/24
Elias/Susan Miller 11/3/29

404. MUMMA (Continued)
    Sam./Eliz. Miller 11/2/34
    Wm./Reb. Pope 12/13/34
    Jc./Barb. Hofman 7/12/36
    Dn. S./Naomi Malone 5/4/40
    John/Susan Hoffman 12/5/42
    Dn. G./Adaline Albert 12/17/46
    Jc. H./Ann M. Miller 1/30/47
    Sam./Ann Cath. Alter 12/20/47
    Sol./Susan C. McWinn 11/16/47
    Abr./Cath. Grimes 5/19/51
    Abr. H./Elenora Finegan 1/14/51
    Sam./Am. Alter 11/5/55
    Hn. C./Mary Jane Rohrback 11/9/57
405. MUMMERT (MUMMART)
    Wm./Eliz. Carpenter 2/9/08
    Wm. L./Rachel Cox 10/5/34
406. MUNDY
    Hn./Cath. Dusing 4/5/40
    John/Eliz. Bragonier 11/27/55
407. MUNGAN (MUNGIN)
    Jm./Mary Poffenberger 10/25/34
    John/Na. Davis 5/15/38
408. MUNSON
    Sam./Cath. Doyle 5/1/41
    Josephus W./Julian Boyer 9/14/58
409. MUNTHY
    Ph./Mary McLaughlin 4/24/19
410. MURPHY
    John/Marg. Murphy 6/1/33
    Dennis/Marg. S. Harry 3/5/34
    Pat./Bridget McKee 9/5/39
    Jm./Ann Eliza Jarrett 9/22/41
411. MURRAY (MURAY, MURRY, MURRA)
    Jm./Marg. Baker 6/13/10
    John R./Sus. Bevans 12/7/11
    Jm./Eliz. Slusser 2/6/18
    Joshua Jr./Ann Maria Schleigh 7/2/22
    Stephen/Mariah Sensell 7/17/24
    Tho./Mary Beard 6/22/30
    Dn./Marg. Stake 7/23/33
    Ed. Bennett/Sallie A.P. Fechtig 9/3/53
    Jackson/Na. Bowman 10/4/54
412. MUSE
    Wm./Ros. Snavely 12/29/10
    Warner/Mar. Stewart 1/6/30
413. MUSEWINKLE
    Sam./Lydia Buzzard 3/15/37
414. MUSGROVE (MUSGRAVE)
    Pt./Cath. Iseminger 3/27/01
    Pt./Mary Iseminger 5/5/09
415. MUSSA
    Gottleib Fred./Cath. Stock 9/13/53
416. MUSSELMAN (MOOSELMAN)
    Mich./Eve Bouch 2/14/04
    Mich./Barb. Shirk 10/25/13
417. MUSTIN
    John/Mary Weaver 7/18/15

418. MYER (MYERS)
    Jc./Mary Shanefield 3/14/00
    John/Cath. Albright 3/29/00
    Abr./Cath. Gilbert 2/9/02
    John/Cath. Shatt 10/26/02
    Pt./Cath. Vincenhenner 9/18/02
    Jc./Eliz. Myers 4/19/03
    John/Peggy Parks 2/28/03
    Abr./Mary Springer 4/3/04
    Wm./Cath. Carson 10/22/04
    Fred./Sr. Myers 7/23/08
    Dv./Eliz. Householder 5/17/09
    Geo./Na. Welty 3/9/09
    Jc./Cath. Heinz 5/21/12
    Hn./Mary Kephart 5/25/13
    Ph./Eliz. Muse 8/3/13
    Pt./Mary Roulette 7/9/14
    Jc./Sus. Householder 6/28/15
    Fred./Cath. Boley 7/10/17
    Pt./Am. Binkley 6/14/17
    Jc./Eliz. Sheets 3/3/18
    Adam/Eliz. Neybert 11/16/22
    Jc./Anna Poffenberger 8/17/22
    Jc./Eliz. Glass 4/8/22
    Jc./Mar. Zimmerman 6/27/22
    Bear/Sr. Lape 4/25/23
    Jc./Mary Ann Myers 5/25/24
    John/Mary Russell 12/13/25
    Hn./Eliza Lutz 1/12/26
    Jc./Eliz. Oiler 12/13/26
    Mt./Mary Myers 6/7/26
    Is./Lane Miller 12/5/27
    John/Mary Domer 12/4/27
    Jos. S./Ellenor Ann Hant 5/28/28
    John/Mary Myers 5/25/30
    Dv./Jane K. Gordon 12/6/31
    Pt./Mary Tenant 3/1/34
    Jc./Eliza Shay 9/3/35
    Benj./Mary Rothraick 12/1/36
    Emanuel/Tamzin Myers 4/12/36
    Pt./Cath. Hoss 12/27/36
    Sam./Mary Price 3/19/36
    Wm./Rachel Myers 4/12/36
    Elie/Na. Ann Mills 3/21/37
    Jon./Mary Startzman 8/2/38
    Nimrod/Mary Lorshbaugh 3/29/38
    Sam./Ellen McClanahan 2/5/41
    Zachariah/Mary Smith 3/23/42
    John/Ann Eliz. Gouter 8/27/44
    Sam./Cath. Deitrich 11/19/44
    Jm. B./Eliz. Shoop 3/19/45
    John/Susan Myers 3/7/46
    Dn./Eliz. Litton 5/20/48
    Alford/Mary Netz 7/28/49
    Jos. A./Eliz. Heitshire 12/4/49
    Wm. H./Mary Jane Souders 2/19/51
    Chn./Ann Hoffman 1/27/53
    Hn./Francina Hiltebridle 4/21/53

76

418. MYER (MYERS) (Continued)
    Jc./Mary Ann Summers 11/2/53
    John/Malinda Snyder 10/17/53
    Jc./Ann Cookerly 1/24/54
    Pt./Marg. Miller 5/27/54
    Levi/Angeline Longman 12/24/55
    Wm. H./Malinda E. Shilling 12/24/57
    Jc./Eliz. Miller 5/11/58
    John V./Mary E. Knode 3/29/59
    Dv./Louisa Long 11/5/60
    John/Susan Carr 10/12/60

419. NADRY
    Jm./Lydia Antrim 9/28/14
420. NAFE
    Dv./Sus. Singer 10/3/09
421. NAFF
    Hn./Susan Marker 8/13/32
    Hn. A./Cynthia Ann McNutt 1/19/39
422. NAIL
    Adam/Susan Kershner 4/21/58
423. NALLY
    Sam./Ros. Myers 11/11/33
    Sol./Mary Ann Moresburgh 1/1/33
    Dv./Sr. Sweitzer 4/12/38
    Jc./Mary Buzzard 1/6/55
    Jos./Susan Moats 3/23/58
424. NARR
    And./Cath. Beard 7/10/27
425. NATHAN
    Pt./Marg. Karl 12/27/40
426. NAVE
    Fred./Eliz. Smith 4/27/03
    Jos./Marg. Murray 1/26/46
427. NAYLOR
    Wm./Ellen Holt 1/13/42
428. NEAL (NEEL, NEALL, NEELE)
    Lewis/Eliz. Perkins 5/7/00
    Hn. R./Mary Burton 3/7/04
    Jm./Na. Jones 3/10/18
    Elias O./So. Alter 2/16/25
    Dv./Eleanor Olliver 8/6/32
429. NEEDY (NEADY)
    Wm./Cath. Garhart 11/22/24
    Jc./Malinda Gollocher 12/6/45
    Sam./Louisa Susan Hauer 3/21/59
430. NEFF
    Jc./Mary Sottory 7/31/02
    Geo./Cath. Beard 5/2/09
    Jc./Mag. Shipley 8/21/17
    John/Ros. Lorshbaugh 3/6/17
    Dv./Susan Wateman 9/2/24
    Ezekiel/Sr. Hyatt 3/29/25
    Geo./Eliz. Keplinger 3/12/30 or
        3/12/31 (2 dates given in cross-
        indexes)
    Jc./Eliz. Snyder 3/8/33
    John Hn./Eliza Stouffer 12/23/46

431. NEGLEY (NAGLY)
    Chn./Barb. Newcomer 4/26/15
    Dr. Elias/Mary C. Brewer 12/7/48
    Pt./Laura Rickenbaugh 5/7/49
    John A./Mary Eliz. Rowland 9/15/57
432. NEIBERT (NEYBERT)
    John/Marg. Fox 8/7/15
    John/Eliz. Deal 1/12/24
    Ph./Eliz. Householder 11/22/25
    John/Theresa Roman 2/19/38
    Ph. H./Juliann Wolf 5/25/48
    Wm. H./Eliza Ann Mace 8/31/54
433. NEIDIG
    Benj./Mary M. Smith 4/30/49
434. NEIKIRK (NIKIRK, NYKIRK, NEYKIRK, NIKARK)
    Hn./Na. Furry 4/16/05
    Geo./Marg. Shiffler 5/6/06
    John/Barb. Summers 1/22/14
    Geo./Mary Mondebaugh 2/11/17
    Geo./Eliz. Bowser 2/22/22
    Sam./Sus. Bealer 4/2/22
    Dv./Sus. Pry 8/4/31
    Mannassus/Mary Ann Pope 12/21/31
    Dv./Eliz. Hill 1/1/40
    Hn. F./Mary Miller 2/17/45
    Mich./Na. Wolfkill 7/28/46
    And./Marg. E. Hammer 12/10/51
    John W./Barb. Ann Neikirk 2/13/55
435. NEILL
    Alex./Sr. Owens 12/9/00
    Tho./Reb. Neill 5/13/24
    Wm./Grace A. Kennedy 11/14/33
    Wm./Priscilla Ingram 8/30/47
    Lewis/Ann Taylor 3/14/51
    Jm./Mrs. Louise Paquine 8/9/56
    Stansberry/Eliza J. Charlton 7/30/60
436. NELSON
    Wm./Molly Earhart 4/6/09
437. NEMAN
    Hn./Sus. Brantner 11/26/03
438. NEPPER (NEPPLER)
    Wm./Hen. S. Howard 5/31/27
    Jc./Mary Francis 5/1/29
439. NESBIT (NESBITT)
    Jc./Cath. Tyler 5/3/00
    Jon./Polly Cownaver 12/4/02
    Pt./Eliz. Davis 7/2/04
    Nath./Eleanor Dickey 12/30/13
    Jon./Ann R. Meixsell 3/23/30 or 3/23/31
        (2 dates given in cross-indexes)
    Jon./Mary Johnson 12/17/58
440. NETZ
    John/Polly Deck 7/19/31
    Jc./Luema Drenner 8/1/35
    John/Marg. Easterday 9/26/45
    Sam./Har. Ann Stiffler 10/13/56

441. NEWBANKS
Strother/Sr. Larick 11/20/29
442. NEWCOMER
Dn./Sus. Shupe 4/6/01
Jc./Anne Funk 3/20/04
Emanuel/Cath. Funk 3/31/06
Chn./Barb. Barr 6/14/08
Joel Sr./Eliz. Newcomer 4/10/13
Pt./Barb. Sharrick 9/20/14
Pt. Jr./Anna Good 2/26/20
Dn./Barb. Stoner 11/18/22
John/Cath. Nafe 3/15/22
John/Cath. Newcomer 12/9/22
John/Lydia Jane Hawthorn 5/1/23
Sam/Sr. Friendly 12/6/23
Chn./Sr. Keller 1/8/25
Jc./Sus. Brewer 12/19/27
Hn./Mary Ann Seibert 10/22/28
Dv. C./Eleanor C. Grieves 4/25/29
Jc./Lea Beard 3/15/30
Is./Eliz. Emmert 1/24/33
Joel/Sr. Adam 1/22/33
Pt./So. Fockler 9/21/33
Sam. F./Amanda I.C.R. Schrader 5/6/34
Mich./Mar. Krotzer 11/17/36
Joshua/Mary Ann Ankeney 1/26/37
Jos./Susan Coffman 4/10/40
Jonas/Am. Summers 9/13/41
Wm./Eliz. Trenner 12/23/41
Dv. C./Virginia C. Hamm 9/27/42
Dv. H./Ruanna Thomas 3/7/42
John/Eliz. Keedy 3/28/43
Zachariah/Sr. Ann Adams 8/19/43
Hn./Marg. Spigler 12/7/44
Jos./Lydia Thomas 7/22/45
Jc./Reb. Bell 12/31/49
Simon P./Reb. A. Creager 2/28/49
Geo./Sus. Faulder 2/19/50
John/Cath. Boyer 12/10/50
Pt. S./Mary F. Monroe 1/28/51
Jos./Eliz. Eavey 2/1/53
John N./Ann Cath. Mentzer 10/16/54
Cyrus P./Eliz. Hause 3/19/55
John D./Eliz. Landis 1/27/55
Jos./Ellen Black 4/30/55
Dv./Eliz. Cain 9/29/56
John/Anna Ridenour 8/26/57
John B./Na. Barkdoll 10/31/57
John H./Ellen Williams 3/30/58
Jos./Sr. Richards 11/6/58
V.H./Anna Sherrick 5/19/58
Wm./Eliza H. Witmer 4/25/59
John W./Barb. A. Keller 8/7/60
443. NEWKIRK
Mary H./John K. Robbins 1/17/33

444. NEWLER
John/Marg. Hughes 4/6/39
445. NEWLON
Al./Chna. McIlhenney 3/20/49
446. NEWMAN (NUMAN)
John/Mary Price 4/9/08
Sam./Ann Maria Fauver 9/4/23
Jc./Eliz. Kausler 7/25/27
Jc./Cath. Long 5/26/28
Geo. R./Lucy Ann Baylis 11/2/31
447. NEWSON
Jos./Sus. Snyder 7/1/09
Abr./Lucinda Friend 1/31/15
Tho./Cath. Young 12/1/19
John/Na. Dickson 12/11/24
Alex./Susan Byers 8/15/27
Jos. M./Marg. Dorsey 11/16/35
448. NICELY
Abr./Sr. Clem 12/26/29
Hn./Mary Daugherty 9/2/30
Geo. W./Mary Davis 4/18/32
449. NICHOLAS
Matthias/Mary Poorman 10/30/19
John C./Kate Clare Rench 1/30/55
450. NICHOLS (NICHOLIS)
Jc./Sus. George 6/7/00
Wm./Jane Cartwright 11/6/00
Jm./Mar. Beard 8/13/17
Jos./Eliz. Ann Morsburg 5/27/22
Jc./Eliz. Koyner 8/8/37
Jc./Eliz. Yerty 3/1/44
John/Charity Brown 5/20/45
Sam./Ru Annetta Smith 11/3/46
Sam./Eliz. Royer 12/30/56
Emanuel/Mahala Brown 1/21/57
451. NICHODEMUS (NICODEMMS)
Hn./Hetthy Funk 12/29/03
John/Peggy Potter 2/9/05
Jc./Rowana Hess 12/9/26
John/Ann Maria Motter 6/9/26
Joshua/Cath. Sheney 8/11/27
Jc./Am. Drenner 12/12/44
Tho./Eliz. Heck 1/13/47
John/Eliz. Emerson 3/1/49
Fred./Mary Ann Medcalf 2/21/50
Hn. C./Isa. Cray 12/12/50
Jc./Han. Miller 3/24/52
John H./Tracilla Keedy 11/20/60
452. NICKERSON
Benj./Na. Oldham 10/8/56
453. NICKSON
Jm./Mary Snyder 10/1/17
454. NIER (NEIR)
Conrad/Polly Bottenberger 6/4/05
Wm./Dorcas Colbert 1/3/35

78

455. NIGH
Geo. Jr./Sus. Knode 8/20/03
Pt./Polly Smith 8/5/10
Sam./Eliz. Rench 10/27/18
Dv. R./Susan Miller 2/23/53
Sam./Mary Lowman 12/31/60
456. NIGHSWANDER (NISHWANDER, NEY-
SWANDER, NIGHSWANGER, NEIS-
WANGER)
Abr./Eliz. Hoffer 8/22/08
John/Na. Avey 8/27/08
Abr./Eliz. Newcomer 9/12/11
Jos./Lydia Avey 2/11/12
Jc./Barb. Snider 10/24/20
Dn./Susan Slanker 11/7/21
Wm./Louisa Davis 4/8/26
Wilson/Delilah Brown 12/1/32
Hn./Milley Toner 7/26/34
Jc./Eliza Brown 12/25/35
457. NIGHT
Hn./Sr. Wolf 11/17/17
458. NISS
Adam/Sus. Hoverstick 11/13/10
459. NISTINE
Jc. E./Barb. Dahoof 3/30/36
460. NITZEL (NEITZEL)
John/Eliza Hammon 2/1/27
461. NOERR
John C./Malinda M. Beard 9/25/57
462. NOLAND (NOWLAND)
Dn./Eliz. Neall 1/7/10
Sam./Sr. Sellers 5/13/16
Tho./Sus. Lambert 2/9/30
463. NOLL (NOLLS, NOLE, NOLES)
Wm./Barb. Bowman 8/9/08
Conrad/Char. Frick 11/9/11
464. NORRED
Sam./Serena V. Showman 3/17/34
465. NORRIS (NORRISS)
John/Rachel Ault 6/1/07
Pat./Sr. Ott 9/8/09
Stephen/Char. Madara 7/24/13
Geo./Cath. Keefauver 4/18/18
Jc./Polly Arnsberger 3/14/21
Wm./Mary Long 11/22/25
John/Sr. Ann Posey 12/28/35
Hn./Ann Thum 11/3/38
Geo./Cath. Foutch 8/14/41
Wm./Mary Himes 2/26/41
Wm./Ann Eliz. Matthew 5/5/46
Jesse/Marg. Morgan 11/25/47
Geo./Marg. Rice 8/6/50
Tho. Hn./Caroline Carter 11/8/51
Milton V./Cath. Stine 1/24/53
Horatio/Susan Biesshing 1/25/55
Jm./Sr. Jane Laypole 11/18/58

466. NORTH
Geo./Mary Edwards 4/21/15
467. NORTHCOTT
Jm. H./Cath. Hershey 5/17/41
468. NOTT
Jm./Cath. Itnire 10/19/25
469. NOTTINGHAM
Enoch/Sr. Hager 3/27/02
John/Savilla Brown 1/25/45
470. NOUSE
Pt./Na. Moore 10/9/38
Pt./Marg. Beckley 5/12/51
471. NOWELL (NEWELL)
Jm./Eliz. Malott 8/14/10
Wm. T./Mary Ann Lambert 11/16/11
John/Char. Crunkleton 11/6/23
Gilbert/Maria Ribblet 6/9/25
John/Reb. Thomas 10/3/36
472. NUFER
John W./Ellen Sheiss 11/20/44
Mich. B./Na. Waltz 10/19/44
473. NULD
John/Susan Moudy 2/13/45
474. NULL
Hn./Mary Miller 12/5/07
Rob./Susan Boren 1/18/43
475. NULUM
Elijah/Mary Furr 9/29/01
476. NUNAMAKER (NUNIMAKER, NUNEMAKER, NUNA-
MACHER, NUNAMACKER)
Dn./Eliz. Fausnaught 11/6/04
Sam./Eliz. Bragonier 5/10/21
John/Lydia Shoop 2/15/30
Hn./Ros. Kinnell 5/3/38
Rezin I./Ann E. Hoffman 1/22/56
Theodore/Hen. Turner 7/22/57
Hn./Ruann Marsilles 2/13/60
477. NURSE
Chas./Cath. Snively 8/12/36
478. NUSE
John/Mary McKesick 7/18/15
John W./Barb. Bagent 9/24/49
Jos./Sr. Reynolds 12/30/57
479. NUTZ
Sam./Mag. Bridendale 12/31/27
480. NYMAN
Mich./Eliz. Christian 11/23/32
Dn. G./Wilimini Stephens 10/6/35
Geo./Mary Smith 1/23/43
Jos./Jane Reb. Miller 9/20/43
Mich./Eliza Ann Spielman 12/6/54
Rob. V./Frances Miles 10/17/59

481. OAK
Wm./Sr. Hollis 4/1/46
482. OBERLIN
Sam./Mary E. Hoffman 8/21/48

483. OCKER
Sam./Cath. Bowman 11/13/58
484. OCKS
And./Mary Rishoh 8/23/00
485. O'CONNOR
Bernard/Marg. McCaffey 8/31/33
Tho./Bridget Hurlekee 11/15/58
486. O'DONNELL
Constantine/Ros. McGinley 11/28/09
John/Sus. Tolen 10/24/20
John/Har. Coss 4/29/36
Domenick A./Mary A. Bevans 8/8/37
487. OFFERD
Jm./Ruth Chaney 4/29/06
488. OFFNER
Geo./Letitia Dearing 3/25/15
489. OGDEN
Phenias/Lucretia Bowles 3/10/38
490. OGILBY
Sam./Sr. Robertson 9/28/46
491. OGIN
Pt./Jane Jenkins 9/26/01
492. OGLE
Sam. V./Marg. Freaner 12/25/48
493. OGLETON
Caleb/Eliza Duckett 5/12/43
494. O'KEEFE
Nich./Helena Adams 9/1/47
495. O'LAUGHLIN
Dennis/Sr. Young 1/3/20
496. OLDHAM
Ed./Jane Gardner 5/3/00
497. OLIVER (OLLIVER)
John/Mary Beck 4/28/07
Benj./Susan Yates 9/29/38
Denton/Reb. Mann 1/3/40
Joshua/Ann Maria Kale 7/11/48
498. OLMS
Jm./Jane Williamson 9/21/48
499. OMWECK
Mt./Eliz. Pence 8/30/10
500. ONDERDONK
Wm./Maria F. Mayhugh 10/29/50
501. O'NEAL (O'NEILL)
Wm./Reb. Chaney 5/3/00
Horatio/Mary Shaw 8/29/07
Law./Cath. Root 6/20/17
Jos./Mary Donnelly 8/2/59
502. ORBAKER
Jc./Cath. Burkhart 4/28/10
503. ORDENBARGER
Ph./Lydia France 2/26/27
504. ORDERLY
Jos./Sr. Ann Grove 9/25/38
505. ORDNER
Stephen/Mary Ann Dagenhart 2/1/43

506. O'REILEY
John/Bridget O'Reily 12/27/36
Jm./Susan McGovran 2/2/37
507. ORNDORFF (ORONDORFF)
Chn./Mary Wireman 6/7/00
Hn./Ella Miller 8/30/00
Jc./Sr. A. Greenwood 9/21/41
Wm./Eliz. A. Foyles 11/3/52
508. ORR (OHR)
John Jr./Sr. Arnold 10/9/05
Jc. J./Eliz. Rohrer 6/7/34
Elias J./Leah E. Rohrer 10/30/44
John H./Sr. I. Deavers 9/23/51
509. ORRICK
Cromwell/Mary Johnson 1/22/16
John/Urilla Stonebraker 9/17/33
Constantine/Sr. E. Larew 8/10/44
Geo. W./Mary A. Fausnaught 9/13/51
510. ORT
Jc. J./Eliz. Boerstler 2/3/10
Hn./Sr. Smith 3/18/20
511. ORTMAN
John/Cath. Baker 8/14/04
Hn./Mary Shilling 9/20/08
Wm./Eliz. Ann Harlin 8/18/35
Jer./Lue C. Holbert 9/16/56
512. OSBORNE (OSBORN, OSBOURN)
Hn./Marg. Spessard 10/31/32
Nathan/Ellen B. Link 8/8/41
Nathan/Eliza Ann Bean 11/6/45
J.W./Sr. Jane Herr 9/1/57
513. OSTER
John/Sus. Westerberger 4/5/06
Dn./Cath. Barkman 6/11/14
Dn./Mary Barkman 6/20/46
John/Marg. Snyder 12/19/57
514. OSWALD (OSWALT)
John/Eve Garver 9/19/01
Benj./Sally Keyser 9/23/09
Benj./Sr. Ann Brinem 4/16/27
John/Marg. Stiffy 3/30/33
Dv./Susan Beard 12/20/41
Ph./Talina R. Fogler 3/13/41
Benj. F./So. Bell 10/25/47
Sam. K./Lydia A. Spessard 8/28/54
515. OTT
Hn./Eliz. Stover 9/5/09
John D./Mary Ann Quantrill 5/10/32
Barney/Marg. Welch 11/2/39
Jc./So. Hunstbery 9/7/47
Dn./Mary C. Renner 3/15/49
Dn./Mary Eliz. Doyle 7/2/58
516. OTTO
Matthias/Sr. Miller 12/22/15
Hn./Ann Miller 2/8/26
Hn./Mary Dick 12/6/31
Hn./Eliz. Reeder 5/28/39

516. OTTO (Continued)
  John/Cath. Gardenour 3/24/49
  Dv./Eliz. Ecker 12/24/50
  Chn./Ann G. Stant 1/24/50 or
    1/24/51 (2 dates given in cross-
    indexes)
517. OVELMAN
  Wm./Mary Faberitz 8/13/11
518. OVER
  D.J./Sally Bomberger 3/18/58
519. OVERCASH
  Sol./Barb. A. Rowland 2/21/55
520. OVERPECK
  Jc./Sr. Trout 11/16/12
521. OWENS
  Dn./Eliza Dougherty 10/26/33
522. OYESTER
  Dn./Patience Lewis 3/17/40

523. PADEN (PAYDEN)
  John/Eliz. Lewis 7/12/22
  John/Mary Jones 11/21/35
  Lewis Alex./Susan Gimple 6/14/49
524. PADER
  Wm./Mary Farrow 8/6/31
525. PAGE
  John/Mary Lynch 4/16/08
  Ed./Na. Williams 8/13/14
526. PAINE (PAYNE)
  Hn./Eliz. Cartz 4/12/03
  John/Sr. Powers 12/22/07
527. PAINTER
  Dn./Mary Piper 9/18/00 ("now Bender"
    pencil note after Daniel)
  Jc./Mary Abell 10/24/17
  Jc./Barb. Kline 10/21/30
  Jc./Eliz. Sheckles 8/31/46
528. PALMER
  Jc./Barb. Otto 5/30/01
  Jos./Cath. Engleman 5/21/03
  Geo./Sus. Heller 5/26/07
  Jos./Cath. Knodle 11/24/09
  Pereguine/Ann Cole 2/4/13
  Chn./Eliz. Burgan 6/1/19
  Chn./Eliz. Knodle 12/14/22
  John/Eliz. Welty 3/11/24
  Jos./Sr. Ann Mossburgh 7/24/24
  Jc./Cath. Knodle 3/21/25
  John/Ann Knodle 11/7/25
  Jc./Na. Moggins 10/24/26
  Jos./Sr. Moates 3/31/26
  Dn./So. Smith 10/20/27
  Dn./Eliza Knodle 7/30/31
  Wm./Cath. Ridenour 9/13/34
  John/Rachel Wilkinson 1/21/40
  Benj./Levina Welsh 4/29/44
  Sam. I./Marg. S. Eckman 11/16/48
  Dv./Evaline Long 8/18/49

  Jos./Sr. Jones 9/20/51
  Wm./Amanda Cath. Smith 4/13/52
  Sam./Susan Davis 2/25/57
529. PALMORE
  Jc./Nelly Boyer 4/24/16
  Pt./Peggy Orh 6/8/16
530. PAMOT
  Rich./Debly Roby 12/12/04
531. PANAFATHER
  John/Ellen Powers 10/23/32
532. PARKER
  Is./Marg. Criner 10/19/08
  John/Cath. Evilhock 5/15/31
  John/Cath. Formes 10/23/34
  Rev. Jos./Mrs. Mary Repler 12/10/38
  John W./Katie E. Miller 10/26/55
533. PARKS (PARKE, PARK)
  Timothy/Char. Inngold 4/1/00
  Jc./Marg. Hill 3/6/01
  Tho./Eliz. Roof 10/8/05
  John/Reb. Sigler 2/21/34
  Jos./Sr. Sauntman 3/28/34
  Jos./Mary Finafouck 1/15/39
  Geo./Eliz. Warner 9/28/53
  Jos./Aleathy Ann Horman 10/7/56
534. PARMER
  Perry/Susan Kitzmiller 4/10/24
  John/Susan Kepplinger 3/29/45
535. PARSON (PARSONS)
  Jc./Na. Eachs 6/5/29
536. PARTON
  Jos./Mary Susan Spangler 12/18/54
537. PASH
  Wm./Mary Ann Dowell 7/16/08
538. PASS
  John/Eliz. Mauggins 11/7/31
539. PATRICK
  Jm./Esther Lester 11/14/07
540. PATTERSON (PATTISON)
  Arch./Mary Calimel 6/22/18
  Jer./Sus. Dickey 11/23/18
  Zachariah/Maria Benn 11/24/19
  Sol./Sus. Parrell 8/24/26
  Wm. U./Ann H. Anders 4/2/49
541. PATTON (PATTEN)
  Jm./Sr. Christi 7/3/10
  Jm./Eliz. Etnire 6/6/34
542. PAULSGROVE
  Hn./Eliz. Wagner 12/7/02
543. PAXTON
  Dn. D./Na. Kidwell 9/10/49
544. PEAKE
  Bennett/Eliz. Marshall 2/16/14
545. PEARCE
  John/Rua Taylor 12/27/45
546. PEARSON
  Geo./Ellen S. Hoye 2/5/42
  Jos. Jr./Mary L. Rickenbaugh 10/11/42

547. PECK
  And./Sus. Miller 1/4/12
  Wm. J./Marg. Brannon 12/27/17
  Jerome/Emly Frances McCormack 1/27/60
548. PECKMAN
  Jos./Mary Fultz 9/17/12
549. PEDDICORD
  Wm./Mary Collier 12/14/03
550. PELTZ
  John/Na. Figaley 1/20/25
551. PENCE (PENTZ)
  Dv./Barb. Aerberger 7/2/01
  Wm./Eliz. Adams 1/14/06
  Jc./Marg. Turnbecker 8/2/22
552. PENDLETON
  Benj./Har. Stephens 8/19/30
  Benj./Rachel Lyles 5/1/51
553. PENNELL (PANNELL)
  Geo./Marg. Martin 12/22/01
  Jon./Han. Cunning 11/5/12
  John/Eliz. Pake 4/25/28
554. PENNER
  Hn./Cath. Ott 10/4/05
555. PENNINGTON
  Tho./Eurydice Mann 8/7/39
556. PEPLE
  Tho./Mary Chew 12/7/08
557. PEPPER
  Wm./Ros. Cramer 12/3/04
558. PERIN
  John/Am. Ingram 10/29/03
559. PERRELL
  Wm./Am. Pitsnogle 10/27/45
560. PERRY (PEREY)
  Jon./Eliz. Kelsinger 4/18/26
  Dr. Hemen F./Louisa M. Prather
    5/3/56
561. PETER (PETERS)
  Dn./Eliz. Nigh 8/4/04
  Geo./Caroline Reynolds 3/8/31
  Fred./Mary Chrissinger 1/19/37
  John/Eliz. Mary Phillips 6/1/38
  Chas./Louisa Kline 2/14/59
562. PETERMAN
  Jc./Mary Moudy 7/27/25
  Jc./Har. Baxter 3/8/28
  Wm. T./Ann C. Spitler 10/15/39
  John F./Pamelia Rosine Grosh 6/19/44
  Geo./Mary Magraw 12/19/49
563. PETERSON
  Israel/Na. Falker 12/24/00
564. PETRY (PETRE, PETRI, PETERY)
  Ph./Eliz. Hogmire 5/28/06 ("s/o Jc."
    pencil note)
  John/Cath. Line 3/10/14 ("s/o Jc."
    pencil note)
  Jonas/Emeline Wever 2/27/30
  Geo./Cath. Welty 3/12/31

  Jm./Anna Eliz. Friedhofin 4/30/38
  John S./Eliz. G. Clopper 3/8/60
565. PEYTON
  Chambers/Mary Brannon 1/1/16
566. PFAGING
  Frod./Cath. Shilling 5/9/55
567. PHILLIPPY
  Resin/Mary Byers 4/30/33
568. PHILLIPS
  Wm./Sus. Hufford 10/20/21
569. PHILPOTT
  Horatio/Ann Allen 4/5/08
570. PICKETT
  Jm./Eliz. Horine 5/1/58
571. PICKLE
  Jc./Eliz. Weaver 6/21/03
572. PIEKING
  Jc./Eleanor Williams 1/17/27
573. PIER (PEIR)
  Wm./Reb. Goodwin 1/16/10
  Hn./Mary Ann Watts 6/26/15
574. PIFER
  Dn./Mar. Brown 12/6/05 ("s/o Jc. Sr."
    pencil note)
  Leuvenen/Har. Allen 10/8/36
575. PIKE
  Francis/Mary E.L. Haver 2/22/39
  D.A./Cath. Rett 2/28/60
576. PINDER
  Benj. S./Sr. Ann Small 6/7/28
577. PINE
  Wm./Anna Cutshaw 2/12/18
  Edwin/Susan Lindonman 7/4/49
578. PINEBRECH
  Jc./Sus. Herlinger 9/11/17
579. PINKEY
  Gutlip/Barb. Shank 4/3/05
580. PIPER (PIPERS)
  Jc./Eliz. Darby 4/5/02
  Conrod/Mary Reynolds 10/19/03
  Mich./Mary Locker 4/12/14
  Dv./Eliz Kitsmiller 5/11/25 (Dv. crossed
    out; pencil note "Dn. buried near For-
    reston, Ill." added)
  Hn./Eliz. Keedy 11/18/28 ("s/o Dn. Sr."
    pencil note after Hn.; "d/o Jc." pencil
    note after Eliz.)
  Jc./Ann Kitzmiller 12/9/28
  Elias/Mary Hammond 7/26/22
  Aaron/Marg. G. Martin 10/5/30
  Elias/Eliza Palmer 6/7/31
  Jc./So. Moats 4/2/31
  Dn./Tracilla Stine 3/23/35 ("had no child-
    ren" pencil note)
  Dv./Maria Nicholas 3/4/37
  Elias/Barb. Thompson 6/25/39
  Dn. D./Mary Baker 11/30/41 ("Mary Sophia,
    d/o Elias" pencil note)

82

580. PIPER (PIPERS)(Continued)
    Jm. N./Mary Ann Covell 3/19/55
    Sam./Mary Etta Cost 11/5/58 ("s/o
    Hn." pencil note)
581. PITMAN (PITTMAN)
    John/Cath. Aldray 11/17/11
    Dv. H./Am. S. Ritenour 10/8/25
    Geo. H./Hester McGovern 12/1/53
582. PITSNOGLE
    Levi/Matilda Long 6/1/47
583. PITTINGER
    Wm. S./Mary C. Bowman 10/30/48
    Dv. S./Mary Ann Spickler 12/29/54
    Jc./Mary Matilda Zellers 12/21/54
584. PITZER
    Wm./Cath. Kitchens 11/11/37
    Mathias/Sus. Davis 8/1/38
    Geo. I./Sr. Bender 2/5/46
585. PLANK
    Jesse/Cath. Marker 12/15/37
586. PLECHER
    John/Marg. Lorshbough 11/24/14
587. PLUMMER
    John/Na. Hose 4/30/32
588. PLUNKETT
    John/Ann Clarke 1/31/18
589. POE
    Jm. R./Ann Harter 4/1/47
    Isaiah S./Mary Eliz. Gans 12/27/59
    Oliver/Susan McAfee 9/10/60
590. POFFENBERGER (POFFENBURGER)
    Dn./Mary Somer 11/8/03
    Hn./Mary Lantz 8/3/09
    John/Phebe Roberts 10/24/09
    Chn./Mary Brantner 11/24/13
    And./Am. Smith 9/28/16
    Hn./Annet Montgomery 6/6/17
    Jc./Na. Rohrer 3/22/20
    John/Na. Miller 10/23/24
    Jc./Milly Stouffer 1/24/26
    Hn./Susan Zittle 3/12/30
    Dn./Eliz. Mose 3/5/31
    Mich./Barb. Pitman 2/9/31
    Tho./Mary Ann Thomas 2/19/31
    Sam./Cath. Shemmel 4/6/32
    Wm./Mary Fink 4/18/33
    Dn./Mary Malone 5/12/34
    Elias/Ros. McCreary 8/15/35
    Jos./Mary Ann Coffman 2/7/38
    Dv./Barb. Miller 9/5/39
    John/Sr. Ann Fink 12/18/46
    John/Marg. Weck 4/7/48
    Elias/Mary E. Showman 2/10/52
    Hn./Chna. Speaker 9/25/52
    Lawson W./Lavina Coffman 2/3/52
    Hn. A./Mar. S. Schlosser 5/8/54
    And./Susan A.R. Riddlemoser 12/24/57

    Lawson W./Ann H. Knode 4/28/57
    Al./Har. Hutzel 3/2/58
    John H./Sr. Jane Geltmacher 4/3/58
    Hiram/Cath. Snavely 12/5/59
    John Reuben/Amanda H. Moose 10/18/59
    Wm./Cath. Schamel 12/11/60
591. POINT (POINTS)
    Dv./Sidney R. Taylor 10/29/21
592. POLAND
    John/Emily Baylis 9/30/11
    Shepphard/Cath. Turk 4/8/30
    Wm./Han. Ronemous 9/12/35
593. POLLOCK (POLLICK)
    John/Cath. Flora 4/30/03
    Jm./Francis Gibson 6/4/08
    Jc. T./Sr. Massey 8/7/19
    Jm. C./Jane N. Bowen 12/25/24
    Jos./Sr. Collins 12/7/24
594. POOL (POOLE)
    Rich./Reb. Malott 7/16/17
    Dn./Mary Ann Ridenour 5/9/55
595. POORMAN
    Jc./Cath. Fox 11/1/09
    Jc./Na. McClain 3/7/26
    Is./Juliann Kreigh 9/9/37
    Jc./Eliza Price 3/2/40
596. POPE
    Wm./Ros. Thomas 8/14/10
    Ed./Easter Miller 8/13/18
597. PORSAL
    Chas. W./Mary E. Leathers 7/26/49
598. PORTER
    John/Eliz. Kealhowe 7/2/08
    Chas./Eliz. Laub 9/14/17
    Dn./Eliz. Cooper 1/5/21
    Levi/Rosella Delauney 7/30/45
    Chas. W./Mary Ann Stiffler 11/28/53
599. PORTERFIELD
    Arch./Han. Towson 10/27/14
    Chas. T./Marg. J. Hollman 11/28/54
    Wm. R./Hellen O'Donnelly 3/19/55
600. PORTZ (PORTS)
    Dv./Susan Miller 3/17/38
    Otho J./Mary A. Mades 8/1/60
601. POSEY
    Fred. J./Eliz. McCardle 12/18/39
    Boliver/Adeline Dalrymple 10/3/49
602. POST
    Tho. C.R./Ann Eliza Groves 5/22/34
    Geo. W./Sr. Ann Smith 2/17/35
603. POTTER
    Ralph/Eliz. Arnold 10/29/22
    Jm./Eliz. Moore 10/17/23
    Benj./So. Grim 9/6/25
    Jm./Reb. Dennison 8/22/25
    Dv. G./Eliz. Olliver 3/3/38

604. POTTS
    Hn. J./Comfort Am. Worley 11/6/57
    Dv./Han. Bridgeman 4/28/10
    Sam./Eliz. Bartmess 12/9/17
    Chas./Eliz. Snyder 3/27/20
    Geo. M./Cornelia Ringgold 11/16/26
    Alex./Cath. Toms 6/14/31
    Alex./Chna. Ropp 7/16/33
    Geo. Wash./Sus. Jones 12/19/45
    Marcus S./Virginia K. Sycafoos 4/17/51
605. POWELL
    Jm./Jane Malone 4/4/07
    Tho./Han. Chambers 2/9/13
    Is./Marg. Hall 12/5/15
    John/Na. Bowers 4/9/18
    Upton/Ann Smith 3/19/28
    Sam./Sr. Root 9/7/31
    Elisha/Eliz. Winnell 9/23/34
    Moses/Maria Price 10/28/37
    Warner/Eliz. Sponsler 11/4/47
    Wm. U./Ann H. Anders 4/2/49
    Wm./Mary Rowe 8/6/56
    Wm./Mary Jones 11/15/60
606. POWERS
    Wm./Mary Rhodes 4/8/21
    John L./Eliz. Cook 7/19/60
607. POWLAS (POWLES)
    John/Juliana Ditch 3/23/05
    Wm./Mary Hanna 2/25/46
    Upton/Sevilla Newman 2/25/46
    Jc./Anna King 2/15/59
608. PRAINE
    Sol./Orphit Taylor 4/20/26
609. PRAISER
    Wm./Mary Coffroth 4/8/05
610. PRATHER (PRAITHER)
    Hn./Louisa Bell 11/23/09
    Jm./Letha Greenwall 9/10/11
    Sam. Jr./Eliz. Jacques 4/25/11
    Friend/Mar. Amos 1/12/19
    Perry/Char. Johnson 3/29/28
    Sam. S./Jemima McBee 4/21/28
    Basil/Temperance Mason 4/22/29
    Elie/Cath. Hanes 4/13/29
    Benj./Cath. Miller 11/23/30
    John/Cath. Barr 12/13/30
    Perry/Eliz. Troxall 8/3/30
    Tho./Susan Ambrose 12/4/32
    Rich./Sr. Ann Moore 3/5/33
    Sam. T./Maria Blair 3/17/35
    Sam. G./Amanda L. Reitzell 9/10/58
611. PRATT
    Hn./Na. Arecy 5/24/03
612. PRENTICE
    John/Polly Garber 5/8/04
613. PRESCOTT
    Dn. W./Ann V. Rohrback 12/12/49

614. PRESTON
    Wm. H./Mary C. Swartzweller 5/21/44
615. PRETZLER
    Chas./Regina Diedenruder 12/4/54
    Chn. G./Clara Brown 3/17/56
616. PRICE
    Geo./Sus. Sillhart 1/18/00
    Josiah/Sr. Scott 3/5/06
    Levi/Francis Baird 12/11/06
    Ig./Isa. McGowan 1/30/07
    Jc./Cath. Hose 3/6/07
    Sacia/Nelly Hammond 1/26/08
    Emanuel/Sr. Price 11/29/10
    John/Na. Albert 5/2/10
    Sam. D./Cath. B. Chapline 9/18/11
    Absolom/Sr. Hammond 1/2/13
    Wm./Mary Mechs 12/7/13
    John/Cath. Gehr 5/20/14
    Geo./Cath. Hout 9/26/15
    Wm.Esquire/Sally Duckett 5/14/18
    Hn./Julia Ann Ong 10/25/30
    John/Cath. Barr 12/13/30
    Sam./Julia Ann Houser 3/18/31
    John/Chna. Friedly 5/6/33
    Benj./Sr. Ann Kennedy 5/20/34
    Dv./Reb. Jackson 3/1/34
    Abel/Eliz. Ann Davis 7/17/35
    Rob./Mary B.F. Denner 12/1/35
    Amos/Cynthia Ann Ingram 9/16/36
    Dv. E./Sr. Ann Brosius 1/21/37
    Jos. D./Han. M. McVitty 6/13/40
    Jc./Mary Gehr 9/21/41
    Jc./Susan Moreland 3/1/44
617. PRIM
    Mark/Na. Daugherty 7/16/31
618. PRINCE
    Val./Mary Harbaugh 11/1/14
619. PROCTOR
    Abner/Cath. Smith 9/15/32
620. PROFY
    Tho./Sr. Digner 6/29/37
621. PROTASTINGER
    Geo./Eliz. Schilhass 7/14/38
622. PROTZMAN (PRETZMAN)
    Pt./Sus. Ridenour 12/22/27
    Sam./Mary Bender 4/8/28
    Jos. G./Sr. Smith 7/24/30
623. PRY (PREY)
    John/Marg. White 2/17/03
    Sam./Mary Ann Cost 12/17/44
    Ph./Eliz. Ellen Cost 12/2/47
    John Wolfgang/Ann Cath. Most 5/12/58
624. PRYOR (PRYER)
    Pt./Leah Forrest 10/1/12
    Benj./Cath. Lewis 6/16/32
    Sam./Marg. King 11/10/32

625. PUMMELL
John/Mary Ann Fauver 7/1/34
626. PURCELL
Pat./Bridget Maurice 7/16/43
627. PURDY
Tho./Mary Keefer 1/25/48
628. PUSEY
Wm./Eliza Jane Friend 2/12/50
629. PUTMAN
Ph./Cath. Smith 4/21/08
Noah/Marg. Himes 12/14/40
630. PUTT
Benj./Barb. Lowman 1/22/13
631. PUTTERBAUGH
Is./Ruann Snavely 3/26/51
632. PUTTERMAN
Warren/Na. Gull 8/22/39
633. PYLE
John I./Cath. Myers 5/9/32

634. QUAKER
And./Eliz. Bolsh 3/8/06
635. QUINLIN
John/Marg. McCune 2/9/33

636. RADFORD
Chas. J./Eliz. B. Woodbury 9/29/42
637. RADY
Anthony/Cath. Barrett 11/3/40
638. RAFFERTY
Jos./Reb. Beall 12/16/14
639. RAGAN (REAGAN)
John Sr./Barb. Orondorff 9/22/99
Rich./Eliz. Ragan 12/31/05
John Jr./Am. Harry 10/16/10
Jon. H./Sr. Ann Cramer 4/1/34
Dv./Winney Werrick 10/31/35
Rich. Jr./Lydia Brooke 5/1/38
Wm./Sr. S. Williams 11/24/46
Jon. Hager/Sr. Ann Young 11/9/53
640. RAGER
Mich./Eliz. Gittinger 6/18/08
Rufus/Lydia Suman 3/4/46
Hiram/Mary Ann Gower 9/17/51
641. RAHM
Jc./Sr. Eakel 9/25/12
Dv./Eleanor Howard 9/17/14
642. RAINOR
John/Rosey Mentruse 2/27/04
643. RAIRDEN
Mich./Mary Cramer 4/15/28
644. RALPH
Wm./Jane Johnson 10/3/02
645. RAMER
Fred./Eliz. Smith 4/5/05
Benj./Na. Edwards 4/12/08

646. RAMSBURG (RAMSBURGH)
Stephen/Cath. Whip 4/13/15
Hn./Cath. Hilliard 10/28/40
647. RAMSEY
Jm./Cath. Snyder 2/13/17
Sabret/Marg. A. Herd 10/11/49
648. RAMSPARK
Hn./Cath. Link 6/3/05
649. RAMY (RAIMY)
Benj./Han. Painter 10/12/02
Is./Eliz. Perry 10/12/35
650. RANCH
Jos./Eliz. Schnebly 2/23/37
651. RANDALL (RANDELL)
John/Rachel Mackfee 4/25/09
Jos./Mary Jones 12/13/32
Clagett W./Ann Reb. Kershner 11/22/49
652. RANEY (RANNY)
Hugh C./Mary Wolfersburger 7/31/26
Willis/So. Leight 11/7/37
653. RANKIN (RANKEN)
Mat./Na. Smith 4/7/02
654. RAUSCHKALB
Sam./Sr. Miller 1/25/12
655. RAUTH
Pt./Fredricka Rousenberger 9/28/54
656. RAWLINS
Francis W./Arianah Drew 10/19/36
657. RAY
Wm./Marg. Moore 6/20/37
Hn./Caroline Graham 5/10/45
658. REACH
John/Cath. Shafer 12/30/13
Rob./Cath. Miller 1/27/14
659. REAM
Hn./Nelly Cauffman 3/2/27
Dv./Ann So. Julius 11/18/33
660. REAMER
Wm. C./Abby Mann 3/12/44
John D./Isa. Bowman 10/1/45
661. REASON
Jm./Mary More 12/13/23
662. REATH
John Arch./Susan Ann Hursh 9/1/53
663. REDDICK
John/Susan Milligan 11/18/34
664. REDGRAVE (REDGRAVES)
Jm./Eliz. Dalrymple 11/19/03
665. REDMAN
John R.A./Har. P. Flood 4/2/44
666. REED (REID, READ)
John/Han. Huntt 7/11/01
Ninian/Polly Shank 4/23/11
Wm./Cath. Blackwell 5/8/18
Benj. Josephus/Arabella Eliza McCleland
10/6/25
John/Am. Robinson 4/9/30

666. REED (REID, READ) (Continued)
    Chas./Vialetta Creigh 12/26/33
    Wash./Sr. Deaner 4/23/33
    Jos. H./Mary Donoho 4/17/35
    Jc./Julia Ann Kepler 3/17/40
    Wm./Mary Ann Shaman 10/30/40
    Geo. W./Frances Eliz. Hart 12/22/43
    Geo. W./Sr. Ann Crawford 11/1/43
    Jc./Cath. Eliza Morgan 12/30/43
    Dn./Susan Eakle 1/1/46
    Jc./Mary Sellers 2/27/49
    John C.T./Hen. Newcomer 12/12/53
    Geo./Roz. Newcomer 12/29/54
    Jer./Isa. Colbert 9/26/59
667. REEDER (READER)
    Henson/Sus. Berry 3/19/08
    Kenellem B./Sr. Watts 5/30/14
    Jesse/Na. Green 12/28/15
    Fred. B./Sus. Watts 12/23/18
    Dv./Ruth Alexander 7/22/27
    Hiram/Ros. Longman 9/20/37
    Tho. A./Cath. Brewer 3/30/42
    Alex./Eliz. Masters 3/27/44
    Chas./Mary M. Russell 9/7/46
    Hn. W./Marg. A. Hershey 5/3/47
    Wm./Mahetable Tanner 3/23/47
    Zachariah/Marg. Ann Poffenberger
        11/25/47
    Geo./Cath. Martz 2/7/49
    A.B./Mary E. Rowland 2/10/58
668. REEDY (Keedy in cross-index)
    Chn. M./Mary E. Carr 11/7/49
669. REEL
    John/Holday Toncray 9/15/04
    Jos./Marg. Schnebly 4/17/17
    Hn./Eliz. Pierce 5/29/20
    John/Reb. Smith 5/29/22
    Abr./Mar. Beasley 1/5/35
    Hn./Mary Stine 12/14/36
    Jc. Jr./Eliz. Schlagel 6/6/37
    Sam./Maria Loshbaugh 9/15/40
    Hn./Maria Houser 3/15/42
    John/Cath. Wolfersberger 2/28/43
    Dv./Ann Maria Banford 4/15/44
    Hn;/Barb. Stonebraker 1/11/49
    Sam./C.R. Price 10/14/58
670. REESE (REECE, REES)
    Hn./Cath. Beard 7/22/19
    Wm./Elisa West 6/26/28
    Joel/Rachel G. Dannell 6/14/36
    Isaiah/Sr. Jane Conrad 12/20/43
    Dv. F./Balinda Rinehart 3/1/52
    John/Susan Coy 9/15/53
671. REICHARD (REICKARD)
    Jc./Eliz. Wolf 3/26/38
    Val./Cath. Wolf 10/25/41
    John/Julia Ringer 1/1/47
    John A./Susan E. Stickle 2/26/55
    Dn. M./Reb. U. Boyd 1/4/58

672. REIFF
    John/Eve Stouffer 11/29/41
673. REILLY (REILY)
    Jm. R./Mary Orondorff 8/31/19
    Hugh/Ellen Thornton 2/11/36
    Ed./Maria Lantz 6/15/44
674. REINER
    Pt./Eve Rowell 10/15/02
675. REITZEL (REITZELL)
    John/Marg. Feterick 8/26/06
    Jc./Eliz. Middlekauff 1/23/33
676. REMICK
    Wm./Abigail Talbert 11/2/17
677. REMLY
    Conrad/Delilah Jones 5/27/15
678. RENCH (RENTCH)
    Pt./Polly Downey 3/24/01
    Tho. H./Jane Hamilton 8/1/20
    And./Jane S. Price 5/28/29
    Sam./Eliz. S. Swearinger 2/23/29
    John A./Mary A. Malott 8/7/33
    Dn. S./Savilla Stonebreaker 12/2/45
679. RENKER
    Adam/Cissey Keisinger 12/18/15
680. RENNER
    Jc./Mary Creager 9/24/02
    Ph./Reb. Albright 10/15/02
    Geo./Chna. Sarver 1/4/03 (female "Chn."
        in both indexes)
    Adam/Mary Young 11/21/08
    Hn./Cath. Newcomer 1/27/14
    Pt./Eliz. Haymaker 4/11/23
    Wm./Susan Highswander 12/31/27
    Jc./Polly Coss 3/9/29
    Jc./Cath. Byers 9/26/32
    Jon./Eliz. Longanecker 11/8/36
    Simon/May Cunningham 1/12/36
    Pt./Cath. Fultz 11/16/40
    Edwin T.B./Mary Hine 6/13/43
    Sol./Eliz. Smith 3/27/44
    Herman/Caroline Renner 2/7/49
    Jos./Reb. M. Wiles 7/21/56
    Hn./Barb. Hawthorn 2/22/58
681. REPP (REPPS, RAPP)
    John/Chna. Lantz 6/5/13
    John/Eliz. Protzman 10/12/15
    Jc./Sr. Bowers 3/26/16
    Jc./Marg. Rutter 5/25/25
    Lewis P./Julia Sheneberger 3/16/47
682. REPPLE
    Ludwick/Maria Cromry 6/18/05
683. RESH
    Jc./Mary Hob 11/14/07
    Benj./Agnes Pittinger 4/14/47
684. RESLEY (RESSLY, RESSLEY)
    Geo./Mary Priest 2/12/07
    Fred./Mary Boyd 3/27/37
    Jm./Eleanor Craig 10/9/46

685. RESS
    Francis/Sus. Huddle 6/12/15
686. RESSLER
    Mich./Sr. Doherty 4/23/01
687. RESSNER
    Hn./Phebe Shupe 12/5/12
688. RETCLIFF
    Wm./Eliz. Williard 2/26/39
689. REYNARD (RYNARD)
    Dn./Barb. Bowers 3/6/02
690. REYNOLDS
    Geo./Mary B. Delashmutt 9/6/03
    Lloyd/Eve Steace 1/21/06
    Wm./Mercy Walling 12/5/09
    John (Dr.)/Maria Sprigg 5/11/19
    Jesse/Caroline Unseld 10/22/25
    Wm. R.S./Chna. A. Boult 2/23/32
    Jm. W./Susan Herr 10/16/34
    Francis/Cath. Ryan 12/30/36
    Jm./Maria Kelly 4/21/36
    Sam./Eliza C. Nettz 10/2/44
    Ezra/Marg. Moles 6/4/45
    Wm./Sr. A. Bowers 1/5/45
    Wm. M./Eliz. Grimes 8/14/45
    Wm./Sr. Jane Deaver 11/27/50
    Jm. Wm./Sr. A. Welck 6/29/51
    Dv./Eliz. Fogler 2/2/55
    Hn./Laura Eliz. Saylor 8/16/55
    Dn. P./Annie C. Sigler 10/42/58
691. RHIND
    John/Eliza Snider 7/12/37
692. RHINEBERGER
    Wm./Grace Stewart 11/22/32
693. RHODE (RHODES)
    John/Eliz. Dutrow 6/16/15
    Hn./Eliz. Sidle 6/12/28
    Jos./Mary Ann Telly 2/11/31
    Jc. Jr./Marg. Weisel 3/15/32
    Arther/Rosa Anna McGurley 7/13/40
    Jos./Mary Leckroon 3/22/45
    John M./Na. Plum 12/8/54
694. RIBBLETT
    Dn./Char. Sease 5/9/17
695. RICAND
    And./Mary Shaw 9/23/41
696. RICE
    Jc./Mary Rowland 3/6/09
    John Jr./Eliz. Hartzog 1/27/19
    Hn./Han. Friedly 2/5/23
    Hn./Na. Mauggins 11/27/24
    Sam./Sr. Beard 4/14/35
    Dv./Cath. Avey 1/9/36
    Hn./Fanny Stine 8/21/43
    Dn. J./Maria Stine 12/28/46
    Jm. Wm./Sally Ann Donaldson 9/12/48
    Sam./Louisa B. Borden 2/26/48

697. RICHARDS
    Hn. R./Elvira Biser 10/23/25
698. RICHARDSON
    John/Cath. Smith 9/16/02
    Jm./Jane Smith 5/9/08
    Jos./Mary Keefer 10/28/16
    Elijah/Eliza Allen 12/5/34
    Rob./Na. Ridenour 5/10/49
    John/Ferlinda Frazier 6/26/50
699. RICHES
    Rufus/Mary Crunkleton 12/26/15
700. RICK
    Lau./Mary Moore 4/26/09
701. RICKENBAUGH
    Hn./Eliz. Cushwa 3/23/14
    Mt./Mary Lewis 4/10/18
    Dv./Marg. Sprecher 2/26/23
702. RICKMAN
    Geo./Mary Colyer 7/16/17
703. RICKTER (REICHTER)
    Chn. I./Na. Gruber 4/26/36
    Chas./Caroline Potts 7/9/60
704. RIDDLE
    Wm. N./Eliz. Ragan 5/3/49
705. RIDDLEMOSER
    Wm. A./E.A.M. George 1/5/47
706. RIDENOUR
    Chr./Eliz. Bowers 3/28/00
    Geo./Molly Coon 6/4/03
    Mt./Sus. Lizer 4/23/03
    Conrad/Barb. Hufman 4/30/04
    John/Dorothy Funk 12/11/05
    Benj./Mary Renner 11/29/06
    Jc./Marg. Shupe 10/15/08
    Fred./Sus. Hower 6/26/11
    John/Eliz. Goll 2/13/13
    Mt./Ann Clapsaddle 7/20/13
    Nich./Mary Brewah 1/16/13
    Is./Cath. Startzman 12/21/15
    Jc./Eliz. Flory 12/2/15
    Jc./Sr. Hose 1/5/15
    Matthias/Eliz. Hunt 11/8/17
    Nich. Jr./Cath. Holtzman 12/1/18
    John/Cath. Kendle 11/4/19
    Dv./Eliz. Brewer 3/28/21
    Jon./Elenor Ridenour 12/28/21
    Jos./Eliz. Markin 5/22/21
    John D./Sr. Protzman 9/14/24
    Jon./Sr. Reed 3/14/25
    Dv./Susan Ebreht 11/25/28
    Geo./Susan Unger 3/16/28
    Dn./Sr. Bean 1/13/30
    Dv./Cath. Harbine 11/2/30
    Dv./Marg. Kausler 4/8/30
    Hn./Mary Ann Hyland 9/23/30
    Dn./Eliz. Brown 7/27/31
    Mt./Marg. Grush 5/21/32

706. RIDENOUR (Continued)
Sam./Eliz. Flory 3/28/32
Sam./Eliz. Burkhart 5/9/33
Is./Sr. Deal 3/8/38
Chas./Susan Welshans 12/25/41
Benj./Mary E. Harsh 7/3/46
Jc. Adam/Sr. Kline 10/3/49
Jc./Jane R. Jumper 8/19/52
Sol./Sr. C. Fisher 1/29/56
Benj./Susan Houser 8/1/57
John E./Maria R. Carver 10/1/57
Benj./Ann M. Prier 1/7/58
Hiram Cyrus/Mary Ann Eliz. Hultz
   9/15/58
Wm. F./Eliz. A. Stevenson 11/23/58
Jc. H./Keziah Stottlemyer 10/16/60
707. RIDGLEY
Rich./Louisa Snyder 10/22/41
708. RIFFEY
Geo./Mary Baugh 8/6/21
709. RIGGES
Ed./Eliza Robey 2/4/06
710. RIGHT
Jm./Patty Hibbins 5/16/99
711. RIGLER
Stephen/Mary Showaker 3/23/13
712. RILEY
Tho./Na. Brown 4/9/10
Dennis/Mary Galrock 3/31/15
John/Ros. Prior 6/26/49
Geo./Lydia A. Dennis 10/19/52
713. RINEHART (RHINEHART, REINHARD)
And./Mary Cretzinger 8/14/12
Dv./Cath. Wolfe 5/27/16
Jon./Sus. Bovey 6/21/17
Jc./Eliz. Westenberger 3/1/27
Sam./Lydia Pritt 5/3/30
Dv./Anna Prett 9/21/35
Sam./Eliz. Bevans 10/23/38
Chn./Cath. Grove 3/3/41
Hn./Ellen Maria Beard 2/14/44
Dv./Cath. Faulder 2/25/46
John/Mary Powers 9/10/47
Dn./Eliza Miller 3/29/51
Hn./Malinda Young 9/21/53
714. RINGER
Pt./Mary Powless 12/2/05
John/Eliz. Reed 6/21/18
Jc./Cath. Gardner 5/19/19
John/Mary Witmer 11/23/22
Rich./Sr. Smith 12/4/24
Sam./Evy Ann Shriner 11/18/33
Pt./Elmira Slifer 9/16/40
John H./Barbary Eavey 4/11/48
Jobaretha E./Adeline Hanna 8/5/55
Pt./Orinda Lowman 12/29/57
715. RINOLL
Pt./Na. Shank 4/16/10

Pt./Cath. Row 6/11/12
Sam./Eliz. Baker 12/9/12
716. RIPLEY
Jc./Matilda Hayes 4/6/10
717. RIPPLE
Lewis Jr./Eliz. Ann Newcomer 2/13/50
John/Mary Ann Longanecker 4/25/45
718. RISER (RIZER)
Geo./Eliz. Potter 8/10/19
Wm./Eliz. Myers 7/20/52
719. RISSLE
John/Sus. Haye 9/26/11
720. RITCHIE
John/Mary Ann McElroy 10/12/22
721. RITTER
Jc./Mary Bowers 3/7/27
Jm./Sr. Cath. Davis 6/20/59
722. RITZ (RITIS)
Jos./Eliz. Grove 10/20/01
Sol./Mary Wise 10/17/08
723. RIVER
Pt./Eliz. Roach 3/11/19
724. RIXEY
Wm./Mary Brent 10/3/14
725. ROACH
Rob./Cath. Miller 1/27/14
Thornton/Eliz. Dorsey 6/3/39
Thornton/Marg. Brolier 4/8/51
Rob. S./Kate Rowland 2/14/54
726. ROANE (RHONE)
Ed./Nora Murphey 5/9/33
Hn./Susan Slice 4/25/44
Hn./Cath. Guringer 7/11/53
727. ROARK
Barney/Anna I. Hoffman 11/25/34
728. ROBBINS
John K./Mary H. Newkirk 1/17/33
729. ROBERTS
Wm./Eliza Cease 1/19/04
Sam./Han. Davis 6/20/12
Jos./Marg. Rager 1/29/16
John/Mar. Little 8/11/19
Lemmon/Eliz. Simmons 12/23/30
Jos./Na. Palmer 2/3/35
John/Rosa Ann McLaughlin 6/4/40
Edmond H./Am. A. Seibert 6/13/43
John/Emily Seiss 4/21/47
Wm. M./Susan V. Helfestay 2/15/53
Jm. F./Sirena E. Hiltabridel 8/2/58
730. ROBERTSON
John/Mary Harry 1/7/12
Tho./Marg. McKee 1/13/19
Is./Marg. Albert 4/19/21
Wm./Eliza Grieves 6/25/22
Wm./Sr. Ann Clark 12/29/36
Tho. G./Caroline V. Powles 9/9/44
John/Mary C. Smith 1/24/53

731. ROBINET (ROBINETTE)
Elijah/Han. Chaney 8/1/12
732. ROBINSON
Wm./Eliz. Windell 5/5/00
Jm./Eve Verrow 7/24/24
Wm./Phebe Poffenberger 8/13/27
John/Han. Thomas 9/15/30
Chas./Mary Billmyer 4/14/31
N.B./Maria Dillon 11/18/33
Ed./Mary Bushels 12/4/35
Alex./Sus. Masener 2/16/40
Hez./Mary Gruver 6/29/41
Elias/Ellen Knipple 12/22/42
Geo. W./Cath. Smith 10/12/48
733. ROBY (ROBEY)
Owen/Priscilla Hayes 9/7/12
Wm./Cordela Lynch 4/6/14
734. ROCH
Hugh/Mary Little 8/21/40
735. ROCK
John/Mary Graham 11/26/32
736. ROCKWOOD
Mich./Esther Albright 5/6/08
737. RODERAUF
Jm./Cath. Hussang 1/10/11
738. RODGERS
Pat./Sr. Karogyl 1/30/34
Jos./Maria Alison 11/29/45
739. RODRICK (RHODERICK)
Dn./Mary Ann Sullivan 7/24/09
Perry/So. Blessing 12/20/44
Geo./Ann So. Smith 4/3/46
Geo. W./Mary Hedrick 4/1/56
Geo W./Ann Coffman 2/28/60
740. ROGAN
Pat./Ann Loan 8/16/40
741. ROGERS
Jos./Tracy Carry 4/19/02
Ruben/Mary Ann King 3/18/30
742. ROHE
John Hn./Ann Wyland 12/2/45
743. ROHRBACK
John/Eliz. Hill 2/11/02
Hn./Barb. Barber 1/22/06
Jc./Mary Smith 3/24/17
John/Mary Smith 12/9/18
John/Ros. Myers 5/26/28
Dn./Mary Hill 3/7/40
Jc. Jr./Na. Ann Haynes 1/7/40
Benj. F./Ann S. Wagoner 2/24/51
Noah/Sr. Ann Rohrer 12/16/51
Jos./Kate Boyd 10/29/56
Dn./Deana Rohrback 9/23/59
744. ROHRER
John/Eliz. Keplinger 12/13/00
Dv./Sus. Funk 9/29/01

Dn./Mary Koon 4/1/02
Mt./Esther Bachtell 9/5/03
Fred./Maria Burr 4/16/05
John/Eliz. Funk 8/31/08
Sam./Mag. Rohrer 6/18/10
Jc./Mag. Rohrer 3/2/11
Sam./Reb. Fink 3/22/12
Hn./Marg. Hedrick 7/31/13
John/Mary Nichodemus 5/4/16
Fred. Jr./Eliz. Thomas 5/11/18
John/Sus. Poffenberger 8/16/19
Jc./Mary Funk 5/16/20
Chn./Eliz. Huffer 4/9/21
Sam./Eliz. Crampton 3/9/22
Jc./Eliz. Hill 3/31/25
Jc./Ros. Keefauver 4/8/25
Jc. M./Mary Smith 12/29/25
John M. Jr./Mary Hildebrand 11/10/25
Benj./So. Grim 7/25/26
Jos./Eliz. Thomas 11/18/28
Hn./Sus. Allabaugh 2/23/30
Mt./Mary Funk 10/19/30
Hn./Ann Maria Householder 12/20/31
Hn. B./Mar. Ann Piper 3/21/35
Josiah C./Caroline A. Showman 2/18/35
Dv./Am. Syderstick 3/15/36
John/Eliz. Ridenour 2/24/38
Fred. B./Har. Rohrer 6/1/40
Is./Eliz. Byers 3/23/41
Benoni/Reb. Loose 3/19/42
Jer. E./Malinda J. Mullendore 12/7/43
Geo. C./Mahala A. Mullendore 3/4/44
Jc./Mahala Poffenberger 7/6/44
Jos./Eliz. Ann Bargesser 3/11/44
Abr./Mary Geltmaker 3/4/45
Mahlon/Mahala Leaser 1/12/47
Mt./Tracy Stine 8/18/47
Ph. T./Matilda Creamer 4/10/47
Geo. C./So. E. Deaner 5/2/48
Hn. C./Mary Mumma 12/20/49
John/Ros. Finebruck 11/21/49
Mt./Ann Zimmerman 2/16/49
Jos./Susan Palmer 3/13/50
Sam./Har. E. Rohrer 1/20/52
Mt. T./Marg. Ann Eavey 2/28/53
Sam./Eliz. C. Ohr 2/20/56
Hn./Cath. Bowers 2/25/57
Hn./Eliza Ann Rohrer 11/22/57
John Hn./Cecelia Ann Herd 8/3/58
745. ROMAN
Jm. D./Louisa M. Kennedy 9/26/37
Benj. F./Sr. Jacques 3/16/52
746. ROMINE
Jesse/Han. Stump 11/20/10
747. RONEMOUS
Lewis/Maria Jane Peacher 1/29/58
748. RONEY
John/Chna. Ambrose 4/19/14

89

749. ROOF
Jc./Eliz. Albert 10/17/14
Sam./Cath. Weddle 12/5/60
750. ROOP
John/Cath. Hine 12/26/35
751. ROOT (ROOTS)
John/Cath. Moore 3/24/12
Hn./Mary Massillias 1/1/27
Dn./Sus. Room 3/13/30
Jc./Mar. Browning 11/9/39
752. ROOTHS
Conrad/Eve Lout 11/20/50
753. ROPER
Jm./Na. Curuthers 1/18/10
Jm./Eliz. Laley 4/30/38
754. ROSCOE
Dv. C./Mary Ever Edwards 6/19/17
755. ROSE
Geo./Cath. Serbey 9/27/07
Hugh/Polly Thresher 8/3/09
Wm./Na. Green 4/14/10
John/Char. Anderson 9/7/12
756. ROSEBERRY
Joshua/Reb. Bell 8/27/52
757. ROSENBERGER
Bart./Marg. A. Watson 1/30/47
Fred./Mary C. Watson 8/12/50
758. ROSENSTOCK
Sam./Sr. Coffman 5/27/54
759. ROSS
Geo. G./Eliza Pindell 5/2/09
Lampkin/Eliz. Beckley 12/31/19
Wm. S./Eleanor Dagenhart 4/24/23
Al./Mary Miller 5/28/35
Sam./Sus. Wyant 3/8/37
Rich./Cath. Mooney 11/18/43
760. ROSSER
Jm. W./Ann C. Thompson 11/8/28
761. ROTHRACK (ROTHRICK)
Ph./Sus. Ollabaugh 6/13/38
762. ROUCH
Jm./Marg. Lynch 6/25/36
763. ROUGH
Mich./Cath. Weitzell 10/21/05
764. ROULETT (RULETT)
Tho./Sus. McKesick 3/30/07
John/Sr. Hoffman 9/13/21
Wm./Marg. Ann Miller 3/2/47
765. ROUP
John/Cath. Bloomanour 5/3/37
766. ROUSH (ROUSCH)
And./Betsey Biddle 2/28/11
Mt./Marg. Patton 6/26/17
767. ROUSKULP
Upton/Joanna Weis 7/22/44
768. ROUTZHAN
Jm./Eliz. M. Heaberly 1/20/46

769. ROW (ROWE)
Wm./Mary Stare 2/23/02
Ph./Eliz. Harshberger 10/10/06
Abr./Eliz. Crouse 11/22/14
Hn./Sr. Zimmerman 4/8/18
Sam./Eliz. Hinty 4/11/21
John/Marg. Billmyer 3/14/26
Rich./Mary Monninger 12/24/27
Anthony/Ann Tho. McWilliams 3/12/38
Rich./Susan L. Snider 4/23/40
Sam./Mary Ann Leggett 3/24/45
Hiram/Cath. Boward 3/6/51
Jc./Levina Gaylor 2/27/51
Benj./Ann R. Yeakel 2/15/54
Ed./Eliz. Sharey 7/6/58
770. ROWENGAN
Sol./Eliz. Dusing 10/6/14
771. ROWLAND (ROLAND)
John/Cath. Null 4/10/04
John Jr./Anne Timmerman 3/31/06
Abr./Eliz. Funk 6/5/10
Sam./Lydia Harden 8/9/16
Chn./Barb. Bear 9/30/17
Is./Eliz. Rowland 5/11/23
Jos./Mary Hefflebower 3/20/23
Emanuel/Na. Stover 3/22/24
Jc./Eliz. Stover 3/1/25
Is./Chna. Avey 3/25/29
Jonas/Ann Gilbert 3/1/32
Dn./Eliz. Rhinehart 10/8/33
Is./Mar. Adams 5/4/33
Is./Na. Gruber 4/26/36
Jos./Reb. Resley 2/16/42
Hn./Eliz. Myley 5/21/45
And./Mary Ann Bear 1/26/46
John F./Cath. Shafer 1/26/50
Benj./Eliz. Funk 1/9/55
Dv. B./Sr. Ann Conrad 12/17/55
Dn. G./Na. Stoner 1/28/57
Jer./Cath. Fessler 5/19/58
Amos/Eliz. Bowman 1/17/59
John F./Lydia Ann Stifler 9/2/54
Dv. B./Cath. Coup 10/8/51
772. ROWLER
Jc./Kitty Burckhartt 9/6/21
773. ROYER
Jc./Mary Kaigy 4/9/14
Sam./Mary Hamaker 3/6/39
774. RUBT
Dn./Eliz. Piper 10/11/14
775. RUCH
Hn./Barbary Middlekauff 11/4/33
776. RUDISILL
Geo./Sr. Ann Lowery 10/23/39
Mich./Mar. M. Lewis 2/15/44
Jc./Marg. Tenant 8/10/46
Dv./Tracey Bomberger 12/11/47

777. RUDY (ROODY)
    Jos./Barb. Miller 11/21/14
    Emanuel/Sr. Westenberger 9/9/18
    Emanuel/Eliz. Miller 12/22/32
    Wash./Levinia Huntsberry 7/28/46
    Emanuel/Eliz. Young 10/15/57
778. RUFFNER
    John/Eliz. Long 6/20/17
779. RUMBURGER
    Fares/Sr. Shaneberger 11/20/38
    Phares/Mary Monroe 6/4/46
780. RUMMELL
    Wm./Eliza Edwards 1/5/32
781. RUNKLE
    John/Polly Emmerick 10/27/14
782. RUNNER
    Wm./Reb. Miller 6/23/17
    Mich./Sr. Hamm 6/13/21
783. RUSH
    Jon./Peggy Rush 11/1/10
    Benj./Ann Robertson 3/26/30
    Wm./Eliza Jane Turner 5/15/49
784. RUSSELL
    Sam./Eliz. Ground 8/28/06
    Hugh/Ann Webb 2/21/07
    John I./Susan Flory 10/11/30

    Benj./Sr. Bender 2/26/31
    Dv./Eliz. Poffenberger 3/30/33
    Tho./Charity Crowl 5/15/39
    Jc./Eliz. Hedden 5/29/48
785. RUTH
    Wm./Julia Ann Wolf 4/2/51
786. RUTHRAUFF
    Jc. A./Eleanora Eakle 11/27/48
787. RUTTER
    Walter/Peggy Moninger 8/15/99
    Edmund Jr./Eliz. Sibert 10/19/05
    Benj./Sr. Muse 6/10/12
    John/Mary Kinsell 6/20/15
    Mt./Mary Garver 11/23/19
788. RYAN
    Nich. P./Na. Garrity 7/22/24
    Rody/Mary Donnelly 5/30/24
    Hn./Eliz. Agnes Baker 10/29/56
789. RYE
    Hn./Eliz. Wade 1/3/35
    Jm. W./Susan M. Johnston 9/27/42
790. RYENULL
    Hn./Anna Kailer 2/10/41
791. RYNER
    Pt./Mary Huffman 6/7/07

1. SACKETT
   Milton/Ann Sterrett 12/10/06
2. SAGER
   John/Mary Beard 8/2/15
   Jc. Jr./Mary Newcomer 8/17/19
   Dn./Char. Carn 12/21/39
   John/Cath. Swope 8/10/54
3. SAILOR (SAILER, SALOR, SAYLOR, SAYLER)
   Pt. Jr./Cath. Rowland 4/8/06
   John/Eliz. Miller 11/22/10
   Fred./Sus. Thumb 8/25/18
   John/Tereshia Shecter 11/26/31
   Jos./Eliz. Phillips 3/17/40
   Jc./Cath. Matilda Hahn 7/7/42
   Dn./Barb. Pretzler 10/27/57
   Ed./Matilda Hewett 8/4/57
   Hn./Marg. Gray 11/16/57
4. ST. CLAIR
   Wm./Mary Embigh 5/7/06
5. ST. JOHN
   John C./Eve Marshall 6/18/17
6. ST. MIRE
   Dv./Eve Welty 7/23/03
7. SALLY
   Wm./Mary Davit 5/17/38
8. SAMMONS
   John/So. Lee 12/14/58
9. SAMS
   Carlton C./Char. D. Wever 11/4/42
10. SANDERS (SAUNDERS, SONDERS)
    Jm./Sr. Smith 9/6/00
    Geo./Eliz. Locker 2/23/05
    Crayton/Cath. Ebersole 10/14/31
    Wm./Eliz. Smice 1/1/33
    W.N.H./Sr. E. Garnheart 7/19/48
11. SANDMAN
    Geo./Cath. Schnider 8/26/19
12. SANDS
    Geo. W./Ann Marie Cronise 8/18/21
    Wm./Ann M. Campbell 1/18/55
    Rob./Hen. L. King 9/8/60
13. SANGIRE
    Abr./Marg. Tritle 4/19/31
14. SANNERS
    Vincent Jr./Sus. Hudgell 3/15/24
15. SANTMAN (SAUNTMAN)
    John/Mary Snyder 8/1/11
16. SANTZ
    John F./Ann Eliz. Hartman 3/23/60
17. SAPPINTON
    Tho./Mary Shutz 4/3/13
18. SAVAGE
    John/Adalaide H. Hughes 12/30/30
19. SAVILLE
    Arthur/Ann R. Myers 2/23/52
    Arch./Ellen Orrick 4/11/54
20. SAWVILLE
    John/Han. Pottorf 3/18/23

21. SAYLES
    Tho./Cath. Miller 2/4/51
22. SCHAMER
    Hn. Wm./Amanda H. Zimmerman 8/2/47
23. SCHETTON
    Dv./Mary Emmert 11/14/20
24. SCHILDNECHT (SHILDNECHT)
    Wm./Massey Guyder 12/26/25
    Hn./Susan Snyder 1/10/48
    Wm. H./Eliz. Carver 10/25/59
    Ezra/Kate Welsh 8/16/60
25. SCHLECHT
    John M./Eliz. C. Ridenour 9/29/29
26. SCHLEY (SCHLEIGH, SLEIGH)
    Sam./Cath. Rape 7/16/04
    John Jr./Ann Maria Artz 12/1/19
    Wm./Ann C. Ringgold 9/28/24
    Geo./Mary Hill 6/26/39
    John/Cath. Louisa Mittag 8/15/39
    Jm. M./Ellen Stull 2/6/38
    Jc. Brown/Sr. Ann Ragan 12/27/42
    Fred. A./Barb. Hall 6/15/43
    John Ed./Mary Virginia Towner 10/21/44
    Chas. A./Augusta Boyd 4/24/60
27. SCHLOCKERBECK
    Jc./Cath. Smith 11/18/56
28. SCHMITT
    Bernadotte/Barbary S. Bender 4/20/54
29. SCHMUCKER
    Sam./Eleanora Geiger 2/28/21
30. SCHNEBLY
    Dn./Cath. Rench 4/8/06
    John/Sus. Kershner 7/24/10
    John/Betsy Shaey 4/5/11
    Hn./Mary Schnebly 1/23/12
    Jm./Cath. Dunn 7/24/13
    Dn. H./AnnMarie Rench (Reach) 1/3/14
    Hn. C./Hen. M. Chew 4/26/14
    John/Eliza Kealhofer 3/24/19
    Dn./Marg. Rench 7/4/20
    John/Lydia Ressly 2/28/22
    Dn./Jane E. Turner 3/16/39
    Jos. R./Sr. Middlekauff 2/1/40
    Dn. H./Susan S. Miller 3/21/48
    Jos. Sprigg/Ann Eliz. Stonebraker 2/4/56
    Jc./Frances M. Rowland 9/8/57
    Melchor M./Ann Reb. Alter 2/8/59
    Al./Kate S. Hollman 6/26/60
31. SCHNECKENBERGER
    Sam./Barbary Bowers 8/20/34
32. SCHNIRES
    Geo./Maria C. Russi 9/2/34
33. SCHOOBE
    Cratch/Eliz. Keefer 6/22/55
34. SCHOPPERT
    Abr. Alex./Aire Ellen Merchant 9/21/60
35. SCHREIDER
    Hn./So. Rapp 8/4/54

36. SCHROY
John/Rachel Domer 9/24/11
37. SCHUBERT
Hn./Eva Freidland 8/14/47
38. SCISTER
Dv./Reb. Evans 11/23/09
39. SCOGGINS
John/Cath. Matzebaugh 3/24/10
40. SCOTT
Chas./Eliz. Newell 9/25/06
Pat./Mary Kenney 3/31/34
Wm./Susan Shafer 10/1/35
Hn./Anna Virginia Murray 1/28/45
41. SCRIVNER
Ed./Mary Carey 3/9/18
42. SCUFFINS
Chas./Caroline Muck 1/28/52
43. SCURY
John/Mary Burns 5/5/35
44. SEAGER
Benj./Susan Thompson 12/28/42
45. SEALEY
John/Sr. Ann Perry 7/19/30
46. SEAMAN
Jc. Kelb/Mariah Legett 2/10/19
Wm./Cath. Forney 4/14/46
Geo./Sr. McCaffrey 6/15/59
47. SEAPORD (SEAPORT)
Adam/Mary Beiterly 3/23/09
48. SEATJUIRO
Jc./Mary Protzman 12/13/13
49. SECKMAN
Benj./Mary Ann Lowry 11/13/30
50. SECORE
Wm./Sr. E. Spessard 12/23/46
51. SEDGWICK
Sam./Jane Nevit 12/20/15
52. SEELER
Is./Eliz. Judy 8/15/40
53. SEEVERS
Ph./Sr. Ohr 10/10/16
54. SEIBER
Dn. P./Eliz. Spangler 2/25/46
55. SEIBERT (SIBERT, SIABORT, SEYBERT)
Jc./Mag. Stonebraker 3/13/02
John/Mag. Springer 7/23/04
John/Ann Shoop 10/19/05
Hn./Cath. Butterbaugh 4/8/08
Jc./Mary Jordon 8/8/08
Pt./Mary Seibert 3/21/08
Jc./Eliz. Seibert 5/29/11
Hn./Mary Hoss 8/4/12
Mich./Eliz. Brewer 1/3/12
Geo./Cath. Ridenour 10/3/15
John/Dorothy Tysher 6/22/15

Mich./Rosa Troup 1/19/36
Sam./Lydia Bentz 12/28/37
John/Mary Ann Frazier 1/3/39
Jos./Susan S. Stake 2/23/46
Sam./Ann Troup 2/3/52
Dv./Julia Eliz. Ankeney 8/27/53
56. SEIGHMAN
John/Han. Point 9/3/25
Wm. V./Isa. J. Cunningham 3/13/54
Geo. H./Sr. Needy 3/20/56
John D./Mary C. Warble 2/18/58
S.T./Annie Benner 11/3/59
57. SEIGLER (SIGLER)
Hn./Mag. Keefauver 9/4/04
Fred./Eliz. Lantz 8/13/05
Abr./Eliz. Beltzer 6/12/18
John/Sr. Ann Baker 2/7/18
John/Cath. Spielman 12/21/19
And./Sr. Marker 12/6/25
Geo./Na. Shaw 4/2/25
John Jc./Mary Ellen Howard 3/19/47
58. SEISS
Hiram S./Mary Cramer 12/11/58
59. SEITZ
John/Mary Pinkstaff 10/30/10
60. SELL
Dn./Mary Ann Ickes 10/26/52
61. SELLERS (SELLARS)
John/Sus. Miller 4/13/15
Dv./Eliz. Lantz 4/25/28
62. SELLMAN
Howard J./Nanny S. Hebb 3/16/55
63. SELSAM
John C./Mary Ann Cunningham 8/3/54
64. SELSER
Jm./Lydia Rembrow 10/17/06
65. SEMBARGER
Jos. (or Levi?)/Chna. Seber (or Leber?)
4/16/35
66. SEMLER (SIMLER)
Lewis/So. Rupp 5/28/55
And./Mary C. Creamer 8/15/58
Gotleib/Mary Butts 1/6/59
67. SEMMES
Tho./Mary Miller 11/8/03
68. SENEINDIVER
Lewis/Mary E. Choppert 4/14/53
69. SENSEL
John/Cath. R. Schnebly 12/16/28
Mt./Mina Stuck 8/10/49
70. SENSENBAUGH
Jc./Cath. Kline 4/13/24
71. SENTMYER
Dn./Molly Zeigler 3/16/18
72. SERGANT
Arch./Reb. Reynolds 1/13/16

93

73. SEYMORE
    I.H./Caroline V.P. McCardle 2/7/54
    W.W./Sr. Cath. Ramy 1/4/58
74. SEYSTER
    Mich./Mary Wolfkill 12/1/21
    And. K./Cath. G. Harry 11/15/52
    Dv./Cath. H. Newcomer 2/16/54
75. SHACK
    Geo./Matilda Emerson 2/27/41
76. SHACKLE (SHACKLES)
    Pt./Eliz. Harris 11/26/14
77. SHACKLEFORD
    John/Mary Ellen James 5/17/28
    John/Rachel Nighswander 3/9/33
    Coleman/Marg. Sourbeer 5/27/44
78. SHAFFER (SHAFER, SCHAFFER)
    Geo./Cath. Locker 3/16/01
    Ph./Ann Monser 4/6/01
    Leo./Mary Shraeder 1/21/06
    John/Cath. Miller 1/17/09
    John/Cath. Warner 3/28/09
    John/Peggy Writs 5/12/12
    Paul/Eve Funk 3/19/12
    Jc./Gertrude Kauffman 8/21/13
    Geo./Eliz. Hersh 4/28/14
    Dn./Eliz. Giltner 10/2/17
    John/Susan Curtis 9/21/20
    Jon./Sus. Ringger 12/25/20
    Geo./Mar. Swearinger 11/30/24
    Jc./Lydia Eavey 1/19/25
    Sam./Eliz. Petre 3/3/25
    Dn. A./Eliz. Dutro 11/25/31
    John Jr./Mary Ann Hershey 11/23/31
    Alex./Leah S. Eakle 9/10/34
    John/Susan Conner 7/30/34
    John P./Chna. Finkabine 5/1/38
    Jos./Maybelle M. Smith 6/28/42
    John/Mary E. Gregory 9/15/43
    Adam M./Mary Long 4/1/44
    Pt./Barb. Wisner 2/27/49
    Alex./Cath. Long 1/21/50
    Dn./Sabret Ann Creager 7/21/51
    Rob. J./Mary E. Chambers 10/2/51
    Wm./Susan Pickett 12/4/54
    Sam./Eliz. Stouffer 4/7/55
    Benj. F./Han. V. McCauley 12/30/58
    I.P./Amanda Stillwell 2/11/59
79. SHAFFNER
    John/Mary Wickert 7/13/15
    Hn. S./Rachel Meredith 4/16/27
80. SHAM
    Jos./Pheby Taylor 4/22/37
81. SHAMEL (SCHAMEL)
    Pt. H./Mary Carty 10/16/39
    Jc./Sr. Poffenberger 8/19/53
    Josiah/Eliz. Myers 1/25/54
82. SHANEBARGER (SHANABERGER)
    Jc./So. Grosh 3/15/35

83. SHANEFELT (SHANEFELTS, SHANEFIELD,
    SHANEYFIELD, SHONEFIELD, SHONEYFELT)
    Hn./Sus. Sailor 5/15/00
    And./Eliz. Sailor 4/10/01
    Dv./Mary Nighswander 5/25/01
    Wm./Mary Earlywine 10/24/01
    Pt./Eliz. Funk 5/8/22
    And./Sr. Ann Louisa Brannon 3/21/22
    Hn./Han. Hartle 3/1/24
    Abr./Na. Leckrone 10/24/26
    Dn./Sr. Funk 3/16/30
84. SHANER
    Jc./Marg. Miller 9/17/31
85. SHANK
    Chn./Cath. Lautehaw 9/4/04
    Jc./Betsy Resh 1/14/04
    Jc./Cath. Dutterow 11/27/04
    Abr./Na. Resh 5/3/06
    Hn./Barb. Meshell 2/13/10
    Adam/Peggy Muck 2/14/11
    Dn./Mary Hoffman 12/26/11
    Jc./Cath. Fogler 10/5/11
    Geo./Cath. Adams 3/15/14
    Pt./Mary Little 8/10/20
    Hn./Cath. Cox 11/20/22
    And./Esther Hoover 2/20/27
    Jc. R./Mary Hoover 2/16/30
    Abr./Lau Hoover 3/11/34
    Sol./Sr. Kayler 2/19/34
    Hn. B./Ann Eliza Myers 5/21/42
    Noah/Susan Shank 4/10/43
    Jc./Leah Shank 11/26/45
    Hn. J./Lydia Rowland 9/7/47
    Geo. W./Susan Malone 12/26/48
    Jc./Eliz. Shoop 3/3/49
    Jon./Jane Eichelberger 1/3/49
    Benj./Reb. Krouse 3/24/51
    Chn. P./Eliz. Gower 12/23/51
    Wm./Susan Easterday 8/25/51
    Lancelotte/Mary A. Miller 12/22/52
    Jos. S./Mary Ann Snavely 3/24/53
    John D./Mary C. Brewer 5/30/53
    Hn./Cath. Harpman 8/11/54
    And. J./Rose M. Martin 4/10/55
    Tobias/Cath. Stite 10/24/55
    Is./Eliz. Unger 5/15/57
    Jc./Am. Eddy 11/30/59
    Jm. M./So. Strause 10/6/59
    Emanuel/Mary Cath. Palmer 10/9/60
    John/Ann Ferena Starr 12/20/60
86. SHANNON (SHANON)
    Jos./Eliz. Artz 8/24/17
87. SHARER (SHEARER)
    Sam./Eliz. Rew 6/12/02
    John/Na. Newcomer 4/19/06
    Jc./Am. Root 3/13/30
    Fred./Susan E. Gordon 1/15/38
    John/Priscilla Burns 5/30/46

94

88. SHARKEY
   Geo./Elitia McKiernan 8/4/03
89. SHARP
   Geo./Phebe Downing 8/31/09
   John/Cath. Kessane (Keesecker in
      cross-index) 4/9/14
90. SHARRARD (SHERRARD)
   Jm./Anna Smith 3/10/23
   Wm./Har. E. Daniels 9/24/49
   Hugh Lyle/Amanda C. Easterday 1/3/60
91. SHARRICK
   Jos./Sr. Hamm 4/15/28
92. SHATT
   Geo./Mary Critzer 8/20/03
93. SHATTENSE
   O.S./Maria Stake 10/3/39
94. SHATZLEY
   Jos./Mar. A. Ingman 12/16/51
95. SHAW
   Jc./Sus. Meyers 11/24/03
   Jc./Sus. Pence 9/21/05
   John/Julian Coon 2/7/26
   Jc./Betsey Ridenour 3/24/31
   John/Marg. Kretser 6/2/34
   Levi R./Mary Morrison 3/23/52
96. SHAWEN
   Cornelius/Isa. V. Albert 2/17/47
97. SHAY (SHEA)
   Tho./Marg. Gannon 11/14/35
   Bennett/Matilda Chambers 8/30/43
98. SHECKLES
   Rich./Elisha Worster 7/11/32
   Rich./Maria Gearing 7/18/37
99. SHECTER (SCHECHTER)
   Hn./Mary Nicodemus 2/27/02
   Hn./Sus. Wolf 4/29/09
   Jc./Lydia Rowland 11/24/14
   Sam./Marg. Bond 4/3/24
   Hn./Terecy Easterday 12/22/25
   Joshua/Milly Beltzer 6/16/28
   And./Willimina Youtz 5/6/42
100. SHEDERICK
   Mich./So. Mouse 10/16/47
101. SHEELEY (SHEELY, SHEALY, SHEALEY)
   Fred./Cath. Barnhiser 10/7/09
   Hn./Sr. Ridenour 10/13/40
   John/Maria Hose 7/22/40
   Sam./Ann Middlekauff 11/20/56
102. SHEESE
   Geo./Cath. Buckhart 3/25/09
103. SHEETS (SHEETZ, SHEITZ, SHEITS, SHEATS)
   Mich./Marg. Conrad 9/2/09
   John/Polly Yeakle 4/15/11
   Pt./Eliz. Coon 12/2/13
   Dn./Eliz. Sheetz 1/9/17
   Jos./Ann Horine 9/19/18
   Tho. O./Eliz. Hamm 10/4/24

   Jos./Char. Cook 12/23/37
   Reuben/Anna Harbaugh 1/22/50
104. SHEHAN
   Ed./Frances McIlheny 11/21/43
105. SHELLER
   Chn./Cath. Bostater 2/14/42
   Dn. L./Marg. Ann Rowland 11/15/55
   John/Eliz. Dunbarger 9/17/57
106. SHELLMAN
   John/Sus. Miller 10/28/13
107. SHELLY (SHELLEY)
   Jm./Mary Pindell 7/28/06
108. SHELTER
   John/Rachel Meharter 4/12/17
109. SHEPHERD (SHEPHARD, SHEPPARD)
   Pt./Sus. Leckrone 6/16/10
   Jm./Han. Hall 1/13/12
   Wm./Jane Johnston 10/5/12
   John/Mary L. Thompson 3/19/15
   Levi/Sr. Wilkins 4/4/16
   Sam./Eliz. Stephens 2/26/18
   Jm./Jane Claycomb (Claycomp) 8/12/21
   Wm./Eliza Dick 11/30/22
   Jm./Am. Sharp 5/5/28
   John/Marg. Souder 4/1/51
   Dv./Marg. Howard 11/7/54
110. SHEPLY
   Sam./Sus. Knave 5/11/15
111. SHERVIN
   Wm./Reb. Downs 1/25/45
112. SHEWBRIDGE
   Sam./Reb. McBride 12/7/31
113. SHEWEY
   John Jr./Ros. Keedy 5/17/05
114. SHICK
   Law./Eliz. Ebbert 7/15/00
   John/Sus. Servin 12/23/11
115. SHIFFLER
   John/Susan Thomas 8/31/33
   Sam./Ruana A. Snider 9/16/37
   Geo./Cath. Ifirt 7/30/50
   Geo./Eliz. Huffer 12/26/56
   Otho J./Ann C. Neikirk 1/28/60
116. SHILLING (SCHILLING)
   Hn./Eliz. Meligy 1/23/02
   John/Maria Dusinger 4/26/11
   Dv./Na. Siderstick 4/11/19
   Jonas/Marg. Lancaster 9/3/27
   Wm./Sus. Springer 2/6/43
   Hn./Har. South 11/20/45
   Lewis Hn./Debora Ann Walters 9/30/45
   John H./Mary Amanda McCoy 3/29/49
   Wm./Han. S. Long 3/25/50
   Fred. P./Marg. A. Kindell 4/6/53
   Joachim/Eliz. Markoe 2/21/53
   Sam./Isa. French 10/22/56

117. SHIMMEL
   Hn./Eliz. Poffenberger 11/17/08
118. SHINDLE (SCHINDEL, SCHINDLE)
   Dn./Susan Newcomer 12/23/33
   John/Marg. Neikirk 3/20/37
   Dv./Mag. Emmert 10/13/40
   Jon./Frances Tice 2/17/42
   Geo./Commella Winders 1/13/47
   Lewis/Susan Meyley 2/19/48
   And. J./Lavina Emmert 5/7/55
   Wm./Annie L. Funk 12/20/60
119. SHINDLER
   Dv./Mrs. Cath. Hewett 11/16/40
120. SHINGLE
   Ph./Cath. Hate 3/18/08
121. SHINNEBECK
   Fred./Maria Stoner 4/21/40
122. SHIPLER (SHIPPLER)
   Paul/Eliz. Albert 10/7/11
   Mt./Sr. Frey 12/1/59
123. SHIPLEY
   Rich. A./Ellen Alberts 8/7/34
   Tho./Caroline McCoy 8/8/46
124. SHIREMAN
   Jc./Moly Wilkins 6/15/13
125. SHIVES
   John W./Eliz. Lutz 11/26/56
126. SHLEGTER
   John/Caroline Sirt 11/28/40
127. SHNELL
   John/Rachel Keepers 1/1/08
128. SHOAFSTALL
   Geo./Ann Simpson 2/4/01
129. SHOCKEY
   Jc./Barb. Heffner 1/3/20
   Abr./Susan Hoover 9/25/38
130. SHOEMAKER
   Hn./Mary Shaffer 8/1/01
   Dn./Amanda Cassell 11/19/52
   Jc./Marg. England 3/28/56
131. SHOLL
   Mountjoy/Cath. Browning 11/16/25
132. SHOLLEBURGER
   Dv./Chna. Newcomer 4/13/25
133. SHOOK
   Wm./Marg. Huff 2/27/54
   And./Marg. Ann Silvers 6/21/56
134. SHOOP (SHOUP, SHUPE, SHUP, SHUPP)
   Conrad/Mary Fisher 3/20/01
   Dn./Eliz. Sholl 2/11/06
   Mich./Catey Grubb 8/29/15
   Sam./Eliz. Barlap 9/8/20
   Pt./Mary Hohn 8/17/22
   Jc./Sr. Dennison 4/30/23
   Jc./Cath. Dooble 12/8/23

Jos. S./Caroline H. Lincoln 5/24/28
   Chn./Eliz. Dellinger 10/27/41
   Geo./Mary C. Kinsell 10/20/42
   Abr./Ann Smith 11/28/48
   John/Eve Long 11/28/49
   John/Mary Ann Hinkle 2/18/50
   Hn./Cath. Burris 2/26/53
   Levi/Sr. Irwin 11/8/54
   Benj. F./Mary Ann Myers 1/8/57
135. SHORT
   Dv./Mary Pence 11/9/07
136. SHOUSE
   Ph./Mary Poffenberger 12/27/00
137. SHOVER
   Dv./Hester Blackmore 5/22/28
138. SHOW (SHOWE)
   Fred./Ellender Wells 7/12/99
   John/Mary Welty 2/28/35
   Hn./Mary Harper 7/18/35
   Hn./Marg. Atkinson 5/21/36
   Jc./Cath. Moninger 1/29/40
   Sam./Eliz. Knodle 11/29/41
   Geo./Eliz. Funk 3/23/47
   Tho./Sr. Mitchell 2/10/47
   Jc. Wesley/Susan Dovenberger 1/22/59
   Wm. H./Cath. A. McCoy 1/19/60
139. SHOWAKER (SHOWECKER)
   Wm./Na. Slice 3/23/20
   Jc./Ellen Welsh 2/7/26
140. SHOWALTER
   Chn./Sr. Bowman 10/2/38
141. SHOWER (SHOWERS)
   Abr./Eliz. Miller 3/28/07
   Emanuel/Han. Lindsay 11/4/11
   Ezekel/Sus. Seibert 7/21/14
142. SHOWMAN
   Jc./Sr. Grove 4/11/03
   John/Eliz. King 10/31/12
   Dv./Frances Sheets 11/28/13
   Dv. C./Kesia Dedie 2/6/13
   Pt./Cath. Snavely 9/4/16
   Adam/Na. Funk 4/20/19
   Dr. Sam./Chna. Newcomer 4/20/19
   Geo./Rachel Thompson 11/2/24
   Jc./Phebe Morrison 12/2/24
   John S./Louisa Hammond 3/14/36
   Hiram/Eliz. Hammond 4/11/43
   Milville S./Eliz. Jane Thomas 8/21/43
   Lorenzo K./Eliz. Snyder 10/19/52
   Al./Caroline E. Firey 5/19/53
   Ezra D./Susan E. Carty 1/13/59
   Raleigh/Eliz. R. Piper 11/26/60
143. SHRADER (SHREDER, SCHRADER)
   John/Reb. Lowe 4/10/00
144. SHRECK
   Conrad/Cath. Campbell 4/28/04

96

145. SHRIVER (SCHRIVER)
    Hn./Eliz. Shuck 2/21/12
    Dv./Eliz. Grush 11/25/20
    Elias/Jane Seyler 4/12/22
    Dn./Cath. Dundor 1/25/41
    John/Susan Neikirk 5/4/43
    Cyrus/Laura H. Elizabeth 11/9/57
146. SHRODES
    Rich./Na. Hastings 6/7/51
147. SHROEDER
    Hn./Chna. Shewey 2/5/03
    Hn./Cath. Longman 10/29/12
    Hn./Maria F. Burkett 3/23/15
148. SHROYER
    Adam/Marg. Shank 8/1/11
    Lewis/Delilah R. Pryer 8/28/60
149. SHRUM
    Geo./Sr. Alter 7/12/00 (in cross-
    index, Stuam is crossed out, re-
    placed with Shrum)
150. SHRYOCK (SCHRYOCK)
    Geo./Eliz. Lewis 1/12/08
    Dv./Sr. Wilson 11/9/15
151. SHUCK
    Is./Eliz. Wievel 6/10/15
152. SHUEY
    Wm. H./Cath. V. Baker 4/17/47
153. SHUFF
    Sol./Eliz. Smith 9/27/06
    Benj./Marg. Duff 7/8/30
154. SHUGARTS (SHUGARS)
    Zachariah/Sr. Binkley 6/22/11
    Wm./Mary Binkley 1/31/15
    John/Mary Reed 10/1/18
    Zachariah/Mary Keller 10/31/39
    Zachariah/Marg. Kelley 9/15/46
155. SHULL
    Pt./Eliz. Sharks 8/25/00
    Leo./Cath. Young 11/9/12
    John/Na. Homes 12/30/24
156. SHULTZ
    John/Nanny Lair 2/8/19
    Nich./Eliz. Shank 7/29/20
    Joshua/Cath. Fulton 12/22/38
    Chauncey F./Hadassah C. Brown
        5/24/41
157. SHUNK
    Casper/Mary I. Van Lear 1/17/55
158. SHUR
    Jc./Louisa Shafer 4/20/35
159. SHUTT
    Hn./So. Geeding 1/19/20
    Elias/Mary Keedy 12/22/30
    Geo. W./Eliza S. Bennett 5/20/34
    And./Cath. Fultz 8/22/48
    Pt./Cath. Burns 3/24/52
160. SHUTZ
    Jc./Mary Sheetz 2/8/16
    John/Eliza Mahugh 4/18/16

161. SIDEBOTTOM
    John/Eliz. Kraig 9/16/16
162. SIDLE (SYDEL, SEIDLES)
    Geo./Caty Nicholas 7/12/99
    Hn./Mary Weaddle 5/4/99
    Dv./Cath. Mann 2/11/19
    Adam/Mary Mann 5/9/20
163. SILER (SYLER)
    Geo./Roz. Dampsy 7/19/34
    Benj./Mary Wilson 6/9/41
    Earhart/Eliz. Anthony 3/26/56
164. SILVER (SILVERS)
    Ed./Mary Locker 9/28/18
    Sam./Na. Blackman 1/3/22
    Ed./Mary Landis 12/23/35
    John/Marg. Hagerman 10/24/60
165. SILVERSTICK
    John/Mary Driver 1/29/35
166. SIMKINS (SIMKINES)
    Darius/Roena Kadle 3/26/22
167. SIMMER (SIMMERS)
    Pt./Cath. Coss 1/2/07
168. SIMMERMAN
    John/Reb. Stephens 11/30/27
169. SIMMONS
    Jc./Eliz. Drury 3/28/12
    Tho./Mary Donnelly 3/24/18
    Jm./Susan Whetzel 12/15/40
170. SIMON (SIMONS)
    Chas. I./Ann B. Anderson 6/1/32
    Benj./Eliza Hill 12/4/55
171. SIMPSON
    Alex./Na. Sly 4/30/00
    Jesse/Na. Cathurs 12/30/00
    Eph./Tracey Rohrer 12/22/47
172. SINGER (SENGER)
    Fred./Molly Ridenour 2/27/06
    John/Han. Steffey 3/6/19
    Israel/Cath. Emmert 1/16/23
    Dn./Eliz. Bayers 11/4/44
173. SINGES
    Ph./Mary Ann Hartman 10/8/38
174. SINGHASS
    Chn./Ros. Baker 12/22/23
175. SIPE
    Tho./Marg. L. Hedden 12/17/53
176. SISLER
    John/Mary Bulott 7/7/23
    Wm./Sr. Twigg 12/18/24
    Mich./Bry Ann Newcomer 12/6/47
    John/Mary Himes 3/5/57
177. SISNLER
    Chn./Louisa Ridenour 1/2/54
178. SISSON
    Jesse/Eliz. Chapline 5/31/15
179. SKELLEY
    John/Eliz. Hose 12/30/46
180. SKIDMORE
    John/Matilda Bowers 6/5/35

97

181. SKINNER
    Jos. S./Susan E. Smith 4/12/36
    Jos. A./Barb. Martin 5/18/48
182. SLAGLE (SLAGEL, SCHLAGEL)
    John/Barb. Kelbertz 9/18/00
    Jc./Mag. Booby 12/8/02
    John/Sus. Gelwicks 10/14/08
    Dn./Minerva Hodge 2/15/58
183. SLIFER
    Stephen/Eliz. Flenner 1/25/02
    John/Mary Wolf 6/11/18 ("3d" pencil
      note after John)
    Dn./Ann Gantz 11/10/24
    Jon./Levenia Avey 11/7/45
    Mt./Ruanna Finefrock 10/4/48
    Randolph/Mary Ardinger 12/7/49
    Mt./Clara E. Shafer 6/4/57
    And./Maria Rowe 3/18/58
    John L./Amanda Hutzell 11/8/58
184. SLINKER (SLENKER, SLENCKER)
    Dn./Sr. Poffenberger 8/18/23
    Sol./Susan M. Ridenour 2/11/35
185. SLOAN
    Arch./Marg. Kephart 10/27/17
    Hn./Eliz. Myers 1/27/27
    John/Sr. Whetstone 12/20/38
186. SLOSSER (SLUSSER, SCHLOSSER)
    Geo./Mary Painter 9/10/05
    Pt./Eliz. Smith 3/12/05
    Dn./Eliz. Wolf 5/4/28
    Simon/Eliz. Keedy 5/31/30
    Simon/Mar. Neikirk 8/25/34
    Elie/Cath. Buterbaugh 12/17/39
    Dv./Magdalen Adams 4/18/45
    Tobias/Sus. Bender 2/22/47
187. SLOTHOVER
    Geo. Ed./Maria R. Randall 9/4/55
188. SLOWIE
    Hugh/Mary Reed 1/27/39
189. SLUSSMAN
    Geo./Cath. Henty 11/16/11
190. SLYER (SLYERS)
    Sam./Sr. Walters 1/23/31
191. SLYMAN
    Jm./Cath. Barnhart 9/2/39
192. SMALL
    Jc./Mag. Spangler 1/17/12
    Rob./Char. Malott 6/20/22
    John/Eliz. Venrick 9/4/30
    Rob. M./Joan E.M. Howard 9/5/38
    Sam./Ros. Wells 3/31/46
193. SMALLWOOD
    Van/Peggy Dowell 1/1/04
    Permenas/Deborah Brown 6/22/07
194. SMALTZER
    Leo./Cath. Barkman 8/14/24

195. SMART
    Dn./Rachel Lewis 8/5/02
196. SMAY
    Dn./Eliz. Fleson 10/23/06
197. SMELTZER
    Jc./Mary Ann Leighter 10/17/39
    Adam R./Mar. C. Knode 1/2/45
198. SMITH
    Jos./Eliz. Huffman 11/30/99
    Tho./Betsy Crovever 5/13/99
    John/So. Pultz 8/23/00
    John/Eliz. Richardson 11/27/00
    Matthias/Barb. Baechtel 11/4/01
    Tho./Mary Hogmire 1/8/01
    Geo./Polly Shall 2/25/02
    Jc./Mary McClain 5/30/04
    Jm./Eliz. Sibert 11/27/04
    Dv./Mary Wolslager 7/15/05
    Eph./Mag. Lantz 6/27/06
    Jos./Mary Swope 10/14/08
    Geo./Eliz. Dusinger 7/24/09
    Mich./Sus. Neybert 4/8/09
    Hn./Sus. Line 6/20/11
    Joshua/Cath. Koons 3/25/12
    Dv./Ros. Burner 10/11/15
    Jc./Mary Cramer 6/30/15
    John/Mary Williard 6/23/15
    Setatial/Mary Baringer 5/15/15
    Dn./Cath. Woleslager 3/7/16
    Dv./Peggy Harrow 4/9/16
    Geo./Sus. Federell 11/28/16
    Jc./Mary Brunner 4/13/16
    John/Peggy Middlekauff 11/12/16
    Hn. C.W./Mary Ensminger 4/17/17
    John/Eliz. Hammer 3/28/18
    John/Chna. Farst 6/19/18
    Jc./Eliz. Smith 2/17/19
    John/Sr. Poffenberger 9/4/19
    Zebina/Sr. Towson 3/25/20
    Jos./Na. Reel 1/5/21
    Josiah/Mary Dillman 10/6/21
    John/Mary Ann Otto 3/21/22
    Jos./Peggy Show 12/7/22
    Sam./Mary Hoover 11/6/22
    Wm./Marg. Downey 3/21/22
    Sam./Mary Robinson 11/29/23
    Chn./Reb. Sensenbaugh 8/24/24
    Geo./Eliz. Steiner 9/25/24
    Jc./So. Poffenbarger 3/23/24
    Jos. P./Maria Louisa Meredith 6/9/24
    John/Na. Rowe 7/25/25
    Jonas/Reb. Poffenberger 11/12/25
    Wm./Na. Huffer 3/28/25
    Ed./Eliz. Eustachins 9/23/26
    Jc. S./Sr. Ann Yoe 10/12/26
    Jc./Isa. Dugan 10/2/27
    John/Marg. Harmon 9/26/27

198. SMITH (Continued)

Hn./Jane Staley 8/14/28
Jc./Eliz. Smith 10/6/28
Jm./So. Long 11/18/28
Jon./Dorothy Bruner 3/25/28
Geo./Mag. Miller 9/10/29
Tho./Eliz. Itnire 8/8/29
Israel/Ary Downes 12/21/30
Jc./Tyett Davis 3/29/30
Geo./Eliz. Augustine 4/14/31
Mich. P./Cath. Dellinger 5/12/31
Abijah/Mary Christian 3/27/32
Hn./So. Thomas 3/12/32
John L./Mag. Hershey 5/24/32
Dv./Sus. Beck 8/17/33
Geo./Lydia Marker 1/19/33
Jm. H./Sr. Ann Poetz 11/26/33
Jon./So. Wiseninger 6/3/33
Pt./Mary Smith 7/23/33
Sam. B./Mary Shepherd 11/14/33
Jc./Mary Grim 6/11/34
John A./Eliza Powell 12/24/34
Abr./Eliz. Smith 2/3/35
Dn./Mary Donovan 7/11/35
Elie/Marg. Watson 1/17/35
Geo./Eliza Green 10/3/35
Levi/Mary Wilson 9/10/35
Sam./Eliz. Nyman 10/6/35
Elias/Eliz. Watson 4/20/36
Mich./Bridget Donnelly 8/27/36
Otho J./Jennett Y. Blackford 3/31/37
Fred. C./Mary E. Shaw 2/21/38
Geo./Caroline Henry 1/2/38
Geo./Eliz. Boyers 9/22/38
Is./Sidney McDonald 8/27/38
John K./Eliz. Adams 4/21/38
Jc./Susan Lowman 2/22/39
Hn./Julia Ann Lyday 4/25/40
Simon/Caroline Shafer 6/15/40
Wm. A./Eliz. Kiner 10/6/40
Geo./Anna Palmer 4/20/41
Geo./Mary Kreps 12/6/41
Geo. I./Mary A. Shafer 3/25/41
Jos. B./Mary Brewer 3/1/41
Louis H./Susan Stotler 5/3/41
Dv./Matilda Knode 2/10/42
John C./Barb. Ann Negley 4/18/42
John H./Sr. Kretzer 9/6/42
Sol./So. Thomas 3/29/42
Dv./Mary Ann Coffman 1/17/43
J. Irvin/Mar. S. Towson 2/15/44
Jc./Na. Nikirk 10/23/44
John W./Jane Norris 11/7/44
And./Ann Jane Ardinger 10/6/45
Geo. A./Eliz. Stinemetz 8/2/45
John M./Lydia I. Hoffman 8/23/45

Dv./Marg. Ridenour 11/13/46
Jos./Mar. Jones 9/2/46
Dn./Mary Palmer 5/27/47
Geo. F./Indiana B. Craft 6/9/47
Wm. F./Susan Slifer 8/5/47
Al. H./Mary Ellen Curry 1/13/48
Conrad H./Reb. Giddinger 2/3/48
Wm. K./Sr. Ann Powell 10/9/48
Geo. W./Lydia E. Keadle 9/28/49
Ezra/Sr. Ann Stouffer 2/18/50
Geo./Reb. Flora 11/9/50
Mahlon/Susan Young 12/4/50
Sol./Eliz. Moats 12/30/50
Geo. P./Ann M. Biershing 1/7/51
Jc./Maria Stine 4/5/51
John C./Leah Ann Huldeboyer 3/15/51
John N./Marg. Leonard 4/14/51
Dn./Matilda Geltmacher 2/12/53
Hn./Eliza Vernon 2/17/53
John/Cath. Lyboldt 1/3/53
Sam./Sr. Ann Huntsberry 3/8/53
Gerrit/M.A. Fitzhugh 10/17/54
John W./Eliz. Stine 3/4/54
Jos. C./Cath. A. Grove 10/28/54
Rob. B./Ann A.R. Smith 12/24/54
Amos/Mary Ellen Portis 12/26/55
John T./Ann M. Maugins 9/10/55
Lauson/Cath. Zeigler 9/6/55
Jc./Eliza Ann Monigan 10/28/56
John/Ann Maria Bingham 6/21/56
Jos./Roz. Grove 12/8/56
Sol./Marg. S. Reynull 12/24/56
Abr./Mary Eliz. Miller 3/3/57
Ezra/Eleanora Shilling 11/5/57
Geo. W./Julia Ann Gouff 6/2/57
Geo. W./Isa. Glass Thompson 12/22/57
Hn./Lucinda Watson 4/25/57
Mahlon/Susan C. Gloss 3/6/57
And. K./Sr. A.E. Thomas 1/26/58
Dv./Mary Ann Eliz. Jacobs 12/27/58
Dv. L./Ellen Maria Heyser 6/3/58
F.M./Am. McKee 1/26/58
John/Cath. Seele 10/12/58
John R./Anna Bair 11/15/58
Lewis H./Georgiann Baker 2/15/58
And./Frances V. Potter 12/6/59
Dv./Ann Rowland 12/12/59
Fred./Barb. Mallahan 6/9/59
Gotleib/Susan Maisack 8/2/59
Otho/Anna Thomas 11/2/59
Sam./Marg. Ann Gross 7/23/59
Al./Sus. Lambert 1/3/60
And. Wm./Eliz. E. Palmer 12/18/60
Dn. Jr./Na. Bruner 3/28/60
Nathan/Mary A. Avey 2/7/60
Pt./Marg. Hoover 9/18/60

199. SMOOT (SMOOTE, SMOOTZ, SMOOTS)
    Abr./Cath. Fye 9/18/99
    Geo. C./Matilda Stull 1/24/09
    Chn./Esther Gardner 5/3/17
    Jc./Mary Slenker 8/26/24
    Jc./Jane Tecumseh 5/28/25
200. SMURR
    John/Ellenor Kimes 11/27/23
    Napoleon B./Sr. Jane Parker 5/1/57
201. SMUTZ
    Dv./Mary Thomas 5/23/09
202. SNAVELY
    Hn./Jean Donaldson 1/2/06
    Jc./Chna. Hoover 4/18/18
    John/Sus. Foltz 4/3/27
    Jc. M./Lucretia A. Zimmerman 4/28/59
203. SNEARY
    John R./Eliz. C. Eakle 11/21/46
204. SNECKEBARGER
    Geo./Eliz. Barkdoll 3/25/46
205. SNELL
    Dn./Edna Malott 11/27/01
206. SNIVELY
    Jc./Eliz. Stoner 5/27/99
    Jc./Mary Lyons 1/8/02
    Geo./Eliza Baker 6/7/30
    Hn./Sr. Hershey 12/17/31
    Jos./Mary Planker 5/16/36
    Jc./Cath. Snyder 1/25/39
    John C./Mary Stonebraker 3/25/39
    John H./Lydia Dennison 9/12/39
    Dv./Han. Bayer 12/23/46
    Wash./Eliz. Staubs 10/20/46
    Dn./Malinda C. Bell 5/6/59
    Fred. B./Cornelia G. Hammond 12/5/60
207. SNODGRASS
    Stephen R./Eliz. Brethed 1/11/41
208. SNODDY
    B.I./Lucy Flory 6/26/60
209. SNOOK
    Sam./Har. Smith 6/20/33
    J.F./Eliz. S. Dodd 11/10/41
    Simon P./Marg. Grim 4/25/42
    John/Susan Underwood 1/3/48
210. SNORTERLY
    Geo./Sus. Burkhart 7/3/10
211. SNOW
    Dv./Loretta Flory 5/1/49
212. SNOWBURGER
    Dv./Rachel Horn 3/7/09
213. SNYDER
    Abr./Polly Snyder 8/12/01
    Jc./Cath. Wyantine 10/10/01
    John/Eve Boosier 8/12/02
    Fred./Cath. Allender 9/16/03
    Geo./Jane Wallace 12/28/03
    John/Sr. Miller 8/31/03

    Abr./Matilda Winders 3/10/04
    Abr./Mary Kyser 3/31/04
    Adam/Marg. Brook 7/6/05
    Geo./Ann Berry 5/23/06
    John/Eliz. Null 3/31/09
    Geo./Mary Davis 3/14/10
    Dv./Darkey Thoughts 5/1/12
    Gerhard/Reb. Spitsnogle 9/29/12
    Jc./Har. Bryan 8/20/12
    Pt./Eliz. Gray 2/26/12
    Fred./Nelly Rose 4/26/14
    John/Reb. Beard 3/27/15
    And./Rachel W. McCoy 12/7/17
    Adam/Eliz. Hammond 12/30/18
    John/Mary Merteny 3/28/18
    Leo./Reb. Charlton 11/19/18
    John/Eliz. Hass 8/7/19
    Mt./Rachel Moudy 3/8/19
    Chn./Eliz. Glaze 5/3/21
    Sam. C./Ann Gibbs From 11/4/22
    Hn./Precilla Mosteller 5/17/23
    John/Na. Smith 4/12/23
    Pt./Mary Shanefelt 2/15/23
    Geo./Na. Davis 12/24/24
    Hn./Cath. Aubert 11/27/24
    Chn./Jane Wright 10/10/25
    Hn./Cath. Lahnor 12/27/25
    Jc./Eliz. Stouffer 8/31/25
    Anthony/Marg. M. Boyd 2/21/28
    Jc./Lucinda Grim 6/9/30
    Sam./Ann Maria Chany 2/20/30
    Jm./Mary Ann Giles 3/31/31
    John/Maria Eichelberger 4/3/32
    And./Am. Smith 5/23/33
    Dv./Ann Taylor 6/5/33
    Dv./Sr. Hutzell 8/21/33
    John/Marg. Lichty 2/27/34
    Anthony Jr./Eliz. Wever 3/12/35
    John/Eliz. Ann Benner 3/24/35
    Ezra I./Sr. Ann Staubs 11/6/37
    John/Reb. Long 2/11/37
    John R./Cath. R. Prather 1/9/37
    Elias A./Cath. Thomas 3/27/38
    Ezra A./Na. Hutzel 11/1/38
    John/Mary Wolf 11/26/38
    Simon W./So. Grow 10/31/38
    Geo./Mary Stinemetz 3/18/39
    Geo./Mrs. Ann M. Troubtman 3/19/39
    Anthony/Ann M. Clark 3/20/40
    Pt./Susan D. Gordon 12/13/41
    Dn. O./Mary A. Cooney 9/19/44
    Hn./Frances Brewer 8/17/44
    Geo. of A./Eliz. Stinemetz 8/2/45
    Dn. G.W./Cath. A.F. Glaze 4/6/46
    Jos. H./So. Staubs 11/12/46
    Dv./Eliz. Ann Snyder 10/7/47
    Oliver H./Ann Bender 9/15/47

100

213. SNYDER (Continued)
    Pat./Malinda Lancaster 11/11/47
    Geo. N./Sr. M. Bombarger 3/16/48
    Sol. G.N./Mary A. Negley 1/20/48
    John A./Ann R. Rinehart 7/30/51
    Simon/Susan Goody 12/2/51
    Jc. H./Ann Marg. Myers 11/16/52
    Emanuel/Delilah Kretzinger 11/16/54
    Fred. B./Virginia Jones 9/7/54
    Wm./Mary Ann Funk 10/5/54
    Irvin/Eliza Jane Harris 5/19/55
    John/Marg. E. Sterling 3/24/55
    Hn./Mrs. Susan Olliver 2/19/56
    Lewis/Mary Eliz. Remley 5/15/56
    Simon P./Ruann Snyder 3/24/57
    John T./Sue M. Edden 11/2/58
    Wm. M./Alice V. Irvin 3/14/60
214. SOARD
    Conrad/Eliz. Kife 5/2/01
215. SOCKE
    Geo./Eliz. Kershner 12/19/45
    Geo./Eliz. F. Shafer 3/18/59
216. SOHN
    Conrad/Ann Christian 5/15/17
217. SOLTMAN
    John/Mary C. Warrel 10/16/52
218. SONNER (SONER)
    Jos./Sus. Copenhaver 8/12/13
    John Hn./So. Mutshler 3/31/34
219. SOUDER (SOUDERS)
    Dn./Marg. Beeler 1/3/15
    Jm./Eliza Crow 10/17/21
    Hn./Ros. Rager 10/11/34
220. SOUTH
    Tho./Barb. Wolf 3/28/03
    Wm./Cath. Brouchmyer 3/29/04
    Garey/Rachel Newson 12/23/05
    Wm./Matilda Tracy 7/30/07
    John/Barb. River 12/8/18
    Gera/Sr. Watts 5/20/30
    Jos./Eliz. Watts 12/4/43
    Benj./Chna. Shank 3/20/47
    Benj./Marg. Young 5/18/48
    Wm./Sr. Ann Shilling 10/11/48
221. SOUTHERLAND
    Hugh McKay/Cath. Miller 4/19/47
222. SOUTHWOOD
    Ed. E./Han. F. Hurst 10/27/51
223. SOWERS
    Fred./Mary Brewer 3/14/33
    Dv./Marg. Barkes 3/16/41
    Elie/Na. Kreps 1/27/51
    Pt. Jm./Mary Jane Knepper 2/1/58
    Sam./Sr. Krepps 1/13/59
224. SOZEY (SOSSY)
    Abr./Eliza Chew 7/23/29
225. SPAED
    John/Emily Koch 1/4/51

226. SPALDING (SPAULDING)
    Jm./Mary Bowers 1/19/13
    Raphael/Cath. Hornish 6/17/15
    Wm./Mary Edwards 3/30/22
227. SPANGLER (SPENGLER)
    John/Reb. Lingenfelter 5/9/04
    Jos./Polly Smith 3/12/14
    Matthias/Eliza Buckise 9/13/27
    Chas./Ann Reb. Artz 12/15/29
    John F./Susan M. McClanahan 6/18/50
    Dv./Milly Ann Burd 8/12/54
    Jc./Ann E. Seibert 10/19/59
228. SPARROW
    Wm./Susan Highbarger 4/24/41
    Wm./Har. Highberger 11/11/51
229. SPEAKER
    Hn./Mary Ann Ardinger 12/26/46
    Fred. Wm./Ellen Eliz. Bowers 10/13/47
    Noah/Cath. A. Garvin 3/7/49
    Wash./Caroline Garvin 1/22/50
    Wm./Mary Bovey 1/30/50
    Chr./Marg. Taylor 3/21/57
230. SPEAR
    Mat./Mar. N. Anderson 5/19/26
231. SPEARAUGH
    Geo./Sr. Eakel 10/18/00
232. SPECHER
    Mt. L./Priscilla Hammer 7/30/60
233. SPECK
    Pt./Chna. Gushwa 11/21/07
    Mt./Na. Spieler 10/12/10
    Dv./Reb. Stouffer 12/28/43
    Fred./Mary Ann Wolfersberger 8/20/44
    Mt./Isa. Pittenger 2/7/44
    Pat./Mary Dillahunt 8/3/46
234. SPEIGLER (SPIGLER)
    Sam./Mary Oderfer 12/7/16
    John/Matilda Young 10/19/20
235. SPELAHAN
    Dn./Marg. Cuky 8/23/38
236. SPENCER
    John/Na. Simkins 9/11/17
    Jarvis/Cath. Ragan 12/30/38
237. SPERO
    Geo./Sr. Warner 3/16/05
238. SPESSARD (SPESARD, SPESSART)
    Pt./Cath. Weaver 9/18/02
    John/Cath. Stover 4/4/14
    Chn./Mary Ann Hershey 2/9/37
    John/Ann Thorper 8/11/39
    John/Eliza Ann Cook 4/3/47
    Dn./Reb. Rhinehart 3/14/48
    Dn. W./Mary Ann Hartel 11/16/54
    Wm. R./Susan Immel 3/28/57
    Sam. H./Susan Hawkins 1/30/58
239. SPICKER
    Sam./Na. Miller 12/18/24

240. SPICKLER (SPECKLER)
    Frisby Tilghman/Sus. Sheeler 11/15/47
    Tho. P./Susan Middlekauff 1/15/48
    Hn. M./Cath. W. Gabriel 12/13/52
    C.B./Sr. Plum 2/1/58
    Calvin B./Ellen Newcomer 2/9/60
241. SPIELMAN (SPEELMAN, SPEALMAN)
    John/Betsy Morgan 5/31/05
    Dv./Ros. Neybert 3/24/09
    John/Polly Seigler 4/25/20
    Dv./Cath. Wentling 9/22/24
    Mich./Mary Shrader 6/22/27
    Dv./Cath. Sailor 3/16/30
    Dv./Susan Rohrer 5/1/33
    Jc./Eliza Houpt 8/4/34
    Sam./Barb. Sailer 10/30/34
    Jc./Sr. Boward 1/1/36
    John/So. Wolf 4/11/36
    Jon./Caroline S. Steffey 9/5/44
    John M./Julia Myers 1/9/45
    Jc./Sr. Neikirk 4/23/46
    Wm. H./Ann M. Rohrback 6/11/49
    Hiram/Mary Hose 4/30/51
    Dv./Mary Ellen Blessing 8/11/53
    John D./Susan Welsh 1/19/53
    Dv./Emiline Stouffer 9/16/57
    Ezra/Eliz. Geigis 10/1/57
    Emanuel/Mar. Beaughly 4/16/59
242. SPITZEL
    John/Han. Grove 8/15/26
243. SPITZNOGLE (SPITSNAGLE)
    John/Barb. Myers 6/30/01
    Geo./Eliz. Varner 3/6/02
244. SPOHN (SPONG)
    John/Sus. Miller 6/28/04
    Matthias Jr./Sr. Shepherd 6/10/17
    Dv./Eliz. Arnsberger 12/23/19
    Elias/Cath. Weaver 1/8/29
    Matthias/Susan Sulser 3/9/47
    John L./Julia Roulett 6/7/56
    Elias/Mar. E. Fry 5/31/58
245. SPONSELLER
    Fred./Eliz. Evilhock 1/19/18
    Fred./Har. Ellis 10/5/25
    Fred./Cath. Kreps 3/5/53
246. SPOTTS
    Geo. Wm./Mary S. Watters 8/29/37
    Geo. W.L./Eve R. Gatrell 9/26/50
247. SPRAGUE
    Asa/Esther Hughes 10/28/40
248. SPRECHER (SPRICHER)
    Geo./Mary Houck 5/20/16
    Ph./Cath. Houcke 2/22/20
    Dv./Mary Ankeney 4/19/24
    John/Sr. Bowser 3/17/25
    Jc./Marg. Miller 8/8/29
    Ph./Eletha E. Castle 3/9/40

    Elias/Mary Hammer 1/20/46
    Is./Cath. Ankeney 8/1/53
    Dv./Eliza Jane Boteler 7/22/54
    Ph./Mar. Jane Eckman 12/22/57
    Geo. W./Susan Norris 1/26/58
    Jc./Mary Jane Mong 2/9/59
    John/Virginia King 7/26/60
    Ph./Sr. A. Masters 1/3/60
    Sam./Marg. McNamee 10/4/60
    Wm. H./Eliza A. Stouffer 9/22/60
249. SPRIGG (SPRIGGS)
    Dv./Eliz. Chesby 10/11/13
    Wm./Eleanor Blair 2/15/42
250. SPRING
    Pt. M./Mary Ann Petry 4/27/41
251. SPRINGER
    Geo./Marg. McNamee 7/22/01
    Emanuel/Cath. Sudgick 12/17/11
    John/Marg. Sellinger 7/2/14
    Francis/Mary Kreigh 4/8/37
    John/Matilda Kitzmiller 12/29/46
252. SPRINKLE
    John W./Emily C. Shered 6/21/51
253. STAFF
    Sam./Mary Ann Palmer 10/20/47
254. STAHL (STOLL)
    Simon/Cath. Stemple 2/5/03
    John I./Prudence Williams 9/10/05
    Otho H.W./Lettice S. Hall 2/21/09
    Geo./Marg. Ensminger 2/5/23
    John Jc./Maria Cath. Russe 12/17/34
    John/Rachel McCoy 3/28/53
    Dn./Athalinda Renner 10/14/54
    Law./Mar. Ann Maysilles 12/20/57
    Hiram R./Mary Hartle 4/16/60
    Law./Mary E· Maysilles 12/17/60
255. STAKE
    Wm./Esther Zeakman 9/27/99
    Pt./Ros. Moudy 7/25/12
    Elie/Ellen Monahan 9/14/20
    Jc./Mary Boroff 4/19/31
    John M./Har. Shrives 3/24/32
    Ed. G.W./Ann E. Miller 4/30/39
    John/Marg. Iseminger 5/2/39
    Wm./Maria Moudy 1/10/42
    A. Kershner/Adaline S. Oster 4/2/44
    Jc./Cath. Miller 11/27/45
    Jc./Cath. Hammond 2/6/54
256. STALEY
    Dn./Sr. Thornborough 3/7/12
    Dn./Isa. Anderson 11/21/16
    Stephen/Mary Lively 9/27/18
    Pt./Cath. Medaria 11/4/20
    Warfield D./Mary A. Horn 11/19/35
257. STALLSMITH
    John/Eliz. Binkley 9/7/11
258. STAMY
    Sol./Cath. Sheller 10/3/53

102

259. STANES
     Leo./Cath. Bashow 5/14/05
260. STANHOPE
     Lewis/Louisa Miller 6/3/45
     Lewis G./Eliz. Newcomer 4/6/47
261. STANLEY
     Jm. Smith/Sr. Ann Figally 10/28/24
262. STANTON (STAUNTON, STAUNTEN)
     Jm./Sr. Gardner 12/29/12
     Wm. N./So. S. Johnson 7/28/46
263. STARKEY
     Enoch/Eliz. McAtee 5/2/51
264. STARLING
     Abr./Mar. Hammond 5/25/13
     Abr./M.I. Watson 6/25/34
     Abr./Susan Hawkey 7/16/36
     Sam./Ellen Williams 3/8/37
     Wm./Matilda A. Murray 9/3/53
265. STARR
     Abr./Eve Cline 11/23/99
266. STARRY
     Jos./Char. I. Shirley 1/27/34
267. START
     Nathan/Barb. Ridenour 10/28/01
     Wm. Hadley/Cath. Henry 6/16/07
268. STARTZMAN
     Dv./Marg. Smith 8/26/09
     Dv./Sus. Little 1/13/00
     Pt./Polly Holtzman 10/24/15
     Sam./Sus. Startzman 9/8/19
     Jc./Ann Jack 4/24/20
     Dv./Ann Stahl 3/21/26
     Wm./So. Miller 4/15/30
     Wm./Susan Startzman 9/16/34
     John W./Sr. Householder 2/10/35
     Lewis/Cath. Ward 9/24/36
     Elias/Susan Bentz 11/29/37
     Mt./Eliz. Watkins 1/1/40
     Dv./Susan McNamee 2/22/41
     John/Susan Comfort Little 7/15/41
     Chn./Eliza Ankeney 1/10/46
     Dv./Eliz. Shriver 5/13/51
     Jc. M./Ann Cath. Schindel 11/26/59
269. STATLER
     John/Prudence Schnebly 3/29/16
270. STAUB (STAUBS, STAUPS, STOUB)
     Jc./Eliz. Shank 6/11/14
     Geo./Mary Miller 4/13/17
     Elie/Ellen Brannon 3/25/19
     John/Reb. Longanacre 7/23/31
     Jm./Har. Huntzberry 5/14/39
271. STAUM
     Dn./Sr. Shank 12/20/38
272. STAYLER
     Cornelius/Ruenna Snavely 11/16/29
273. STECH
     Mt. Luther/Lydia A.A.T. Payne 8/30/56

274. STEECE (STEACE, STEESE)
     Hn./Sus. Murphy 7/29/17
275. STEEL (STEELE, STEAL)
     Abr./Na. Palmer 2/15/06
     Rob./Esther Long 3/9/13
     John N./Anna Ogh Buchanan 9/30/19
     John/Sus. Peritz 12/8/28
     Wm./Sally Prechfield 11/5/28
     Wm. C./Mary Hetzer 10/19/35
     Jm./Am. Anaton 8/22/36
     John H./Mary Ann Gehr 9/17/38
     Pat./Cath. Kaesmann 6/15/39
     John/Mary Forsythe 11/16/47
     Levi B./Cynthia Inglebright 3/25/58
276. STEFFEY (STEFFLEY, STEFFIE, STEFFY,
     STEPHY)
     Mich./Mary Wake 12/12/01
     Ph./Mary Bear 3/17/17
     Wm./Eliz. Oswald 9/6/17
     Pt./Mary Protzman 2/1/23
     Jc./Regena Stump 7/29/24
     Dv./Ann Ridenour 8/22/25
     Geo./Ann Mary Winders 4/25/25
     Dv./Sr. Hartle 3/27/27
     And./Mary Beard 3/19/31
     Sam./Mary Ann Garver 2/25/34
     Is./Susan Durbler 9/29/35
     Jc./Cath. Munday 8/29/37
     Jc./Mary Ann House 1/21/39
     Wm./Caroline Baker 9/27/43
     Jos./Sr. Hill 6/13/44
     Emory E./Cath. E. Grosh 10/38/48
     Ed. P./Eliz. A. Conley 1/17/60
277. STEGERS
     Baltis/Cath. Hunter 2/11/45
     Adam/Roz. Breisch 4/22/56
278. STEIN
     Pt./Ann Lowman 4/4/05
     Barnett/Cath. Huffer 11/26/16
279. STEINBAUGH,(STINEBAUGH)
     John/Mary Harsh 6/27/04
     Geo./Mary Sheller 1/6/17
     Ph./Cath. Bowser 6/29/19
280. STELLE
     Wm. R./Susan Robertson 2/4/39
281. STELTON
     Hn./Marg. A. Sweitzer 5/23/48
282. STEMAN
     Pt./Molly Herr 3/17/19
283. STEMNER
     Jos./Marg. Souders 1/19/58
284. STEMPLE
     John/Marg. Lohm 3/22/21
285. STENNETT
     Jm. M./Chra. Spessard 9/9/15
286. STEOLE
     Dv./Jane Lilly 3/1/32

103

287. STEPHENS
Chn./Sr. Babb 10/31/05
Dv./Har. McFerran 3/29/06
Lewis/Mary Shepler 3/26/21
Alex./Mary Cahill 3/23/29
Sam. M.T./Eliza A. Carter 6/9/32
Orlando/Han. Hill 9/21/44
288. STEPHENSON (STEVESON)
Ferdinand/Phillipe Strider 3/23/25
Jos./Na. Grove 10/12/30
289. STEPPE (STEPPEE)
Pt./Cath. Trytle 12/13/04
290. STERLING
Wm./Marg. Adkinson 1/28/07
O.C. Jr./Marg. E. Logan 7/19/56
291. STERNE
Geo./Francis Douthal 10/10/00
Wm./Mary Cath. Emory 12/23/52
292. STERRETT (STERRETTE)
Jm./Sus. Grubb 2/17/07
Jm./Eliz. Rench 6/10/07
Jos. I./Rachel Hogg 6/18/14
Benj./Na. Hogg 12/29/18
293. STEVENS
H.S./Eliz. L. Blackwell 9/25/43
294. STEWART
John/Sr. Malott 12/25/02
Tho./Jane Jack 11/15/04
John/Ros. Sheeler 12/8/08
Rob./Mary Daniel 2/13/09
Wm./Eliz. S. Watts 12/17/30
John L./Sus. Mitchell 6/14/33
Wm. T./Susan Hammaker 2/22/44
John R./Caroline C. Buckhart 11/17/46
295. STEWICK
Dv./Eliz. Myers 12/31/25
296. STEY
Conrad/Cath. Witmer 3/27/38
297. STICKLE
Wm./Sr. Ridenour 11/1/31
Hiram R./Am. R. Albers 11/8/49
298. STICKLER
Sam./Sr. Miller 4/11/22
299. STIFFLER
John/Cath. Kitzmiller 9/26/23
Cornelius/Eliza James 7/18/31
300. STIGN
Alex./Lucinda Corbett 11/22/55
301. STILWELL
Dv./Maria Fouke 9/14/13
Johnson/Sr. Yates 12/3/42
Abr. M./Eliz. A. Deaver 5/15/48
302. STINE
John/Marg. Frankenberger 1/1/03
Matthias/Eliz. Yakel 3/16/12
Nich./Na. Lorshbaugh 11/14/14
John/Mag. Bovey 1/4/19

Ph./So. Smith 5/4/20
Barnet/Fanny Hersh 3/18/25
Geo./Eliz. Smith 7/27/25
Jc./Mary Haines 12/21/25
Casper/Mary Beltzer 3/3/27
Benj./Leah Cretzer 1/22/39
Augustus/Eliz. Weller 5/14/41
John/Reb. Gloss 4/20/42
John N./Amanda Rohrer 12/26/44
Jc./Maria Ann Thomas 2/22/51
Ezra/Cath. Price 10/4/53
Jos./Mary A. Gloss 12/27/53
Jc./Na. Greenawalt 2/13/54
Geo. B./Har. L. Clopper 10/22/55
Josiah A./Eliz. Rohrer 11/12/56
Abr./Caroline E. Hoover 6/25/59
303. STINEMETZ (STINEMERTZ)
Hn./Eliz. Speigler 2/7/16
Geo./Rachel Leiter 6/26/21
John/Susan Myers 3/4/22
Abr./Na. Nicholas 3/29/23
Wm./Mary Ann Cyester 12/20/45
304. STINGER
John/Sr. Wolf 6/3/33
305. STIPES
Benj./Isa. Green 11/27/23
306. STIPP
Abr./Ann Comega 1/17/33
307. STITELY
Geo./Mary Booser 2/11/50
308. STITZEL
John/Cath. Hoffman 6/7/25
309. STITZMAN
Dv./Eliz. Kline 11/19/07
310. STOCK (STOCKES, STOKES)
Geo./Han. Ann Cross 12/10/10
John/Na. Davidson 1/12/21
Mich. F./Chna. Eliz. Buner 12/27/52
311. STOCKSLAGER (STUCKSLAGER)
John/Regina Slanker 11/30/22
Hn./Mary Ann Line 11/5/25
Ph./Sr. Schmutz 4/8/29
Jc./Salome Line 11/8/34
Pt./Sr. Carn 1/12/39
John/Mary Thomas 1/23/49
Geo. A.H./Caroline Stockslager 12/20/52
Mt. L./Caroline R. Waller 11/10/58
John/Ann R. Longnecker 11/2/59
312. STOCKWELL
Is./Mary Smith 12/9/03
313. STOCY (STOCEY)
Geo. W./Julian McCouley 6/3/19
314. STODDARD
Jm./Eliz. Brosius 11/20/13
315. STOLTZ
Pt./Eliz. Shupe 6/25/05

316. STONE
Wm./Sus. Leighter 6/14/00
Ezra/Lucy Ann Smith 12/6/32
317. STONEBRAKER (STONEBREAKER)
Geo./Eliz. Nafe 12/27/00
Garrett/Cath. Shroeder 1/22/03
Pt./Reb. Draper 2/20/05
John/Naomy McCoy 1/31/11
John/Lydia Avey 8/21/13
Jos./Na. Landis 10/24/14
Jc./Mary Reynolds 4/24/16
Jc./Eliz. Ward 10/10/27
John/Eliz. Davis 9/8/32
Wm. H./Elisa M. Huyett 3/11/33
Sam./Margaretta Pennel 8/3/37
Hn./Engeline Rench 11/20/37
Sam./Marg. Rench 4/10/39
Oliver/Cath. Baker 2/10/41
Perry/Reb. Alter 12/24/42
Sam. A./Sr. R. Knode 5/27/45
John/Susan Line 4/25/46
Jm. W./Laura L. McCardell 9/27/48
Wm. G./E.S. Clagett 6/5/49
A.S./Kate E. Pearce 8/30/56
John M./Mary C. Malott 6/3/59
318. STONER
Mich./Eliz. Snively 7/2/99
Abr./Mary Holmes 10/24/01
Abr./Sr. Stover 8/25/07
Is./Anne Newcomer 8/25/07
Mt./Na. Bachtell 1/31/14
Dv./Na. Tiches 9/6/23
John/Cath. Brantner 5/23/26
Jc./Eliz. Shockey 5/18/38
Sam./Reb. Young 5/29/41
And. L./Eliz. Shank 1/24/43
Mt./Maria Gehr 10/17/43
Benj./Mary Shank 1/19/44
319. STOOPE (STOOPS, STOUPS)
Wm./Am. Startzman 1/24/27
Jc./Sr. Conn 3/28/45
320. STOPS
Jc./Eliz. Middlekauff 4/26/22
321. STORMAN
Hn./Cath. Hoffman 3/13/05
322. STOTLER
Jc./Susan Rohrer 1/27/41
John P./Han. Rinehart 3/23/41
Dv./Eliza Jane Speaker 3/1/43
Sam./Mary Davis 3/22/43
Chn./Eliz. Newcomer 10/27/45
323. STOTTLEMYER (STOTTLEMEYER)
Geo./Sus. Pry 2/8/14
Jc./Barb. Protzman 10/28/15
Dn./Han. Racker 11/19/19
John/Sus. Wolf 11/19/19
Dv./Isa. Hayes 2/17/25

Nelson/Han. Pryor 7/25/30
John M./Hen. Hays 10/10/32
Jos./So. Hays 1/16/35
John/Sus. Buzzard 3/5/44
Isaiah/Mary Gilday 12/30/56
Rob. F./Am. C. Wolverton 1/19/59
324. STOUCH
Hn./Hetty Carson 7/26/41
Hn./Eliz. C. Huyett 11/19/42
325. STOUFFER (STOUFER)
Abr./Eliz. Newcomer 10/14/05
Dv./Julia Attahouce 6/11/11
John/Barb. Welty 3/16/11
Jc./Marg. Stover 1/24/14
Jc./Cath. Reneberger 1/5/24
Chn./Na. Varner 10/7/26
Matthias/Betsey Draper 8/20/28
Elias/Rachel Robinson 8/12/29
Pt./Sr. Ott 11/24/29
Chn./Eliz. Shank 12/13/31
Dv./Eliz. Ensminger 6/11/31
Abr./Susan Fahrney 2/20/32
Dn./Elisa Bowman 11/3/32
Sam./Eliz. Doub 3/30/33
Jc./Cath. Eakle 10/22/36
Chn./Ros. Thomas 1/16/39
Jc./Maria Parks 3/21/43
Emanuel/Mary Ann Rinehart 1/13/45
Pt./Susan Mase 1/16/45
Hn. S./Na. Mase 6/18/46
John H./So. Smith 9/5/49
Pt. B./Mary A. Miller 9/9/50
Jc./Maria Wolfkill 4/9/51
Pt./Caroline Virginia Lewis 1/26/53
Benj. F./Mary Koontz 8/25/55
Jon./Ellen Mace 12/13/55
Wm./Cath. Matilda Lewis 4/4/55
Al. W./Sr. H. Smith 11/5/57
And./Mary Cath. Gouker 12/1/57
Hiram W./Clara M. Grosh 2/17/57
Simon/Isa. Bostater 3/12/57
Dn. F./Drusilla Cheney 11/1/58
Frisby/Amanda E. Snyder 10/5/58
Dn. H./Julia Myers 11/28/59
Jc./Eliz. Bope 1/4/60
John R./Susan Shilling 1/18/60
Josiah/Susan Am. Thomas 8/9/60
Wm. C./Ann Maria Miller 11/22/60
326. STOUT (STOUDT)
Geo./Cath. Beltzhoover 11/2/04
John/Sus. Essinger 8/20/05
John T./Eliz. Campfield 2/27/16
Aaron/Mary Dorsey 1/14/33
327. STOVER
John/Eliz. Kline 2/7/05
Dn./Sus. Funk 2/17/10
Dn./Marg. Tishingham 9/2/19

105

327. STOVER (Continued)
Sam./Sr. Snider 3/6/21
Geo./Eliz. Welty 4/13/24
Jc./Eliz. Emmert 10/28/25
John/Marg. Petre 3/14/26("now
Stouffer" note after John)
Dv./Mary Hill 9/3/27
Dn./Cath. Stover 11/16/29
Mich./Eliz. Chichester 9/23/33
Hn./Na. Ensminger 3/4/34
Jc./Polly Baker 3/15/36
Sam./Eliz. Wolgamot 10/16/37
Jon. H./Eveline Tolbert 5/9/38
Wm./Angeline L. Bigham 10/14/56
Jc. T./Susan R. Moury 3/25/57
Levi/Marg. Ann Fockler 7/31/58
Sam./Chna. Severs, no date
328. STRAIN
Tho./Sr. Hammond 6/16/05
329. STRAILMAN
Abdiel L./Mary Shill 1/10/57
330. STRAITH
Alex./Eleanor Hunter 4/7/12
331. STRASBURG
Dn./Cath. Potts 8/16/52
332. STRAUSE
Geo. R./Mary Eliz. Herr 11/25/50
333. STRAYER
Nich./Emma Snyder 7/9/27
334. STRECKER (STRICKER)
Jc./Julianna Smith 5/29/07
335. STRICKLER (STRICKLEAR)
Hn./Cath. Brubaker 5/13/19
John B./Barb. Brubaker 6/4/24
336. STRICKLEY
John/Sus. Celler 11/15/21
337. STRIDE
Rufus/Eliz. Domer 12/18/55
338. STRIDER
Jc./Sr. Ann Trider 3/8/36
John/Cath. Adams 3/3/38
339. STRIGER
John/Biershiba Bennett 1/6/17
340. STRIPE
Dv./Mary Smith 3/12/05
341. STRITE
John/Eliz. Summers 3/5/21
John/Hen. L. Hitchcock 2/11/57
Hn./Susan Bear 2/7/60
342. STROCK
Hn./Cath. Middlekauff 2/16/52
Wm./Alethia Hildebrand 11/1/54
343. STRODE
Theodore S.R./Eliz. Barbery Heck
5/30/57
344. STROHL
Ph./Char. Stuter 5/9/01

345. STRONG
Dv./Mary Price 4/7/02
346. STROUSE
Jc./Chna. Eavey 1/29/30
347. STROVINGER
John/So. Miller 12/23/58
348. STRUNK
And./Mary Ann Deitrick 12/20/39
349. STUBBLEFIELD
Geo./Ellen Edwards 7/15/34
350. STUDERS
Mt./Patty Wiggins 2/16/09
351. STUFF
Hez./So. McClane 9/8/54
352. STULTZ
Geo./Fanny Nesbit 4/6/01
353. STUMBAUGH
Jos./Maria A. Miller, no date
354. STUMP
John/Susan Butt 2/29/32
355. STURR
Jc./Sr. Allison 2/27/08
Jc./Eliz. McDill 4/6/15
Sam./Leticia Webb 6/8/24
John/Eliz. Hess 3/19/25
Wm. H./Susan Hess 8/22/31
Joshua/Sr. Force 7/28/45
356. STUTZMAN
Geo./Sus. Householder 6/2/00
357. SUFF
Fred./Cath. R. Craver 11/6/38
358. SULLIVAN
John/Ann Cross 1/20/13
Wm./Marg. Carroll 11/9/33
Elijah W./Eliz. Flory 8/28/38
Timothy/Helena Healy 2/27/38
Jer./Ann Twa 7/4/40
359. SULTZER
And. J./Lydia Ann Smith 7/27/27
360. SUMAN
Garrett/Anna Buzzard 12/19/09
Wm./Lavinia Albert 3/28/49
Sam./Ruann Dagenhart 3/20/52
John/Cath. Row 8/3/58
361. SUMMERS (SUMER)
John/Eliz. Petre 1/21/01
Felty/Reb. Linton 10/5/02
Jc./Eliza Summers 5/14/03 ("2d marr."
after John; "d/o Jc. Petery Jr." after
Eliza)
Pt./Marg. Cloppbaugh 1/10/03
Wm./Eliz. Miller 9/2/04
Nath./Sr. W. Wade 7/3/20
Adam/Na. Hymes 2/11/27
John/Sr. Rowland 1/13/27
Nath./Mary Wade 8/20/27
Jc./Anna Miller 3/2/31

361. SUMMERS (SUMER) (Continued)
    Wm./Ellen Neall 3/5/33
    Elie/Han. Ford 11/14/37
    Geo./So. Miller 8/10/38
    Sam./Sr. Ann Mertz 9/24/39
    And./Cath. E. Davis 11/10/49
    John Wesley/Cath. Hart 2/8/51
    John/Marg. Sayer 10/9/56
    John/Ann M.E. Baechtell 9/8/57
    Elias/Almira B. Fouke 2/2/59
362. SUTER
    Jc./Eliz. Miller 10/1/16
    Pt./Cath. Martin 4/6/30
    Geo. W.W./Julia Ann Pryor 7/30/58
363. SUTTON
    John/Eliz. Miller 11/2/12
    John Jr./Hester L. Roberts 11/8/51
364. SWAGELY
    Mich./Mary Young 12/28/14
365. SWAIN
    Geo./Eliz. Harper 5/13/39
    Wm./Mary Smith 1/27/42
    Wm./Mar. Smith 4/5/45
    Sam./Sam. Swain 1/11/48 (written
      in index this way)
    Benj./Elizth Boyer 6/21/51
366. SWANLEY
    Jc./Polly Thompson 1/7/01
367. SWANN (SWAN)
    Geo. M./Louisa L. Graham 2/5/24
    Rob./Ellen E. Macgill 11/28/55
368. SWARRICK
    Jm. A./Eliz. Clark 8/21/60
369. SWART
    Jc./Cath. Zollinger 4/13/13
370. SWARTZ (SCHWARTZ)
    Francis Ph./Char. Gruber 5/5/18
    Wm./Cath. Dunn 11/30/18
    And./Reb. McDavid 6/19/23
    Geo./Miranda Myers 1/4/49
371. SWEANY (SWEENY, SWENEY)
    Jc./Eliz. Hogans 9/23/14
    Gararet/Bridget Langing 4/19/37
    Francis/Ann Miller 10/13/42
372. SWEARINGER
    John/Milly Daily 5/15/99
373. SWEITZER
    Leo./Eliz. Hemsworth 12/14/13
    Hn./Betsey Holbert 8/29/15
    Hn./Mary Betts 6/4/16
    Wm./Eliz. Maysilles 11/17/40
    Wm. H./Cath. Buzzard 12/5/51
    John/Mary Ann Rice 12/29/55
374. SWHIER
    Jc./Mary Ann Hott 8/13/29
375. SWIGERT
    Ph./Sr. Carver 1/26/01
    John/Marg. McDill 2/18/03

376. SWINEY
    Wm./Mag. Oats 6/21/08
377. SWINGER
    And./Cath. Figley 11/27/34
378. SWINGERT
    Lewis R./Frances A. Seckman 3/6/60
379. SWINGLE
    Mich./Mary Newcomer 2/7/15
380. SWINGLEY (SWINGLY)
    Leo./Prudence Brentlinger 4/1/05
    John/Eliz. Hoffman 8/18/06
    Nath./Eliz. Sharer 2/27/25
    Sam. R./Maria Rice 10/13/31
    Wm./Eve Cath. Fiery 6/5/32
    Benj./Cath. Hershey 11/28/37
    Sam. N./Ann Mary Locher 12/27/42
    Geo./Ann Eliz. Locher 4/6/48
    Otho/Cath. M. Shoop 4/27/52
    Sam. K./Ruth Prather 8/10/57
381. SWOPE (SWOOP, SWOAP)
    John/Mary Stemple 1/26/08
    Jc./Betsy Hartle 4/5/11
    Barnet/Mary Bowman 7/31/18
    Barnett/Eliz. Cow 2/27/18
    Mich./Cath. Cow 3/16/18
    John/Marg. Stine 5/7/19
    Sam. H./Susan Marie Ingram 1/4/19
    Jc./Eliza Light 6/11/21
    John/Mary Ann Petre 12/17/28
    Dv./Mary Renner 4/3/30
    John/Na. V. Castor 3/25/31
    Noah/Matilda Kendle 12/6/33
    John/Marg. Hogmire 1/26/35
    Ig./Mar. A.S. Castor 3/14/36
    Jc./Mary Caster 4/13/37
    Barnhart/Eliz. Nave 9/11/39
    Dn./Sr. Ann Merchant 12/21/40
    John C./Eliz. Knieriem 9/11/48
    Dv. Ig./Mary Ann Swope 5/28/55
    Geo. Hiram/Barb. Fulton 12/24/55
382. SWORD (SWORDS)
    Wm./Mary Albert 4/17/02
    Dn./Sus. Holmes 5/31/08
    Pt./Mary Miller 10/18/15
    Jc. R./Marg. Cook 12/19/60
383. SYESTER
    Dn. W./Hen. C. Herr 6/27/55
384. SYTHE
    John/Mary Summers 10/19/05
385. TABBS
    Moses/Jane Maria Carroll 10/8/11
386. TABLER
    Jm./Cath. Myers 3/29/27
    Levi/Ruth Welshans 4/9/40
    Ph. H./Mary E. Welshance 4/11/46
    John Hn./Ann C. Mallory 5/22/49

107

386. TABLER (Continued)
    John A./Mary E. Cox 3/25/50
    Alvin J.P./Ann R. Mason 1/9/51
    Jm. W./Ann A. Shindel 2/24/59
387. TAGGERT
    Chas./Jane Brady 12/3/60
388. TALBERT
    Wilson/Na. Hedge 9/24/17
    Benj./Malinda Hedge 7/20/19
    Lewis/Jemima Kemp 8/10/50
    John/Ann Berger 4/12/52
389. TALBOTT (TALBOT)
    Hillary/Marg. L. Bennett 10/21/26
390. TALL
    John/Mary Neybert 12/21/14
    Wm./Sr. Ann Hood 3/20/41
    Benj./Evaline Ashbay 12/28/57
391. TALLEY (TALLEIN in cross-index)
    John/Sr. Newcomer 2/24/18
392. TALLMAN
    John/Fanny Tutwiler 11/9/21
393. TANEY (TENEY)
    Arthur/Na. Mulon 5/23/33
    Augustine Brooke/Louise Ellen Bowles
        12/9/54
    Jos./Mary V. Moore 8/13/60
394. TANEYHILL
    Jm./Eliz. Huffmaster 6/8/30
395. TANNER
    John/Cath. Sosey 3/17/51
396. TARLTON
    Kaleb/Marg. Bear 4/12/00
    Stephen/Marg. Adams 1/1/29
397. TATE
    John/Eliz. Long 1/21/19
398. TAWNEY
    Geo./Rachel Showman 7/27/47
399. TAYLOR
    Wm./Na. Reynolds 11/11/99
    Jc./Edith Gawthrop 10/21/05
    Geo./Sr. Wooden 12/10/19
    Jm./Cath. Burkett 4/11/21
    Jos. F./Mary Bryan 2/3/27
    Sam./Na. Mummert 6/22/30
    Rob./Am. Moninger 12/24/39
    Hn./Reb. Poffenberger 12/22/41
    Sam./Eliz. Bowers 9/11/44
    Wm./Sr. Deitrick 1/5/45
    Wm./Maria Lynch 2/16/47
    Zachariah/Sr. Slifer 10/14/48
    Hn./Matilda Sprinkle 6/5/50
    Jm./Ellenora Harper 9/3/50
    Chas./Eliz. Lake 1/30/58
    Jeptha H./Mary Cath. Baker 1/21/60
    Wm. W./Elenora Carty 10/5/60
400. TEAS
    Wm./Sus. Smith 8/31/15

401. TEDBALE
    Rob. M./Maria Antonet Ringgold 6/15/33
402. TEDRICK
    John/Mary Ann Ditto 7/23/33
403. TEMMER
    Fred./Marg. Jane Frey 6/6/44
404. TEMPLE
    Conrad/Maria Wilson 5/21/04
405. TENBY
    Dennis/Eve Stahlworth 11/6/16
406. TENNENT (TENNANT, TENANT)
    Jm./Polly Avey 4/11/11
    Mich./Cath. Coffman 11/8/46
    Wm./Mary E. Spielman 3/1/48
    Jm./Sr. Henry 5/15/56
407. TENNIS
    Sam./Louisianna Myers 7/14/57
408. TERNEY
    Jc./Eliz. McCoy 2/19/10
409. TERRY
    Mich./Norry Dillon 8/12/37
    Rob./Bridget Farrell 11/11/37
410. THARP
    Lody/Sus. Bowers 11/27/15
    John/Cath. Tice 8/5/40
411. THAYER
    Oscar B./Mary Cath. Gehr 5/7/56
412. THOMAS
    Jc./Sus. Shecter 3/9/02
    Tho./Miama Armsworthy 1/23/02
    Mich./Mary Painter 11/19/05
    Dn./Cath. Geeding 4/14/08
    Hn./Cath. Shecter 11/12/08
    Sam./Jane Paine 11/5/08
    Abr./Eliz. Thomas 12/29/12
    Chr./Cath. Buzzard 10/21/14
    Dv./Eliz. Hawkey 8/5/15
    Lodwick/So. Silver 4/13/15
    Dv./Peggy Carpenter 1/16/21
    John/Cath. Hose 11/3/21
    Geo./Sus. Rohrer 2/14/22
    Geo./Sr. Schlosser 3/17/23
    Mich./Mary Waltz 8/6/23
    Elias/Mary Ann Moore 11/29/25
    Wm./Mary Casebar 9/14/25
    Is. P./Har. Harn 9/11/26
    John/Eliza Edmonds 6/20/26
    Jon./Roz. Mumma 4/13/29
    Kelley/Jane Hunter 2/6/29
    Pt./Sr. Kingery 4/3/29
    Sam./Mary Hill 3/30/31
    Joshua/Salina Landis 1/29/33
    Chr./Jemima K. Dutrow 6/27/34
    Gideon/Eliz. Rohrer 12/1/34
    Fred./Sr. Oswald 11/24/35
    Jc./Mary Kendle 4/12/16

108

412. THOMAS (Continued)
　　Geo./Chra. Carns 5/21/36
　　Jc. A./Sr. Hammond 12/9/37
　　Fred./Eliz. Feigley 9/11/39
　　Joel/Mary Alter 10/5/40
　　Jos./Mary Ann Johnston 7/22/40
　　Wm./Cath. Roger 11/10/40
　　Abr./Caroline Yontz 1/26/42
　　Dv./Susan Stops 5/20/44
　　Jc. G./Ann Long 7/28/44
　　Benj./Eliz. Faulkler 3/11/47
　　Josiah/Mary C. Deaner 6/10/50
　　Mt./Susann Rinehart 1/24/52
　　Jasper N./Caroline Lampert 12/24/53
　　Sol. S./Eliz. Huffer 11/21/53
　　John/Marg. Smith 4/4/54
　　Dn. Jr./Susan Maria Keedy 5/3/55
　　Jc./Eliz. Grim 1/16/55
　　Noah G./Sallie Thomas 10/27/56
　　Hn./Rachel Miller 11/26/57
　　Benj./Mary Smith 3/2/58
　　Jc./Ros. Kitzmiller 3/26/59
　　Rob./Malinda Kepler 5/14/60
413. THOMBURG
　　Sol./Mary Lefevre 3/13/22
　　Is. W./Mary Susan Magruder 10/2/56
414. THOMPSON (THOMSON)
　　Is./Reb. Prather 3/14/12
　　Jc./Susan Spielman 1/13/14
　　Jm. M./Sus. Snyder 8/17/16
　　Jm./Eliz. King 2/26/18
　　Jm./Judith Funk 5/15/19
　　Dn./Sr. Ann Cross 12/4/23
　　Benj./Mary Reel 9/8/28
　　Conrad/Sr. Keyser 6/21/33
　　John/Susan Kitzmiller 10/5/36
　　Sam. A./Hen. C. Thornsburg 3/13/43
　　Rob./Ann Colbert 3/13/44
　　John T./Mary V. Hurst 1/13/52
　　Wm./Marg. McGonigal 4/14/57
415. THOMTON
　　Jos./Mary Ann Wilson 11/13/07
416. THONSBURG
　　Geo. T./Sr. Ohlweiler 3/29/21
417. THORNBURG (THORNSBURG)
　　Rob. C./Savilla Ridenour 12/27/49
　　R.C./Mary E. Carson 4/1/57
418. THRASHER (THRESHER)
　　Is./Har. Durff 7/3/19
　　Jos. E./Mary E. Bowles 4/28/59
419. THRONE
　　Geo./Eliz. Hose 8/3/13
420. THRUSH
　　John/Rachel Mann 12/6/50
421. THUMB (THUM)
　　Geo./Marg. Waughtell 10/3/25
　　Dv./Polly Troup 3/24/47
　　Wm./Jane McCoury 9/18/54

422. THURSTON
　　Tho./Sr. Beasley 4/15/11
　　John B./Eleanor Albert 1/15/38
423. TICE
　　Mich./Mary Kershner 11/26/01
　　Pt./Mary Hower 1/31/07
　　Jc./Mary Syster 3/2/13
　　John/Na. Newcomer 3/17/21
　　John/Maria McClain 1/2/27
　　Jon./Reb. Melown 1/7/28
　　Dn./Susan Sheitz 10/20/32
　　Sam./Marg. Ann Hershberger 4/19/34
　　Wm. M./Ann C. Kinkle 1/10/37
　　Hn. K./Mary McCardle 3/7/38
　　Emanuel/Susan Bragonier 2/10/40
　　Franklin N./Cath. E. Felker 11/28/50
　　Sam./Ann E. Masters 4/3/50
　　Wm. M./Kate A. Hockley 10/7/51
　　Dn. H./Eleanora Mills 8/16/58
424. TIETIAN
　　Chn./Julianna Wagelly 9/9/02
425. TILGHMAN
　　Emanuel/Sr. Howard 8/12/06
426. TIMBERLAKE
　　Geo. W./Eliza P. Minsies 7/4/99
427. TIMMERMAN
　　Wm./Eliz. Gray 11/3/14
　　Benj./Mary Wiant 9/21/24
428. TIMMONDS (TIMMONS)
　　John/Sr. Mullen 11/29/09
　　Rich./Sr. Cath. Davis 9/18/52
429. TINTERMAN
　　Lewis/Barb. Gouger 8/18/49
430. TIRLEY
　　Geo. W./Narcissa Y. Fechtig 9/16/56
431. TITLOW
　　Emanuel/Am. Talen 9/8/36
　　Emanuel/Eliz. Rhodes 8/12/54
　　Dn./Sus. Stonebraker 1/31/55
432. TOBY (TOBEY)
　　Mich./Mag. Miller 12/22/11
　　Hn./Mary Renner 11/2/15
　　Hn./Mag. C.S. Rohrer 12/22/35
　　Mich. T./Cath. Rohrer 2/22/36
433. TOLHELM
　　Jos./Reb. Miller 12/9/35
434. TOLL
　　Tho./Sr. Williams 1/25/11
435. TOLSTON
　　And./Peggy Hornbraker 2/4/09
436. TOM (TOMS, THOMS)
　　Wm./Mary Staule 10/19/05
　　Jc./Sus. Armsley 10/16/10
　　Sam./Mary Hoover 3/2/10
　　John/Eliz. Lyon 10/12/13
　　Jon./Mary Markle 2/26/19
　　John/Deborah Barnheiser 11/22/32

436. TOM (TOMS, THOMS) (Continued)
Lewis/Cath. Dutree 4/9/36
Ezra/Jane Perry 3/6/38
Sam./Mary Ann Wolf 1/27/47
Dn./Malinda Brandeburg 10/16/60
Dv./Emeline Smith 11/5/60
Josiah/Ann Virginia Schindel 10/6/60
437. TOMEY
Pat./Johanna Kennedy 9/8/40
438. TONLAY
Wm./Am. Dennison 12/14/29
439. TOOBLE
Hn./Sus. Baer 9/1/18
440. TOOLE
Tho./Eliz. McMurren 12/7/00
Jm./Ros. McAfee 6/7/04
441. TOPP
Nath./Mary Reedy 6/16/27
442. TOUCHSTONE
Benj./Eliz. Hamilton 3/30/05
443. TOUPMAN
Abr./Cath. Thomas 5/25/05
444. TOWSON
Jc. T./Hen. M. Bishop 1/2/57
445. TOY
Dn./Marg. Maxwell 5/11/40
446. TRACY (TRACEY)
Pt./Eliz. Malone 5/16/07
John/Peggy McCleary 2/25/10
Mat./Mary Harley 3/31/21
John P./Mary Webb 5/16/32
John W./Eliza Bomburger 10/18/55
Hiram/Mary Boren 7/19/58
447. TRAIL
Sam./Eveline Brown 2/18/32
448. TRAVER
Fred./Cath. Geeler 8/2/30
And. J./Mary Eliz. Bowles 10/29/55
449. TREE
John/Ann Eliz. Stover 8/7/17
450. TREIBER
John G./Chna. Knieriem 12/30/46
451. TRESLER (TRISLER)
Dv./Chna. Brouchmyer 3/26/05
452. TRIBBET
John/Eliz. Sypes 4/7/00
453. TRIDAY
Wm./Pamelia Kate Snyder 3/11/56
454. TRIMBLE
Jos. H./Har. J. Grifith 3/31/53
455. TRINE
Chn./Mary Eliz. Gelwise 11/20/29
456. TRITCH(TRITSCH)
Hn./Eliz. Sillhart 12/10/08
Wm./Marg. Cline 1/17/16
Jc. J./Eliz. Dundore 12/31/27
Jc. Ezra/Har. Rohrer 11/12/41
Benj. F./Lavina Smith 10/18/44

457. TRITLE (TRIDLE, TRYTLE)
Jc./Eliz. Mart 11/7/01
Jc./Anna Winters 2/9/29
Ludwick/Cath. Martin 12/23/29
Jc./Sr. Mentzer 1/2/39
Dn./Eliz. Hammett 9/22/58
458. TROT
Hn./Na. Snell 8/12/15
459. TROUP
John/Mary Snyder 8/1/08
Jc./Peggy Snyder 2/23/11
Dv./Cath. Weaver 3/28/12
Dv./Eliz. Cushwa 5/20/23
John/Polly Tysher 2/1/27
Dv./Mary Wachtel 2/6/32
Jos./Sr. Cushwa 2/12/39
Hn./Ann Cath. Schnebly 11/30/43
Dv./Susan Null 12/6/52
John A./Sr. Jane Keisecker 1/16/55
Sol./Lydia Troup 12/24/59
460. TROVINGER
Sam./Mary Dickson 9/10/99
Cath./Abigale Smith 3/23/22 (cross-index
also indicates Cath.)
John/Sr. E. Leonard 10/31/48
461. TROXELL (TROXALL)
Jc./Eliz. Brewer 11/22/06
Pt./Marg. Early 3/28/09
Jc./Sus. Rhodes 8/20/12
Abr./Sr. Raugh 8/19/13
John/Eliz. Cooper 10/8/14
John/Mary Alter 3/1/16
John/Livia Hatherly 5/15/26
John/Chna. Sponsler 7/18/38
Levi/Eliz. Shilling 3/1/49
Abr./Susan Jenkins 6/24/50
Ph./Mar. J. Schleigh 1/22/51
John P./Ellen Jenkins 6/2/54
Wm./Louisa C. Staley 11/15/57
462. TRUBY (TRUBEY)
Dv./Cath. Mautter 3/19/14
Dn./Polly Stover 6/11/17
463. TRUE
Tho./Eliz. Night 12/29/08
Wm./Julia Pettet 4/2/11
464. TRUEMAN
John/Mary Brown 11/18/50
465. TRUMPHOWER
Geo./Mary Myers 3/20/40
466. TSCHNEDY
Dv./Mary Bovey 8/5/20
467. TSCHUDY
Dv./Cath. Fitz 11/27/58
468. TUCKER
Wm. G./Eliz. Gift 1/12/58
John Hn./Han. Jane Gift 4/30/59
Tho. L./Mary Jane Greenfield 9/10/59

110

469. TUCKERMAN
   Tho./Betrice Forman 8/30/99
470. TURNBOLT
   Darlington/Susan Hose 9/2/48
471. TUNNEREUTHER
   Fred./Mary Mundabaugh 2/18/51
472. TURNER
   Edmund H./Reb. Porter 4/7/02
   John/Eliz. Harpe 4/21/03
   Sam./Mar. Brannon 1/4/07
   Simon/Am. Parrott 5/26/08
   John/Sr. Evans 12/30/11
   Edmund H./Jane Davis 5/30/14
   Wm./Hen. Maria Mitchell 12/21/40
   Anthony/Har. Ann Pitzer 11/6/44
   Tho. M./Marg. Ellen Feron 5/1/47
   Tho./Sr. Ann Thompson 11/9/49
   John Lister/Eliza Stewart 2/25/51
   John D./Mary McIlhenney 5/13/51
   Jos./Ann Lowe 4/19/51
   John R./Marg. Ann Popp 2/12/53
   Wm. R./Ellen Fulk 1/11/53
   Jos./Ann M. Myers 5/10/54
   Franklin P./Fannie A. Miller 12/4/55
473. TUTWILER
   John/Peggy Wright 8/7/05
   Jc./Eve Miller 11/3/21
474. TWIGG
   Rob./Sr. Harmon 10/23/13
   Elias/Eliz. Chaney 1/20/16
   Wm./Mary Jane Medler 4/6/36
   Wm./Mar. Cunningham 4/15/44
475. TYSON
   John/Susan Buckwalter 12/28/50
476. TZSANT (TZSART)
   Dv./Betsey Fulton 11/17/30
477. UHLER
   Geo./Eliz. Basore 3/16/13
478. ULERICH
   Chas./Cath. Freytinger 4/3/37
479. ULERY
   Jc./Isa. Corbut 9/30/30
480. ULHUM
   Wm. Wesley/Mary Eliz. Doren-
   berger 12/6/59
481. ULIUS
   John/Cath. Nunimaker 1/1/08
482. ULRICH (ULLRICH)
   Stephen/Maria Mowen 11/9/03
   John Pt./Mary Stump 3/21/22
   Sam./Annie Skinner 6/2/59
483. ULLUM
   Tho. J./Marg. A. Stouffer 5/5/57
484. UMBAUGH
   Mich./Jane R. Herbert 7/8/19
485. UMPENHOUR
   Mich./Rachel Henry 12/26/20

486. UNCKELSBEE
   Ph./Mary Poffinberger 1/12/16
487. UNDERDONK
   Hilliary/Mary Slyer 9/24/50
488. UNDERWOOD
   John J./So. A. Snyder 2/15/42
489. UNGER
   Fred./So. McClure 12/3/07
   Fred./Eliz. Fishaugh 12/22/27
   Fred./Polly Fishaugh 2/19/28
   Jos./Eliz. Hammett 3/2/30
   Dv./Mary Oswald 3/18/39
   Fred./Eliz. Dibert 2/12/39
   Elias/Eliza Mull 4/6/41
490. UNSELD
   John C./Sr. L. Perry 7/18/28
491. UPDEGRAFF
   Ambrose/Cath. Robinson 3/4/13
   Sam./Susan Boyd 5/6/19
   Geo./Eliza Boyd 9/26/22
   Sam./Fanny S. Irwin 11/26/50
   Wm./Laura A. Mobley 1/16/55
492. UPPERMAN
   John/Eliz. Will 4/13/04
493. UPTON
   John/Eliz. Locker 10/27/34 or 10/27/35
   (2 dates given in cross-index)
494. VALENTINE
   Dn./Susan Adams 9/20/51
   Eli D./Roz. Finefruck 3/29/53
   Calvin L./Mary Ann Goff 8/4/55
495. VANDRUFF
   Adam/Caroline Hershberger 7/31/51
496. VANFOSSAR
   Jesse/Cath. Griner 9/11/07
497. VANFOUKE
   Tho./Calanthia Jane Huyett 12/30/57
498. VAN HORN
   John/Na. White 12/22/18
499 John/Jane Rush 8/3/40
499. VAN LEAR
   Jos./Han. Powell 9/12/18
   Geo. W./Anna Miller 5/5/43
   Mat. S./Sidney McClelland 8/29/43
500. VAN METER
   Abr./Maria C. Van Meter 3/20/27
   A./Eliza Jane Russell 6/25/34
   Jm. A./Mahala Cath. Welchhonce 8/16/49
   Nath./Har. C. Carper 10/9/51
501. VAN SANT
   Peregrine/Eliz. Clayton 2/7/11
502. VARNER
   Abr./Eliz. Thomas 3/8/00
   Abr./Julianna Friend 1/20/05
   John/Freany Buck 8/18/20
503. VASE
   Ambrose/Mary Wood 10/31/08

111

504. VAUGHAN
Gary/Lyida Fagins 9/12/22
505. VEANT
Sam./Agnes Fisher 8/24/49
506. VERBLE
Pt./Barb. Mumma 8/26/03
Matthias/Eliz. Staup 6/20/07
Dn./Sr. Thomas 1/12/22
507. VERMILYEA
Curtis/Polly Artis 6/24/37
508. VERROW
John/Eve Brunner 5/17/17
509. VICKERS
Joshua/Rachel James 1/13/29
Wm./Jerusha Mullen 1/5/56
Rob. D./Ann M. Stripe 8/9/60
510. VINSONHELLER
Rob./Eliz. Hammond 10/30/28
511. VINT
Beniah/Lucy M. Crist 11/7/57
512. VOCIAL
John/Sr. Peterson 10/14/12
513. VOESNER
Jc./Louisa Gelwicks 2/15/43
514. VOGLE
John Leo./Amanda R. Sigler 10/18/53

515. WACHTEL (WAUCHTEL, WOCHTEL, WAUGH-
TELE, WACHTELL)
John/Eliz. Thumb 6/20/08
Val./Marg. Bovey 12/2/22
Jon./Pamelia Barton 1/10/26
Benj. H./Cath. Stull 7/7/49
Dn./Cath. Derr 12/27/56
Benj./Har. Kurley 9/10/57
516. WADE
Cabel/Arey Hall 2/27/04
Wm./Mary Bash 5/28/08
Rich./Mary Ann Ditto 12/1/10
Charley B.F./Am. Miskivens 2/21/20
Hn./Abigail Yertz 4/25/23
John/Eliz. Weaver 6/1/22 (John "of
Henry")
Hn./Na. Crampton 5/12/25
Sol./Sr. Myers 8/16/36
Sol./Mar. Snyder 3/1/45
John Hn./Mary Marg. McCoy 4/1/48
John Hn./Ellen McCoy 1/6/55
Elie/Eliza Roulett 1/17/57
517. WADSWORTH
Geo. W./Mary Ortman 7/19/52
518. WAGAMAN
Dv./Na. Beck 9/28/12
519. WAGELLY (WAGELY, WEAGLEY)
John/Cath. Kneedy 7/8/06
John/Eliz. Showman 3/15/19

John P./Ellen Hilliard 3/27/32
Wm./Susan Zimmerman 6/25/40
Sam. C./Eliz. Renner 2/28/52
520. WAGNER (WAGONER, WAGGONER, WAUGNER)
Fred./Barb. Coon 8/18/01
Jc./Rachel Smith 6/16/09
John Jr./Sus. Rice 3/16/15
Hn./Eliz. Roads 1/13/20
Jc./Mary Welty 12/20/20
Benj./Mary T. Hamm 2/20/21
Chn./Eliz. Haber 4/19/21
Hn./Eliz. Hoover 4/2/22
Sam./Cath. Mumma 5/8/28
Sam./Emma Chaney 3/19/31
Jos./Susan Shecter 12/7/37
Fred./Eliz. Simler 2/19/38
Fred./Debby Oldon 1/19/39
John H./Marg. Gearhart 3/2/52
Jos./Sr. Hartle 12/26/57
Jos./Susan Gearhart 3/7/59
521. WAICKNIGHT (WAKENIGHT, WEIGHNEIGHT)
Dn./Isa. Powell 7/15/16
Jc./Mary Ann Dutrow 12/7/41
John U./Lydia Ann Young 3/24/48
522. WALDICK
And. J./Lavinia Gristle 10/20/59
523. WALKER
Wm./Eliz. Smith 12/26/00
Dn./Mary Keesecker 6/5/17
Sam./Eliza Dean 5/15/17
Aaron/Mary Horsenest 12/31/25
Hugh/Anna Thornton 9/23/33
Tho./Ann W. Fowler 7/23/34
Jm./Reb. Jones 12/15/35
Ed. T./Ann E. Eckard 9/15/48
524. WALLACE (WALLIS)
Jm./Sus. Stack 9/4/99
Wm./Eliz. Steffey 6/11/04
Otho H./Eleanor R. Dugan 1/18/20
Otho/Susan Albert 12/22/29
Wm./Na. Welty 2/9/33
Jm./Sr. Emmert 3/26/36
525. WALLER
Hn./Cath. Adams 11/8/17
526. WALLICK (WALLICH)
Conrad/Cath. Beard 3/2/05
Matthias/Na. Leckrone 4/17/18
John/Susan Fausnaught 8/24/21
Wm./Eliz. C. Long 1/8/53
527. WALLING
Hn./Sr. Cake 6/19/15
528. WALPER
John/Cath. Myers 6/14/15
529. WALTER (WALTERS)
Mich./Marg. Painter 4/24/10
Wm./Sr. Myers 11/23/39
Augustus/Marg. A.B. Tronce 6/30/41

112

529. WALTER (WALTERS) (Continued)
    Bennet G./Emma Murphy 1/8/42
    John/Ann S. Poffenberger 8/6/44
    Geo./Adelaide Giles 7/26/54
530. WALTMYER (WALTMERRY, WALTERMYER)
    Ph./Barb. Wagely 12/14/10
    Hn./Eliz. Zorr 3/22/27
531. WALTON
    Corbin/Cath. Roof 8/29/19
532. WALTZ
    Jc./Sus. Kessler 2/10/00
    John/Ann Winters 4/1/33
    Mt./Sus. Thomas 11/2/43
533. WANTZ (WANSE)
    Dn./Eliza Keller 4/8/37
    Alex./Julian Shup 12/21/41
    Adam/Eliza Ripp 6/7/43
534. WARBLE
    Jc./Am. Eakel 3/27/27
    Amos E./Caroline Eliz. Hoover
      12/31/35
535. WARD
    Jos./Eliz. Agleston 9/17/07
    Jm./Patty Ward 9/8/09
    Tho./Sus. Karrells 12/11/12
    Rich./Lydia Alley 2/16/14
    Jc./Rachel Miller 12/11/16
    Jc./Hester Miller 5/10/27
    Wm./Eliz. Bouce 1/29/35
    Aaron/Marg. Ann Rohrer 6/2/40
    Wm. S./Lucinda H. Yost 8/2/45
    Sam./Eliz. Shaw 11/17/52
    Zelophed/Mary Miller 9/20/53
    Jm./Maria Shank 3/7/54
    Jos./Eliz. Jane Nichodemus 11/27/60
536. WARDEN
    Sam. R./Mary Eliz. Saylor 5/9/55
537. WAREHAN
    Dv./Ann Simmers 9/30/56
538. WARFIELD
    Pruety/Cath. Johnston 5/1/15
    Nich./Eliz. Leggett 6/15/20
    Wm./Jane Jackson 6/22/25
    John/Ruth Lemonds 8/11/32
    Ph. P./Mary Hill 10/24/44
539. WARNER (WARNAR)
    Dv./Polly Shank 11/2/04
    Jos./Marg. Wright 5/16/07
    Dv./Eliz. Dugan 7/29/19
    Abr./Eliz. Geeding 5/21/25
    John/Mary Ann Cook 1/2/26
    Dv./Mary Ann Shaw 1/26/33
    Hn./Chna. Bovey 11/28/38
    Geo./Ann Bowers 4/27/39
    John/Rose Ann Marshall 7/19/49
    Pt./Marg. Miller 1/16/51
    John/Susan Spotts 10/19/53
    Rob./Mary Eliz. Shafer 4/5/53

    Geo. An./Susan Kath. Foutz 6/26/55
    Zebedee/Sr. C. Snively 9/9/56
540. WARRENFELTZ (WANERFELS, WEAREFELTZ,
    WERENFELS)
    John/Mary Leatherman 12/13/09
    Ph./Cath. Leatherman 4/27/12
    Dn./Susan Ludy 2/3/43
    John/Marg. Jane McGruder 6/26/48
    Jc./Susan L. Stonebraker 12/16/54
    Sol./Tracy Ann Easterday 12/14/58
541. WARSELL
    Jm./Rachel Diddle 1/10/03
542. WART (WURT)
    Harman/Sus. Miller 10/1/99
543. WASERMAN
    Jc./Eliz. Brosh 8/31/12
544. WASHABAUGH
    Dv./Marg. Houseman 11/9/01
    Sam./Sr. McLaughlin 9/6/26
545. WASHINGTON
    Elias/Reb. Hamilton 3/13/26
    W. Fairfax/M.A. Dorsey 10/5/52
546. WASSON
    Augustus/Mary Hagenberger 10/26/54
547. WASSON
    Jm./Mary A. McLanahan 4/15/43
    Wm./Maria Hess 1/15/43
548. WATERMYER
    Jos./So. Adams 4/30/37
549. WATERS (WATTER)
    Hn./Eliz. Sturr (Sture) 3/29/15
    Hiram S./Eliza Bargwar 9/6/43
    Ansolum/Mary Nikirk 2/21/44
    Jos. G./Mar. Clagett 11/5/53
550. WATKINS
    Horatio/Hen. Sterling 8/7/05
    Benj./Marg. Haverstick 12/31/29
    Is./Eliz. Gearheart 7/27/29
    Dv./Marg. Panal 1/30/34
    Rich./Ros. Startzman 3/17/34
    Ed./Susan Wolf 3/23/36
    Rob./Helena Bevans 2/12/38
    Jm./Roz. Bragonier 2/20/51
551. WATSON
    Hn./Marg. Richardson 10/6/02
    Wm./Sr. Beck 8/9/04
    Abr./Eliz. River 9/23/06
    Rich./Sr. Hovermale 2/5/08
    Conrad/Eliz. Hose 3/22/21
    Simon/Rachel E. Friend 1/30/24
    Lewis/Eliz. Grim 5/21/32
    Jm./Sr. Donnelly 2/28/35
    Matthias/Sr. Ann Rulett 6/8/35
    Rob./Mary Rohrer 12/14/38
    Jos./Eliz. Eakle 2/1/42
    Jos. N./Mary E. Clabaugh 2/25/51
    Dn./Mary Ann Knode 10/11/59
    Geo. A./Caroline Sager 3/26/58

552. WATT (WATTS)
    Tho./Sr. Newson 5/4/03
    John/Eve Bower 11/8/06
    Jos./Susan Alter 12/11/33
    Jc./Frederica Biser 8/14/41
    Tho. B./Lydia A. Shecter 1/11/41
    Frisby D./Na. South 8/11/45
    Abr. N./Mary McCoy 9/15/46
    Ed./Sally A. Hollingsworth 12/23/56
553. WAUGH
    Arch. M./Cath. Hager 1/5/04
    John/Jane Connelly 11/22/13
    Tho. M./Eliza Muria Kealhofer 8/14/26
554. WAY
    Grantham/Mary Ann Anderson 4/28/32
555. WAYMAN
    Peregrine/Julia Herbert 5/16/11
556. WEAKFIELD
    Chn./Barb. Krailey 10/13/09
557. WEARHAM
    Wm./Sr. F. Williams 9/27/32
558. WEAST
    Jos./Sus. Speelman 11/16/14
    Hn./Sus. Hufford 6/24/22
    Jos./Jane Lesley 7/28/24
    Hn./Lucinda Dagonhart 2/28/33
    Hiram/Susan Horine 6/27/36
    Geo. L./Isa. G. Remley 11/22/49
559. WEASTER
    Pt./Cath. Adams 9/7/14
560. WEAVER (WEVER, WEABER)
    Mich./Mary Spessart 11/15/02
    Lewis/Har. O'Neal 1/18/03
    Hn./Agnes Morrison 10/1/07
    John/Eliz. Harmon 11/17/10
    Jm./Cath. Glass 1/18/12
    Mich./Eliz. Wisinger 4/25/15
    John/Phebe Waters 2/8/30 ("John Waters"
      in cross-index)
    Ambrose/Cath. Diffenbaugh 12/21/33
    Dv./Amanda Burns 9/18/33
    Ferdinand/Mary Beyers (Boyers) 12/20/37
    Hn./Cath. Butler 6/13/39
    Jon./Mary A. Hammer 5/14/46
    Ph./Mary McMullen 5/9/46
    Dv./Ann Reb. Davis 5/18/50
    Geo./Ellenora Spickler 1/8/51
    Pt./Marg. Miller 1/16/51
561. WEBB
    Wm. Jr./Mary Baker 4/28/04
    Jos. B./Eliz. Wilson 11/18/06
    Geo./Anna Allender 10/27/07
    Pointon/Mary Webb 10/13/19
    Nath./Har. Allender 11/29/20
    Pointon/Mary Young 5/23/27
    Arthur B./Mary Ann Young 5/3/36
    Jackson/Eliz. Cridler 9/21/48
562. WEBER
    Geo. R./Susan Shepherd 4/25/32

    Jon./Mary Ruth 2/19/44
    Abr./Na. Schnebly 12/17/60
563. WEBSTER
    Tho. D./Sr. Jane Ott 5/15/41
564. WECKSER
    Mich./Char. Boteler 6/13/12
565. WEDDLE (WETTLE)
    John/Eliz. Wissinger 10/9/28
    Sam./Elizth Welty 9/10/50
566. WEDDOWS (WIDDOWS)
    John/Polly Whetstone 4/4/15
567. WEEKS
    Moses/Marg. Snapp 12/28/12
568. WEGENAST
    Chn./Barb. Bernhart 2/15/53
569. WEIBEL
    Wm./Maria Arndt 4/25/43
570. WEIGHTMAN
    And./Sr. Ormston 10/24/32
571. WEINBOROW
    Wm./Rachel McCoy 12/7/19
572. WEIS (WEISE)
    Dn./Mary Steffy 6/24/24
    Rich./Sr. Kline 4/7/25
    Wm./Mary Swartzwelder 10/15/29
    John/Adaline G. Lancaster 1/30/30 or
      1/28/30 (2 dates given)
    John C./Susan McMullen 1/2/37
    Wm./Louisa Heitzler 3/27/38
    Ezra/Cath. McCardle 11/16/41
    Wm./Emma Jane Kealhofer 4/6/48
573. WEISEL (WEISELL)
    Dn./Matilda Davis 10/16/27
574. WELCH (WELCK)
    Rich./Marg. Gower 5/13/29
    Elias/Eliz. Johnson 5/20/30
    John/Am. Kreek 9/22/32
    Sylvester/Rachel E. Rector 9/25/34
    Jer./Eliza Mason 12/13/36
    Jos./Reb. Smith 2/19/38
    Lawson B./Julia Horine 5/15/43
    Chas./Ann E. Knode 12/20/55
575. WELDIN
    Jc./Allas Grush 12/29/37
576. WELHELM
    Dv./Ann Maria Bowers 11/25/31
577. WELHOUSE
    Geo./Eliz. Nighswander 11/18/20
578. WELLER
    Barnabus/Rachel England 4/5/56
579. WELLS
    Is./Eliz. Herring 6/28/20
    Tho./Susan Petery 1/3/33
580. WELSH
    John/Cath. Snyder 8/24/07
    Jm./Eliz. H. Smith 8/28/21
    Levi/Sr. Hill 1/25/31
    Mich./Julian Robertson 1/22/33
    Rich./Joanna Carroll 10/2/33

580. WELSH (Continued)
    Benj. B./Eliz. B. Gilbert 5/18/40
    Wm. B./Mary Jane Crissman 12/29/46
581. WELSHANS
    Ph. H./Sr. Jane Mallory 11/24/56
    Hn./Cath. Eliz. Dollwick 5/18/58
582. WELSLAGER
    Sam./Mary Welsh 3/13/23
583. WELTY (WELDY)
    John/Sus. Holms 2/11/04
    Hn./Mag. Newcomer 10/14/05
    Jc./Eliz. Hohn 8/24/10
    Dv./Mary Gehr 11/2/13
    Hn. C./Eliz. Keedy 12/22/13
    Chn./Mary Trubey 1/29/14
    Jc./Mary E. Coon 12/20/23
    Sam./Eliz. Middlekauff 11/29/27
    Geo./Frances Hammond 1/28/30
    John H./Sally Emmert 1/26/31
    John/Mary Wolf 12/1/32
    Chn./Cath. Hiett 6/29/39
    Mich./Am. South 8/17/39
    John/Eliz. Bovey 10/11/41
    Dn./Ann S. Zuck 9/8/48
    Hn. S./Chna. Newcomer 1/18/50
    Hn. S./Susan Coffman 2/18/50
    Chn./Maria Coffman 12/27/52
    Tyrus/Amanda A. Nyman 10/24/54
    Dv./Laura A. Shafer 2/23/59
    Jc. E./Emma E. Albaugh 9/6/59
584. WENTEMOYER
    Hn./Sr. Kretzer 1/6/27
585. WENTLING (WENDLING)
    John/Cath. Server 8/16/06
586. WERNER
    Wm. R./Reb. Emerson 5/2/40
587. WEST
    Mat./Prudence Hathorn 12/16/24
    Dv. P./Otillia Heaflich 4/14/29
    Tho./Cath. Hoffmaster 2/18/36
    Wesley/Ann Powell 7/1/37
    Wm./Eliz. Nichols 8/11/41
    Jer./Sr. Mull 2/28/42
    Dn. P./Emily Pattison 10/9/44
    Tho./Cath. Deter 5/20/44
    Wm. H./Francis Wolfenberger 12/16/50
588. WESTENBERGER (WESTERBERGER, WESTE-
    BERGER, WESTENBARGER)
    Dv./Sus. Oxx 4/11/00
    John/Eliz. Sands 5/4/11
    John/Susan Hines 2/14/29
589. WHARTON
    John O./Eliz. A.T. Mason 4/9/29
    Rob./Sr. J. Duvall 5/30/53

590. WHEELER
    Jos./Anna Bond 3/13/12
    Jos. Jr./Lavinia Reynolds 6/15/39
591. WHERROTT (WHERRITT)
    Geo./Barb. Grush 3/11/01
    Geo./Sr. McIntosh 9/2/16
    John/Eliz. Downs 4/21/17
    Sam./Eliz. Hyatt 6/25/29
592. WHETSELL (WHITESELL, WHETSEL)
    John/Eve Hass 5/31/00
    Pt./Ann Moyer 5/8/28
    Alford/Ellen Betz 12/29/47
593. WHETSTONE (WHITESTONE)
    John/Eliz. Renner 9/20/01
    Jc./Sr. Armstrong 12/23/24
    John/Drusey Biderman 8/15/32
594. WHIP (WHIPP)
    Sam./Maria O'Neall 12/25/15
    Pt./Sr. House 8/30/39
595. WHITE
    Jesse/Lydia McIntire 9/3/01
    Is./Mary Grove 5/19/06
    Is. S./Mary Rench 9/21/09
    Wm./Na. Stephens 8/6/10
    Joshua/Na. Hayes 11/30/13
    Wm./Am. Clinetage 3/9/18
    Jesse/Cath. Fraley 12/10/21
    Ed./Polly Kuhn 10/1/34
    John H./Eliz. Leasure 1/25/40
    Dn./Marg. Burkhart 3/2/48
    Madison/Ann Highbarger 3/26/49
596. WHITEFOOT
    Tho./Lydia Emerson 6/27/29
597. WHITEKENNACK (WITHENNECK, WETHKNECHT)
    John/Ann Shook 3/31/10
    Jc./Mary Apeier 8/12/24
598. WHITEMAN
    Chn./Cath. Steffy 6/1/13
599. WHITESIDE
    Sam. H./Anna Stewart 9/26/11
600. WHITING
    Dv./Sr. Duckett 6/13/44
601. WHITLOCK
    John/Na. Haysted 10/23/99
602. WHITMORE
    Pt./Polly Shank 12/21/02
603. WHITSON (WITSON)
    Is./Phoebe Pussmore 1/14/01
    Rob./Mary Ann Jamison 1/17/38
    Wm. A./Lydia Schappart 2/22/51
604. WICK (WICKES)
    Addison/Jane Savage 7/7/35
    Elias/Belinda Unclesbee 3/28/39
605. WICKARSHIP
    Jon./Jane Beason 8/29/03

606. WIDENER
Jc./Mary Ann Beard 5/7/26
607. WILAND (WILEN)
John/Eliz. Troup 3/19/14
Wm./Sr. Bickley 4/21/15
Nich./Marg. Doople 1/24/18
Dv./Mary Jane Turner 1/20/44
608. WILCOX
Wm. G./Mar. A. Nixon 10/22/42
609. WILCOXEN
Hanson T./Mary K. Mason 1/30/55
610. WILDERS (WILLDERS)
Jer./Eleanor McGinley 4/28/09
Jm./Cath. Judy 8/23/14
Nich./Marg. Dooble 1/24/18
611. WILES
Dv./Mary Teiderick 6/11/17
John/Emma C. Brewer 11/17/58
612. WILEY
John A./Mary L. Kidwell 5/7/49
613. WILHELMS (WILLHAM)
John/Reb. Thomas 6/18/03
Ph./Ruhannah Willchantz 8/7/17
Sam./Mary Seibert 11/27/37
614. WILKINSON
Hn./Julian Wilkinhood 3/7/24
Tho./Sr. Funk 6/28/32
615. WILKS
Fred./Mary Ann Thumb 8/28/46
616. WILLARD (WILLIARD, WILLYARD)
Elias/Mary Baker 3/5/08
John/Barb. Ridenour 8/2/11
Perry/Lydia J. Allen 12/5/39
617. WILLHIDE
Fred. Lewis/Eliz. Moxley 12/13/41
618. WILLIAMS
Otho H./Eliz. Bowie Hall 10/7/00
Rob./Eliz. Austin 5/16/02
Elisha/Lydia Boyer 12/12/07
John/Eliz. James 7/30/07
Tho. O./Sr. Lykens 8/15/10
Ed./Marg. Davis 12/26/11
Elijah/Cath. Snyder 2/7/11
Abell/Cath. Horine 4/8/14
John/Eve Guyer 4/3/17
John/Maria Greenwell 4/26/21
Otho Holland/Eliz. England Van Lear
7/14/23
Abner/Mary Shecter 8/16/28
Pheneas/Mary Miller 1/29/29
Tho./Barb. Wisman 11/4/29
John/Han. Cunningham 12/23/34
Sam. H./Mary E. Marmaduke 5/2/35
Ed. C./Sr. C. Sheppart 9/28/36
Jc./Cath. Coon 3/21/36
Elie/Eliz. Reed 3/25/40
John/Cath. E. Ireston 3/4/43
Dv. A./Matilda Weagley 8/31/47
Burton/Marg. J. Anderson 10/14/50

John/Marg. M. Kailor 2/19/51
John R./Cath. Bowman 12/20/51
619. WILLIAMSON
Sam./Ann Nicols 12/23/00
Sam./Ann Johns 4/21/08
Jm. H./Cath. Shaffer 10/1/28
Dv./Eliz. R. Keighn 9/29/34
Warren R./Ann Maria Lutter or Sutter
11/23/37
Wm. S./Cath. E. Powles 9/22/47
620. WILLIS
Wm./Eliz. Coon 3/24/04
Levin C./Eliza Orndorff 10/22/14
Geo./Lavinia Slusman 2/8/39
Wm./Reb. Bridges 10/27/56
621. WILLS
Tho./Na. I. Stephens 12/16/33
622. WILSON
Wm./Lydia Owings 9/29/04
John/Isa. Getty 2/15/05
Jm./Sr. Sinicke 8/26/13
Jos./Mary Beard 12/21/13
Dv. T./Ann Mary Cramer 4/18/16
Is./Cholie Ann Louise Doans 2/26/16
Jm./Mar. Ditto 9/16/17
Rob./Eliz. Caldwell 1/14/17
John/Sr. Hayes 1/6/18
Rob./Eliz. Simmers 4/14/18
Jm./Mary Frazier 3/16/19
Jm./Ann Eliza Gordon 11/14/20
Shipwitt C./Sr. Weisel 5/6/20
Tho./Har. Peterson 1/31/20
John K./Susan N. Chapline 4/10/21
Dv. T./Susan Bean 12/27/26
Greenbury Barker/Louisianna Orndorff
5/23/26
Asaph/Na. Olock 5/17/32
Jm./Maria Spangler 7/21/32
Sam./Am. Stouffer 12/20/34
Wm. H./Sr. Knodle 3/8/37
John/Eleanora Cross 9/1/38
Tho./Sus. Tucker 2/24/41
Wm./Rose Ann Mills 9/23/41
Tho./Mary Scuffins 10/14/47
Is./Susan R. Baker 11/6/48
John G./Mary Jane Brent 5/1/48
Jm./Jane McGraw 10/22/51
Jesse Jr./Ann E. Hytle 7/17/51
Joshua G./Eliza Petre 1/10/54
Jc./Cath. Titlow 4/22/56
H.B./Eliz. E. Kennedy 11/18/57
John R./S. Georgetta Anderson 8/28/60
Wm. H./Susan Newcomer 9/18/60
623. WINDEL (WINDLE)
John/Eliz. Frorisburry 4/7/06
Tempel/Phebe Zirk 9/5/15
Wm./Marg. Harmon 7/25/25
John/Ruann Boyd 12/10/44

116

624. WINDER (WINDERS)
John/Sr. Adams 9/7/99
John/Eliz. Ridenour 3/22/03
Geo./Jane Burns 10/7/19
Sam./Sus. Newcomer 6/9/23
Jc./Sr. Landis 10/25/25
Dn./Cath. M. Knode 9/2/26
John/Reb. Slenker 4/3/30
John/Lydia Ann Shoop 12/27/48
John/Susan Powell 12/14/50
Sam. Jr./Fanny Kreps 9/27/51
Elias/Eliz. Eyerly 11/9/53
625. WINDERHALTER
Jc./Rachel Miley 7/29/33
626. WINEBRENNER
Jc./Mary Goll 4/17/13
Chn./Mary Winders 6/11/14
John/Cath. Esminger 5/18/16
627. WINGERT
John/Cath. Rowland 11/18/11
John/Mary Newcomer 8/12/19
A.B./Mary Zellers 11/12/22
Adam/Marg. Zeller 10/7/46
John C./Huldah Miller 10/22/47
Jc./Na. Miller 8/15/48
Ph. H./Eliza Jane Fiery 3/17/56
628. WINKFIELD
John/Eliz. Tracey 11/19/31
Dv./Susan Snyder 6/15/57
629. WINSH
John Jc./Marg. Baker 10/15/56
630. WINTER (WINTERS)
Wm./Mary Keller 10/14/11
Geo./So. Keller 8/29/23
Joshua/Eliz. Kretzer 11/17/27
Chn./Cath. Cramer 9/12/29
John/Mary B. Mason 4/9/33
J.G./Susan Tritle 2/7/37
John/Marg. Oswald 10/31/38
Dn./Sr. Ann Bowser 12/31/40
Jos./Agnes A.M. Allender 1/8/42
Dv./Ann M. Colliflower 10/28/45
Wm. R./Mary Maysilles 8/18/57
631. WINSEL
Benj./Allice Cammerron 11/13/24
632. WISE
John/Chna. Keller 12/27/02
Jc./Emeally Moore 11/29/06
Sam./Cath. Miller 4/27/13
Geo./Mary Kreps 11/25/15
Dn./Na. Greenawalt 7/26/30
Geo./Eleanor Hammer 12/14/35
Joshua D./Sr. E. Flinn 11/4/42
Hn./Sr. Zellers 6/3/44
Jc. H./Cath. Middlekauff 12/12/53
John C./Amanda Flory 9/7/57
Rich. H./Mary E. McGlone 2/4/58

633. WISENER
Hn./Rachel Howard 2/3/41
634. WISHARD (WISHART)
Jc./Rachel Myers 11/4/09
John/Eliz. Coal 11/27/15
Ed./Amanda A. Smith 2/26/50
John D./Tracy R. Eavey 4/10/54
Wm./Lydia Bear 1/20/55
635. WISMER
John Jr./Sr. Hiskey 3/12/28
636. WISNER
Hn./Chna. Smith 12/30/12
637. WISSINGER
S.D./Eliz. Acor 8/22/56
638. WITHER (WITHERS)
Jc./Cath. Zerbe 11/10/18
639. WITHINGTON
Hn. A./Priscilla A. Kershner 3/19/44
640. WITMER
John Jr./Ros. Brewer 1/31/20
John/Susan Smith 1/24/25
Dv./Mary Horine 12/21/29
Abr./Lydia Newcomer 2/24/30
Benj./Cath. Hammond 12/18/32
Geo./Ann Maria Gilper 3/3/32
Pt./Cath. Farst 1/24/33
John Sr./Mary Silvers 8/30/38
Fred./Na. Dick 8/21/44
Hn. B./Sr. Char. Crammer 6/12/48
Dv./Eliz. Hoffman 12/5/57
Calvin/Han. M.W. O'Neal 2/1/58
Milton/Sr. Ann Foultz 2/7/60
641. WITTER
Benj./So. Nichodemus 11/9/31
Emanuel/Sr. Baker 4/6/33
Jc./Amanda Huffer 1/12/57
642. WOESTLER
Jc./Eliz. Stokes 5/7/10
643. WOLF (WOFF, WOLFE)
Dn./Mag. Springer 11/3/01
Fred./Motlina Smith 1/27/01
Jos./Mary Springer 6/2/01
John/Eliz. Middlekauff 3/19/11
Conrad/Sus. Potter 8/24/13
John/Cath. Ward 8/7/13
Dv./Sus. Middlekauff 10/23/16
Jc./Sr. Snyder 8/15/16
John/Cath. Walper 7/24/17
Pt./Mary Owings 8/7/17
Wm./Cath. Metz 2/3/18
John/Mariah Museter 7/3/20
Geo./Ann Eliz. Brunner 8/24/20
Sam./Mary Coon 9/19/20
Dn./Eliz. Bennett 12/28/22
John/Eliz. Miller 7/31/24
Jm./Eliz. Shilling 8/26/30
Sam./Barb. Witmer 7/26/31

643. WOLF (WOFF, WOLFE) (Continued)
Dv./Cath. Hauver 10/19/32
Jos./Anna Kretzer 1/14/32
Jos. M./Cath. Thomas 2/14/37
John/Lucretia McClain 9/17/39
Mt./Eliz. Kemp 11/19/39
Pl./Mary Druner 11/23/39
Dv./Eliz. Bowers 11/11/40
John/Matilda Sager 7/27/40
John/Mary Ann Rowland 2/8/40
John/Lucretia Knodle 12/21/40
Dv./Marg. Rinehart 5/15/41
Simon/Eliz. Warwell 8/23/43
Dv./Susan Yaler 9/21/44
John W./Sr. Snyder 8/16/45
Adam/Victoria Schleigh 7/4/46
Dv. Jr./Mary Long 2/11/46
Geo. W./Mary Hoffman 10/19/49
John/Eliza A. Middlekauff 12/19/49
Jos./Mar. Taylor 2/20/49
Jos./Joan Protzman 8/2/49
Dn./Ann M. Rowland 10/14/50
Dv./Eliz. Carson 10/31/50
Jc./Mary Ellen Albaugh 12/9/51
Dv./Rachel Hawthorn 1/26/53
Hn./M.A.J. McClain 10/26/53
Geo. Y./Louisa Knave 3/11/54
Wm./Na. Maugins 4/1/56
John Hn./Sr. Ann Shatzer 3/25/57
Geo. Y./Marg. McMullen 1/1/59
644. WOLFENSBERGER (WOFELSBURGER,
WOLFERSBERGER)
John/Sr. Sailer 5/29/12
Jos./Sus. Shanefelt 1/11/25
Jos./Mary Ann Dibert 12/8/34
Jos. S./Sr. S. Neibert 11/13/47
645. WOLFINGER
Mich./Sr. Fultz 11/6/02
Jc./Na. Iahn 12/3/33
646. WOLFKILL
John/Eliz. Reynolds 9/26/07
John/Eliz. Price 1/25/20
Jc./Eliz. Mace 3/30/21
Elie/Mary Ann Clarke 4/27/43
Jc./Jane Brinham 12/13/48
647. WOLFORD (WOOLFORD)
Hn./Eliz. Knodle 12/25/01
Mich./Cath. Bowman 6/8/05
John/Sus. Knodle 12/7/07
John/Eliz. Bowers 4/16/16
John/Ann Noll 11/18/19
Hn./Sus. Knodle 1/14/23
Tho./Ann Huyet 12/5/32
John Hn./Marg. Ann Painter 8/24/46
Jc. B./Sr. E. Brewer 1/28/53
Tho./Lucretia Downs 9/26/57
Jc. E./Eleanor Popp 11/11/58
Upton H./Celinary Cramer 3/30/58

648. WOLGAMOT (WOLGAMORE)
Sam./Mary Beard 9/28/11
John/Julianna Abell 6/28/15
Jos./Nancy Baer 5/20/15
John/Susan Martin 10/26/19
And./Mary Tice 5/13/22
John/Mary Ann Fiery 7/28/27
649. WOLKE
Wisset/Eliz. Rohr 12/13/48
650. WOLTZ
John/Leah Updegraff 3/2/09
Wm./Polly Simkins 3/21/09
Sam./Cath. Bowman 4/10/10
Elie/Eliz. Walling 6/29/16
Jm./Louisa Petre 12/31/38
Chas. W./Am. Stake 4/15/50
Sam. A./Cath. Wolf 2/26/50
John R./Cath. C. McCusker 7/26/51
651. WOLVINGTON
Jm. W./Cath. M. Garlin 6/1/49
652. WONDERLICK
Dv./Sr. Newman 4/24/32
653. WOOD
Jos./Mary Crampton 10/21/99
Rich./Mary Hall 11/10/07
Wm. H./Mary Welch 2/22/38
Israel/Eliz. Jordan 11/3/47
654. WOODEN (WOOTEN)
Randolph/Cath. Sydel 5/13/99
655. WORLAND
Chas./Polly Damsey 3/12/00
656. WORLEY
John/Eve Tice 8/4/08
657. WOTRING (WOODRING)
Nich./Polly Sheats 3/31/00
Abr./Eliz. Rahauser 3/15/25
658. WRIGHT
Pt./Sus. Lefever 7/29/06
Tho./Mar. Cromley 3/28/12
Jesse/Na. Tracy 7/22/14
Jesse/Na. Fogle 10/21/15
Tho./Mag. Hose 11/14/16
John/Mary Ann Rickenbaugh 2/14/18
John/Eliz. King 5/21/18
Tho./Eliz. Snyder 7/20/29
Wm./Susan Miller 10/29/31
Wm./Maria Doup 4/20/33
Tho./Mar. Rohrer 7/24/35
Jm. R./Eliz. Hill 10/5/48
Lewis/Ann Maria Hill 11/2/48
Pt./Lydia Feigley 11/29/55
Ezra/Susan Wyand 12/23/56
Wm. H./Frances Reid 3/18/58
Wm. E./Mary E. Thornsburg 11/17/59
659. WROE
John A./Mar. Jane Barr 1/15/44
660. WURSTER
Fred./Chra. Eidel 3/8/08

118

661. WYAND (WYANT, WYIANT, WIANT)
     Hn./Eliz. Warner 7/19/10
     John/Eliz. Kealhofer 9/11/10
     Jc./Sus. Ridenour 6/1/14
     Hn./Cath. Krise 12/10/16
     Chn./Mercy Cost 4/8/25
     Wm./Rhinhandle Sturn 7/18/26
     Yost/Eliz. Neikirk 12/17/27
     Simon/Reb. Geeding 10/27/30
662. WYND
     Joshua/Ann M. Middlekauff 3/7/59
663. WYNKOOP
     Garrett/Julia A. Moutz 11/17/41
664. WYSONG
     John/Helen Marietta Hebb 2/24/29

665. YAKLE (YAKEL)
     John/Cath. Eastachins 9/5/25
     Wm./Har. M. Hoye 10/27/28
     Tho./Am. Wolford 10/9/32
666. YANDERS
     Simon/Reb. Trovinger 9/7/12
667. YEAKLE
     John/Sus. Miller 10/26/99
     Jc./Eliz. Wilson 9/25/02
     Amos/Cath. Specart 11/5/03
     John/Chna. Teeterly 2/22/03
     Geo./Eliz. Clarke 11/9/16
     Dv./Eliz. Boward 1/1/36
     Pt./Louisa Seavers 9/26/38
     Sam./Mary E. Stover 3/2/53
     John C./Jocana Shirey 9/3/56
668. YERGER
     Mich./Marg. Shull 11/17/00
669. YERKESS
     Joshua/Marg. Reed 9/11/06
670. YERTY
     Dn./Eliz. Rohrback 2/16/35
671. YESLER (YESSLER)
     Hn./Cath. Statler 12/26/10
     John/Sus. Baker 8/12/37
     Jos. H./Eliz. Doub 2/9/52
     Sam./Eliz. Bowers 12/23/58
672. YETNYRE
     Hn./Betsey Yetnyre 2/14/49
673. YOE
     Benj./Narcissa Ann Post 10/8/29
674. YONSON
     Pt./Mary Gassman 11/21/60
675. YONTZ (YOUNCE)
     Wm./Sus. Swope 8/1/01
     John/Prudence Entler 10/30/28
     Mt./Cath. Deale 8/15/29
     Reason/Mary Shoop 9/17/31
     Jc./Emily Harp 9/4/32
     Jos./Mary Kanine 4/5/32
     John/Har. Windle 2/27/41
     Wm. H.H./Marg. Kochenor 12/23/58

676. YORTY
     Geo./Mary Mahan 1/23/28
677. YOUNG
     Geo./Mary Bowser 6/28/02
     John/Eliz. Deitsch 3/15/11
     Geo./Peggy Swagely 4/16/16
     Sam./Na. Dibert 6/1/16
     Jc./Marg. Bowman 2/3/18
     Sam./Har. Strain 9/15/18
     John/Mary C. Shaffer 2/28/29
     John/Barb. Huffer 3/24/32
     John/Cath. Spielman 8/24/32
     Wm./Ann Dellinger 12/25/33
     Wm./Na. Long 4/7/34
     Wm. H./Susan Poffenberger 1/6/36
     John W./Maria Edwards 3/25/39
     Ph./Eliz. Nichodemus 9/24/39
     John/Eliz. Kimler 6/2/40
     Geo./Susan Bowman 1/25/42
     Greenbery/Sr. Hutzell 5/14/44
     Elie/Caroline Bear 3/22/47
     Gideon/Frances Bowers 2/28/48
     Matthias/Ann Maria Geltmaker 11/12/49
     Wash./Sr. Cath. Lock 8/6/49
     John D./Maria Keyser 2/1/51
     Elias/Roseann Bear 2/7/54
     John H./Hen. Coffman 11/15/55
     Augustus/Laura Frances Claggett 12/29/5
678. YOUNKER
     Adam/Cath. Poffenberger 3/5/14
679. YOUNKIN
     A.C./M.C. Jones 2/28/54 (no indication
        of the female)
680. YOUTZ
     Benj./Polly Hammond 4/15/11
     Jos./Mary Snyder 2/8/15
     Cornelius G.W./Mary Wise 7/28/40
681. YOWLER (YOULER)
     Geo./Eliz. Bowers 10/31/16
     Sam. B./Mary A. Nufer 5/19/51
     Geo. W./Reb. Shafer 11/1/58
682. YRO
     Benj./Mary Helm 3/23/11

683. ZEIGLER (ZIEGLER)
     Lewis/Cath. Lantz 11/29/09
     Jc./Marg. Stenger 3/6/18
     Geo./Sus. Russell 10/9/21
     Tho./Cath. Smith 9/10/36
     Arch./Maria Mayhew 6/17/37
     Geo./Elenora Bigler 7/28/40
     Lewis/Eliz. Myers 10/5/44
     Sam. F./Louisa J. Barr 1/23/49
     Wm./Rose Ann Myers 7/19/49
     Geo./Ann R. Hoffman 4/8/50
     Chas. W./Amanda Springer 1/27/58

119

684. ZELLER (ZELLAR, ZELLERS, ZELLARS)
    Otho/Barb. Spiegler 4/16/08
    Otho/Eve Pollinger 6/7/20
    Dn./Eliz. B. Fouke 2/21/25
    Dv./Theresa Rench 5/11/26
    Sam./Marg. Young 12/20/26
    Sam./Susan McLaughlin 4/7/27
    Otho/Mary Harry 12/1/36
    Dn./Rachel Pheasant 4/6/37
    Hn./Adelaide M. Anderson 4/26/38
    Dn./Mary Long 3/27/41
    John/Eliza McLaughlin 10/2/44
    Hn./Ann Sellers 12/30/51
    Jc./Ann Am. Shelleberger 11/24/56
685. ZENTMYER
    Sam./Lydia Hockley 12/14/40
686. ZIMMERMAN
    Jos./Sus. Kuhn 7/17/23
    Barney/Sr. Sager 12/1/27
    Pt./So. South 12/1/34
    Jc./Mary M. Harr 4/9/35
    Benj./Cath. Cronise 3/21/41

And./Barb. Oertel 9/6/48
Elias/Mary C. Keiper 3/6/56
687. ZINKAND
    Lau./Mary Ann Swinger 9/13/55
688. ZITTLE
    Sam./Lydia Muck 2/23/49
    John H./Eliz. Smith 5/18/52
689. ZIVISLER
    Jm./Ann Waugh 4/30/27
690. ZOLL
    Jc./Eliz. Shafer 3/28/34
    Jc./Amanda Poffenberger 12/23/37
691. ZOLLEM
    Chas. Fred. T./Henietta Brookelman
        12/6/56
692. ZOLLINGER
    Geo./Cath. Myers 10/21/19
693. ZUCK (ZOOK)
    John H./Eliz. A. Downes 9/14/26
    Hn./Sr. Zilhart 9/8/38
694. ZUMBRUM
    Jc./Sr. Hann 11/8/55

-A-
ABELL Julianna, 118
  Mary, 81
ACHLE Cath., 5
ACKERSON Mary, 35
ACOR Eliz., 117
ADAM Sr., 78
ADAMS Am., 61
  Ann Cecelia, 71
  Caroline, 37
  Cath., 47, 94, 106,
112, 114
  Eliz., 82, 99
  Ellen, 61
  Helena, 80
  Loretta, 32
  Magdalen, 98
  Mar., 90
  Marg., 108
  Na., 70
  Peggy, 55
  Reb., 19
  So., 113
  Sr., 117
  Sr. Ann, 11, 78
  Sus., 54
  Susan, 111
ADAMSON Ann, 17
ADKINSON Marg., 104
ADLEY Mary Ann, 49
ADLUM Mary, 35
AERBERGER Barb., 82
AGLESTON Eliz., 113
  Mary, 37
AINSWORTH Eliz., 16
  Mary Ann, 41
  Na. Ann, 17
  Sus., 42
AKEY Ann Matilda, 59
ALABAUGH Mary, 2
ALBAUGH Cath., 42
  Emma E., 115
  Marg. Ann, 17
  Mary Ellen, 118
ALBERS Am. R., 104
ALBERT Adaline, 76
  Am. Ann, 47
  Ann Maria, 5
  Cath., 35, 38, 58,
64
  Char. E., 36
  Eleanor, 109
  Eliz., 90, 96
  Isa. V., 95
  Lavinia, 106
  Marg., 30, 88
  Marg. E., 41
  Mary, 65, 67, 69,
107
  Mary E., 66

Na., 84
Sus., 69
Susan, 2, 112
ALBERTS Ellen, 96
ALBREGH Betsy, 11
ALBRIGHT Cath., 76
  Esther, 89
  Marg., 38
  Reb., 86
ALBURTIS Rosa E., 70
ALDRAY Cath., 83
ALDRIDGE Eliz., 9
ALEXANDER Eliz. P., 46
  Ruth, 86
  Sr. Ann, 66
ALEY Cath., 51
ALISON Maria, 89
ALLABAUGH Cath., 12
  Mary, 2
  Sr., 44
  Sus., 89
ALLEN Ann, 82
  Edith, 64
  Eliza, 87
  Har., 82
  Lydia J., 116
  Mar., 29
  Mar. K., 10
  Reb., 44
  Reb. Miller, 10
ALLENDER Addrilla, 74
  Agnes A.M., 117
  Anna, 114
  Cath., 100
  Har., 114
  Mary Ann, 34
ALLEY Lydia, 113
ALLISON Cath., 46
  Ellen, 12
  Mary, 48
  Sr., 106
ALLSIP Eliza, 40
ALSOP Julian, 35
ALTER Am., 76
  Ann Reb., 76
  Ann Reb., 92
  Mary, 109, 110
  Reb., 105
  So., 77
  Sr., 97
  Susan, 114
AMBROSE Cath., 29
  Chna., 89
  Eveline, 29
  Na., 49
  Susan, 59, 84
AMEN Cath., 45
AMOS Mar., 84
ANATON Am., 103
ANDERS Ann H., 81, 84

Chna. C., 43
ANDERSON Adelaide M.,
120
  Ann A., 71
  Ann B., 97
  Ary Ann, 16
  Char., 90
  Eliza J., 45
  Georgetta, 116
  Isa., 102
  Jane, 29
  Mar., 36
  Mar. N., 101
  Marg. J., 116
  Mary Ann, 114
  Priscilla, 1
  Sr. Ann, 18
ANGLE Alice Jane, 9
  Cath., 66
  Eliz., 1
ANIBA Ann E., 65
  Ellen N., 4
  Mary B., 43
ANKENEY Cath., 55, 102
  Eliz., 10, 57
  Eliza, 103
  Julia Eliz., 93
  Mag., 57
  Marg., 12
  Mary, 72, 102
  Mary Ann, 78
  Na., 43
  So., 33
  Susan, 72
ANSMINGER Char., 1
ANTHONY Eliz., 97
  Gertrude, 15
ANTRIM Lydia, 77
APEIER Mary, 115
ARDINGER Ann Jane, 99
  Eliz., 27
  Mary, 98
  Mary Ann, 101
ARECY Na., 84
AREHEART Mary, 115
ARMESTROUT Cath., 56
ARMSLEY Na., 43
  Sus., 109
ARMSTRONG Cath. A., 38
  Eliz., 57
  Sr., 115
ARMSWORTHY Miama, 108
ARNDT Maria, 114
ARNOLD Eliz., 75, 83
  Hulda, 47
  Matilda, 24
  Miriam, 26
  Na., 65
  Paulina, 62
  Sr., 80

INDEX TO BRIDES

ARNSBERGER Cath., 12
  Chna., 18
  Eliz., 102
  Ester, 23
  Mary, 9
  Polly, 79
ARNSPERGER Eliza Ann, 37
ARTER Cath., 60
ARTIS Polly, 112
ARTMAN Caty, 19
ARTZ Altha Ann, 21
  Ann, 19
  Ann Cath., 64
  Ann Maria, 92
  Ann Reb., 101
  Annie E., 48
  Cath., 48
  Eliz., 94
  Helen, 20
  Maria, 24
  Reb., 61
  Ruey, 75
  Sr., 48
  Sus., 72
ASH Mary Ann, 15
ASHBAY Evaline, 108
ASHBERRY Mary, 45
ASHTON Naomi E., 17
ATHEY Eliz., 20
  Har., 7
  Lucretia, 26
ATKINSON Marg., 96
ATTAHOUCE Julia, 105
ATTOM Mary, 13
AUBERT Cath., 100
  Eliz., 2
AUGUSTINE Eliz., 99
AULT Anne, 61
  Eliz., 7
  Ellen, 30
  Rachel, 79
  Susan, 54
AULUM Eliz., 73
AUSTIN Eliz., 116
  Na., 63
AVEY Am. Ann, 5
  Cath., 49, 87
  Chna., 90
  Eliz., 4, 66
  Levenia, 98
  Lydia, 79, 105
  Mary A., 99
  Na., 26, 79
  Polly, 108
  Sr., 11
  Sus., 27
  Susan, 70
AYERLY Bridget, 74

-B-
BABB Har., 36
  Sr., 104
BACHTEL Reb., 34
  Sus., 5
BACHTELL Chna., 50
  Esther, 89
  Na., 72, 105
  Reb., 33
BAECHTEL Barb., 98
  Hen. B., 64
BAECHTELL Ann M.E., 107
  Mary E., 56
BAER Ann Cath., 21
  Eliz. Hortensia, 20
  Nancy, 118
  Sus., 110
BAGENT Barb., 79
  Cath., 3
BAGFORD Ruth, 68
BAILEY Na., 6
BAIR Anna, 99
  Chna., 48
  Eliz., 70
BAIRD Francis, 84
BAKER Ann M., 25
  Caroline, 103
  Cath., 67, 80, 105
  Cath. V., 97
  Eliz., 10, 47, 88
  Eliz. Agnes, 91
  Eliza, 100
  Ellen, 52
  Georgiann, 99
  Louisa, 54
  Magdalene J., 68
  Marg., 76, 117
  Mary, 20, 36, 58, 75, 82, 114, 116
  Mary A., 73
  Mary Cath., 108
  Polly, 106
  Ros., 97
  So., 38
  Sr., 117
  Sr. Ann, 93
  Sus., 22, 119
  Susan R., 116
BALCH Cath. E.S., 18
BALDWIN Cornelia D., 73
  Eliz., 28
  Jane, 40
BALT Mary Jane, 41
BALTES Mary, 16
BANE Sr. Eliz., 48
BANFORD Ann Maria, 86
BANGLY Cath., 44
BANKS Ellen, 61

BARBER Barb., 89
  Eliz., 75
  Marg., 34
  Mary, 7
  Matilda, 25
  Susan J., 11
BARGER Matilda, 23
BARGESSER Eliz. Ann, 89
BARGETT Na., 36
BARGWAR Eliza, 113
BARINGER Mary, 98
BARKDOLL Eliz., 100
  Mary Ann, 27
  Na., 78
  Susan, 44
BARKES Marg., 101
BARKMAN Cath., 80, 98
  Dorothy, 47
  Eliz., 11
  Mary, 80
  So., 66
  Sr. Ann, 26
BARKS Eliz., 13
  Lavania, 24
  Mary, 28
BARLAP Eliz., 96
BARLIP Marg., 73
BARLUP Eliz., 4
BARNES Cath., 66
  Eliz., 53
  Mary, 52
  Maryan, 11
  Rachel, 53
BARNETT Agnes, 46
  Ann, 60
  Cassandra, 3
  Cath., 68
  Eliz., 53, 66
  Louisiana, 10
  Sus., 53
BARNHART Cath., 98
BARNHEISER Deborah, 109
BARNHISER Cath., 95
  Eliz., 15
  Mary, 63
  Sr., 1
BARR Ann Mary, 24
  Barb., 78
  Cath., 71, 84
  Louisa J., 119
  Lydia Ann, 56
  Mag., 48
  Mar. Jane, 118
  Mary, 15
  Susan R., 70
BARRET Marg., 27
BARRETT Cath., 85
BARRINGER Sr., 69

BARRY Mary, 39
BARTGISS Eliza Ann, 22
BARTLETT Mary, 69
BARTLY Prudence, 43
BARTMAN Eliza, 37
BARTMESS Eliz., 84
BARTON Mary, 4
  Pamelia, 112
  Wiley, 2
BARYMAN Eliz., 26
BASH Mary, 112
BASHOW Cath., 103
BASORE Eliz., 15, 111
BASSAW Han., 56
BAUGH Mary, 88
BAUGHER Eliz., 42
BAUGHMAN Na., 60
BAUMBARGER Eliz., 15
  Lydia, 62
BAUNERING Leonora, 42
BAXTER Har., 82
BAYARD Mary Matilda,
  71
BAYER Han., 100
BAYERS Eliz., 97
BAYLIS Caroline, 64
  Emily, 83
  Lucy Ann, 78
BAYLOR Marg., 30
BAYLY Char., 63
  Hen., 55
  Reb. C., 68
BEACHTEL Susan F., 17
BEACKLEY Na., 45
BEAGLER Cath., 48
BEALCH Sus., 23
BEALER Barb., 27
  Cath., 70
  Eleanor, 57
  Eliz., 39, 54, 74
  Mary, 44
  Sally, 30
  Sr., 71
  Sus., 77
BEALL Cath., 60
  Lucy, 70
  Mercy S., 40
  Reb., 85
BEAN Barb., 9
  Eliz., 74
  Eliza Ann, 80
  Frances, 5
  Mary Ann, 18
  Reb., 52
  Sr., 45, 87
  Susan, 116
BEAR Ann, 41
  Barb., 90
  Caroline, 119
  Eliz., 3, 72

Lydia, 117
Mag., 45
Marg., 108
Mary, 75, 103
Mary Ann, 39, 90
Na., 19, 61
Roseann, 119
Sr. C., 29
Susan, 106
BEARD Cath., 29, 77,
  86, 112
  Cath. L., 5
  Cath. M., 44
  Eliz., 40, 65
  Ellen Maria, 88
  Han., 17
  Hellen M., 54
  Lea, 78
  Louisa, 16
  Malinda M., 79
  Mar., 78
  Mar. A., 21
  Marg., 58
  Mary, 3, 65, 76, 92,
    103, 116, 118
  Mary Ann, 116
  Mary M., 36
  Peggy, 6
  Reb., 100
  Sr., 10, 87
  Sus., 34
  Susan, 80
BEARINGER Eliz., 12
BEARN Cath., 20
BEASLEY Mar., 86
  Mary, 49
  Sr., 109
BEASON Jane, 115
BEATTY Eliz. C., 11
  Marg., 33
BEAUGHLY Mar., 102
BEAVER Lucinda, 50
  Mary, 40
  Mary Ann, 71
BECK Eliz., 71
  Eliz. R.V., 5
  Mar., 64
  Mary, 80
  Mary Ann, 59
  Na., 112
  Sr., 113
  Sus., 99
BECKENBAUGH Eliz., 70
  Mary, 56
BECKLEY Am., 25
  Ann S., 33
  Eliz., 90
  Mar. Ellen, 69
  Marg., 75, 79
  Mary, 74

BECKLY Sr., 73
BECKS Mary Ann, 45
BEECHER Sr., 32

BEECHLER Barb., 26
BEECRAFT Mary, 59
BEELER Eliz., 22
  Eliz. Helen, 37
  Eliza, 35
  Ellen, 13
  Marg., 101
  Mary E., 18
  Sr., 50
BEERBOWER Marg., 38
  Sr., 4
BEICHEL Cath., 2
  Mary, 49
BEIGLER Eliz., 15
BEITERLY Mary, 93
BELL Eliz., 72
  Louisa, 84
  Malinda, 50
  Malinda C., 100
  Maria, 62
  Mary, 8, 66
  Mary Ann, 7, 75
  Reb., 78, 90
  Reb. T., 71
  Ros., 58
  So., 80
  Sus., 45
  Viney, 70
BELLEM Cath., 15
BELT Char., 55
BELTZER Eliz., 93
  Mary, 104
  Milly, 95
BELTZHOOVER Cath., 105
  Sr., 1
BENCE Cath., 1
  Mary, 41
BENDER Ann, 100
  Ann Eliz., 60
  Ann Mary C., 67
  Barbary S., 92
  Eliza, 41
  Marg., 11
  Maria M., 25
  Mary, 75, 84
  Sr., 75, 83, 91
  Sus., 98
  Susan, 44
BENKER Marg., 43
BENN Maria, 81
BENNER Annie, 93
  Eliz., 12
  Eliz. Ann, 100
  Merinda Etta, 14
  Pauline, 47
  Reb., 69

Ruan, 14
BENNETT Biershiba, 106
Delilieh, 13
Eliz., 117
Eliza, 41
Eliza S., 97
Marg. L., 108
Mary, 51
Mary Ann, 20
BENTZ Cath., 44
Eliz., 72
Lydia, 93
Marg., 12, 59
Mary, 42
Susan, 103
BERGER Ann, 108
BERGMAN Sus., 75
BERGONIER Jennie, 65
BERIER Mary, 44
BERKELEY Ann M., 63
BERNHART Barb., 114
BERRY Am., 1
Ann, 100
Maria, 23
Mary, 26
Sus., 86
BERTIE Cath., 10
BESORE Mary, 19
Mary S., 10
BEST Susan, 45
BETERBENNER Lucinda,
46
BETON Eliz., 41
BETTERBENNER Susan, 13
BETTS Ann, 9
Louisa V., 33
Mary, 24, 107
Na., 48
Rosini, 8
BETZ Ann Maria, 52
Cath., 9, 53
Eliz., 34, 42
Ellen, 115
BETZER Lydia, 44
BEVANS Ann, 25
Eliz., 74, 88
Eveline L., 8
Helena, 113
Marg., 34
Mary A., 80
Sus., 76
BEYERS (BOYERS) Mary,
114
BIAYS Margaretta M.,
13
BICKLEY Sr., 116
BIDAMON Ann, 46
Drucilla, 54
BIDDLE Betsey, 90
BIDERMAN Drusey, 115

BIERSHING Ann M., 99
BIESSHING Susan, 79
BIGGAM Mary Ann, 10
BIGHAM Angeline L.,
106
Cath., 62
Eliz. A., 50
BIGLER Elenora, 119
BIGNOLL Eliz., 34
BILLINGS Mary, 28
BILLMYER Cath., 44
Hester, 62
Judith, 20
Marg., 90
Mary, 89
BINDERIN (BIMLERIN)
Nanie, 53
BINGHAM Ann Maria, 99
BINKLEY Am., 76
Eliz., 102
Eve E., 63
Isa., 50
Mary, 43, 97
Sr., 14, 97
Sr. Ann, 39
Sr. Cath., 22
BINKLY Ann E., 74
BIRELY Caroline Eliz.,
34
BIROAD Mary, 45
BISER Elvira, 87
Frederica, 114
BISHOP Han., 72
Hen. M., 110
BITERBENNER Marg., 4
BITZENBURG Susan, 18
BIVENS Na., 27
BLACK Anna, 65
Cath., 10
Ellen, 78
BLACKER Cath., 40
BLACKFORD Jennett Y.,
99
BLACKMAN Na., 97
BLACKMORE Hester, 96
Sr., 70
BLACKWELL Cath., 85
Eliz. L., 104
BLAIR Delilah, 13
Eleanor, 102
Esther, 73
Fanny, 61
Maria, 84
Mary, 22
Mary E., 9
Na., 33
Sr., 31, 63
BLAKE Rosamond C., 62
BLECHER Larah, 50
Marg. Ann, 44

Mary Ann, 15
Reb., 29
Susan, 56
BLECKER Cath., 75
Eliz., 5, 56
BLENTLINGER Cath., 24
BLESSING Ann Cath., 11
Cath., 17
Eliza, 55
Maria, 75
Mary Ellen, 102
So., 89
BLEW Sus., 69
BLICKENSTAFF Cath., 68
Eliz., 32, 74
BLOCHER Marg., 56
BLOOD Eliz. L., 23
Mrs. Clarine S., 36
BLOOM Ann, 73
Marg., 73
BLOOMANOUR Cath., 90
BLOOMINGOUR Am., 64
BLOOMINOUR Caroline,
43
BLOYER Eliz., 75
BOARD Eliz., 39
BOBST Polly, 59
BODY So., 70
BOEMAN Ann E., 42
BOERSTH Caroline, 25
BOERSTLER Eliz., 80
Marg. M., 29
BOGGS Mary A.S., 71
BOLEY Cath., 76
BOLSH Eliz., 85
BOMBARGER Ann, 33
Eliz., 8
Mary, 1
Sr. M., 101
Susan, 42
BOMBERGER Anna, 70
Cath., 4
Mary E., 37
Reb., 11
Sally, 81
Tracey, 90
BOMBURGER Eliz., 69
Eliza, 110
BOMGARDNER Molly, 30
Sus., 33
BOND Anna, 115
Eliz., 19
Marg., 95
Mary Ann, 40
Sr., 66
BOOBY Mag., 98
BOOKER Ros., 69
BOON Sr., 21
BOONE Cath., 32
Marietta, 54

Mrs. Cath., 29
Sus., 70
BOOSER Eliz., 69
Mary, 104
BOOSIER Eve, 100
BOOTH Maria, 36
Susan S., 57
BOPE Eliz., 105
BOPP Mary, 67
BORAUFF, Eliz., 29
BORDEN Louisa B., 87
BOREHOFF Cath., 48
BOREN Mary, 110
Patsey, 11
Providence, 66
Susan, 79
BOROFF Mary, 102
BOSTATER Cath., 95
Eliz., 51
Isa., 105
BOSWELL Eliz. Ann, 3
BOTELER Am. E., 7
Char., 114
Eliza Jane, 102
Heziah, 1
Mary Ann, 74
Mary Ellen, 10
Mary Jane, 44
Priscilla, 18
Ruth S.A., 7
Sr., 58
BOTLER Aletha M., 4
BOTTELL Sr., 51
BOTTENBERGER Polly, 78
BOUCE Eliz., 113
BOUCH Eve, 76
BOULT Chna. A., 87
Narcissia, 44
BOVEY Cath., 54
Chna., 113
Eliz., 7, 55, 115
Mag., 104
Marg., 112
Mary, 21, 52, 101, 110
Mary Ann, 37
Reb., 10
Sus., 88
BOVIE Barb., 43
BOWARD Cath., 90
Eliz., 30, 119
Emily, 18
Marg., 8, 27, 74
Na., 19
Sr., 102
BOWART Marg., 33
BOWEN Eliz., 37
Eliza A., 72
Jane N., 83
BOWER Cath., 16

Eliz., 16, 18
Eve, 114
Jeanette, 74
Mary, 22
BOWERD Mary Ann, 23
Sr., 22
BOWERS Ann, 113
Ann Maria, 9, 114
Barb., 87
Barbary, 92
Cath., 40, 69, 89
Eliz., 7, 10, 17, 20, 21, 87, 108, 118, 119
Ellen Eliz., 101
Eve Marg., 36
Frances, 119
Han., 2
Hen., 69
Kate Cordelia, 25
Lavina, 53
Louisa, 23
Mar. Ann, 11
Marg., 18, 22, 53
Marg. Ann, 39
Marg. Eliz., 3
Mary, 21, 39, 88, 101
Mary Ellen, 63
Matilda, 97
Na., 15, 84
Na. Ann, 13
Polly, 55
Reb., 55
Ros., 57
Sr., 86
Sr. A., 87
Sus., 108
BOWERT Chna., 58
BOWLES Ann, 7
Eliz., 24
Juliet, 22
Louise Ellen, 108
Lucretia, 80
Mariah, 17
Mary, 13, 24
Mary E., 109
Mary Eliz., 110
Sr. W., 67
BOWMAN Am., 25
Annie A., 7
Barb., 79
Barbary, 50
Cath., 80, 116, 118
Eliz., 14, 26, 50, 90
Isa., 85
Marg., 26, 31, 119
Mary, 35, 54, 73, 107

Mary C., 83
Mary Cath., 11
Matilda, 40
Na., 70, 76
Ruan, 70
Sr., 96
Susan, 60, 119
BOWORD, Marg., 9
BOWSER Barb., 32
Caroline, 28
Cath., 103
Chra., 27
Eliz., 77
Mary, 12, 64, 119
Polly, 50
Sr., 102
Sr. Ann, 117
BOXWELL Eliz., 11
BOYD Ann A., 65
Augusta, 92
Eliz., 23
Eliza, 111
Kate, 89
Marg., 66
Marg. M., 100
Mary, 86
Mary M., 49
Mary Susan, 21
Na., 14
Nelly, 35
Reb. U., 86
Ruann, 116
Sr., 18, 19
Susan, 111
BOYER Cath., 6, 78
Eliz., 16, 68
Elizth, 107
Julian, 76
Lydia, 116
Mahala M., 25
Na., 39
Nelly, 81
Reb., 39
Sabina, 42
Sus., 36
Tracy A.C., 68
BOYERS Barbary Ann, 74
Eliz., 52, 74, 99
Marg. E., 74
Mary, 21
Na., 6
BRACHER Eliz., 49
BRADLY Biddy, 75
BRADSHAW Sr., 21
BRADY Jane, 108
Marg., 16
Philipi, 17
BRAFORD Phillis, 63
BRAGONIER Cath., 35
Eliz., 12, 76, 79

Mary, 71
Peggy, 68
Roz., 113
Sr., 10
Susan, 109
BRAINHALL Mary Ann, 41
BRAMHALL So., 45
BRAMHILL Sr., 50
BRANDEBURG Malinda, 110
BRANDNER Sr. Ann, 73
BRANDT Jane, 68
BRANNER Mary, 48
BRANNIGAN Jane, 65
BRANNON Eliz., 59
  Ellen, 103
  Mar., 111
  Marg., 82
  Mary, 82
  Reb., 63
  Sr. Ann Louisa, 94
BRANSON, Peggy, 29
BRANSTATER, Eliz., 61
  Mary, 33
BRANTNER Cath., 105
  Eliz., 24, 73
  Mary, 19, 83
  Mary Ann, 33
  Sus., 77
  Susan, 9
BRATTER Eliz., 2
BREAKER Eliz., 55
BREATHED Jane, 28
BREHM Maria A., 60
BREISCH Roz., 103
BRENDLE Cath., 44
BRENGLE Sr. E., 32
BRENNER Peggy, 72
BRENT Lucretia L., 18
  Mary, 88
  Mary Jane, 116
  Matilda, 43
BRENTLINGER Prudence, 107
BRETHED Eliz., 100
BREWAH Mary, 1, 87
  Sr., 48
BREWER Ann, 58
  Ann E., 28, 33
  Ann Mary, 33
  Cath., 86
  Chra., 13
  Eliz., 33, 48, 64, 66, 87, 93, 110
  Emma C., 116
  Frances, 100
  Mar., 15
  Marg., 75
  Mary, 26, 65, 99, 101

Mary Ann, 6
Mary C., 77, 94
Na., 21
Ros., 117
Sr., 56, 70
Sr. E., 118
Sus., 43, 78
BREWNER Ann, 35
BRIDENDALE Mag., 79
BRIDGE Cath., 27
  Sr., 44
BRIDGEMAN Han., 84
  Marg., 30
BRIDGEMENT Jane E., 70
BRIDGES Cath., 16
  Mary, 13
  Reb., 116
BRIDGES (BUDGES)
  Marg., 34
BRIDGEWATER Keziah, 13
BRIESH Sus., 35
BRIGHAM America, 44
BRIGHT Drusilla, 32
BRILL Adriana, 57
BRIMET Lucinda, 72
BRINEM Sr. Ann, 80
BRINHAM Ellen R., 38, 42
  Jane, 118
  Margaretta, 53
BRISCOE Clarissa, 23
BRITTEN Eliz., 28
BROADSTONE, Chrz., 11
  Eliz., 36
BROKENBROUGH Lucy, 21
BROLIER Marg., 88
BROOK Eliz., 18
  Marg., 100
  Sr., 62
BROOKE Louisa, 46
  Lydia, 85
  Reb., 66
BROOKELMAN Henietta, 120
BROOKS Lucy N., 18
BROSH Eliz., 113
BROSIUS Cath., 41
  Eliz., 50, 104
  Eliza, 40, 62
  Mary Ann, 69
  Mary J., 13
  Sr. Ann, 9, 84
BROUCHMYER Cath., 101
  Chna., 110
BROUTZMAN Sus., 60
BROWN Ann Lavina, 38
  Ann M., 52
  Annie E., 26
  Cath., 17, 67
  Charity, 78

Chna. Jr., 21
Clara, 84
Dassy, 27
Deborah, 98
Delilah, 79
Eleanor, 56
Eliz., 23, 46, 87
Eliza, 49, 79
Eliza Jane, 57
Eveline, 110
Hadassah C., 97
Han., 13
Isa., 25
Jenny, 19
Lydia, 60
Mahala, 78
Mar., 41, 82
Marg., 66
Marion, 13
Mary, 39, 68, 110
Mary E., 62
Mary M., 13
Matilda, 61
Na., 1, 88
Reb. Ann, 7
Savilla, 79
Sus., 5, 61
BROWNING Cath., 96
  Mar., 90
BROZIER Ann Reb., 48
BRUBAKER Barb., 106
  Cath., 106
BRUCE Mary, 31
BRUMBAUGH Eliz., 72
  Eveline, 8
BRUNER Cath., 14
  Cath. E., 59
  Dorothy, 99
  Marg., 6
  Mary, 118
  Na., 99
  Sarepta A., 15
BRUNNER Ann Eliz., 117
  Eve, 112
  Marg., 69
  Mary, 98
  Na., 17
BRYAN Ann, 74
  Har., 100
  Mary, 108
  Mary Ann, 17
  Sus., 43
BRYROUN Sr., 50
BRYSON Sr., 56
BUCHANAN Ann Victoria, 45
  Anna Ogh, 103
  Har., 28
  Mary S., 68
  Meliora, 27

126

BUCK Eliz., 4
　Eliza, 39
　Freany, 111
　Mary, 43
BUCKHART Caroline C., 104
　Cath., 95
BUCKISE Eliza, 101
BUCKLEY Mary Ann, 42
BUCKWALTER Susan, 111
BUDGE Julia Ann, 12
BUHRMAN Ann M., 44
　Cath., 35
　Diana, 13
　Savilla, 13, 44
　Sus., 25
BULOTT Mary, 97
BUNER Chna. Eliz., 104
BURCH Mar., 20
BURCHART Cath., 35
　Louisa M., 30
BURCKHART Almira, 33
　Caroline C., 52
　Caroline E., 34
　Laretta L., 60
BURCKHARTT Kitty, 90
BURD Milly Ann, 101
　Sr. Ann, 74
BURGAN Eliz., 81
　Maria, 57
　Mrs. Eliz., 18
　Patsy, 42
　Reb., 1
BURGER Barb., 55
BURGESS Anna, 14
BURGESSER Julia Ann, 34
BURGESSOR Mary Ann, 10
BURGET Mary, 56
BURGHER Barb., 38
BURHMANN Juliann, 61
BURKE Eliz., 1
　Mary, 36
BURKETT Cath., 108
　Eliz., 10, 15, 50
　Marg., 10, 35
　Maria F., 97
　Sr. M., 51
　Sus., 20
BURKHARDT Sr., 26
BURKHART Cath., 80
　Eliz., 88
　Marg., 115
　Mary, 51
　Phebe, 73
　Sr., 48
　Sus., 100
BURNER Ros., 98
BURNES Reb., 66
BURNS Amanda, 114

Cath., 97
　Jane, 117
　Mary, 37, 61, 93
　Priscilla, 94
BURNSIDE Hester Ann, 63
BURR Hetty, 30
　Maria, 89
BURRELL Eliz., 57
　Mary, 1
BURRIS Cath., 96
BURROWS Har., 25
BURTON Mary, 77
　Nelly, 21
BUSH Cath. T., 4
　Mary, 64
BUSHELS Mary, 89
BUSSARD Cath., 45
　Eliz., 25
　Eliza, 23
　Mary C., 13
BUSSERD So., 35
BUTERBAUGH Cath., 98
BUTLER Am., 16
　Cath., 114
　Eliz., 1
　Jane, 71
　Mariah, 46
　Priscilla, 75
　Sr., 29
BUTT Cath., 53
　Susan, 106
BUTTERBAUGH Cath., 93
　Eliz., 27
　Mary, 71
BUTTON Mary, 29
BUTTS, Mary, 93
　Ros., 69
BUZZARD, Anna, 106
　Cath., 107, 108
　Lydia, 76
　Mary, 77
　Sus., 105
BYERS Cath., 72, 86
　Eliz., 89
　Eliza, 66
　Emily Louisa, 7
　Hen., 28
　Isora M., 9
　Marg., 27
　Mary, 28, 82
　Mary E., 6
　Sr. Jane, 2
　Susan, 50, 78
　Susan Cath., 6, 58
BYRD Mary, 22

—C—
CABLE Sr., 29
CADDERS Jane, 65

CADEL Sr., 46
CADWALDER Lydia, 62
CAFFELT Mary, 35
CAHILL Mary, 104
　Priscilla, 68
CAIN Eliz., 78
　Ellen, 2
CAKE Sr., 112
CALDWELL Eliz., 116
　Mary, 37
　Na. B., 47

CALENS Mary, 74
CALIMEL Mary, 81
CALVERT, Mary Ann, 16
　Matilda, 65
CAMERER Barb., 73
　Han., 64
CAMMERRON Allice, 117
CAMPBELL Ann M., 92
　Cath., 96
　Eliz. C., 50
　Mary, 61
　Reb., 51
CAMPFIELD Eliz., 105
CAREY Ephla, 24
　Mary, 93
CARLIN Reb., 66
CARLISLE Mary E., 51
CARLS Marg., 32
CARN Char., 92
　Sr., 104
CARNEY Ellen, 71
　Susan, 21
CARNS Chra., 109
　Marg., 10
CAROTHER Cath., 63
CAROTHERS Han., 54
CARPENTER Eliz., 16, 76
　Peggy, 108
　Polly, 38
CARPER Frances, 36
　Har. C., 111

CARR Eliz., 28
　Ellen, 39
　Marg., 9
　Maria T., 26
　Mary A., 37
　Mary E., 56, 86
　So., 44
　Susan, 77
CARREL Eliz., 6
CARRELL Mary, 57
CARROLL Jane Maria, 107
　Joanna, 114
　Judy, 23
　Marg., 106

Na., 67
CARRY Tracy, 89
CARSON Cath., 76
  Eliz., 118
  Hetty, 105
  Mary E., 109
CARTER Ann, 13
  Caroline, 79
  Eliza A., 104
  Mary, 6, 39
  Sus., 43
CARTWRIGHT Jane, 78
CARTY Cath., 41
  Elenora, 108
  Mary, 94
  Mary Ann, 69
  Susan E., 96
CARTZ Eliz., 81
CARVER Eliz., 92
  Ellen C., 73
  Maria R., 88
  Peggy, 8
  Sr., 107
  Sr. O.A., 33
CASEBAR, Mary, 108
CASH Eliz., 32
CASPER Mary, 45
CASSELL, Amanda, 96
  Ann Parmelia, 23
  Margarette, 12
CASSON Esther, 26
CASTER Mary, 107
CASTLE Am., 60
  Eletha E., 102
  Lydia, 52
CASTOR Cath. Lavinia,
75
  Mar. A.S., 107
  Na. V., 107
CATHER Mary Jane, 70
CATHURS Na., 97
CATLETT Na., 24
CAUFFMAN Nelly, 85
  Sus., 17
CAUSGROVE Bridget, 26
CAW Am. L., 73
  Cath., 50
CEASE Cath., 15
  Eliza, 88
CEAVIER Eliz., 6
CELLER Sus., 106
CELLERS Marg., 43
CHAMBERS Ann, 64
  Han., 84
  Maria So., 75
  Mary, 58
  Mary Ann, 46, 57
  Mary E., 94
  Mary M., 71
  Matilda, 95

CHANEY Aletha, 18
  Amey, 36
  Clarissa, 48
  Eliz., 111
  Ellen, 67
  Emma, 112
  Han., 89
  Mary, 59
  Matilda, 74
  Mrs. Sr., 62
  Prudence, 10
  Reb., 80
  Ruth, 80
CHANY Ann Maria, 100
  Drusila, 47
  Fannie, 51
  Mary, 46
CHAPLIN Indiana, 12
CHAPLINE Cath. B., 84
  Eliz., 97
  Sr., 31
  Susan N., 116
CHAPMAN Han., 50
  Han. C., 56
  Maria, 9
CHARLES Barb., 26
  Eliz., 71
  Mary Ann, 11
CHARLTON Eliza J., 77
  Reb., 100
  Sus., 5
CHENEWITH Mary, 60
CHENEY Drusilla, 105
  Prudence, 56
CHENOWETH Han. E., 18
CHERNUTT Marg., 30
CHESBY Eliz., 102
CHEW Eliza, 101
  Hen. M., 92
  Mary, 82
CHICESTER Ann, 15
CHICHESTER Eliz., 106
CHIPLEY Eliz. W., 55
CHOON Eliz., 14
CHOPPERT Mary E., 93
CHRIKE Ann Eliz., 69
CHRISMAN Ruey, 25
CHRISSINGER Laura, 67
  Mary, 82
CHRISTI Sr., 81
CHRISTIAN Ann, 101
  Eliz., 79
  Francis Paten, 75
  Mary, 99
  Rachel M., 14
CHRISTINE Cath., 54
CHRISTMAN Mary, 52
CHRISTOPHER Eliz., 59
CLABAUGH Mary E., 113
CLAGETT Aletha, 10

E.S., 105
  Eliz. Ann, 53
  Mar., 113
  Sr., 27
CLAGGETT Ann Eliz., 42
  Eleanora, 24
  Eliz., 18, 41, 46
  Eliza, 19
  Laura Frances, 119
  Mary A., 41
  Mary Ann, 38
  Matilda, 18
  So., 34
  Sr., 10
CLAM Mary, 41
CLAPPER So., 56
CLAPSADDLE Ann, 87
CLARK Ann M., 27, 100
  Eliz., 107
  Julia, 8
  Mary Ann, 75
  Sr. Ann, 88
  Sr. S., 17
CLARKE Ann, 51, 70, 83
  Cath., 28, 72
  Cath. Ann, 1
  Eliz., 119
  Hen., 27
  Mary Ann, 28, 50,
118
  Susan, 68
CLAYCOMB (CLAYCOMP)
Jane, 95
CLAYTON Eliz., 24, 111
  Sr. M., 8
CLEATON Mary, 54
CLELIN Mrs. Matilda,
23
CLEM Sr., 78
CLEVIDENCE Cath., 26,
57
  Eliz., 56
  Mary A., 26
CLINE Eve, 103
  Har., 22
  Marg., 41, 110
  Mary, 10, 60
CLINETAGE Am., 115
CLOPER, Cath., 3
  Mary, 3
CLOPPBAUGH Marg., 106
CLOPPER Eliz., 22, 50
  Eliz. G., 82
  Har. L., 104
  Leah, 56
  Mary, 8, 13
  Reb., 73
  Reb. B., 14
  Ros., 6
  Sus., 19

CLOWSER Susan, 33
CLUGSTON Na. A., 2
CLUM Eliz., 17
COAL Eliz., 117
COALER Cath., 23
  Esther, 10
COATS Eliza, 21
COBERT Reb., 56
COBLER Reb., 40
COCHLAN Eliz., 37
COCHRAN Ann, 7
COCHRANE Ann, 74
COFFMAN Ann, 89
  Barb., 15
  Cath., 19, 108
  Eliz., 3, 54
  Hen., 119
  Lavina, 83
  Maria, 115
  Mary Ann, 83, 99
  Rachel, 59
  Rozanne, 1
  Sr., 90
  Sr. A., 71
  Susan, 78, 115
COFFROTH Mary, 84
COHILL Mary, 5
COLBERT Ann, 109
  Ann Divine, 54
  Dorcas, 78
  Eliz., 54
  Isa., 86
COLE Ann, 81
  Eliz., 58, 67
COLEMAN Eliz., 54
COLER Susan, 47
COLLEFLOWER Eliz., 29
  Louisa, 34
COLLIER Mary, 38, 82
COLLIFLOWER Ann M.,
  61, 117
  Cath., 41
  Eliz., 6
  Isa., 44
  Mary D., 42
  Susan, 36
COLLIMAN Susan, 62
COLLINS Mary, 5, 54
  Mary Ann, 20
  Sr., 83
COLLISON Na., 18
COLVIN Ellen, 70
COLYER Mary, 87
COMBS Mary, 29
  Na., 23
  Ruth, 43
COMEGA Ann, 104
COMPTON Marg., 20
  Mary, 65
CONLER Sr., 64

CONLEY Eliz. A., 103
CONN Cath., 58
  Sr., 105
CONNELLY Ann, 66
  Bridget, 65
  Jane, 114
CONNER Jane, 22
  Sr., 4
  Susan, 52, 94
CONRAD Eliz., 70
  Marg., 95
  Sr. Ann, 90
  Sr. Jane, 86
CONRADT Ann Maria, 27
CONROD Eliz., 22
CONWAY Eliza, 34
COOK Caroline, 66
  Cath., 36
  Char., 95
  Eliz., 53, 84
  Eliza, 45
  Eliza Ann, 101
  Fanny, 39
  Marg., 107
  Mary, 17
  Mary Ann, 62, 113
  Peggy, 72
  Sus., 12, 21
COOKAS Mary, 16
COOKE Marg., 59
COOKERLY Ann, 77
COOKEY Ann Eliz., 75
COON Barb., 112
  Cath., 116
  Eliz., 23, 33, 95,
116
  Frances, 36
  Julian, 95
  Marg., 32, 63
  Mary, 3, 117
  Mary E., 115
  Molly, 87
  Na., 46
  Sr., 43
  Sus., 53
COONEY Mary A., 100
COONS Cath., 65
  Juliet, 10
  Sr., 10, 17
COONTZ Mary E., 21
COOPER Eliz., 67, 83,
110
  Mar. E., 11
COPENHAVER Eliz., 20
  Sus., 101
CORBERT Jane, 75
CORBETT Lucinda, 104
CORBEY Eliz., 40
CORBUT Isa., 111
COROGAN Ann, 61

CORSE Na., 75
CORSEN Wettimince, 42
COSS Cath., 97
  Eliza, 66
  Har., 80
  Polly, 19, 86
  Sr., 12
COST Cath., 75
  Eliz. Ellen, 84
  Mary, 10
  Mary Ann, 84
  Mary Etta, 83
  Mercy, 119
COTTINGHAM Mary, 55
COUCHMAN Sr., 30
COUP Cath., 90
  S. Eliz., 55
COURTNEY Mary, 66
COUSLER Ros., 42
COVELL Mary Ann, 83
COW Cath., 107
  Eliz., 107
COWNAVER Polly, 77
COWTON Eliz., 12
  Mar., 17
  Sr. Jane, 42
COX Cath., 59, 94
  Eliz., 71
  Hen., 3
  Marg. A., 45
  Mary, 18, 41, 51,
59, 69
  Mary E., 108
  Rachel, 76
COY Cath., 67
  Drucilla F., 37
  Mary, 52
  Susan, 86
CRABILL, Eliza, 46
CRAFT Indiana B., 99
  Peggy, 6
CRAIG Cath., 13
  Eleanor, 86
  Jane, 43
CRAIGLOW Barb., 24
CRAIGWELL Jane, 48
CRALEY Adelaide So.,
67
CRAMER Ann Mary, 116
  Cath., 72, 117
  Celinary, 118
  Eliz., 24, 42
  Leah, 46
  Marg., 46
  Mary, 85, 93, 98
  Ros., 42
  Sr. Ann, 85
  Sus., 42
CRAMMER Sr. Char., 117
CRAMPTON Eliz., 56, 89

Elmira, 30
Mary, 118
Mary E., 54
Na., 112
CRAVER Cath. R., 106
Mary, 70
CRAWFORD Sr. Ann, 86
Susan, 17
CRAY Isa., 78
CRAYTON Cath. M., 58
CREAGER Am., 29, 46
Ann Maria, 65
Barb., 63
Cath., 20
Hen., 64
Mar. Ann, 47
Mary, 20, 69, 86
Reb. A., 78
Rose Ann, 17
Sabret Ann, 94
Sr. Ann, 16
CREAMER Ellen, 60
Mary C., 93
Matilda, 89
Sr., 14
CRECINGER Cath., 9
CREEK Ann, 54
Barb., 40
Eliz., 73
CREIGH Cath., 26
Vialetta, 86
CRESWELL Marg., 38
CRETZER Eliz., 13
Leah, 104
Mary, 49
So., 59
CRETZINGER Char., 40
Eliz., 21, 25
Mary, 88
Na., 72
Sus., 64
CRIDLER Eliz., 114
Marg. S., 72
CRINER Marg., 81
CRIOR Layer, 19
CRISMAN Eliz., 2
CRISSINGER Ellen E.,
19
CRISSMAN Mary Jane,
115
CRIST Cath., 72
Lucy M., 112
CRISVILE Mary, 60
CRISWELL, Eliz., 56
Frances, 58
CRITZER Mary, 95
CROFFORD Sr., 63
CROMER Eliz., 20
Han. C., 6
CROMLEY Cath., 25

Mar., 118
CROMRY Maria, 86
CROMWELL Eliz. G., 23
Eliz. Rench, 12
CRONISE Ann Marie, 92
Cath., 58, 120
Jane E., 57
Mary, 9
CROP Margaretta, 6
CROSS Ann, 106
Cath., 64
Eleanora, 116
Eliz., 1
Han. Ann, 104
Ketturah, 2
Maria Ann, 53
Sr., 52
Sr. Ann, 109
CROUSE Eliz., 44, 90
Mary A., 25, 33
CROVEVER Betsy, 98
CROW Cath., 26, 70
Eliz., 17
Eliza, 27, 101
Han., 43
Malinda, 7
Mary Jane, 5
CROWER Sr., 3
CROWL, Charity, 91
Mary, 72
CROWN, Lucy Ann, 6
CRUM Reb., 4
CRUMBACK Mary, 10
CRUNKLETON Char., 79
Mary, 87
Ruth, 49
CRUTHERS Eliz., 23
CRUTZWELL Eliza Ann,
43
CUDDY Cath., 18
CUHN Matalina, 15
CUKY Marg., 101
CULBERTSON Kate, 74
Mary A., 66
Matilda, 24
CULLER Char. E., 64
CULLERSON Eliz., 52
CUNNING Han., 82
CUNNINGHAM Cath., 38
Eliz., 74
Han., 116
Isa. J., 93
Mar., 111
Mary Ann, 93
May, 86
CUPPENHOUSE Sr., 72
CURDY So., 1
CURFFMAN Cordelia, 73
CURFMAN Susan, 16
CURNICUM Mary, 43

CURRELL, Barb., 63
CURRY Eveline, 27
Mary Ellen, 99
CURTIS Mary, 40
Mary A.E., 52
Sr., 2
Susan, 94
CURUTHERS Na., 90
CUSHWA Cath., 68
Eliz., 87, 110
Mary, 40
Mary Ann, 52
Sr., 8, 110
CUTSHALL Jane, 59
Sr., 59
CUTSHAW Anna, 82
CYESTER Mary Ann, 104
So., 40

-D-
DAGANHART Motlena, 29
DAGENHART Ann Maria, 4
Barb., 8
Eleanor, 90
Ellen, 24
Mary Ann, 80
Ruann, 106
DAGONHART Lucinda, 114
DAHL Eliz., 16
DAHOOF Barb., 79
DAILY Milly, 107
Sus., 22
DALL ELiz. B., 55
Har. B., 2
DALONG Sus., 33
DALRYMPLE Adeline, 83
Eliz., 85
DAMPSY Roz., 17, 97
DAMSEY Polly, 118
DANIEL Mary, 104
Mary Ann, 24
DANIELS Han., 24
Har. E., 95
DANNELL Rachel G., 86
DANNER Ann Eliza, 68
DANT Eliz., 67
DARBY Eliz., 82
DARK Eliz., 28
DASHER Adalaide, 2
DAUGHERTY Mary, 78
Na., 84
DAVIDSON Eleano, 36
Na., 104
DAVIS Adelaide E., 57
Ann, 4
Ann Maria, 54
Ann Reb., 114
Barb., 11
Cath., 15
Cath. E., 107

Cath. S., 66
Desia, 2
Eliz., 55, 74, 77, 105
Eliz. Ann, 84
Eliz. D., 8
Eliz. M., 27
Eliza, 56, 63
Elleanora, 28
Han., 54, 88
Har., 22, 72
Holly, 62
Jane, 111
Louisa, 73, 79
Marg., 29, 116
Maria, 54
Maria L., 73
Mary, 28, 78, 100, 105
Mary Jane, 71
Matilda, 114
Matilda J., 44
Matty, 23
Na., 76, 100
Narrisa, 17
Reb., 40
So., 41
Sr., 2, 5, 18, 61, 68
Sr. Cath., 88, 109
Sus., 59, 83
Susan, 81
Tyett, 99
DAVIT Mary, 92
DAVY Mary, 20
DAY Esabella, 55
DEACON Eliz., 25
DEAL Anna, 27
Eliz., 38, 51, 77
Ellen, 40
Maria, 58
Sr., 88
Susan, 57
DEALE Cath., 119
DEAN Eliza, 112
DEANER Mary C., 109
So. E., 89
Sr., 86
DEARING Letitia, 80
DEAVER, Ann R., 3
Eliz. A., 104
Jane, 87
DEAVERS, Sr. I., 80
DECK Polly, 77
DECKER, Marg. Ann, 44
DEDIE Kesia, 96
DEEDY Barb., 50
DEENER Mary Ann, 73
DEEVERS Maria, 49
DEGAN Ellen, 19

DEIBERT Mary, 44
Reb., 37
Susan, 3
DEITRICH Cath., 76
Mary, 60
DEITRICK Han., 70
Lydia, 1
Mary, 12
Mary Ann, 106
Sr., 108
DEITSCH Eliz., 119
DELASHMUTT Mary B., 87
DELAUGHNEY Eliza M., 36
DELAUNEY Mar. Ann, 7
Rosella, 83
DELAWTER Mary, 15
DELKOUR Margaretta, 23, 25
DELLINGER Almira V., 41
Ann, 119
Anna W., 17
Cath., 40, 61, 99
Eliz., 96
Eliz. Jane, 73
Sr. Ann, 73
Susan, 13
DEMPSTER Eliz., 19
DENNER Eliz. B.F., 84
DENNIS Lydia A., 88
DENNISON Am., 110
Clarissa, 21
Lydia, 100
Rachel, 27
Reb., 83
Sr., 55, 96
DENNY Julia Ann, 40
DENOON Eliz., 55
DENURE Ellen, 24
DERR Cath., 112
DERRER Lucinda, 13
DERRY Eliz. C., 6
DESMOND Ellen, 53
DESPORTS Fleuretta, 16
DETER Cath., 115
DETRICK Sus., 18
DETWILER Eliz., 25
DEVIER Mar. Jane, 14
DEVORE Eliz., 26
DEVOREM Mary, 20
DIBERT Eliz., 111
Magdalene, 55
Mary Ann, 118
Na., 119
DICK Cath., 57, 72
Eliza, 95
Ellen, 59
Marg., 40
Mary, 80

Na., 117
DICKEY Eleanor, 77
Isa. W., 75
Sus., 81
DICKSON Mar. Ann, 37
Mary, 110
Na., 78
DIDDLE Rachel, 113
DIEDENRUDER Regina, 84
DIFFENBAUGH Cath., 114
Eliz., 48
DIGNER Sr., 84
DILAHUNT Eliza, 30
DILLAHUNT Mary, 101
Mary Ann, 23
DILLEHART Mary M., 48
DILLEHUNT Louisa, 1
DILLMAN Am., 75
Han., 58
Mary, 98
DILLON Ann, 4
Cath., 13
Maria, 89
Norry, 108
Sr., 53
DINGER Cath., 41
DINGES Mary Cath., 30
DINGLER Caty, 34
DINKLE Mary Ann, 25
DITCH, Juliana, 84
Sus., 66
DITCHER Cath., 37
DITTO, Ellen Jane, 2
Mar., 116
Mary, 49
Mary Ann, 108, 112
Reb., 43
DIXON Cath., 68
Elisa I., 44
Susan, 45
DIZARDS Fiscey, 34
DOANS Cholie Ann Louise, 116
DOCHARTY Cath., 68
DODD Ann Cath., 54
ELiz. S., 100
DOHERTY Sr., 87
DOLAND Ellen, 48
DOLL Mary, 25
DOLLWICK Cath. Eliz., 115
DOMBAUGH Fany, 45
DOMER Eliz., 7, 106
Marg., 50
Mary, 76
Rachel, 93
Ros., 7
Sally, 73
DONAGHE Marg., 16
DONALDSON Eliza, 48

Jean, 100
Mary, 59
Mary Ann, 75
Sally Ann, 87
DONER, Hetty, 51
DONNELLY Bridget, 99
Cath., 17
Louisa, 17
Mary, 80, 91, 97
Matilda, 69
Sr., 113
DONOHO Anne, 3
Mary, 86
DONOVAN Marg., 17
Mary, 99
DOOBLE Cath., 96
Marg., 116
Sr., 57
DOOPLE Marg., 116
Mary, 67
DORENBERGER Eliz., 22
Mary Eliz., 111
DORNBAUGH Mary, 61
DORRANCE Mary A., 35
DORSEY Ann C., 34
Eliz., 88
M.A., 113
Marg., 78
Mary, 105
Mary J., 34
DOTERLY Eliz., 12
DOUB Ann Eliz., 45
Caroline, 21, 29
Cath., 37
Eliz., 44, 105, 119
DOUBBLE Cath., 30
DOUBLE, Maria, 60
DOUD Eliz. Susan, 71
DOUDLE Alsenah D., 7
DOUGHERTY, Eliza, 81
Judith, 45
DOUGLASS Amy E., 69
Ellenor, 56
DOUP Maria, 118
DOUPLE Har., 51
DOUTHAL Francis, 104
DOVENBARGER Sr., 2
DOVENBERGER Mar., 64
Matilda A., 64
Susan, 96
DOWELL Mary Ann, 81
Peggy, 98
DOWNES Ary, 99
Eliz. A., 120
Mary, 40
DOWNEY Cath., 19, 63
Chna., 63
Eliz., 16
Eliza, 40
Eveline, 74

Hadassah, 64
Marg., 98
Maria, 27
Mary, 19
Na., 67
Polly, 86
DOWNING Phebe, 95
DOWNS Amy, 49
Eliz., 115
Eliz. P., 27
Eliza, 24
Fedelia, 15
Hen., 27
Laura L., 2
Lucretia, 118
Mary, 54
Reb., 95
Sr. E., 3
DOYLE Ann E., 49
Cath., 76
Chna., 8
Eliz. A., 66
Ellen, 51
Kate B., 68
Mary Eliz., 80
Reb., 7, 48
DRAKE Cath., 16
DRAMS Louisa, 13
DRAPER Betsey, 105
Reb., 105
DRENNEN Mary, 34
DRENNER Am., 78
Luema, 77
Lydia Ellen, 32
Mary Cath., 19
DREW Arianah, 85
DRILL Mary B., 61
Sr., 52
DRIVER Mary, 97
DRONDORE Chna., 11
DRURENBURGH Rachel, 58
DRURY Eliz., 97
Matilda, 20
Sr., 2
DUBBEL Cath., 30
DUBBLE Eliz., 54
So., 38
DUBLE Na., 12
DUCKETT Eliza, 80
Mariane, 62
Mary L., 2
Sally, 84
Sr., 115
DUCKS Helinco, 20
DUFF, Marg., 97
DUFFIELD Eliz., 4
DUFFY Mary, 53
DUGAN Eleanor R., 112
Eliz., 27, 113
Isa., 63, 98

Marg., 41
Maria, 26
Mary, 33
Na., 54, 62
DUGINER Mary, 67
DUKE Mary Jane, 28
DUNBARGER Eliz., 95
DUNDOR Cath., 97
DUNDORE Eliz., 110
Susan, 29
DUNHAM Eliza S., 21
DUNN Cath., 92, 107
Eliz., 43, 62, 63
DUPLE Cath., 50
Eliz., 11
Sus., 59
DURBLER Susan, 103
DURFF Har., 109
Mar., 64
DUSING Cath., 35, 76
Eliz., 90
Eliz. M., 28
Mar., 70
DUSINGER Eliz., 98
Maria, 95
DUST Alsinda Isa., 13
Reb. E., 50
DUTEROW, Susan, 54
DUTREE Cath., 110
DUTRO Eliz., 94
Mary, 52
DUTROW Eliz., 87
Jemima K., 108
Mary, 31
Mary Ann, 112
DUTTEROW Cath., 94
DUVALL Am., 49
Sr. J., 115
DYCE Betsey, 47

-E-

EACHS Na., 81
EACHUS Mary, 16
EAGEN Cath., 29
EAGLE Lucinda, 75
EAKEL Am., 113
Cath., 21, 46, 50
Eliz., 44, 50, 58
Leah, 53
Marg., 50
Mary, 27, 49
Sr., 85, 101
EAKLE Cath., 70, 105
Eleanora, 91
Eliz., 113
Eliz. C., 100
Leah S., 94
Malinda, 31
Mary, 29, 42
Mary E., 15

Na., 59
Sr., 47, 64
Susan, 86
EARHART, Molly, 77
EARLY Marg., 110
Marg. Ann, 11
EARLYWINE Mary, 94
EASTACHINS Cath., 119
EASTERDAY Amanda C., 95
Ann So., 35
Barb. Ann, 41
Eliz., 1
Esther, 24
Marg., 77
Mary, 62
Mary A., 36
Susan, 94
Terecy, 95
Tracy Ann, 113
EASTON Am., 15
Eliz., 10
EATON Mar., 52
EATY Han. M., 42
EAVEY Barbary, 88
Chna., 106
Eliz., 78
Lydia, 94
Marg., 10
Marg. Ann, 89
Mary, 19
Rachel, 64
Reb., 30
Tracy R., 117
EBBERT, Eliz., 95
EBERLY Cath., 67
EBERSOLE Cath., 92
EBERT, Mary, 42
EBREHT Susan, 87
ECKARD Ann E., 112
ECKENBARGER Ann, 11
Dolly, 60
ECKER Cath., 3
Eliz., 81
Matilda, 73
ECKERT Cath., 71
Maria, 43, 50
ECKMAN Mar. Jane, 102
Marg. S., 81
EDDEN Sue M., 101
EDDY Am., 94
EDEMAN Peggy, 16
EDMONDS Eliza, 108
Mary Ann, 46
Mary C., 3
EDWARDS Editha, 45
Eliza, 23, 91
Ellen, 106
Har., 23
Jane, 2

Maria, 119
Mary, 79, 101
Mary Ever, 90
Na., 85
EFFINGER Mary, 7
EICHELBERGER Cath., 49, 58
Eliz., 17
Jane, 94
Mahala, 45
Marg., 46
Maria, 100
Mary, 25
EIDEL Chra., 118
EIFERT, Mary Ann, 49
EL RUTHERFORD Marg., 62
ELDER Clotilda, 13
ELIFRITZ Mary Ellen, 8
ELIZABETH Laura H., 97
ELLER Fanny, 19
ELLIOTT Ann, 52
Cath., 59
Mar., 36
Marg. M., 21
Polly, 32
ELLIS Har., 102
ELY Eliz., 5
EMARICK Nully, 15
EMBERSON Hepsey, 23
EMBIGH Cath., 24
Mary, 92
EMBREY Amanda, 73
EMERSON Chra., 56
Eliz., 78
Lydia, 115
Matilda, 94
Reb., 115
Udolphus, 68
EMLICK Char., 51
EMMERICK Marg., 17
Mary, 6
Polly, 91
Ros., 52
EMMERSON Han., 46
EMMETT Amanda H., 33
Cath., 71, 97
Cath. J., 33
Eliz., 32, 62, 78, 106
Eliz. A., 60
Lavina, 96
Louisa, 63
Mag., 49, 96
Magdalon, 35
Mary, 92
Na., 34
Sally, 115
Sr., 112
EMORY Mary Cath., 104

EMPICH Eliz., 8
ENDRES Susan, 70
ENGLAND Marg., 96
Rachel, 114
ENGLE Ann C., 8
Mary, 58
ENGLEMAN Cath., 81
Han., 57
ENNIS Eliz., 14
ENSMINGER Ann Eve, 2
Eliz., 105
Marg., 75, 102
Mary, 1, 98
Na., 106
Sr., 43
ENSTEIN Hen., 33
ENSWORTH Cath., 57
ENTLER Cath., 30
Eliz., 13
Ellen, 22
Prudence, 119
ERISMAN Ann Maria, 1
ERNST Eliz., 41
ERVIN, Sus., 56
ESMINGER Cath., 32, 117
Eliz., 17
Mary, 69
Sr., 27, 69
ESSINGER Sus., 105
ESTELL Maria, 34
ETNIRE Eliz., 81
Sr., 48
EUSTACHINS Eliz., 98
EUSTIS Sr. Ann, 69
EVANS Julianna, 23
Marg. E., 59
Mary, 65
Reb., 93
Sr., 111
EVERHAND Lydia, 8
EVERHART Eliz., 7
EVERLY Marg., 72
EVERSOLE Eliz., 8
Eliza, 35
Eve, 63
Mary, 13, 29
EVES Mar. E., 69
EVILHOCK Cath., 81
Eliz., 102
EYERLY Eliz., 117
Har., 35
EYLER Ann Maria, 7

-F-
FABERITZ Mary, 81
FACHLER Barb., 1
FAGAN, Na., 9
FAGINS Lyida, 112
FAHRNEY Elisa, 105

133

Eliz., 67
Mary A., 37
Sus., 60
FAIR Sr. E., 15
FALDER Reb., 66
FALES Mary, 47
FALKER Na., 82
FARE Barb., 28
FARIS Ann, 1
FARLTON Alice, 50
FARNESWORTH Lucinda, 54
FARNSWORTH Han. O., 63
FARQUHAR Alice, 66
Eliz., 1
Jane, 59
Mar. May, 49
FARRELL Bridget, 108
Bridgett, 32
Maria, 34
FARREN Ann, 53
FARROW Louisa, 69
Mary, 59, 60, 81
FARST Cath., 117
Chna., 98
FASNAUGHT Sus., 22
FATE Mary, 4
FAUCET Lydia, 51
FAUCKLER Eliz., 51
FAUGHER Hellen L., 64
FAULDER Cath., 88
Sus., 78
FAULDERS Ann, 28
Eliz., 5
Han., 22
Mary Ann, 32
FAULKISELL Sr., 43
FAULKLER Eliz., 109
FAULKWELL Eliz., 14
Reb., 75
Ruth S., 7
FAUSNAUGHT Eliz., 79
Julian, 65
Mary A., 80
Sr., 34
Sus., 16
Susan, 112
FAUSS Cornelia, 15
FAUVER Ann Maria, 78
Mary Ann, 85
FAYETTIN Marg., 50
FAYMAN Eliz., 4
FEALY Mary, 65
FEASTER Elizth, 2
FEBRY Marg., 33
FECHTIG Joanna Am., 49
Marg., 2
Mary E., 9
Narcissa Y., 109
Sallie A.P., 76

Sus., 66
Susan F., 48, 52
FEDERELL Sus., 98
FEERY Na., 63
FEIDT Mary Ann, 74
Mary E., 6
Susan C., 60
FEIGLEY, Cath. Ann, 59
Eliz., 109
Isa., 36
Lydia, 118
Mary, 11
Sr. Ann, 8
FEIRY Mary, 12
Mary Eliz., 11
FELIX Sus., 45
FELKER Cath., 37
Cath. E., 109
Eleanor, 5
Sr., 48
FENCELER Kitty, 66
FERGUSON Jane, 43
FERON Marg. Ellen, 111
FERRELL Frances O., 18
FESSLER Cath., 90
FETERICK Marg., 86
FETTER Mary Ann, 37
FICHTER Mar., 27
FIE Eliz., 64
FIELDS Ann M., 63
Hen., 21
FIERY Cath., 6
Eliz., 12
Eliza Jane, 117
Eve Cath., 107
Mary, 72
Mary Ann, 118
Mary Ann E., 12
Sus., 2
FIGALEY Na., 82
FIGALLY, Mary, 18
Sr. Ann, 103
FIGLEY Cath., 107
FILES Sr., 56
FILLER Eliz., 64
FINAFOUCK Mary, 81
FINCK Na., 33
FINEBRUCK Ros., 89
FINEFROCK Ruanna, 98
FINEFRUCK Roz., 111
FINEGAN Elenora, 76
FINFROCK Sally, 20
Sus., 61
FINGER Marg. Emilie, 59
FINK Barb., 63
Chna., 74
Eliz., 29
Magdalena, 6
Mary, 83

Reb., 89
Sr. Ann, 83
FINKABINE Chna., 94
FIREY Caroline E., 96
Mary, 2
Mary Eliza, 71
Sr., 13
FISCHER Barb., 60
FISHACK, Cath., 20
Hen., 34
FISHAUGH Eliz., 111
Polly, 111
FISHAUK Cath., 32
FISHER Agnes, 112
Eliz., 7, 29
Eliza, 72
Frances Eliz., 48
Mary, 45, 46, 96
Sr., 22, 38
Sr. C., 88
Sus., 55
FITZ Cath., 110
Cornelia Ann, 68
FITZGERALD Bridget, 28
FITZHUGH Adelaid H., 5
Eliza M., 34
M.A., 99
FIZER Cath., 14
FLAGG Iorda E.A., 71
Louisa, 62
FLANAGAN Ann R., 24
Sr., 20
FLANNAGAN Marg., 66
FLEMING Jane, 59
FLEMMING Am., 37
An Eliza, 57
Eliz., 68
Jane, 63
Mary Ann, 67
FLENNER Eliz., 98
Marg., 57
FLESON Eliz., 98
FLETCHER Reb. E., 24
FLINN Sr. E., 117
FLOCHER Marg., 64
FLOOD Har. P., 85
FLOOK Reb., 16
FLORA Cath., 83
Eliz., 67
Mary, 56, 65
Mary Jane, 25
Na., 1
Reb., 99
Sus., 12
FLORY Amanda, 117
Eliz., 20, 87, 88, 106
Loretta, 100
Lucy, 100
Na., 24

Susan, 91
FLOYER Marianna, 52
FLUCK Susan M., 28
FOCKLER Marg. Ann, 106
Mary Ann, 29
So., 78
FOGLE Na., 118
FOGLER Cath., 94
Eliz., 87
Rea Ruth, 29
Talina R., 80
FOGWELL, Polly, 32
Sus., 56
FOILS Eliz. A., 55
FOLDER Ann Maria, 11
FOLTZ Barb., 42
Esther, 50
Mag., 63
Mary, 63
Sus., 100
FORBUS Sr., 27
FORCE Sr., 106
FORD Chna., 54
Eliz., 15
Han., 107
Helen, 56
Mar. M., 56
Sr., 8
Sr. Ann, 71
FORE Eliz., 1
FOREMAN Rachel, 35
FOREST Mary Ann, 51
FOREY Ellen, 69
FORMAN Betrice, 111
Mar., 36
FORMES Cath., 81
FORNEY Cath., 93
FORNY Eliz., 30
FORREST Julian, 11
Lavinia, 65
Leah, 84
Mary, 34
Sus., 45
FORRESTER Mildred, 43
Mildren, 46
FORRY Eliz., 1
FORSYTH Marg., 12
Na., 5
FORSYTHE Cath., 55
Mary, 103
Mary Ann, 28
FORTHMAN Barb., 62
So., 69
FORTNEY, Mary Eliz., 75
FOSTER Caroline, 51
Cath., 5
Frances, 42
Marg., 10
Maria Louisa, 48

Na., 44
Polly, 1
Ros. E., 1
FOTHERILL Polly, 48
FOUBLE Marg. A., 55
FOUKE Almira B., 107
Eliz. B., 120
Maria, 104
Mary Ann, 63
FOULDER Marg., 32
FOULTZ Sr. Ann, 117
FOUTCH Cath., 79
FOUTS Eliz., 5
FOUTZ, Char., 12
Dorothy, 23
Eliz., 32
Eve, 9
Mag., 62
Roz., 60
Sr. M., 34
Susan, 14
Susan Kath., 113
FOW, Sr., 2
FOWLER Ann W., 112
Lucretia O., 34
FOX Cath., 46, 83
Letitia, 66
Marg., 77
Sr. Ann, 67
Virginia, 47
FOY Cath., 6
FOYLES Eliz. A., 80
FRAKER Am., 49
Arabella, 75
FRALEY, Cath., 115
Eliz., 2
FRANCE Lydia, 80
FRANCIS Mary, 77
FRANKENBERGER Marg., 104
FRAVER Eliza Ann, 37
FRAZIER Ferlinda, 87
Julian, 38
Mary, 116
Mary Ann, 93
FREANER Louisa, 73
Marg., 80
Reb., 58
FREANEY Diana, 32
FREDERICK Eliz., 54
Na., 74
FREET Barb., 72
FREEZE Marg., 37
FREIDLAND Eva, 93
FRENCH Ann Maria, 68
Eliz., 73
Han., 55
Isa., 95
Louisa, 60
Marg., 30, 38

FREY Chna., 68
Marg. Jane, 108
Sr., 96
Susan Ann, 59
FREYTINGER Cath., 111
FRICK Char., 79
FRIDINGER Eliz., 49
Marg., 11
Maria, 54
Mary, 49
FRIEDHOFIN Anna Eliz., 82
FRIEDLY Chna., 84
Han., 87
FRIEND Eleanor, 44
Eliz., 45
Eliza Jane, 85
Jane, 54
Julianna, 111
Lucinda, 78
Nelly, 44
Rachel E., 20, 113
Reb., 32
Sr., 49
FRIENDLY Sr., 78
FRILL Na., 27
FRITTS, Mary Ann, 23
FRITZ Cath., 63
Eliz., 32
Malinda, 19
Mary, 43
FROM Ann Gibbs, 100
Ros., 34
FRORISBURRY Eliz., 116
FROZIER Mariah, 18
FRY Har., 43
Jane, 54, 55
Mar. E., 102
Mary, 35
FRYE So., 36
FRYER Emily Virginia, 74
FRYMAN Marg., 73
FULK, Ellen, 111
FULLERTON, Eliz., 21
Nellie, 9
FULTON Barb., 107
Betsey, 111
Cath., 97
Maria, 14
Mary, 28
Mary Ann, 53
FULTZ Cath., 42, 86, 97
Mary, 82
Sr., 118
FUNK Ann, 44
Anne, 78
Annie L., 96
Barbary, 10

Cath., 78
Dorothy, 87
Eliz., 1, 32, 64, 89, 90, 94, 96
Eve, 94
Frances, 33
Francy, 29
Hetthy, 78
Judith, 109
Malinda, 56
Marg., 49
Mary, 8, 10, 36, 44, 68, 89
Mary Ann, 101
Mrs. Anna, 56
Na., 11, 44, 60, 96
Polly, 38
Sr., 3, 94, 116
Sus., 49, 74, 89, 105
Susan, 65
Teresa, 13
Tracy, 18
FURLEY, Eliza Ann, 44
FURR Mary, 79
FURRAY Barb., 8
FURRY, Ann So., 54
Eliz., 39
Mar., 66
Na., 77
FYE Cath., 100

-G-
GABBY Eliza C., 28
Emily, 67
Jane, 54
GABRIEL Cath. W., 102
GAFF Polly, 41
Sr., 29
GAINER Eliz. J., 45
GAITHER, Ann, 11
Mar., 48
GALE Cath., 11
GALEWIX Lovice, 14
GALLAGHER Bridget, 6
Mary Ann, 11
GALROCK Mary, 88
GAMBLE Eliza Jane, 75
Marg., 46
GAN Cath., 58
GANNON Marg., 95
GANS, Mary Eliz., 83
GANTT Maria, 58
GANTZ Ann, 98
Ann Am., 49
Barb., 32
Mary, 19, 64
Sr., 22, 38
GARBER Polly, 84
GARDENOUR Cath., 81

Mahala, 54
Mariah, 52
GARDNER Cath., 88
Eliz., 71
Esther, 100
Eveline, 51
Jane, 80
Sr., 103
Sus., 35
GARDNOUR Julianna, 30
GARHART Cath., 77
GARLIN Cath. M., 118
GARLINGER Eliz., 17
GARMAN, Cath., 13
Sally, 6
GARNAND Reb., 69
GARNER Mary Ann, 4
Sus., 40
GARNETT Mehaly, 8
GARNHEART Sr. E., 92
GARNS Reb. J., 48
GARRAGHTY Mrs., 27
GARRETT Eliz., 18
Mary Ann, 10
Matilda, 38
GARRISH Louisa, 64
GARRITY Cath., 62
Na., 91
GARVER, Eliz., 37
Eve, 80
Mary, 91
Mary Ann, 103
Na., 20
Sus., 50
Susan Eliz., 23
GARVIN, Caroline, 101
Cath. A., 101
GASSMAN Mary, 119
GASTOR Ellen, 41
GATRELL Eve R., 102
GAWTHROP Edith, 108
GAY Char., 26
GAYLOR Levina, 90
GEARHART Cath., 18, 57
Eliz., 7, 61, 113
Eliza, 9
Marg., 112
Mary, 24
Reb., 71
So., 44
Susan, 112
Susan M., 7
GEARING Maria, 95
GEEDING Cath., 108
Eliz., 113
Reb., 119
So., 97
GEEDY Ros., 52
GEELER Cath., 110
GEETING Cath., 26

Eliz., 25
GEGLER Louisa, 66
GEHR Ann Eliz., 11
Cath., 84
Cath. Electa, 71
Eliza, 75
Juliann, 54
Maria, 105
Mary, 84, 115
Mary Ann, 103
Mary Cath., 108
Na., 49
Sarah, 6
Sr., 62
GEIGER Eleanora, 92
Eliz., 18
Eliza, 38
Hen., 54
Sally, 12
Scharlotte, 21
GEIGIS Eliz., 102
GEIGLER Eliz., 34
GEISER Mary, 70
Sr., 34
GELTMACHER Matilda, 99
Sr. Jane, 83
GELTMAKER Ann Maria, 119
Mary, 89
GELTMOCKER Eliz., 41
GELWICK, Mary E., 52
GELWICKS Amanda, 24
Louisa, 112
Marg. Ann, 35
Sus., 98
Virginia, 45
GELWISE Mary Eliz., 110
GELWIX Marg. Ann, 3
GENAWEIN Mag., 58
GEORGE E.A.M., 87
Sus., 78
GERRARD Marion E., 9
GETTER Sr. Ann, 57
GETTY Isa., 116
GIBBS, Eliz., 72
GIBSON Francis, 83
Marg., 22
Phebe, 16
GIDDINGER Reb., 99
GIFT Eliz., 110
Han. Jane, 110
GIGLER Cath., 59
GIGOUS Sr. L., 61
GILBERT Ann, 90
Cath., 76
Eliz., 35
Eliz. B., 115
Eve, 26
Han., 24

Marg. M., 21
GILDAY Mary, 105
GILES Adelaide, 113
  Mary Ann, 100
GILLILAND Mary, 8
GILLIS Eliz., 72
  Han., 27
GILMER Mary I., 31
GILMYER Cath. T., 41
GILPER Ann Maria, 117
GILTNER Eliz., 94
GIMPLE Cath., 54
  Susan, 81
GINGERY Marg., 49
GITTINGER Eliz., 85
GLASS Abigail, 16
  Cath., 114
  Eliz., 48, 76
  Eve, 64
  Na., 3
GLASSBRENNER Cath., 2
  Chna., 24
GLAZE Cath., 72
  Cath. A.F., 100
  Eliz., 100
GLENN Mary R., 11
GLESSNER Amanda M., 46
GLETNER Mary, 64
GLOOZE Susan, 27
GLOSS Elizth M., 75
  Mary A., 104
  Reb., 104
  Susan C., 99
GLOSSBRENNER Cath., 61
GOBLE Mag., 57
GODWIN Polly, 67
GOFF Mary Ann, 111
  So., 43
GOLB Cath., 7
GOLD Marion, 20
GOLDSBERRY Ann, 34
  Har., 4
GOLDSBOROUGH Sr. E.,
  18
GOLDSMITH Rosa, 55
GOLE Cath., 14
GOLL Eliz., 87
  Mary, 117
  Sr., 51
GOLLOCHER Malinda, 77
GONDER Susan, 64
GOOD Anna, 78
  Barb., 70
  Eliz., 36, 71
GOODINTING Marg., 36
GOODWIN Reb., 82
GOODY Lena, 25
  Susan, 101
GORDAN Mary Ann, 14
  Na., 40

GORDON, Ann Eliza, 116
  Jane K., 76
  Mary, 20
  Sus., 57
  Susan D., 100
  Susan E., 94
GORMAN Cath., 65
  Mary Ann, 53
GORRELL Cecelia, 14
GORTIE Mary, 36
GOUFF Caroline, 57
  Julia Ann, 99
  Sr., 26
  Sr. Ann, 71
GOUGER Barb., 109
GOUKER Mag., 68
  Mary Cath., 105
  Mary Eliz., 63
  Mary Kate, 40
  Mary M., 73
GOULDING Ann, 60
  Susan, 12
GOURT Marg., 69
GOUTER Ann Eliz., 76
GOW Cath., 73
  Mahala, 52
  Sally, 18
GOWER Ann, 66
  Cath., 47
  Eliz., 94
  Marg., 114
  Mary Ann, 85
  Polly, 35
  Susan, 11
GOWGER Mary, 35
GOWKER Sr., 63
GRABILL, Rachel, 61
GRAEFF Cath., 8, 13
GRAGEN Dolly, 22
GRAHAM Caroline, 85
  Eliz., 43
  Louisa L., 107
  Mary, 89
GRANT Marg., 2
  Mary A., 34
GRANTHAM Jemima J., 17
  Mary, 20
GRAVE Eliz., 12
GRAVES Ann R., 49
  Eliz., 2
GRAY Ann, 57
  Ann R., 1
  Cath., 34
  Eliz., 44, 47, 55,
  100, 109
  Marg., 92
  Mary, 32
  Mary A.R., 22
  Mary Ann, 62
  Polly, 33

GREAMER (GROMER) Na.,
  4
GREEN Barb., 38
  Eliz., 42
  Eliza, 99
  Isa., 104
  Na., 86, 90
  Rachel, 19
  Reb., 47
  Sr., 47
  Sus., 6
  Theny, 15
GREENAWALT Eliz., 47
  Lavinia, 65
  Na., 104, 117
GREENFIELD, Mary Jane,
  110
GREENWALL Letha, 84
GREENWELL Maria, 116
  Mary, 55
GREENWOOD Sr. A., 80
GREGORY, Ann, 51
  Mary E., 94
  Mehetable, 6
GREY Eliz., 65
GRIEVES Eleanor C., 78
  Eliza, 88
GRIFFITH Mary, 43
  Mary Ann, 69
GRIFITH Har. J., 110
GRIM Arnslia, 29
  Eliz., 36, 109, 113
  Han. P.B., 29
  Hen., 60
  Louisa, 35
  Lucinda, 100
  Lydia, 37
  Marg., 43, 100
  Mary, 99
  Mary Ann, 24
  Mary Jane, 75
  So., 24, 83, 89
  Susan, 43
GRIMES Ann, 22
  Cath., 76
  Eliz., 87
  Jane, 4
  Mary Ann, 7
  Sr., 46
GRIMM Eliz., 25
GRIMMER Eliz., 42
GRINER Cath., 111
GRISTLE Lavinia, 112
GRONTZ Cath., 33
  Mary Ann, 10
GROOMBAUGH Mary, 26
GROOMS Na., 41
GROSH, Am., 50
  Ann Mary, 4
  Cath. E., 103

Clara M., 105
Lucy M., 25
Marg. J., 35
Pamelia Rosine, 82
So., 94
Sr., 35, 69
GROSS Eliz., 73
Han., 1, 42
Marg. Ann, 99
Mary, 56
GROSSNICKEL Mary, 47
GROSUCH Sr. A., 48
GROUND Eliz., 91
Sr., 68
GROVE Am., 4
Ann Maria, 42
Ann Reb., 65
Barb. Ellen, 42
Cath., 88
Cath. A., 99
Dorothy, 42
Eliz., 70, 88
Eliza, 16
Eve, 9
Han., 102
Har., 52
Lavenia, 46
Mary, 42, 63, 69, 115
Mary Ann, 67
Na., 62, 104
Roz., 99
Sarah, 34
Sr., 96
Sr. Ann, 80
Susan, 26
GROVES Ann Eliza, 83
GROW So., 100
GRUBB Catey, 96
Marg., 18
Reb., 70
Sus., 104
GRUBER Char., 107
Eliz., 11
Marg. Ann, 11
Mary, 25
Na., 64, 87, 90
Sr., 9
GRUSH Allas, 114
Barb., 115
Eliz., 97
Marg., 87
GRUVER, Mary, 89
GULL Na., 85
GUNDER Emily, 50
GURINGER Cath., 88
GUSHWA Chna., 101
Eliz., 12
Marg., 39
GUSTARD Ros., 67

GUTHING Marg., 41
GUTHRIE Marie, 7
GUTMAN Reb., 45
GUY Eliz., 59
GUYDER Massey, 92
GUYER Eve, 116
GUYTON Reb., 4
Sr., 19
Sr. Ann, 16
GYER Eliz., 66

-H-
HABB, Sr. T., 9
HABER Eliz., 112
HABLE Jean, 4
HACKNEY Mar., 24
HAGELINE Cath., 74

HAGENBERGER Mary, 113
HAGER Cath., 114
Eliz., 61
Malinda C., 28
Mary, 62
Sr., 79
HAGERMAN Marg., 97
HAHN Cath. Matilda, 92
Han., 12
Marg., 5
Mary, 17
Sally, 47
HAILLER Marg., 15
HAINES Ann Maria, 54
Cath., 43
Eliz., 51
Mar. Ellen, 74
Mary, 20, 104
Susan, 25
Susan G., 58
HAINS Eliz. A., 41
Sr., 55
HALE Sr., 72
HALEY Cath., 61
HALFESTINE Mary, 72
HALL Arey, 112
Barb., 92
Eliz. Bowie, 116
Emily, 18
Han., 95
Han. M.L., 61
Jane E., 20
Lettice S., 102
Marg., 25, 70, 84
Mary, 118
Sr., 9
HALLAM Mary, 38
HALLER Eve, 24
HAMACKER Maria, 40
HAMAKER Mary, 90
HAMIA, Mary, 23
HAMILTON Bolina, 18

Eliz., 110
Eliza, 60
Jane, 49, 86
Juliet, 27
Marg., 61
Mary, 75
Mary B., 70
Reb., 113
Sr., 7, 10
Sus., 23
HAMM Eliz., 95
Mary, 70
Mary T., 112
Sr., 91, 95
Virginia C., 78
HAMMAKER Anna, 3
Susan, 37, 104
HAMMEL Elis., 40
HAMMER Ann Am., 25
Cath., 2
Eleanor, 117
Eliz., 98
Marg. E., 77
Mary, 23, 102
Mary A., 114
Priscilla, 101
Sr., 60
HAMMERSLA Ann Cath., 10
Mary B., 22
Sr. Ann, 71
HAMMET Cath., 9
HAMMETT Eliz., 110, 111
Marg., 46
Sr., 1, 26
Virginia, 73
HAMMON Eliza, 79
HAMMOND Angeline, 8
Caroline, 19
Caroline T., 29
Cath., 102, 117
Cornelia G., 100
Eliz., 24, 59, 96, 100, 112
Ellen, 65
Frances, 115
Han., 17
Helen, 73
Louisa, 96
Louisa Ann, 20
Mar., 103
Mary, 41, 82
Mary A., 29
Mary Ann, 3
Nelly, 84
Polly, 119
Reb. C., 10
Sr., 84, 106, 109
Sus., 17, 24

Susan, 2
HANES Cath., 84
  Eliz., 75
  Mary Ann, 18
  Priscilla, 14
HANN Sr., 120
HANNA Adeline, 88
  Eliz., 56
  Marg., 57
  Mary, 13
  Na., 7
  Reb., 74
  Sr. Ann, 53
  Tracy, 32
  Urilla, 67
HANNAH Na., 38
HANNAN, Mary, 84
HANNANKAMP Mary E., 56
HANSHER Isa., 1
HANT Ellenor Ann, 76
HANY Mary, 25
HARBAUGH, Anna, 95
  Eliz., 66
  Isa. S., 6
  Julianna, 31
  Marg., 60
  Mary, 84
  Sus., 66
HARBIN Susan, 42
HARBINE Cath., 87
  Eliza Jane, 16
  Mary Ann, 39
HARDEN Caroline, 70
  Lydia, 90
HARDY Priscilla, 38
HARE Sr., 38
HARK Grace, 68
HARKER Eliz., 36
HARLEY Mary, 110
HARLIN Eliz. Ann, 80
HARMAN Cath., 29
  Eliz., 11
  Hetty, 22
  Mary, 53
  Na., 60
HARMASON Polly, 37
HARMISTON Sr., 21
HARMON Eliz., 114
  Marg., 98, 116
  Mary Ann, 47
  Sr., 111
HARN Eliz. T., 45
  Har., 108
HARNE Mary Ellen, 40
HARP Emily, 119
HARPE, Eliz., 111
HARPER Eliz., 56, 107
  Ellen, 45
  Ellenora, 108
  Mary, 96

HARPMAN Cath., 94
HARR, Mary M., 120
  Na., 12
HARRIETT Cecelia, 38
HARRIGAN Lydia N., 9
HARRIS Eliz., 94
  Eliza Jane, 101
  Mahala, 62
HARRISON Cath., 52
  Emily, 51
  Marg., 46
  Mary, 34
HARROW Peggy, 98
HARRY Am., 85
  Cath. G., 94
  Eliz., 54
  Han., 53
  Isa., 22
  Marg., 50
  Marg. S., 76
  Mary, 88, 120
  Mary Eliz., 63
  Sally, 6
  Sr. B., 10
  Susan, 7
  Susan B., 64
HARSH Mary, 103
  Mary E., 88
HARSHBERGER Eliz., 90
HARSHMAN Cath., 25
  Eliz., 25
HART Ann, 21
  Cath., 38, 107
  Eliza, 41
  Frances Eliz., 86
  Mary Ann, 67
  Sally, 11
  Susan, 13
HARTEL Mary Ann, 101
HARTER, Ann, 83
HARTLE Ann M., 73
  Betsy, 107
  Cath., 73
  Esther, 16
  Han., 94
  Hetty, 59
  Mary, 102
  Sr., 103, 112
  Sus., 16
  Susan, 69
HARTMAN Ann Eliz., 61,
92
  Eliz., 38, 40, 45
  Eliz. Emiline, 30
  Eliza, 13
  Ellen, 40
  Julia A., 71
  Marg., 27, 65
  Mary Ann, 97
HARTZOG Eliz., 87

HARVEY Eliz., 62
  Marg., 16
HARVIN, Mary E., 21
HAS Ann, 66
HASS Eliz., 100
  Eve, 115
HASTINGS Na., 97
HATE Cath., 96
HATHERDLY, Mary, 46
HATHERLY Livia, 110
HATHORN Prudence, 115
HAUER Caroline, 13
  Louisa Susan, 77
HAUSE Eliz., 33, 78
HAUVER Cath., 9, 118
  Mary Ann, 21
HAVENER Eliz., 25
HAVER Mary E.L., 82
HAVERSTICK, Marg., 113
  Sr., 43
HAVITT Abagail, 43
HAWKEN Julian E., 4
  Marg., 72
HAWKENS Cath. A., 11
HAWKEY Eliz., 108
  Susan, 103
HAWKINS Cath., 11
  Eliz. Susan, 38
  Frances E., 45
  Na., 62
  Susan, 101
HAWN Cath., 74
  Mary So., 53
HAWTHORN Barb., 86
  Lydia Jane, 78
  Maria, 25
  Rachel, 118
HAWTHORNE Mary Jane,
65
HAYDEN Na., 37
HAYE Sus., 88
HAYES Delilah, 65
  Eliz., 70
  Isa., 105
  Mary, 36
  Matilda, 24, 88
  Na., 115
  Priscilla, 89
  Prudence, 46
  Sr., 46, 116
HAYMAKER Eliz., 86
HAYNES Mary, 24
  Na. Ann, 89
  Rachel A., 55
  Reb., 19
HAYS, Caroline, 41
  Cath., 57
  Eliz., 73
  Eliz. P., 42
  Har., 42

Hen., 105
Mary, 17
So., 105
So. B., 71
HAYSTED Na., 115
HEABERLY Eliz. M., 90
HEAFLICH Am. S., 17
Otillia, 115
HEAGLE Cath., 4
HEALY Helena, 106
HEANSON Eliza Jane, 39
HEARTLAND Eliz., 2
HEASON Barb., 19
HEAVNER Sus., 5
HEBB Ann, 68
Cath., 17
Helen Marietta, 119
Nanny S., 93
HEBBERD Jane M., 56
HECK Eliz., 78
Eliz. Barbery, 106
Eliza Ann, 42
Eliza M., 20
Han. E., 6
Sr., 9
Sr. A.C., 64
Sr. Ann, 66
HEDDEN Eliz., 91
Marg. L., 97
HEDGE Malinda, 108
Na., 108
HEDGES Mary Jane, 5
HEDRICK Marg., 89
Mary, 89
HEDRICKS Blanche A.,
12
HEFFLEBOWER Cath., 71
Mary, 90
HEFFLEY, Cath., 8
Eliz., 64
HEFFNER Barb., 96
Hen., 6
HEFLEBOWER Hulda, 72
HEINZ Cath., 76
HEISKELL, Mary, 22
HEITSHIRE Eliz., 76
HEITZLER Louisa, 114
HELFESTAY Susan V., 88
HELLANE Caroline, 22
HELLER Am., 12
Cath., 1
Mary, 12
Polly, 5
Sus., 43, 81
HELM Mary, 119
So. W., 70
HELPHENSTINE Malinda
M., 1
HELSER Lydia, 12
Sus., 3

HEMSWORTH Ann R., 38
Eliz., 107
Louisa, 70
HENDERSON, Isa., 24
Louisa M., 19
HENDRICK Eliz., 16
HENDRICKS Eliza, 64
Mary E., 55
Sus., 17
HENNEBERGER Sus., 8
HENNEBREGER Sr. Ann,
26
HENNESY, Bridget, 57
HENRY Caroline, 99
Cath., 103
Eliz., 41
Rachel, 111
Sr., 108
HENSON Susan C., 13
HENTY, Cath., 98
HERBERT Cornelia M.,
47
Feaby, 66
Jane R., 111
Julia, 114
Phebe E., 12
HERD Cecelia Ann, 89
Louisa, 35
Marg. A., 85
Mary Jane, 15
HERING Na., 58
HERLINGER Sus., 82
HERR Ann, 62
Cath., 59
Eliz., 7, 48
Eliza, 70
Frances, 60
Hen. C., 107
Hetty, 44
Lizzie B., 30
Maria, 51
Mary, 53
Mary Ann, 1
Mary Eliz., 106
Molly, 103
Na., 48
Sr. Jane, 80
Sus., 55
Susan, 87
HERRING Cath., 43
Eliz., 114
Mary, 10
HERSH Eliz., 94
Fanny, 43, 104
HERSHBERGER Caroline,
111
Chna., 47
Eliz., 30
Juliann, 43
Marg. Ann, 109

HERSHEY Ann, 30
Barb., 33, 37, 48,
49
Cath., 15, 79, 107
Eliz., 3, 37
Francy, 3
Mag., 45, 48, 99
Marg. A., 86
Mary, 52
Mary Ann, 94, 101
Matilda, 16
Sr., 100
Susan, 57
HERTZEL Chna., 72
HESKETT Mar., 5
HESLEHAN Ellen, 58
HESLETIN Ann Cornelia,
65
HESLEY (HERLSOY) Mar.
E., 5
HESS Ann Maria, 22
Cath., 42
Eliz., 106
Marg., 28
Maria, 113
Marinda, 68
Mary Ann, 43
Phebe, 17
Rowana, 78
Sus., 42
Susan, 106
HESSELSTINE Eliz. B.,
4
HESSEY Marg., 34
Sr. E., 63
HETENHOUSER Hen., 51
HETZER Caroline, 48
Jane Eliz., 17
Mary, 103
HEWETT Maria, 59
Matilda, 92
Mrs. Cath., 96
HEWITT, Leah, 12
Marg., 50
HEYGISS Mary C., 14
HEYSER Ellen Maria, 99
HIATT Mary C., 39
HIBBINS Patty, 88
HIBERT Ann Arnold, 33
HICKMAN Eliz., 19
Mary, 21
HICKS Cath., 18, 55
Eliza Ann, 25
HIESTAND Frances, 47
HIETT, Cath., 115
HIGGENS Mary, 8
HIGGINS Bridget, 39
Emily I.T., 66
Isa., 74

HIGGS Esther, 42
HIGHBARGER Ann, 115
  Cath., 58, 64
  Marg., 73
  Mary F., 69
  Susan, 101
HIGHBERGER Har., 101
HIGHSHOE, Eliz., 57
HIGHSWANDER Susan, 86
HILDEBRAND Alethia,
106
  Leah, 32
  Lucretia, 53
  Mary, 89
HILE Na., 52
HILL Ann C., 13
  Ann Maria, 118
  Cath., 10
  Eliz., 67, 75, 77,
89, 118
  Eliz. Ann, 74
  Eliza, 97
  Han., 104
  Julia Ann, 4
  Marg., 81
  Marg. V., 52
  Mary, 89, 92, 106,
108, 113
  Mary Cath., 63
  Sr., 50, 103, 114
  Susan, 27, 55
HILLIARD Cath., 85
  Ellen, 112
  Marg., 46

HILTABRIDEL, Sirena
E., 88
HILTEBRIDLE Francina,
76
HIME, Am. C., 7
HIMES Cath., 11
  Eliz., 47
  Hellen E., 34
  Lavinia, 42
  Marg., 38, 85
  Mary, 23, 79, 97
  Mary Jane, 29
  Sr. Ann, 30
HINCH Eliz., 55
HINDS Cath., 14
  Ruth, 59
HINE Cath., 90
  Mary, 86
  Reb., 7
  Susan, 75
HINES Cath., 10
  Eliz., 6, 12
  Susan, 60, 115
HINKLE Mary Ann, 96
HINTY Eliz., 90

HISKEY Sr., 117
HITCHCOCK Charity, 26
  Hen. L., 106
HITE Sus., 45
HOB Mary, 86
HOBBS Mary E., 50
HOBERT Marg., 23
HOBLETZELL Sr. Ann, 22
HOCKEN Ann Eliz., 63
HOCKLEY, Kate A., 109
  Lydia, 120
HODGE Minerva, 98
  Na., 41
HODSON Mar., 62
HOES Mary, 16
HOFECKER Julia Ann, 51
HOFF Du Ann, 44
HOFFER Eliz., 79
  Mary, 72
  Sus., 30
HOFFMAN, Ann, 76
  Ann E., 79
  Ann R., 119
  Anna I., 88
  Cath., 2, 44, 71,
104, 105
  Chna., 50, 69
  Eliz., 48, 72, 107,
117
  Esther, 71
  Han., 20
  Leah, 73
  Lydia, 9
  Lydia I., 99
  Mary, 94, 118
  Mary Ann, 11
  Mary C., 61
  Mary E., 79
  Na., 3
  Polly, 60
  Reb., 37
  Sr., 90
  Sr. C., 29
  Susan, 72, 76
HOFFMASTER Cath., 115
  Mary, 24
HOFMAN Barb., 76
HOGAN Sr., 32
HOGANS Eliz., 107
HOGENS Na., 37
HOGG Na., 104
  Rachel, 104
  Sr. Ann, 22
HOGMIRE Cath., 1, 43,
53
  Eliz., 82
  Marg., 107
  Mary, 6, 98
  Reb., 11
  Sus., 11

HOGMYER Sus., 12
HOHFACKER Johanna, 70
HOHN, Eliz., 115
  Mary, 96
HOLBERT Betsey, 107
  Lue C., 80
  Mary, 74
HOLLER Abigail Jane,
44
  Cath., 28, 34
HOLLEY Sus., 18
HOLLIDAY Mary, 14
  Mary E., 46
HOLLINGSWORTH Eliz.
R., 36
  Lydia E., 57
  Mary Y., 39
  Sally A., 114
HOLLIS Sr., 79
HOLLMAN Kate S., 92
  Marg. J., 83
HOLLY Eliz., 46
  Matilda, 41
HOLMAN Mary, 24
HOLME Kesiah, 18
HOLMES Cath., 61
  Mary, 37, 105
  Na., 51
  Reb., 26
  Sus., 107
HOLMS Sus., 115
HOLT Ellen, 77
  Maria, 15
HOLTZAPPLE Regina, 64
HOLTZMAN Cath., 87
  Eve, 75
  Polly, 103
HOMES Eliza, 43
  Na., 97
HOMPART Kitty, 16
HONENECHT Eliz., 24
HOOBER Eliz., 2
HOOD Sr. Ann, 108
HOOKES Ann Mary, 26
HOOP Jane, 12
HOOPER Eleanor, 66
  Emily, 58
  Lethy Ann, 40
HOOPS Hester, 41
HOOVER Caroline E.,
104
  Caroline Eliz., 113
  Cath., 7, 11, 64
  Chna., 100
  Eliz., 21, 45, 50,
112
  Esther, 15, 94
  Fanny, 56
  Har., 71
  Lau, 94

Marg., 99
Mary, 20, 38, 94, 98, 109
Mary Ann, 38, 70
Mary P., 9
Mrs., 3
Na., 1, 15, 33, 36, 38, 59
Sr., 15, 68
Susan, 21, 96
HOPE Han., 33
HOPKINS Bridget, 68
HOPWOOD Rachel, 70
HORGAN Cath., 61
HORINE Ann, 95
Anna P., 71
Cath., 116
ELiz., 50
Eliz., 50, 61, 82
Julia, 114
Lucinda, 48
Mary, 117
Susan, 114
HORMAN Aleathy Ann, 81
HORN, Anna Marg., 62
Bridget, 27
Louisa C., 42
Marg. E., 13
Mary A., 102
Rachel, 100
HORNBERGER Ann, 49
HORNBRAKER Peggy, 109
HORNER, Sr. E., 21
HORNING Mary, 56
HORNISH Cath., 101
HORSENEST Mary, 112
HOSE Cath., 24, 84, 108
Eliz., 97, 109, 113
Mag., 118
Maria, 95
Mary, 102
Na., 83
Sr., 13, 87
Susan, 111
HOSS Cath., 76
Mary, 93
HOTT Mary Ann, 107
HOTZ Marg., 32
HOUCK Mary, 102
HOUCKE Cath., 102
HOUER Ros., 12
HOUPT Eliz., 9
Eliza, 102
HOUSE Ann Lydia, 53
Mary, 10
Mary Ann, 103
Mrs. Lydia, 58
Sr., 115
HOUSEHOLDER Ann Maria,

89
Cath., 49
Char., 39
Eliz., 76, 77
Frances, 13
Har. A.B., 33
Marg., 37
Mary Ann, 6
Matilda, 42
Sr., 103
Sus., 76, 106
HOUSEMAN Marg., 113
HOUSER Ann Eliz., 8
Barb., 26
Cath., 23, 65
Eliz., 72
Julia Ann, 6, 84
Lavinia, 42
Maria, 86
Mary, 33, 63
Mary R., 25
Rachel, 72
Sr., 29, 54
Susan, 42, 88
HOUT Cath., 84
HOUZE Cardine, 20
HOVER Lenora, 27
HOVERMAILE Eliz., 58
Judith, 72
Marg., 4
Sus., 72
HOVERMALE Sr., 113
HOVERSTICK Sus., 79
HOWARD Eleanor, 85
Eliz., 25
Elleatta Susan, 28
Hen. S., 77
Joan E.M., 98
Marg., 95
Mary, 34
Mary Ellen, 93
Patty, 9
Rachel, 117
Sr., 109
HOWELL Ally, 6
Reb., 69
Sr., 13
HOWER Lacy Ann, 72
Mary, 109
Sus., 87
HOYE Ann, 8
Ellen S., 81
Har. M., 119
HU Ann Malinda, 42
HUDDLE, Sus., 87
HUDGELL, Sus., 92
HUDZELL Eliz., 45
HUFF Marg., 96
HUFFER Amanda, 117
Barb., 119

Cath., 103
Eliz., 7, 89, 95, 109
Lydia, 18
Magdalen, 52
Mary, 18
Matilda, 7
Na., 98
Ruan, 75
So., 18
Sr., 41
HUFFMAN Eliz., 98
Eliza, 74
Mary, 42, 91
HUFFMASTER Eliz., 3, 108
Mary, 3
HUFFNER Ann, 4
HUFFORD Sr., 73
Sus., 82, 114
HUFMAN Barb., 87
HUGHES Adalaide H., 92
Am., 20
Am. I., 18
Ann, 33
Cath. C., 13
Eliz., 35, 67
Eliz. Alice, 67
Esther, 102
Hen., 33
Laura, 4
Louisa Ann, 27
Mar., 54
Marg., 5, 78
Mariah A., 34
Mary Ann, 71
Mary E., 36
HUHGES, Irene, 43
HULDEBOYER Leah Ann, 99
HULL Evanah, 33
HULST Ann Reb., 8
HULTZ Mary Ann Eliz., 88
HUMERICHOUSE Eliza, 32
Marg., 44
Sus., 16
HUMRICHOUSE Sr. A., 73
HUMRICKHOUSE Louisa, 59
HUNSAKER Maria C., 57
HUNSTBERY So., 80
HUNT Ann Maria, 65
Cath., 52
Eliz., 87
Sr., 55
Sus., 34
Susan, 20
HUNTER Ann, 51
Cath., 103

Eleanor, 106
Jane, 108
HUNTSBERRY Eliz., 38
Levinia, 91
Marg., 56
Sr. Ann, 99
HUNTT, Han., 85
HUNTZBERRY Har., 103
HUPP Alice M., 2
HURLEKEE Bridget, 80
HURLEY Char., 28
HURSH Susan Ann, 85
HURST Han. F., 101
Mary D., 74
Mary V., 109
HUSSANG Cath., 89
HUSTON Mary, 39
HUTCHISON Eliz., 15
HUTZEL Har., 83
Mary, 61
Na., 100
HUTZELL Amanda, 98
Cath., 63
Malinda, 59
Sr., 100, 119
HUYET Ann, 118
HUYETT Calanthia Jane,
34, 111
Elisa M., 105
Eliz., 7
Eliz. C., 105
Mar. Ann, 53
Mary A., 66
Sr., 53
HYATT ELiz., 14
Eliz., 115
Sr., 77
HYBARGER Cath., 20
Eliz., 10
HYCHEW Cindarella, 73
HYETT Anna, 74
Eliza, 24
HYLAND Mary, 64
Mary Ann, 87
Rachel, 10
HYMES Na., 106
HYSER, Hen., 7
HYSINGER Mary Ann, 68
HYTLE Ann E., 116

-I-
ICKES Mary Ann, 93
IELAR Marg., 72
IFIRT Cath., 95
ILER Cath., 22
Mary Ann, 14
Ruanna, 58
IMMEL Susan, 101
INGLE Phebe, 20
Rachel Jane, 12

INGLEBRIGHT Cynthia,
103
INGLEBROTE Mary, 35
INGMAN, Mar. A., 95
INGRAM Am., 82
Cath., 48
Cynthia Ann, 84
Eliz., 48
Lavina, 37
Marg., 43
Priscilla, 77
Susan Marie, 107
INNGOLD Char., 81
IRESTON, Cath. E., 116
IRONHEUM Reb., 59
IRVIN Alice V., 101
Lea, 53
IRWIN Eliz. Virginia,
38
Esther, 13
Fanny S., 111
Sr., 96
ISEMINGER Am., 44
Barb., 18
Cath., 76
Eve, 9
Julian, 36
Juliana, 35
Levinia, 11
Marg., 102
Mary, 76
Sr. A., 10
ISENBERGER Marg., 67
Sus., 69
ISLER Susan, 63
ITNIRE Cath., 79
Eliz., 23, 59, 99
Mary, 35
Susan, 51
IVY Mary Ann, 65

-J-
JACK Ann, 103
Jane, 104
JACKSON Anna T., 39
Eliz., 41
Eliza, 16
Emily, 12
Har., 14
Jane, 8, 113
Marg. A., 53
Mary Cath., 74
Reb., 19, 70, 84
JACOBS Mary Ann Eliz.,
99
Sayann, 11
JACQUES Cath., 33
Cath. R., 66
Eliz., 12, 84
Eliza, 30

Louisa, 55
Marg., 12
Nanny, 70
Sr., 89
JAMES Am., 75
Cordelia, 55
Eliz., 116
Eliza, 104
Han., 73
Louisa, 60
Marg., 68
Mary Ellen, 94
Na., 2, 18
Rachel, 112
JAMISON Har. A., 14
Mary Ann, 115
JARRETT Ann Eliza, 76
JENKINS Eliz., 23
Ellen, 110
Jane, 80
Susan, 110
JENNINGS Abigail, 13,
69
Barb., 16
JOHNS Ann, 116
Cath., 13
JOHNSON Ann E., 25
Char., 84
Eliz., 114
Jane, 61, 85
M.E., 5
Mary, 22, 24, 38,
53, 77, 80
Mary Marg., 45
Na., 11
Ruanna, 57
So. S., 103
Sr. A., 60
Sr. Ellen, 4
JOHNSTON Cath., 113
Elenor B., 13
Eliz., 72
Is., 34
Jane, 95
Mar., 9
Maria, 12
Mary, 66
Mary Ann, 109
Na., 16
Susan M., 91
JOLLIFE Mary, 13
JONES Am., 55
Cath., 49
Cath. R., 57
Cecilia, 19
Delilah, 86
Eleanor, 24
Eliz., 20, 26, 39,
63, 71, 74
Eliz. A., 23

Han., 69
Hetty, 17
M.C., 119
Mar., 99
Mary, 16, 32, 35, 72, 81, 84, 85
Mary P., 16
Matilda, 27
Na., 33, 77
Peggy, 10
Rachel, 43
Rachel A., 71
Reb., 4, 34, 112
So. R., 6
Sr., 81
Sus., 84
Susan, 6
Virginia, 101
JORDAN Eliz., 36, 118
Mary, 93
JOY Mar. Ann, 57
Rhuan, 24
JUDITH Doratha, 11
JUDY Cath., 116
Eliz., 93
JULIUS Ann So., 85
Cath., 3
Eliz., 39
Mary, 1
JUMPER Jane R., 88
JURDEN Na., 32
JUSTICE Cath., 25

-K-
KABLE Marg., 52
KADLE Roena, 97
KAEGE Sus., 6
KAESMANN Cath., 103
KAIGY Mary, 90
KAIL Mary, 27
KAILER Anna, 91
Eliz., 7
Marg., 75
KAILOR Eliza, 21
Marg. M., 116
KAIN Marg. B., 47
KALB Amanda, 7
KALE Ann Maria, 80
KANINE Mary, 119
KANNON Eliz., 58
KARL Marg., 77
KARN So., 57
KARNES Rose Ann, 54
Sus., 70
KAROGYL Sr., 89
KARRELLS Sus., 113
KARRINGTON Ann M., 57
KAUFFMAN Cath., 29
Gertrude, 94
KAUFMAN Eliz., 55

KAUSLER Cath. A., 45
Eliz., 78
Marg., 87
Sr., 40
KAYLER Sr., 94
KEADLE Eliz., 55
Lydia E., 99
KEAFAUVER Mag., 14
KEALHOFER Eliz., 119
Eliza, 92
Eliza Muria, 114
Emma Jane, 114
Helen R., 59
Mary B., 29
Susan, 9
KEALHOWE Eliz., 83
KEALTMOCKER Marg., 41
KEARNEY Marg., 28
KEARON Cath., 28
KEEDY Ann Reb., 64
Anna S., 29
Barb. A., 21, 50
Eliz., 78, 82, 98, 115
Mar., 41, 50
Mary, 97
Mary Ann, 6, 19
Rachel Ann, 16
Ros., 95
Susan, 35
Susan Maria, 109
Tracilla, 78
KEEFAUVER, Cath., 79
Mag., 93
Mary Ann, 64
Ros., 89
So., 28
KEEFER Alice V., 10
Eliz., 92
Mary, 85, 87
Peggy, 64
KEELSMAN Anna Mar., 46
KEENE Jane, 74
KEEPERS Eleanor, 41
Rachel, 96
KEESACRE christiane, 3
Eve, 14
KEESECKER Mary, 112
KEETING Cath., 58
KEFAUVER Barb., 37
Lucinda C., 23
KEHLER Sr., 11
KEIFER Mary A., 58
KEIFFER Marg., 36
KEIGHN Eleanor, 20
Eliz. R., 116
KEILER Eliz., 13
KEIPER Mary C., 120
KEISECKER Elizth C., 65

Sr. Jane, 110
KEISINGER Cissey, 86
KELBERTZ Barb., 98
KELLAR Ann Maria, 22
Maria, 39
Mary, 62
KELLENBERGER Eliz., 51
KELLER Barb., 55
Barb. A., 78
Chna., 117
Easter, 52
ELiz., 22
Eliz., 19
Eliza, 113
Mar. B., 26
Mary, 97, 117
Mary M., 22
Na., 5, 74
So., 117
Sr., 78
KELLEY Marg., 97
KELLY Eliz., 40
Marg., 75
Maria, 5, 87
KELSINGER Eliz., 82
KEMP Eliz., 118
Jemima, 108
Reb., 57
Sr. E., 38
Susan, 66
KENDAL Barb., 37
KENDLE Cath., 87
Deborah, 45
Maria S.W., 70
Mary, 74, 108
Matilda, 107
Na., 40
KENNEDY Barb. Ellen, 70
Eliz. E., 116
Eliza, 68
Grace A., 77
Johanna, 110
Louisa M., 89
Maria, 56
Sr. Ann, 84
KENNEY, Am., 57
Eliz., 48
Gertrude, 72
Mary, 93
KENSEY Agnes, 11
KENSLEY Eliz. A., 40
KEOUGH Mary, 55
KEPHART Cath., 7
Marg., 2
Mary, 76
KEPLER Eliz., 4
Julia Ann, 86
Malinda, 109
Maria, 10

Sus., 46
KEPLINGER Eliz., 77, 89
Marg., 15
KEPPLINGER Susan, 81
KERBAUGH, Mary, 55
KERCHEVAL Mary B., 70
KERFORT Mary, 52
KERRON Betsy, 66
KERSHNER Ann Maria, 2, 37
Ann Reb., 85
Caroline, 26
Cath., 10
Eliz., 5, 43, 47, 67, 101
Eliza, 68
Ellenora, 38
Helen V., 21
Marg., 57
Marg. M., 32
Mary, 27, 28, 57, 109
Mary Ann, 8
Na., 2
Priscilla, 117
Ros., 28
Sr., 29
Sus., 92
Susan, 77
Susan P., 55
KESSANE Cath., 95
KESSINGER Chna., 7
Lydia, 6
KESSLER Mary Ann, 20
Sus., 113
KEVENER, Sr., 57
KEYFAUGER Polly, 64
KEYS Sr., 37
KEYSER Cath., 26
Eliz., 6
Judith, 63
Lydia, 3
Maria, 119
Mary, 59
Sally, 80
Sr., 109
Sus., 1, 3
KIDWELL Ann E., 6
Mary L., 116
Na., 81
Sus., 12
KIDWILER Mary, 61
Susan, 26
KIFE Eliz., 101
KIGER Har., 6
KILLERIN Barb., 24
KILOTZ Eliz., 37
KIMES Ellenor, 100
KIMLER Eliz., 119

KINDEL, Eliza, 37
Mary, 42
KINDELL Marg. A., 95
KINDLE Mar., 72
Maria, 75
Mrs. Sus., 74
KINER Eliz., 99
KING Adaline R., 21
Anna, 84
Barb., 59
Chna., 18
Eliz., 56, 96, 109, 118
Eliza, 74
Ellen, 59
Hen. L., 92
Kate, 9
Marg., 84
Mary Ann, 89
Reb., 40
So., 48
Virginia, 102
KINGERY Ros., 49
Sr., 108
KINKLE Ann C., 109
Eliz., 6
Mary, 74
KINNELL Ros., 79
KINNER Latitia, 24
KINNEY Ann Maria, 57
Cath., 55
KINSEL So., 38
KINSELL Mary, 91
Mary C., 96
KIRACOFE Mary, 2
KIRK Eliz., 66
KIRKPATRICK Maria F., 61
KISER Sr., 38
KISTLER, Mary, 42
KITCHENS Cath., 83
KITSMILLER Eliza, 82
KITZMILLER Ann, 82
Cath., 104
Ellen, 26
Marg., 68
Mary, 1
Mary Ann, 65
Matilda, 102
Ros., 109
Susan, 81, 109
KLINE Barb., 81
Cath., 1, 36, 73, 93
Eliz., 8, 72, 104, 105
Eliza, 28
Louisa, 82
Mary Malinda, 4
Rachel, 26
Sr., 88, 114

Sr. M., 15
Susann, 11
KNAVE Eliz., 10
Louisa, 118
Sus., 95
KNEAD Eliza, 72
KNEEDY Cath., 112
Mary, 39
KNEFF Cath., 1
KNEPPER Ann Priscilla, 2
Mary, 3
Mary Jane, 101
KNIERIEM Chna., 110
Eliz., 107
KNIGHT, Levinia S.M., 53
Mary E., 11
Permilia C., 20
KNIPPLE, Ellen, 89
KNODE Am., 45
Am. E., 4
Am. M., 53
Amanda C., 41
Ann E., 114
Ann H., 83
Cath., 15
Cath. M., 117
Clara J., 50
Hen. E., 74
Mar., 73
Mar. C., 98
Marg. C., 29
Mary, 1, 44, 72
Mary A., 72
Mary Ann, 113
Mary E., 77
Matilda, 99
Na., 65
Reb. S., 37
So., 75
Sr., 47
Sr. R., 105
Sus., 3, 79
Susan, 6
KNODLE Am., 68
Ann, 81
Cath., 81
Eliz., 51, 81, 96, 118
Eliza, 81
Han., 10
Levinia, 74
Lucretia, 118
Mary, 15
Mary A., 24
Na., 8
Sr., 116
Sus., 118
KNOTT Sr. Ann, 11

KOCH Emily, 101
KOCHENOR Marg., 119
KOHN Adelia, 54
KOLBY, Cath., 4
KONTZ Marg., 40
KOON Eliz., 3
  Mary, 89
KOONE Cath., 15
KOONS Cath., 98
  Sr., 13
KOONTZ Har., 7
  Leatha, 9
  Mary, 105
  Mary Cath., 11
KOWNSLAR Eveline C.,
53
KOYNER Eliz., 78
KPER Marg., 66
KRAIG, Eliz., 97
KRAILEY Barb., 114
KRAMMER Sr., 12
KRATZER Eliz., 54
KREEK Am., 114
KREGLOW Marg., 5
KREIGH Juliann, 83
  Mary, 102
  Mary A.J., 23
  Mary Jane, 27
KREPPS Sr., 101
KREPS Ann Eliza, 61
  Cath., 8, 55, 102
  Chna., 17
  Eliz., 12
  Eliza Ann, 29
  Fanny, 117
  Lida, 51
  Lydia Ann, 58
  Marg., 5, 46
  Maria, 51
  Mary, 99, 117
  Mary Ann, 47
  Na., 101
  Sr., 23, 62
  Sus., 72
  Susan, 17
KRETSER, Marg., 95
KRETZER Anna, 118
  Cath., 74
  Delana, 25
  Eliz., 50, 117
  Mary Ann, 2
  So., 15
  Sr., 99, 115
  Sus., 45
KRETZINGER Delila, 10
  Delilah, 101
KRIES Sr., 62
KRISE Cath., 119
KROH Sr. L., 23
KROTZER Mar., 78

KROUSE Eliz. C., 51
  Reb., 94
KUCKLE Cath., 15
KUHN Ann Eliz., 18
  Eliz., 60, 64
  Eva, 60
  Mary Ann, 21
  Polly, 115
  Sus., 120
KUNTZ Eliz., 46
  Mag., 71
KURFMAN Ann Reb., 27
  Mary, 34
KURHMAN Mary, 19
KURLEY Har., 112
KYSER Mary, 100

-L-
LAFEVER Mary, 23
LAHN Na., 118
LAHNOR Cath., 100
LAIR Nanny, 97
LAISS Anna C.M., 40
LAKE Eliz., 108
LAKINS Cath. E., 30
LALEY Eliz., 90
LAMAR Susan Ophelia,
16
LAMBERT Eliz., 39, 41,
53, 64
  Esther, 41
  Eve, 38
  Fanny, 31
  Mary, 38
  Mary Ann, 79
  So., 17
  Sr., 28
  Sus., 79, 99
  Susan, 60
LAMBRIGHT Eliz., 4
  Marg., 71
  Mary, 58
LAMPERT Caroline, 109
  Lilay, 44
  Mary, 73
LAMPKIN Eliz., 57
LANCASTER Adaline G.,
114
  Ann, 18
  Jane, 74
  Lavina, 3
  Malinda, 101
  Marg., 95
LANDES Barb., 65
LANDIS Eliz., 37, 78
  Mary, 97
  Na., 105
  Salina, 108
  Sr., 117
  Susan, 59

LANE Ann M., 6
  Eliza, 58
  Marg., 23
  Mary, 1, 27, 61
LANES Har., 2
LANG Jane, 57
LANGING Bridget, 107
LANGLEY Sr., 2
LANTZ Barb., 23
  Cath., 3, 119
  Chna., 86
  Eliz., 15, 93
  Mag., 98
  Maria, 86
  Mary, 14, 45, 83
  Sr. E., 62
LAPE Sr., 76
LAPOLE Reb., 13
LAREW Sr. E., 80
LARICK Sr., 78
LAUB, Eliz., 83
  Mary, 14
LAUER Caroline, 28
LAURENCE Basbar O., 20
LAUTEHAW Cath., 94
LAVELY Ann, 42
LAVERKNECHT Sus., 6
LAWNEYHILL Eleanor, 61
LAWRENCE Alice G., 41
  Ann W., 57
  Matilda, 12
LAWSON Lydia, 53
LAYMASTER Ann Eliza,
20
LAYPOLE Louisa, 28
  Sr. Jane, 79
LEARY Eliz., 3
  Peggy, 13
LEASER Eliz., 56
  Mahala, 89
LEASURE Eliz., 115
  Reb., 8
LEATHERMAN Cath., 113
  Mag., 70
  Mary, 113
  Sus., 39, 41
LEATHERS Mary E., 83
LEBER Chna., 93
LECKRONE Ann Maria, 27
  Dorethy, 72
  Eliz., 3, 72
  Marg., 56
  Maria, 46
  Mary, 56, 72
  Na., 94, 112
  Sus., 95
LECKROOM Mary, 87
LECKROON Cath., 26
LEE Eliz. I., 48
  Emeline S., 48

Mary E., 30
Mazey, 1
Mrs., 32
So., 92
LEEDS Eliz. M., 69
LEFEVER Cath., 52
  Eliz., 15, 23
  Mary, 25, 36
  Mary Jane, 22
  Sr., 25
  Sus., 118
LEFEVRE Mary, 109
LEFLER Eliz., 1
LEGETT Maria, 61
  Mariah, 93
LEGGETT Cath. Eliz.,
28
  Eliz., 45, 113
  Mar. V., 6
  Mary Ann, 90
  Prudence, 42
  Sr., 41
LEGGITT Sr. A., 38
LEIGH Sus., 45
LEIGHT So., 85
LEIGHTER Cath., 52, 63
  Judith, 46
  Mary, 4
  Mary Ann, 98
  Sus., 52, 105
LEIPOLD Rosina Barb.,
56
LEISER, Marg., 29
  Na., 26
  Sus., 74
LEITER Cath., 54
  Eliza Jane, 15
  Julian, 7
  Polly, 46
  Rachel, 104
  Tabitha C., 12
LEMEN Hester Am., 43
LEMON So., 26
LEMONDS Ruth, 113
LENN, Mary, 37
LEONARD Eliz., 46
  Marg., 99
  Mary C., 11
  Sr. E., 110
LEOPARD Marg. Ann, 39
LEPOLE Mary, 10
LESLER Cath., 37
  Mary, 14
LESLEY Jane, 114
LESTER Eliz., 41
  Esther, 81
LETT Raney, 67
LEVI Miriam, 30
LEVY Berthilde, 26
  Lucretia, 45

LEWIS Annetta, 56
  Caroline Virginia,
105
  Cath., 13, 84
  Cath. Matilda, 105
  Eliz., 81, 97
  Eliza, 19
  Mar. M., 90
  Marg., 42
  Mary, 87
  Patience, 81
  Rachel, 98
  Reb., 16
LICHTY Marg., 100
LICKAINS, Mary J., 69
LIDAY Na., 34
  Sr., 62
LIDER Cath., 69
LIFFICH Mary, 46
LIGHT Cath. A., 49
  Eliza, 107
  Mary, 26
  Polly, 44
LIGHTER So., 54
LILLY Jane, 103
LIMEBAUGH Cath., 34
LINCOLN Caroline H.,
96
  Han., 31
LINDONMAN Susan, 82
LINDSAY Han., 96
  Mary Ann, 67
LINE Ann, 66
  Cath., 36, 47, 82
  Marietta, 52
  Mary Ann, 104
  Salome, 104
  Sr., 29
  Sus., 98
  Susan, 105
LINEBAUGH Cath., 6
LINEBERGER Leah, 14
LINEMAN Cath., 71
LINGENFELTER Reb., 101
LINK Cath., 85
  Ellen B., 80
  Mary, 28
  Matilda, 63
LINKHORN Clara R.C.,
24
LINN Eliz., 36
LINTON Reb., 106
LISER Eliz., 49
  Ros., 32
LITER Isa., 34
LITTLE Eliz., 30
  Emmagen D., 3
  Jane, 23
  Mar., 88
  Mary, 89, 94

Sus., 103
  Susan Comfort, 103
LITTON Eliz., 76
LIVELY Mary, 102
LIZER Sus., 87
LOAN Ann, 89
LOCHER Ann Eliz., 107
  Ann Mary, 107
  Ann R., 54
LOCK Eliza, 35
  Har., 65
  Sr. Cath., 119
LOCKART Polly, 20
LOCKE Jane, 8
  Marg., 34, 75
LOCKER Cath., 94
  Eliz., 92, 111
  Mary, 82, 97
  Sus., 48
LOGAN Helen, 2
  Marg. E., 104
  Mary Jane, 41, 74
LOHM Marg., 103
LONG Ann, 109
  Ann E., 51
  Barb., 59
  Cath., 49, 72, 78,
94
  Eliz., 2, 23, 91,
108
  Eliz. C., 112
  Esther, 103
  Evaline, 81
  Eve, 96
  Han S., 95
  Hen., 36
  Jemimah, 70
  Lavinia, 37
  Louisa, 77
  Lydia, 2
  Maria, 12
  Mary, 4, 37, 51, 79,
94, 118, 120
  Mary C., 28
  Mary E., 46
  Matilda, 83
  Mrs. Susan, 73
  Na., 119
  Reb., 1, 61, 66, 100
  So., 99
  Sr., 73
  Sus., 19, 70
  Susan, 41, 48
  Tracy, 15
LONGANACRE Eliz., 16
  Reb., 46, 103
  Sus., 40
LONGANECKER,   Eliz.,
86
  Mary Ann, 88

LONGMAN Angeline, 77
Cath., 97
Eliz., 49
Leah, 73
Mary, 49, 61
Ros., 86
Sus., 18
LONGNECKER Ann R., 104
LOOKENSLAND Mary, 25
LOOSE Reb., 89
LOPP Eliz., 70
Sr. Ann, 29
LORSHBAUGH Ann, 21
Barb., 75
Mary, 55, 76
Na., 104
Ros., 77
Sus., 22
LORSHBOUGH Marg., 83
LOSEBAUGH Mary, 49
LOSHBAUGH Maria, 86
LOUDENSLAGER Na., 4
Sr. R., 6
LOUDERSLAGER Sr., 40
LOUT Eve, 90
LOVIER Sr. Ann, 33
LOWE Ann, 111
Ann Eliza, 45
Isa. K., 45
Reb., 96
Sr., 54
LOWER Reb., 74
LOWERY Sr. Ann, 90
LOWMAN Ann, 103
Barb., 85
Cath., 2
Eliz., 6, 17, 20, 62
Mary, 52, 79
Orinda, 88
Rachel, 45
Ros., 66
Sus., 18, 65
Susan, 99
LOWREY Marg. Ann, 16
LOWRY, Cath., 39
Mary Ann, 93
LUCAS Tabitha, 21
LUCHBAUGH Eliz. A., 4
LUCKETT Mary Ann, 49
LUDY Ann, 65
Mary Ann, 38
Susan, 113
LUM Cath., 22
Maria Cath., 65
Susan, 59
LUNG Eliz., 58
LUPTON Reb. McP., 51
LUSHBAUGH Eliz., 62
Mary H., 15
Virginia M., 4

LUTTER Ann Maria, 116
LUTZ Angeline, 17
Cath., 35
Eliz., 14, 96
Eliza, 76
Marg., 55
Mary, 44
Na., 21
LYBOLDT Cath., 99
LYDAY Cath., 7
Julia Ann, 99
Lizzie M., 62
Mary, 6
LYKENS Sr., 116
LYLES Rachel, 82
LYNCH Am., 64
Cath., 7
Cordela, 89
Eliz., 68
Han., 53
Marg., 11, 90
Maria, 108
Mary, 12, 81
Na., 12
Reb., 41
Sr. B., 52
Susan A., 14
LYNN Har., 47
Jane, 46
LYON Eliz., 109
LYON (LINE) Cath., 4
LYONS Mary, 100
LYSER Julianna, 59
LYSINGER Sus., 14

-M-
MACABA Maria, 13
MCAFEE Cath., 11
Lucy, 11
Ros., 110
Sus., 13
Susan, 83
MCAHAN Mary Ann, 30
MCALLISTER Sus., 21
MCATEE Eliz., 103
Maria, 42
MCBEE Jemima, 84
MCBRIDE Reb., 95
Susan, 35
MCCABE Ludy, 55
MCCAFFERTY Eliz., 20
MCCAFFEY Marg., 20, 80
MCCAFFREY Sr., 93
MCCAIN Eliz., 31
MCCALL Marg., 56
Mary, 32
Na., 22
Peggy, 32
MCCARDELL Isa., 61
Laura L., 105

Lucretia, 28
MCCARDLE Caroline
V.P., 94
Cath., 114
Eliz., 83
Mary, 109
MCCARTNEY Ann Maria,
55
MCCAULEY Cath., 42
Eliz., 51
Han., 44
Han. V., 94
MCCAULLEY Mary, 50
MCCLAIN Am. Ann, 70
Ann C., 58
Ann Maria, 64
Eliz., 54
Eliz. J., 25
Lucretia, 118
M.A.J., 118
Marg., 18
Maria, 109
Mary, 47, 98
Na., 75, 83
MCCLAIRE Rachel, 68
MCCLANAHAN Ellen, 76
Sr., 58, 67
Susan M., 101
MCCLANE So., 106
MCCLAY Mary, 22
MCCLEARY Marg., 60
Peggy, 110
MCCLELAND Arabella
Eliza, 85
Rachel, 66
MCCLELLAND Mrs. Char.,
69
Sidney, 111
MCCLURE Eliz., 70
Mary, 33, 66
So., 111
MCCOHE Mary, 52
MCCOLLISTER Ann C., 53
Emily, 70
MCCOOL Nelly, 66
MCCORMACK Ann, 69
Ellen, 21
Emly Frances, 82
MCCORMICK Na., 3
Reb., 14
MCCOSKAR Marg., 70
MCCOULEY Julian, 104
MCCOURY Jane, 109
MCCOY Am., 34
Caroline, 96
Cath., 19, 60
Cath. A., 96
Eliz., 25, 30, 55,
65, 75, 108
Eliza, 16

Ellen, 22, 112
Elmira, 54
Emaline A., 11
Har., 39
Jane, 49
Jelis, 56
Leah, 37
Marg., 7
Maria, 57
Mary, 32, 61, 75, 114
Mary Amanda, 95
Mary Marg., 112
Minerva, 12
Na., 59, 65
Na. Bell, 61
Naomy, 105
Polly, 54
Rachel, 102, 114
Rachel W., 100
Sally W., 55
Sr., 21
MCCRAFF, Hetty, 50
MCCRAFT Na., 23
MCCRANE Mary, 44
MCCREA Mar., 44
MCCREARY Ros., 83
MCCREY Reb., 22
MCCUMSEY Peggy, 11
MCCUNE Marg., 85
MCCURDY Priscilla I., 48
MCCUSKER, Cath. C., 118
MCDADE Mary, 27
MCDANIEL Marg., 1
Mary, 68
MCDAVID Patty, 11
Reb., 107
MCDERMOT Cath. A.S., 68
MCDILL, Eliz., 106
Marg., 107
Susan, 27
MCDONALD Ann, 40
Ann V., 2
Cath., 22
Mary, 23, 65
Sidney, 99
Sr., 5
MCDOWELL A.M.P., 67
Mary M., 3
MCDUELL Jannette, 56
MACE Eliz., 118
Eliza Ann, 77
Ellen, 105
Sr. Ann, 71
MCELROY Mary Ann, 88
MCELVOY Mary, 67
MACESWINGEL Sus., 10

MCEVOY Ann, 57
MCFADEN Sr., 20
MCFADON Cath., 21
MCFALL Ann, 16
Mariah, 16
MCFARLAND Mary, 24
MCFERRAN, Har., 42, 104
MCGARY Mariah, 28
MCGEEGHAN Mary, 54
MCGETH Mary, 17
MACGILL Ellen E., 107
MCGILL Sr., 19
MCGINLEY Dorothy, 25
Eleanor, 116
Ros., 80
MCGINNESS Peggy, 59
MCGLASSEN, Na., 66
MCGLONE Mary E., 117
MCGLOUGHLIN Cath., 20
MCGOFERTY Mrs. Susan, 7
MCGONAGLE Marg., 56
Mary, 26
MCGONIGAL Marg., 109
MCGOVERN Hester, 83
MCGOVRAN Susan, 80
MCGOWAN Isa., 84
Jane, 52
Mary, 46
MCGRAW Jane, 116
MCGRUDER Marg. Jane, 113
MCGUIN Sus., 70
MACGUIRE Marg., 17
Mary Eliz., 39
Susan, 33
MCGURLEY Rosa Anna, 87
MCHANN Mary, 27
MACHIN Eliz., 23
MCILHENNEY Chna., 78
Mary, 111
MCILHENY Frances, 95
MCINTIRE Bridget, 67
Fanny, 64
Lydia, 115
Mary, 66
MCINTOSH Sr., 115
MACK Sabina, 72
MCKEE Am., 99
Bridget, 76
Marg., 37, 88
Mary, 37, 43
MACKEN Cath., 51
MACKENHEIMER Ann C., 3
MCKENNEY Sr., 16
Sus., 35
MCKENSEY Mary E., 8
MCKESICK Ann, 34
Mary, 79

Sus., 90
MACKEY Eliz. F., 24
MCKEY Isa., 64
MACKFEE Rachel, 85
MCKIERNAR Elitia, 95
MACKIN Mary, 20
MCKINLEY Ellen S., 64
Mary, 67
MCKINNEY, Jane, 6
Sr., 24
MCKINSEY Isa., 47
MCLANAHAN Mary A., 113
MCLAUGHLIN Bridget, 58
Cath., 5, 43, 65, 70
Eliza, 120
Mary, 76
Mary A., 71
Rosa Ann, 88
Sr., 113
Sus., 22
Susan, 67, 120
MCMAHAN Bridget, 16
Cath., 67
MCMAHON Anna, 17
MCMANNUS Marg., 24
Mary, 55
MCMECHEN Mary, 5
MCMILON Marg., 74
MCMULLEN Marg., 118
Mary, 114
Rose, 70
Susan, 114
MCMURREN, Eliz., 110
MCNAMEE Cath., 49
Marg., 102
Mary, 10
So., 7
Susan, 103
MCNEAL Sus., 45
MCNET Hester, 24
MCNIGHT Manerva, 53
Rhea, 19
MCNITTY Rachel, 37
MCNUTT Cynthia Ann, 77
MCPHERSON Ann, 62
Har. A., 68
Mary Jane, 11
Meliora, 18
MCQUAID Cath., 67
MCQUILKEN Is. V., 24
MCVITTY Han. M., 84
MCWILLIAMS, Ann Tho., 90
Mary Jane, 52
MCWINN Susan C., 76
MADARA, Char., 79
MADES Mary A., 83
MAGRAW Mary, 82
MAGRUDER Mary Susan, 109

MAGUIRE Cath., 18
 Phebe, 5
MAHAN Mary, 119
MAHANY Eliza, 54
MAHONY Ellen, 19
MAHUGH Eliza, 97
 Julian, 52
MAIN Cath. E., 19
MAINS Mar., 74
MAISACK Susan, 99
MAIZE Na., 11
MAJERS Sr., 27
MALLAHAN Barb., 99
MALLARY Laura P., 15
MALLEN Leah, 57
MALLIN Mary A., 11
MALLORY Ann C., 107
 Reb., 27
 Sr. Jane, 115
MALLOY Winna, 39
MALONE Eliz., 3, 110
 Jane, 84
 Mary, 83
 Naomi, 76
 Reb., 30
 Susan, 94
MALONEY, Sus., 71
MALONG Han., 26
MALOTT Cath., 37
 Char., 98
 Edna, 100
 Eliz., 79
 Eliza, 52
 Marg. Jane, 57
 Maria, 55
 Mary A., 86
 Mary C., 105
 Na., 23
 Rachel, 25
 Reb., 83
 Sr., 104
 Sus., 13
MALOY Cath., 61
 Marg., 74
 Mary, 75
MANGINA Han., 5
MANION Mary, 27
MANLEY Mary, 75
MANN Abby, 85
 Cath., 97
 Eurydice, 82
 Mary, 97
 Rachel, 109
 Reb., 80
MANSFIELD Cath., 4
MANTLE Lydia, 43
MANTZ Mary, 20
MARGURA Cath., 1
MARKEL Philipine, 70
MARKER, Cath., 83

Eliz., 3, 58
 Lydia, 99
 Mary, 1, 59
 Polly, 45
 Sr., 93
 Susan, 77
MARKIN Barb., 14
 Eliz., 87
MARKLE Mary, 109
MARKOE Eliz., 95
MARKS Mary C., 60
MARKWOULD Marg., 75
MARMADUKE Mary E., 116
 Sr., 43
MARQUIS Anna, 9
MARRETT Deborah, 64
MARSHALL Eliz., 30, 81
 Eve, 92
 Rachel, 16
 Rose Ann, 113
 Sr., 1
MARSILLES Ruann, 79
MARSTILLER, Ann, 75
MART Eliz., 110
MARTENY Eliz., 1, 29
MARTIN Agnes, 41
 Ann, 58, 62, 63, 72
 Ann C., 47
 Ann Maria, 30
 Barb., 98
 Cath., 19, 35, 107, 110
 Cath. Marg., 75
 Eliz., 4, 38
 Eliza, 20
 Eliza Jane, 56
 Har. E., 55
 Marg., 44, 62, 82
 Marg. C., 27
 Marg. E., 69
 Marg. G., 82
 Maria, 10
 Mary, 8, 18, 39
 Mary E., 4, 13
 Reb., 23
 Rose Ann, 94
 Sr., 12, 48
 Susan, 118
MARTZ Cath., 86
 Sr. Ann, 47
MASE Na., 105
 Susan, 105
MASENER Sus., 89
MASON Ann R., 108
 Eliz. A.T., 115
 Eliza, 114
 Mary B., 117
 Mary K., 116
 Ruth, 55
 Temperance, 84

MASSEY Eliz., 55
 Sr., 83
MASSILLIAS Mary, 90
MASTERS Ann E., 109
 Cath., 37
 Eliz., 86
 Roseann, 62
 Sr. A., 102
MATHENY Mar., 19
 Maria, 35
MATHEWS Mary, 31
MATTHEW Ann Eliz., 79
 Cath. J., 54
MATTHEWS, Hetty J., 11
MATTINGLY Cath., 74
MATZEBAUGH, Cath., 93
 Marg., 66
MAUGGINS Cath., 10
 Eliz., 81
 Na., 87
MAUGINS Ann M., 99
 Mag., 46
 Na., 118
MAUGONS Eliz., 3
MAUKEMAN Chna., 69
MAURICE, Bridget, 85
MAUTTER Cath., 110
MAXWELL Marg., 110
MAY Cath., 71
 Maria, 56
 So., 26
MAYER Eliz., 8
MAYHEW Maria, 119
MAYHUGH, Maria F., 80
MAYS Eliz., 50
MAYSILLE Cath., 56
MAYSILLES Eliz., 41, 107
 Mar. Ann, 102
 Mary, 117
 Mary E., 102
MAYSILLIS Eliz. Ann, 11
MEADS Cath., 19
MEALY Sr. Ann, 48
MECHS, Mary, 84
MEDARIA Cath., 102
MEDCALF, Cath., 4
 Mary Ann, 78
MEDLER Mary Jane, 111
MEEKS Han., 21
MEELY Eliz., 27
MEHARTER Rachel, 95
MEIXSEL Eliza, 47
MEIXSELL Ann R., 77
MELCHOR Eliz., 8
MELIGY Eliz., 95
MELONG Mar., 24
MELOWN Reb., 109
MELTON Maria, 41

MELVIN Mary, 16, 45
MEMPIN Cath. W., 72
MENDENHALL, Mary
Susan, 46
MENSOR Eliz., 40
MENTRUSE Rosey, 85
MENTZER Ann Cath., 78
Eliz., 17, 51
Mary, 38
Peggy, 39
Sr., 110
MERCER Matilda C., 63
MERCHANT Aire Ellen,
92
Eliz., 71
Eveline, 18
Mary Ellen, 15
Sr. Ann, 107
MEREDITH Ann, 66
Eliz. D., 52
Hen., 3
Maria Louisa, 98
Mary F., 45
Mary W., 7
Rachel, 94
MERITT Sr. Louise, 29
MERRICK Emma, 53
MERTENY Mary, 100
MERTZ Mary Ann, 41
Sr. Ann, 107
MESHELL, Barb., 94
MESSELY Susan, 56
MESSEN Jane, 32
MESSILLI Eliz., 8
METCALF Eliz. W., 48
METZ Barb., 5
Cath., 4, 117
Mary Jane, 18
Na., 11
MEYERS Sus., 95
MEYLEY Susan, 96
MEYRE Ellen, 49
MICHAEL Lavinia, 42
Mary Virginia, 53
MICHAELS Marg., 20
MICKLE Susan, 40
MICKLEY Anna, 65
Cath., 7
Mary, 7
MIDDCLAF Clarissa C.,
66
MIDDLEKAUF, So. E., 19
MIDDLEKAUFF Am., 24
Ann, 95
Ann E., 62
Ann M., 119
Barbary, 90
Cath., 106, 117
Eliz., 75, 86, 105,
115, 117

Eliza A., 118
Esther, 71
Lavinia, 61
Lizzie A., 62
Mary, 3, 14
Mary Ann, 56
Mary F., 1
Mary L., 32
Peggy, 98
Ros., 33
Sr., 14, 92
Sus., 117
Susan, 56, 102
Susan M., 32
MILES Biddy, 69
Eliz., 5, 15
Frances, 79
Polly, 55
MILEY Cath., 73
Mar., 60
Rachel, 117
MILLER Ann, 31, 80,
107
Ann E., 102
Ann M., 76
Ann Maria, 105
Ann Mary, 50
Ann Reb., 10, 16
Anna, 106, 111
Barb., 42, 64, 72,
83, 91
Caroline, 47
Cath., 2, 9, 14, 19,
35, 38, 46, 50, 58,
60, 73, 84, 85, 88,
92, 94, 101, 102, 117
Cath. B., 46
Easter, 83
Elenora, 14
Eliz., 2, 5, 6, 8,
13, 36, 38, 39, 44,
49, 69, 76, 77, 91,
92, 96, 106, 107, 117
Eliz. R., 8
Eliza, 38, 88
Ella, 80
Ellen, 58
Eve, 46, 111
Fannie A., 111
Frances A., 71
Han., 78
Har., 4, 43, 59
Hen. A., 18
Hester, 113
Huldah, 117
Isa., 1
Jane Reb., 79
Juliann, 30
Katie E., 81
Lane, 76

Louisa, 62, 103
Mag., 56, 99, 109
Mar., 33
Marg., 20, 77, 94,
102, 113, 114
Marg. A., 61
Marg. Ann, 90
Maria, 67
Maria A., 106
Mary, 5, 20, 40, 44,
47, 52, 63, 68, 69,
71, 77, 79, 90, 93,
103, 107, 113, 116
Mary A., 94, 105
Mary Ann, 22
Mary Cornelia, 51
Mary Eliz., 99
Na., 40, 83, 101,
117
Polly, 1
Prudence, 73
Rachel, 109, 113
Reb., 20, 91, 109
Rose Ann, 59
Roz., 74
Sally, 9, 42, 74
Shartelle, 68
So., 56, 103, 106,
107
Sr., 10, 49, 80, 85,
100, 104
Sus., 28, 36, 42,
61, 62, 82, 93, 95,
102, 113, 119
Susan, 42, 58, 66,
75, 79, 83, 118
Susan Lucretia, 59
Susan S., 92
MILLES Milly, 17
MILLIGAN Eliza, 73
Susan, 85
MILLS Ann, 29
Eleanora, 109
Levinia, 16
Matilda, 74
Na. Ann, 76
Rose Ann, 116
Sr., 27
MILTON Am. Eliz., 55
MILUGHLEY Mary, 21
MINSIES Eliza P., 109
MISENER Betsy, 3
Cath., 34
MISH Eliz. C., 30
Mary, 12
Ros., 5
MISKIVENS Am., 112
MITCHELL, Eliza, 44
Hen. Maria, 111
Sr., 96

Sus., 104
MITTAG Cath. Louisa, 92
MITTAUGH Mary, 47
MITTIG Maria, 49
MITTOCH Eliz., 4
MIX Sr., 6
MOATES Sr., 81
MOATS, Eliz., 69, 99
Mary, 69
Motlina, 6
Rose Ann, 25
So., 82
Sus., 59
Susan, 22, 77
MOBLEY Laura A., 111
Mary A.C., 48
MOCK Eliz., 48
Sr., 64
MOFFITT Ann, 35
Susan E., 3
MOGGINS Cath., 35
Na., 81
Sus., 65
MOHLER Eliz., 27
Har., 74
Marg. R., 49
Sr., 27
MOLAS Matilda, 15
MOLENDORE Mary, 29
MOLER Mariah, 63
MOLES Marg., 87
MONAHAN, Ellen, 102
MONCE Anna, 43
MONDEBAUGH Eliz., 3
Mary, 77
MONDONALL Lidia, 1
MONG Am., 21
Cath., 47
Eliz., 38, 44
Marg., 21, 52
Mary Jane, 102
Peggy, 72
MONGHINE, Susan, 70
MONIGAN Eliza Ann, 99
Helen R., 54
Rose Ann, 42
MONINGER Am., 108
Cath., 96
Peggy, 91
MONNINGER Mar. J., 73
Mary, 90
MONROE Mary, 91
Mary F., 78
MONSER Ann, 94
MONTABAUGH Mary Ann, 3
MONTGOMERY Annet, 83
Mary Ann, 22
Susan, 9
MONTZ Barb., 36

MOONEY Cath., 90
Eliza, 71
Sr., 57
MOORE Ann E., 50
Anna, 53
Cath., 90
Delana, 39
Eliz., 83
Ellen, 61
Emeally, 117
Har., 55
Jane, 67
Lizzie M., 52
Lucy, 70
Marg., 9, 85
Mary, 9, 75, 87
Mary Ann, 29, 108
Mary Jane, 33
Mary V., 108
Na., 79
Sr., 8
Sr. Ann, 84
MOOSE Amanda H., 83
Cath., 68
MORE Mary, 85
MOREHEAD Cath., 54
MORELAND Susan, 84
MORESBURGH Mary Ann, 77
MORGAN, Betsy, 102
Cath. Eliza, 86
Marg., 32, 34, 42, 79
Maria, 69
Mary, 10, 18
Sr., 55
Susan, 75
MORGENDALL Sr., 58
MORIN Ann E., 65
MORRIS Eliz., 45
Mary, 67
Mary Jane, 27
Na., 6, 75
Sophronia A., 33
MORRISON Agnes, 114
Ann, 9
Anna, 6
Cath., 42
Eliz., 5
Lavinia, 64
Lucretia A., 42
Malinda, 28
Mary, 95
Mary Jane, 31
Phebe, 96
Susan, 37
MORSBURG Eliz. Ann, 78
MORSEBURG Reb., 73
MORSTETTER Reb., 49
MOSE Eliz., 83

Har., 66
Sr., 49
MOSER Amy, 70
Malinda, 32
MOSHER Am., 72
MOSS Rachel, 24
MOSSBURGH Sr. Ann, 81
MOSSBURY Char., 40
MOST Ann Cath., 84
Mary, 65
MOSTELLER Precilla, 100
MOTES Har., 36
MOTT Mrs. Cath., 36
MOTTER Ann Maria, 78
MOUDY Am., 5
Cath., 48, 55
Eliz., 15, 20, 32, 57
Fanny, 65
Har., 54
Kaskiah, 12
Maria, 102
Mary, 8, 82
Matilda, 2, 13
Rachel, 100
Ros., 64, 102
Sr. Ann, 23
Susan, 79
MOURER Eliz., 41, 44
Sr., 61
MOURY Susan R., 106
MOUSE Eliz., 29
Isa., 70
Mary Ann, 74
Na., 43
So., 95
MOUSER Marg., 10
MOUTZ Julia A., 119
MOWEN Maria, 111
MOWING Cath., 62
MOWRY Cath., 70
Lidia, 13
MOXLEY, Eliz., 116
MOYER Ann, 115
Eliz., 16
Leath Ann, 73
Mary, 30
Na., 30, 33
Sus., 46, 51
MOYERS Cath., 12
Lydia, 3
MUCK Caroline, 93
Lydia, 120
Mary, 22
Peggy, 94
MUIR Ann, 6
MULHERRON Cath., 12
MULHOLLAND Cath., 24
MULL, Eliza, 111

Sr., 115
MULLEN Cath., 5
  Cath. M., 2
  Eliz., 1, 42
  Jeluma, 4
  Jerusha, 112
  Marg., 37
  Mary Ann, 39
  Salome, 5
  Sr., 109
MULLENDORE Cath., 50
  Mahala A., 89
  Malinda J., 89
  Violetta, 47
MULLENIX Reb. H., 55
MULLER Char., 1
MULLIN Eliz., 7
MULON Na., 108
MUMMA Barb., 52, 112
  Cath., 112
  Cath. E., 1
  Eliz., 52
  Eliz. Susan, 34
  Mary, 72, 89
  Roz., 108
MUMMERT Mary, 41
  Na., 108
MUNAHAN Mary Ann, 67
MUNDABAUGH Mary, 111
  Molly, 2
MUNDAY Cath., 28, 103
  Mary, 35
MUNDEBAUGH Sus., 59
MUNDY Na., 68
MUNGAN Reb., 23
MURPHEY, Nora, 88
MURPHY Emma, 113
  Marg., 76
  Mary, 1
  Sus., 103
MURRAY Am. E., 41
  Ann, 37
  Anna Virginia, 93
  Eliz., 66
  Marg., 77
  Matilda A., 103
  Reb., 45
  Ros., 69
  Susan Maria, 35
MURRY Eliz., 58
  Ellen Jane, 38
  Mary Ann, 24
  Sr. Jane, 5
  Susan, 32
MUSE Eliz., 76
  Sr., 91
MUSETER Mariah, 117
MUSSELMAN Esther, 61
  Na., 44
  Sus., 4

MUTSHLER So., 101
MYERS Almira, 53
  Almyra, 50
  Angeline, 74
  Ann, 30
  Ann Eliza, 94
  Ann Eve, 53
  Ann M., 111
  Ann Marg., 101
  Ann R., 92
  Barb., 102
  Cath., 36, 55, 63,
67, 85, 107, 112, 120
  Char., 45
  Delia, 22
  Eliz., 10, 22, 23,
35, 41, 53, 57, 72,
74, 76, 88, 94, 98,
104, 119
  Eliza Jane, 52
  Han., 8
  Helen Eliz., 28
  Julia, 102, 105
  Louisianna, 108
  Mar. Ann, 7
  Marg., 59
  Mary, 9, 55, 57, 58,
76, 110
  Mary Ann, 61, 76, 96
  Milley, 53
  Miranda, 107
  Na., 70
  Polly, 66
  Rachel, 76, 117
  Reb., 41, 62, 75
  Ros., 18, 37, 77, 89
  Rose Ann, 119
  Salome, 44
  Sr., 36, 54, 63, 76,
112
  Sr. Ann, 73
  Sr. E., 38
  Sus., 37
  Susan, 19, 76, 104
  Tamzin, 76
MYLEY Eliz., 90
MYMAN Sr., 72
MYSLEMAN Mary, 4

-N-
NACKEY Mary, 53
NAFE Cath., 78
  Eliz., 105
  Francy, 29
NAFF Am., 69
  Eliz., 49
  Hen., 7
  Sr. Cath., 22
NAVE Eliz., 107
  Mary, 17, 23

NEAL Eliz., 16
  Har., 16
  Linny, 13
  Mary, 55, 74
  Polly, 3
NEALE Reb., 2
NEALL Eliz., 79
  Ellen, 107
  Mary Eliz., 73
NEEDY Ann Maria, 65
  Sr., 93
NEFF Ann Marie, 7
  Eliza, 34
  Reb. E., 24
NEGLEY Barb. Ann, 99
  Eliz., 34, 50
  Mary A., 101
NEIBERT Mary E., 73
  Sr. S., 118
NEIKIRK Ann C., 95
  Barb., 30
  Barb. Ann, 77
  Cath., 58
  Eliz., 43, 47, 49,
71, 72, 119
  Mar., 96
  Marg., 96
  Mary, 16, 28
  So., 9
  Sr., 102
  Susan, 97
NEILL Esther, 21
  Isa. C., 39
  Matilda, 11
  Rachel, 24
  Reb., 77
NEITZELL Eliz., 48
  Mary, 69
NELSON Betsy, 55
  Mar., 12
  Ruth, 17
  Sr., 64
NESBIT Eliz., 3
  Fanny, 106
NESBITT Eliz., 52
  Mary, 44
NETTS Mary Eliz., 27
NETTZ Eliza C., 87
NETZ Caroline, 75
  Mary, 76
NEUMAN Eliza Jane, 6
NEVIT Jane, 93
NEWBY, Eliz., 30
NEWCOMER Am., 68
  Ann, 36, 44, 50
  Ann Maria, 2
  Anne, 105
  Barb., 36, 77
  Bry Ann, 97
  Cath., 5, 36, 44,

71, 72, 78, 86
Cath. H., 94
Chna., 96, 115
Eliz., 47, 56, 71,
72, 74, 78, 79, 103,
105
Eliz. Ann, 88
Eliza, 10, 67
Ellen, 102
Fanny, 38
Frany, 36
Hen., 86
Jane M., 23
Lydia, 19, 117
Mag., 115
Marg., 1
Maria, 33, 65
Mary, 30, 92, 107,
117
Na., 17, 38, 67, 75,
94, 109
Roz., 86
Ruana, 73
Sr., 17, 30, 60, 70,
72, 108
Sus., 117
Susan, 1, 96, 116
Theresa, 71
NEWELL Eliz., 93
Mary, 5
NEWFEN Eliz., 3
NEWKIRK Mary H., 88
NEWMAN Eveline, 48
Mary, 28
Mary Ann, 35
Molly, 52
Sevilla, 84
Sr., 118
Susan R., 3
NEWSON Am., 17
Mary, 66
Rachel, 101
Sr., 114
NEYBERT Eliz., 76
Mary, 108
Ros., 102
Sus., 98
NICELON Mary, 16
NICHODEMUS Cath., 22
Eliz., 119
Eliz. Jane, 113
Leah, 63
Mary, 89
So., 117
NICHOLAS Caty, 97
Letitia, 29
Marg. E., 37
Maria, 82
Na., 104
NICHOLL So., 54

NICHOLS Ann E., 14
Caroline, 34
Cath., 54
Eliz., 115
Marg., 43, 58
Maria, 9
NICHOLSON Mar., 73
Sus., 25
NICKLESS Cath., 29
NICODEMUS Marg. N., 56
Mary, 95
Susan A., 53
NICOLS Ann, 116
NIERNAM Eliz., 41
NIGH Eliz., 82
Marg. C., 2
Sus., 58
NIGHSWANDER Eliz., 19,
52, 114
Mary, 94
Rachel, 94
So., 29
NIGHT Eliz., 110
Urilla, 33
NIGHWANDER Barb., 32
Na., 56
NIKERK Ann, 54
NIKIRK Mary, 113
Na., 99
NIMMEY Nelly, 48
NISSWANER, Char., 46
NITZEL Ann, 73
NITZELL Emma J., 2
Mary Susan, 32
NIXON Mar. A., 116
NOGLE Anne, 65
NOLL Ann, 118
NOOSE Rachel, 7
NORFORD Ann, 46
NORRIS Anna, 29
Cath., 49
Eliz., 24, 29, 50,
64
Ellen, 75
Jane, 99
Maria, 39
Matilda, 35
Na., 69
Rachel E., 22
So., 43
Sr., 18, 40, 52
Sr. Ann, 19
Sus., 1
Susan, 102
NORRISS Eliz., 15
NORTH Am. W., 23
Lydia R., 39
NORTHCRAFT Sus., 23
NOTTINGAPE Mary, 65
NOURSE Ann, 3

NOWEL Sally, 2
NOWELL Eliz., 20
Sr., 32, 71
NUFER Mary A., 119
NULL Cath., 90
Eliz., 100
Mary, 36
Reb., 14
Susan, 110
NUNAMAKER Juliana, 64
NUNEMACKER Susan, 10
NUNEMAKER Joannah, 71
Mary Ellen, 8
NUNIMAKER Cath., 111
NYMAN, Amanda A., 115
Ann, 52
Eliz., 99
Maria, 74
Mary, 59

-O-
OATS Mag., 107
Ros., 41
O'BANNON Georgeanna,
53
O'BANON Julia E., 21
O'BOYLE Julian, 28
O'BRIAN Julia, 61
Mary, 7
Phebe, 32
O'BURN Susan, 62
ODEN Ann Am., 19
Cath., 67
Josephine A., 4
Mary Ann, 33
ODERFER Barb., 44
Mary, 101
O'DONNELL Jane, 32
Mary Ann, 5
Susan, 66
O'DONNELLY Hellen, 83
OERTEL Barb., 120
O'FERREL Mary, 26
OGELSBY Han., 30
OGLE Eliz., 68
O'HARE Eleanor, 59
OHLWEILER Sr., 109
OHR Eliz. C., 89
Sr., 93
OILER Eliz., 76
OKER Caroline, 10
OLDFIELD Sus., 56
OLDHAM Na., 78
OLDON, Debby, 112
OLDWEIN Louisa, 1
OLLABAUGH Sus., 90
OLLIVER Eleanor, 77
Eliz., 83
Mrs. Susan, 101
OLOCK Na., 116

O'NEAL Fanny, 17
Han. M.W., 117
Har., 114
Reb., 34
Reb. E., 6
Susan C., 29
O'NEALL Marg. E.B., 68
Maria, 115
O'NEILL Eliz., 44
ONG Julia Ann, 84
ORDNER Eliza Ann, 1
O'REILY Bridget, 80
ORH Peggy, 81
ORMSTON Sr., 114
ORNDORFF Eliza, 9, 116
Louisianna, 116
ORNER Mary Ann, 51
ORONDORFF Barb., 85
Eliz., 47
Eliza, 60
Mary, 86
ORRICK Caroline, 32
Ellen, 92
Lucy Ann, 42
Sr., 74
ORTMAN Mary, 112
OSBORNE, Mary, 7
OSTER Adaline S., 102
Ros., 46
OSTERDOCK Cath., 60
OSWALD Barbary, 49
Eliz., 34, 103
Lydia, 57
Lydia Ann, 62
Marg., 117
Mary, 111
Sr., 108
Susan, 70
OTMAN Ros., 4
OTT Cath., 82
Na., 29
Sr., 79, 105
Sr. Jane, 114
OTTO Ann Cath., 21
Barb., 81
Eliz., 54
Mary Ann, 98
Sr., 65
OWENS Eliz., 23
Sr., 69, 77
OWINGS Lydia, 116
Mary, 117
OXX Cath., 53
Sus., 115
OYLER Marg., 63

-P-
PADEN Ellen, 44
PAGE Mary, 1, 64
PAIN Susan, 17

PAINE Jane, 108
PAINTER Cath., 50
Eve Cath., 66
Han., 85
Marg., 112
Marg. Ann, 118
Mary, 24, 47, 98, 108
Na., 17
PAKE Eliz., 82
PALMER Anna, 99
Barb., 35
Cath., 3, 27, 34
Eliz., 16, 17, 73
Eliz. E., 99
Eliza, 82
Frances Cath., 52
Mag., 60
Mar., 64
Marg., 24, 74
Mary, 58, 99
Mary Ann, 102
Mary Cath., 94
Na., 17, 88, 103
Sally, 7
Sr., 35
Susan, 24, 89
PANAL Marg., 113
PANNING Mary, 60
PANOTT Na., 24
PAQUINE Mrs. Louise, 77
PARKER Na., 56
Sr. Jane, 100
PARKS Am., 70
Marg., 68
Maria, 105
Mary M., 72
Peggy, 76
Sr., 21
PARRELL Na., 14
Sus., 81
PARROTT Am., 111
Sus., 30
PARSONS Anna, 8
PARTHER Jane, 14
PATTERSON Ann, 52
Eliza, 16
Mary, 56
PATTISON Emily, 115
PATTON Har. H., 72
Jane, 63
Marg., 73, 90
Sr., 14
PATTOON Mary, 22
PAULL Mary E., 32
PAXTON, Na., 45
PAYN Ann Eliz., 51
PAYNE Lydia A.A.T., 103

Maria, 15
Rachel, 17
PEACHER Maria Jane, 89
PEACOCK Mag., 39
PEARCE Kate E., 105
PEDDICORD Rachel, 24
PELTZ Cath., 41, 42
Reb. Ann, 47
PENCE Eliz., 80
Eve, 74
Mary, 96
Sus., 95
PENCER Cath., 44
PENCIL, Mary, 25
PENNEL Margaretta, 105
PENNELL Char. K., 45
Juan, 58
Mary, 10
PERIN Elenor, 29
PERITZ Sus., 103
PERKINS Eliz., 77
Han., 51
PERRY Eliz., 85
Eliza, 39
Han., 60
Jane, 110
Sr. Ann, 93
Sr. L., 42, 111
PETERS Delilah, 57
Eliz., 50
Mary, 23
PETERSON Har., 116
Sr., 112
PETERY Susan, 114
PETRE Cath., 48, 71
Eliz., 94, 106
Eliza, 116
Louisa, 118
Marg., 106
Marg. E., 18
Mary Ann, 107
Mary E., 17
PETRY Mary Ann, 102
Na., 34
PETTER Mary Ann, 36
PETTET Julia, 110
PFOUTS Cath., 60
PHEARS Prudence, 20
PHEASANT, Rachel, 120
PHILBURN Bridget, 53
PHILIP Bridget, 69
PHILLIPS Eliz., 92
Eliz. Mary, 82
PHOUTZ Eliz., 71
PICKERIN Han., 24
PICKETT Susan, 94
PIERCE Ann Eliz., 7
Eliz., 86
Polly, 60
PIERSON Mary, 67

155

PIFER Marg., 58
PILES Eveline, 36
  Mary Ann, 65
PINDELL Eliza, 90
  Mary, 95
PINKLY Barb., 71
PINKSTAFF Mary, 93
PIPER Barb., 54
  Barb. A., 21
  Cath., 59
  Eliz., 30, 90
  Eliz. R., 96
  Gennett, 26
  Mar. Ann, 89
  Mary, 4, 81
  Matilda, 72
  Ros., 13
PIPERS Peggy, 24
PIRKEY Reb. Ann, 71
PITMAN Barb., 83
PITSNOGLE, Am., 82
PITTENGER Isa., 101
PITTINGER Agnes, 86
PITZER Har. Ann, 111
PLANKER Mary, 100
PLUM Na., 87
  Sr., 102
POCKINS Jane E., 57
POCKLEY Cath., 36
POE Ann Eliz., 46
  Barb., 61
  Hen., 28
  Isa. I.A., 4
POETZ Sr. Ann, 99
POFFENBARGER Cath.,
119
  Philbena, 2
  So., 98
POFFENBERGER Amanda,
120
  Ann M., 11
  Ann S., 113
  Anna, 76
  Betsey, 49
  Eliz., 20, 71, 91,
96
  Eliz. A., 63
  Julia A., 11
  Mahala, 89
  Marg. Ann, 86
  Mary, 34, 64, 72,
74, 76, 96
  Matilda, 19
  Phebe, 89
  Reb., 98, 108
  Ruth, 16
  Sr., 42, 94, 98
  Sr. E., 11
  Sus., 89
  Susan, 119

POFFINBERGER, Mary,
111
  Na. C., 4
POINT Han., 93
POLLINGER Eve, 120
POOLE Mary Ellen, 9
POORMAN Eliz., 46
  Mary, 78
POPE Mary, 68
  Mary Ann, 77
  Reb., 76
POPP Eleanor, 118
  Marg. Ann, 111
  Mary, 68
PORIN Cath., 27
PORTER Amanda, 61
  Cynthia, 36
  Eliz., 7
  Mahala, 11
  Mary, 74
  Na., 36
  Reb., 111
PORTIS Mary Ellen, 99
PORTON Uscilla, 45
POSEY Sr. Ann, 79
POST Ann Eliza, 35
  Lucretia, 67
  Narcissa Ann, 119
POTTENGER Marg. B., 73
  Sr. Marg., 34
POTTER Eliz., 39, 88
  Frances V., 99
  Mary Ann, 51
  Mary Cath., 40
  Peggy, 78
  Sr., 24, 39
  Sus., 117
POTTINGER So. B., 46
POTTORF Han., 92
POTTS Caroline, 87
  Cath., 106
  Marg., 47
  Mary, 39
POWELL Ann, 115
  Eliz., 24
  Eliza, 99
  Han., 111
  Isa., 112
  Mary, 13
  Rachel, 21
  Sr., 3
  Sr. Ann, 99
  Susan, 117
POWER Eliz., 64
POWERS, Ellen, 81
  Mary, 88
  Sr., 81
POWLAS Cath., 72
  Sus., 74
POWLES Caroline V., 88

  Cath. E., 116
  Elizth, 25
  Hen. M., 41
  Louisa Ann, 1
  Marg., 65
  Mary, 1
POWLESS Mary, 88
PRANKARD Mary, 63
PRATHER Ann Eliz., 23
  Anna, 41
  Cath. R., 100
  Lethy, 25
  Louisa M., 82
  Mary Ann, 45
  Reb., 109
  Ruth, 107
  Sr., 70
PREADT Marg., 25
PRECHFIELD Sally, 103
PRESTON So. E., 46
PRETT Anna, 88
  Sr., 25
PRETTYMAN Margaretta
F., 67
PRETZLER Barb., 92
PRETZMAN Clara S., 50
  Eliza M., 59
  Mary Ann, 22
PRICE C.R., 86
  Cath., 104
  Eliz., 41, 118
  Eliza, 83
  Jane S., 86
  Louisa K., 24
  Maria, 84
  Mary, 35, 76, 78,
106
  Reb., 40
  So., 18
  Sr., 15, 84
  Sr. Ann, 72
  Sus., 48
  Susan, 20
PRIER Ann M., 88
PRIEST Mary, 86
PRINCE Sr., 13
PRIOR Ros., 88
PRITT Lydia, 88
PROCTOR Mollie C., 63
PROTZMAN Adaline, 5
  Barb., 105
  Cath., 5
  Eliz., 4, 86
  Joan, 118
  Mary, 65, 93, 103
  Reb., 33
  Sr., 13, 87
PROTZMANN Eliz., 28
PRY Sus., 77, 105
PRYER Delilah R., 97

Eliz., 33
Han. C., 60
PRYOR Han., 105
Julia Ann, 107
PULTZ So., 98
PURCELL Lydia Ann, 67
PUSSMORE Phoebe, 115
PUTMAN Sus., 18

-Q-
QUANTRILL Eliza, 62
Mary Ann, 80
Polly, 37
QUARTERS Eliz., 46
QUINN Ann, 65

-R-
RACKER Han., 105
RAGAN Am., 34
Cath., 101
Eliz., 85, 87
Mary, 68
Sr. Ann, 92
Susan, 50
RAGER, Marg., 88
Mary Eliz., 64
Ros., 101
RAHAUSER Eliz., 118
RAIP Marg., 58
RAMSBURGH Eliz., 51
RAMY Sr. Cath., 94
RANDALL Maria R., 98
Mary Jane, 57
RANDELL Marg., 72
RANEY Cath., 49
RANKIN Anna, 61
Na., 28
RAPE Cath., 92
RAPP So., 92
RARE Marg., 20
RAUGH Sr., 110
RAUM Cath., 7
Sus., 52
RAUN Eliz., 50
RAWLINGS Ann, 23
RAY Jane Eliz., 51
Julian, 68
Na., 35
Rachel Ann, 41
RAYNES Darcus, 6
READER Eliz., 72
Han., 40
READS Cath., 61
REAM Mary, 11
Sr., 51
RECHER Rosina, 9
RECKLEY Barb., 39
RECTOR Rachel E., 114
REDGRAVE Louisa, 14
REDGRAVES Eliza, 35

REDMAN Eliz., 33
Reb., 63
REED Adeline M., 74
Eliz., 9, 88, 116
Jane, 72
Marg., 119
Mary, 97, 98
Sr., 67, 70, 87
REEDER Eliz., 80
Mahala, 70
Marg. Ann, 69
Mary M., 61
Na., 22
Nelly, 12
Sr., 23
Sus., 1
REEDY Mary, 110
REEL Barb., 42
Eliz., 74
Mary, 7, 109
Na., 71, 98
Polly, 44
REESE, Han., 9
REICHARD Eliz., 12
M. Kate, 1
Mary, 64
Susan, 5
REICHART Reb., 10
REID Eliza J., 44
Ellen, 45
Emily, 68
Frances, 118
Mary Cath., 30
REILLEY Mary, 17
REITZ Eliz., 26
REITZELL Amanda L., 84
Ann Reb., 70
Eliz., 7
Mary Ann, 73
RELIVE Mrs., 34
REMBROW Lydia, 93
REMLEY Isa. G., 114
Jane, 45
Mary Eliz., 101
R.C., 41
RENCH Cath., 72, 92
Eliz., 79, 104
Engeline, 105
Fanny, 45
Kate Clare, 78
Marg., 92, 105
Mary, 73, 115
Theresa, 120
RENCH (REACH)
AnnMarie, 92
RENEBERGER Cath., 105
RENN Sus., 59
RENNER Athalinda, 102
Caroline, 86
Cath., 74, 75

Chna., 35
Eliz., 112, 115
Eliza, 33
Joanna, 12
Louisa, 3
Maria, 64
Mary, 5, 87, 107, 109
Mary C., 80
Reb., 37
RENTCH Sally, 42
REPLER Mrs. Mary, 81
REPP Eliz., 6, 9
RESH Betsy, 94
Na., 94
RESLEY Reb., 90
RESSLER Cath., 23
RESSLEY Minerva, 6
RESSLY Lydia, 92
RETT Cath., 82
REULITT Har., 39
REW Eliz., 94
REYNOLDS, Ann A., 25
Barb., 57
Caroline, 82
Eliz., 18, 30, 118
Lavinia, 115
Leathia, 29
Louisa, 48
Maria, 47, 54
Mary, 53, 69, 82, 105
Mary Ann, 29
Mary E., 55
Na., 108
Reb., 2, 93
Sr., 79
REYNULL Marg. S., 99
RHINEHART Eliz., 90
Reb., 101
Sr., 22
RHODE Ros., 21
RHODES Cath., 20
Eliz., 109
Marg., 23
Mary, 84
Mary Ann, 58
Sus., 110
Susan, 30
RIBBLE Mary, 32
RIBBLET Maria, 79
RICE Ally, 65
Ann, 15
Barb., 70
Eliz., 4, 37
Eliz. M., 46
Eliza, 57
Emily, 36
Julia, 62
Marg., 79

Maria, 107
Mary Ann, 107
Peggy, 57
Sr., 32
Sus., 112
RICHARD Eliz. A., 45
Mary, 46
Sr., 9
RICHARDS Sr., 78
RICHARDSON Eliz., 98
Marg., 113
Mary, 22
Sr., 46
RICKARD Eliz., 53
RICKENBAUGH Eliza, 38
Laura, 77
Mary Ann, 118
Mary L., 81
RICKERT Mary, 30
RICKLIRD Na., 49
RICKSON Lea, 14

RIDDLEMOSER Susan
A.R., 83
RIDENOUR Am., 17, 56
Ann, 36, 103
Anna, 78
Barb., 103, 116
Betsey, 95
Cath., 17, 25, 65,
81, 93
Cecelia, 63
Char., 15
Chna., 48
Elenor, 87
Eliz., 11, 29, 44,
57, 65, 66, 71, 89,
117
Eliz. C., 92
Fame Ellen, 49
Louisa, 97
Marg., 18, 99
Mary, 11, 18, 20,
51, 60, 64
Mary A.E., 62
Mary Ann, 44, 83
Mary C., 33
Mary R., 41
Molly, 97
Na., 87
Na. Ann, 4
Polly, 33
Reb., 44, 53
Reb. Marg., 18
Savilla, 109
Sr., 15, 35, 95, 104
Sus., 5, 36, 84, 119
Susan M., 98
RIDEOUT, Mary, 37
RIDGEWAY Bula, 18

RIESELER Eliz., 61
RIFE Louisa, 63
RIFFSNYDER Mary A., 59
RIGHTSTINE Marg., 56
RIGNEY Rachel Ann, 37
RILBLITT Eliz., 26
RILEY Ann, 34
Cath., 19
Eliz., 44
Sally, 54
Sus., 11
RINEBERGER Na., 64
Sus., 6
RINEHART Ann R., 101
Balinda, 86
Cath., 10, 27
Eliz., 10, 43
Han., 105
Marg., 118
Mary, 1
Mary Ann, 105
Susann, 109
RINER Betsey, 14
RINGER Cath., 6
Julia, 86
Marg. Emily, 5
Mary L., 58
Reb. C., 52
RINGGER Sus., 94
RINGGOLD Ann C., 92
Cornelia, 84
Maria Antonet, 108
Virginia, 58
RINKER, Mary, 57
RIPLEY Eliz., 6
RIPP Eliza, 113
RIPPLE Eliz., 56
Mary Cath., 5
So., 46
RISHOH Mary, 80
RITCHIE Mary Anna, 1
RITENOUR Am. S., 83
RITTER Eliz., 39
Mary, 68
RIVER Barb., 101
Eliz., 113
RIZER So., 5
ROACH Barb., 58
Cath., 33
Eliz., 65, 88
Ellis, 71
ROADS Eliz., 21, 112
Mary, 54
Massey, 66
ROBACK, Barb., 51
ROBBINS Agnes F., 69
John K., 78
ROBERTS Ann, 72
Hester L., 107
Marg., 52

Mary Ann, 4
Phebe, 83
Reb., 52
ROBERTSON Ann, 91
Julian, 114
Mary, 27
Phebe, 27
Sr., 80
Susan, 103
ROBEY, Eliz., 1
Eliza, 88
Mary, 72
Stasha, 30
ROBINETT Naomi, 59
ROBINETTE Sus., 54
ROBINSON Am., 85
Cath., 111
Deborah, 20
Eliz., 1, 44, 62, 64
Esther, 16
Fanie M., 8
Marg., 58
Maria, 42
Mary, 19, 98
Na., 68
Rachel, 105
Savilla C., 11
ROBISON Sr., 61
ROBY Debly, 81
Edna, 73
Susan, 25
ROCK Mary, 14
ROCKENBAUGH Maria L.,
67
ROCKSBURY Jane, 54
ROCKWELL Sr. C., 11
RODEFER Arbelin R., 69
RODES Cath., 50
RODGERS Matilda Jane,
15
RODNEY Matilda, 73
ROE Ann, 45
ROGER Cath., 109
ROGERS Lucinda Ann, 39
Lucy, 24
Sr., 30
Sus., 8
ROHER Mary, 25
ROHR Eliz., 118
Mary, 25
ROHRBACK Ann M., 102
Ann V., 84
Barb. Ann, 47
Cath., 41, 51
Deana, 89
Eliz., 119
Har., 5
Lavinia, 59
Mary, 52
Mary Jane, 76

ROHRER Amanda, 104
Ann, 62
Ann E., 71
Barb., 61, 71
Betsy, 5
Cath., 44, 53, 109
Eliz., 5, 12, 46, 57, 80, 104, 108
Eliza Ann, 89
Eve, 51
Har., 89, 110
Har. E., 89
Leah E., 80
Mag., 89
Mag. C.S., 109
Mahala, 37
Mar., 118
Marg., 42
Marg. Ann, 113
Marg. E., 24
Maria, 22
Marietta, 55
Mary, 113
Mary Cath., 32
Mary Mag., 59
Na., 32, 83
Sr. Ann, 89
Sus., 41, 59, 108
Susan, 44, 102, 105
Tracey, 97
ROMAN Theresa, 77
ROMINE, Atty, 42
ROMMEL Betsy, 40
RONAMUS Sus., 19
RONE Marg., 26
RONEMOUS Han., 83
RONER Mary, 45
ROOF Cath., 113
Eliz., 81
ROOM Sus., 90
ROOT Am., 94
Cath., 80
Maria, 45
Sr., 84
Teresa Ann, 21
ROOTS Marg., 47
ROPP Chna., 84
RORICK Ann C., 44
ROSAMARIN Eliz. C., 19
ROSE Nelly, 100
ROSEBERRY Eliz., 34
ROSS Elisa, 10
Gertrude, 20
Jane, 11
Lydia, 32
So., 59
ROTHRAICK Mary, 76
ROTHRAUFF Celinda, 27
Marg., 48
ROUCH Barb., 55

ROULETT Eliza, 112
Julia, 102
ROULETTE, Ann
Virginia, 29
Mary, 76
Sr., 43
ROURKE Mary, 35
ROUSENBERGER
Fredricka, 85
ROUSH Cath., 72
ROUX Han., 22
ROUZAHN Mary Ann, 45
ROW Cath., 18, 88, 106
Louisa, 40
Pricilla, 4
Sr., 67
ROWE Ellen, 54
Jane, 17
Maria, 98
Mary, 17, 84
Na., 98
ROWELL Eve, 86
ROWLAND Amy, 67
Ann, 99
Ann M., 118
Annie, 1
Barb. A., 81
Cath., 92, 117
Eliz., 90
Eliza, 2
Frances M., 92
Kate, 37, 88
Kesia, 24
Lena, 65
Lucinda, 41
Lydia, 94, 95
Marg. Ann, 95
Mary, 35, 37, 87
Mary Ann, 118
Mary E., 86
Mary Eliz., 77
Na., 34
Ros., 3
Sr., 13, 106
Sus., 12
Susan, 6, 37
ROYER Eliz., 78
RUDASIL Eliz., 10
RUDISELL Susan, 55
RUDISILL Mar. M., 75
RUDY Eliz., 71
RULETT Mary, 29
Sr. Ann, 113
RUMLER Mary, 13
RUMMELL Marg., 72
RUNIMUS Ann, 60
RUNNER Mary, 72
RUPP So., 93
RUSH Ann Reb., 35
Eliza, 73

Jane, 111
Peggy, 91
RUSSE, Maria Cath., 102
RUSSEL Mary, 60
RUSSELL Ann, 30, 43
Cath., 61
Eliz. J., 19
Eliza Jane, 111
Eliza Maria, 47
Margaretta, 47
Mary, 6, 76
Mary M., 86
Maza, 55
Reb., 43
Sus., 33, 119
RUSSI Maria C., 92
RUSSIA Selma, 62
RUTH Ellen Jane, 58
Mary, 114
RUTLEDGE Esther, 44
RUTTER Eliz., 55
Marg., 23, 86
Mary Ann, 28
RYAN Cath., 87
Ellen, 26
Mary, 27
RYE Ann, 66
Mary, 7
RYNOLD Susan, 3

-S-
SACKETT Rachel, 48
SAGER Barb., 4
Caroline, 34, 113
Cath., 73, 75
Eliz., 47, 73
Leana, 73
Mary, 44
Mary Ann, 21
Matilda, 118
So., 6
Sr., 120
Sus., 6
SAILER Barb., 102
Sr., 118
Susan, 37
SAILOR Cath., 102
Eliz., 94
Han., 71
Mary, 71
Sus., 94
ST. CLAIR Han. Eliz., 46
Mar., 69
SALMON Julia, 62
SANDERS Julian, 66
SANDS Eliz., 115
SANER Cath., 33
SANFORD Marg., 15

159

SANNER Lydia, 59
  Mary, 15
SANTMAN Cath., 75
SANTMANN Louisa, 44
SARVER Barb., 35
  Chna., 86
SAUNDERS Barb. A., 17
  Marg., 59
  Mary, 74
  Mary Ann, 32
SAUNTMAN Sr., 81
SAVAGE Jane, 115
SAYER Marg., 107
SAYLOR Eliz., 63
  Laura Eliz., 87
  Marg., 44
  Mary Eliz., 113
SCAGGS Eliz., 41
SCARBERRY Susan, 6
SCARY Mahala, 26
SCHAFFER Mary E., 18
SCHAMEL Cath., 83
SCHAPPART Lydia, 115
SCHARTZER Sus., 28
SCHILHASS Eliz., 84
SCHINDEL Adaline E.,
72
  Ann Cath., 103
  Ann Virginia, 110
  Chna., 73
SCHINDLE Ann Maria, 71
SCHIPPER Eliz., 4
SCHLAGEL Eliz., 86
SCHLEIGH Am., 67
  Ann M., 13
  Ann Maria, 76
  Anna E., 19
  Mar. J., 110
  Mary Eliz., 5
  Victoria, 118
SCHLOSSER Mar. S., 83
  Mary, 27
  Sr., 108
SCHLUSSER, Cath., 27
SCHMUTS Eliz., 56
SCHMUTZ Sr., 104
SCHNEBLY, Ann Cath.,
110
  Cath., 29
  Cath. R., 93
  Eliz., 56, 85
  Eliz. M., 9
  Eliza, 55
  Ellen, 6
  Marg., 56, 68, 86
  Mary, 17, 75, 92
  Mary R., 5
  Na., 28, 114
  Prudence, 103
SCHNIDER Cath., 92

SCHOLLS Eliz., 49
SCHRADER Amanda
  I.C.R., 78
  Na., 51
SCHRIVER Mary, 22
  Reb., 72
SCHRYOCK Eliza, 67
  Sus., 34
SCHWARTZ Polly, 61
SCHWOPE Cath., 14
SCOTT Ann, 60
  Judith, 36
  Mar., 45
  Sr., 84
SCRINER Paten, 34
SCUFFINS Mary, 116
SEABRIGHT Julia Ann,
73
SEAMAN Cynthia Ann, 49
  Mar. J., 38
SEASE Char., 87
SEAVERS Louisa, 119
SEBER, Chna., 93
SECKMAN Frances A.,
107
SECORE Sr. Ann, 10
SEDON Caroline, 12
SEELE Cath., 99
SEIBERT Am. A., 88
  Ann E., 101
  Cath., 64
  Eliz., 93
  Eliza, 22
  Marg., 39
  Mary, 23, 65, 93,
116
  Mary Ann, 78
  Mary E., 40
  Sus., 96
SEIDERSTICK Mary, 36
SEIFERT Mary, 57
SEIGLER Am., 55
  Han., 40
  Maria, 36
  Polly, 102
SEISS Emily, 88
SELLERS Ann, 120
  Cath. Ann, 37
  Chna., 64
  Mary, 86
  Sr., 79
SELLINGER Marg., 102
SELSER Cath., 35
  Eliz., 33
SENAILE, Ann, 63
SENGER Mary, 38
SENSEL Eliz., 64
  Sr., 54
SENSELL Mariah, 76
SENSEMAN Mariah, 59

SENSENBAUGH Cath., 98
SERBEY Cath., 90
SERVER Cath., 115
SERVIN Sus., 95
SESIAR Susan, 6
SEVERS Chna., 106
SEYBERT Am., 24
  Eliz., 15
SEYESTER Reb., 62
SEYFERT Kunigunde, 53
SEYLER Jane, 97
SHADE Na., 59
SHAEY Betsy, 92
SHAFER Barb., 36
  Caroline, 99
  Caroline B., 50
  Cath., 85, 90
  Chna., 40
  Clara E., 98
  Deliah, 34
  Eliz., 6, 40, 63,
75, 120
  Eliz. F., 101
  Eliza, 50
  Isa., 62
  Laura A., 115
  Levinia, 62
  Louisa, 97
  Mary A., 43, 99
  Mary Ann, 25
  Mary Eliz., 113
  Mary Ellen, 34
  Reb., 119
  Susan, 93
SHAFFER, Cath., 116
  Maria, 36
  Mary, 96
  Mary C., 119
  Polly, 15
SHAFFNER Ann Maria, 58
  Cath., 10
  Eliza, 12
  Juliann, 47
  Marg., 4
  Seville S., 36
SHALE Cath., 56
SHALL Eliz., 40
  Polly, 98
SHAMAN Mary Ann, 86
SHAMEL Susan, 15
SHANABARGER Am., 25
SHANAFELT Susan, 21
SHANAFELTZ Sr., 19
SHANE Chra., 39
  Eliz., 72
  So., 61
SHANEBERGER Cath., 45
  Sr., 91
SHANEBURGER Eliz., 38
SHANEFELT Eliz., 52

160

INDEX TO BRIDES

Mary, 100
Sus., 118
SHANEFIELD Mary, 76
SHANK, Ann E., 7
Anna, 37
Barb., 18, 82
Cath., 25, 58
Chna., 101
Eliz., 6, 97, 103, 105
Eve, 39
Fanny, 42
Leah, 94
Mag., 62
Marg., 97
Maria, 113
Mary, 27, 56, 105
Na., 10, 51, 88
Polly, 85, 113, 115
Sr., 48, 103
Sus., 44
Susan, 4, 94
Susan H., 18
SHANON Jane, 57
SHARD Eliz., 69
SHARER Eliz., 107
Mary, 67
SHAREY Eliz., 90
SHARKEY Alice, 32
SHARKS Eliz., 97
SHARP Am., 95
So., 20
SHARPLESS So. G., 8
SHARRICK Ann, 48
Barb., 78
SHATT Cath., 76
SHATZER Sr. Ann, 118
SHAW Eliz., 23, 52, 113
Ellen Eliz., 26
Mary, 80, 87
Mary Ann, 113
Mary E., 99
Na., 93
Polly, 4
SHAY Eliza, 76
Susan, 7
SHEATS Polly, 118
SHECKLER Eleanor, 54
Louisa, 7
SHECKLES Eliz., 81
SHECTER Cath., 108
Lavinia, 29
Lydia A., 114
Mary, 116
Sus., 108
Susan, 112
Tereshia, 92
SHEELER Mary, 66
Ros., 104

Sus., 102
SHEETS Eliz., 76
Frances, 96
Mary, 44
Mary Ann, 21, 69
SHEETZ Eliz., 95
Mary, 97
SHEISS Ellen, 79
SHEITZ Cath., 46
Eliza, 46
Susan, 109
SHELEBURGER Chna., 14
SHELL Anna, 69
Cath., 45
SHELLEBERGER Ann Am., 120
SHELLER Cath., 102
Eliz., 36, 45
Mary, 103
SHELLETTO Eliz., 72
SHELLY Mary, 36
SHEMEL, Eliz., 75
SHEMMEL Cath., 83
SHENEBERGER Julia, 86
SHENEY Cath., 78
SHEPHERD Eliz., 49
Han. M., 54
Mary, 99
Sr., 102
Susan, 114
SHEPLER Mary, 104
SHEPPART, Sr. C., 116
SHERCKY Margaretta, 66
SHERDON Na., 15
SHERED Emily C., 102
SHERIFF Eliz., 8
SHERRICK Anna, 78
SHERTZ Lavinia, 44
SHERVAN Mary, 62
SHERVIN (SHEWIN) Ros., 66
SHEWEY Chna., 97
SHIESS Cath., 22
Hen., 61
SHIFFLER Amanda E., 73
Eliz., 75
Marg., 77
SHILL, Mary, 106
SHILLING Cath., 34, 82
Eleanora, 99
Eliz., 110, 117
Malinda E., 77
Mary, 80
Sr., 74
Sr. Ann, 101
Sus., 53
Susan, 105
SHINDEL Am. Jane, 67
Ann A., 108
Caroline E., 33

Leah Matilda, 2
SHINDLE Ann Maria, 33
Eliz., 14, 28
Susan, 71
SHIPLER Han., 21
SHIPLEY, Mag., 77
Sr. E., 41
SHIPP Lydia Ellen, 74
SHIRETY Na., 75
SHIREY Jocana, 119
SHIRK Barb., 76
SHIRLEY Char. I., 103
Jenny, 24
Mary, 3
Mary Ann, 24
Patience, 20
SHOAFF Eliza, 19
SHOAFSTALL Sr., 39
SHOCKEY Eliz., 105
Sus., 5
SHOLL Eliz., 96
Mariah, 56
Mary, 8
SHONK Sus., 9
SHOOK Ann, 115
Eliz., 3, 16
Jane, 2
Rachel Ann, 58
SHOOP Ann, 93
Anna, 6
Caroline A., 9
Cath., 37
Cath. M., 107
Chna., 14, 68
Eliz., 76, 94
Lydia, 79
Lydia Ann, 117
Mary, 119
SHOREN Mary Marg., 38
SHOUTS, Mary, 52
SHOW Eliz., 44
Mar., 2
Mary, 60
Peggy, 98
SHOWAKER Mary, 88
SHOWMAN Caroline A., 89
Cath., 19
Elisa Ann, 69
Eliz., 73, 112
Louisa, 18
Marg., 5
Mary E., 83
Rachel, 108
Serena V., 79
SHRACK Marg., 1
SHRADER Barb., 51
Cath., 18
Mary, 69, 102
SHRAEDER Mary, 94

SHRAPP Am., 12
SHRECK Mary, 12
SHREINER, Ann Eliz., 71
SHRINER Evy Ann, 88
  Mary Ann, 46
  Sr., 53
SHRIVER Ann Maria, 24
  Barb., 9
  Cath., 36, 59
  Eliz., 103
  Marg., 52
  Reb., 12
SHRIVES Har., 102
SHRODES Na., 2
SHROEDER Cath., 105
SHROUDER Eliz., 25
SHROUDS Mary, 10
SHROYER Julian, 21
  Sr., 49
SHRYACK Ann Maria, 47
SHRYOCK Elly, 58
SHUBER Ann, 47
SHUCK Barb., 15
  Eliz., 97
SHUFF Har., 42
SHUGART Mary, 72
  So., 69
SHULL Marg., 119
SHULTZ Ann, 8
SHUMAN Sr., 53
SHUP Julian, 113
SHUPE Barb., 36
  Cath., 3, 43
  Eliz., 7, 104
  Marg., 87
  Phebe, 87
  Sus., 60, 78
SHUPP Eliz., 18
SHURK (SHUSH) Mary, 21
SHURMAN, Drusilla, 63
SHUTT Susan, 56
SHUTZ Mary, 92
SHUTZEN Cath., 36
SHUWALTER Eliza, 4
SIBER Chna., 63
SIBERT Eliz., 26, 91, 98
  Mary, 10
SICAFUCE Julian, 15
SICKMAN Barb. L., 19
SIDERSTICK Eliz., 7
  Na., 95
  Susan, 37
SIDLE Eliz., 87
SIESS Eliz. A., 49
SIGLER Amanda R., 112
  Annie C., 87
  Reb., 81
  Susan, 35

SILLHART Cath., 13
  Eliz., 110
  Mary, 71
  Sus., 84
  Susan, 9
SILVER Bersheba, 71
  Esther, 35
  Mar. S., 33
  Mary A., 74
  So., 108
SILVERS Barb., 72
  Ellen, 46
  Marg. Ann, 96
  Mary, 117
SIMKINS, Mazy, 9
  Na., 101
  Polly, 118
  Sus., 7
SIMLER Eliz., 112
SIMMERMAN Esther, 8
SIMMERS Ann, 113
  Eliz., 116
SIMMONS Eliz., 88
SIMPKINS Sr., 43
SIMPSON Ann, 96
SINGER Sus., 77
SINICKE Sr., 116
SIRT Caroline, 96
SISLER Ann, 36
  Mary, 69
SISSERLER Eliz., 41
SITZLER Lydia, 4
SKINNER Annie, 111
SLAEN Ann, 47
SLAGLE Ann Maria, 48
  Louisa, 37
  Mary, 44
SLANKER Regina, 104
  Susan, 79
SLEIGH Cath., 63
SLEISE Mary, 12
SLENCKER Mary, 42
SLENKER Eliz., 39
  Mary, 100
  Reb., 117
SLICE Cath., 58
  Chra., 6
  Eliz., 75
  Marg., 38
  Na., 96
  Susan, 88
SLICER Barb., 7
SLIFER Cath., 53
  Elmira, 88
  Lydia A., 39
  Marg. A., 37
  Orinda, 64
  Sr., 108
  Susan, 99
SLIMMER Mary, 24

SLOAN Sr., 53
SLOSSER Adelia, 19
  Cath., 17
SLUSMAN Lavinia, 116
  Marg., 59
SLUSSER Eliz., 13, 76
SLUSSMAN Susan, 59
SLY Na., 97
SLYE Sr., 54
SLYER Mary, 111
SMALL Anna V., 51
  Mary, 50
  Sr. Ann, 82
  Susan E., 30
SMELSER Eliz., 30
SMELTZER Mary, 11
SMICE Eliz., 92
  Peggy, 35
SMISE, Eliz., 40
SMITH Abigale, 110
  Am., 83, 100
  Amanda Cath., 81
  Amnada A., 117
  Ann, 68, 84, 96
  Ann A.R., 99
  Ann Cecelia, 65
  Ann So., 89
  Anna, 12, 95
  Annie C., 9
  Bridget, 41
  Cath., 3, 20, 52, 53, 54, 61, 68, 84, 85, 87, 89, 92, 119
  Cath. Aloisa, 44
  Char., 42
  Chna., 117
  Eleanora, 28
  Eliz., 7, 13, 20, 22, 37, 38, 39, 45, 47, 48, 49, 50, 66, 77, 85, 86, 97, 98, 99, 104, 112, 120
  Eliz. H., 114
  Eliza, 40
  Eliza Ann, 70
  Ellen, 34
  Emeline, 110
  Eve, 57
  Eveline, 47
  Har., 100
  Hester Ann, 73
  Jane, 87
  Julianna, 106
  Lavina, 110
  Lucy Ann, 105
  Lydia Ann, 106
  Manah, 2
  Mar., 107
  Mar. A., 54
  Marg., 1, 21, 29,

30, 65, 103, 109
Mary, 12, 14, 21,
28, 34, 51, 57, 64,
66, 68, 72, 76, 79,
89, 99, 104, 106, 107,
109
Mary A., 61
Mary Ann, 42, 51
Mary C., 88
Mary E., 43, 49
Mary Eliza, 62
Mary M., 77
Maybelle M., 94
Motlina, 117
Na., 24, 51, 85, 100
Na. Ellen, 58
Polly, 79, 101
Rachel, 112
Reb., 73, 86, 114
Ros., 6, 62
Ru Annetta, 78
Savilla, 28
So., 48, 53, 61, 81,
104, 105
Sr., 19, 42, 59, 80,
84, 88, 92
Sr. A., 39
Sr. Ann, 14, 83
Sr. H., 105
Sus., 72, 108
Susan, 29, 66, 117
Susan E., 98
Teresa, 29
Trusilla, 13
SMITH (SOUTH) Mary, 28
SMOUDER Marg., 26
SMUTZ, Mag., 57
SNAKEABURGER Barb., 75
SNAPP Marg., 114
SNAVELY Ann, 38
Cath., 34, 60, 83,
96
Chra., 13
Mary Ann, 56, 94
Ros., 76
Ruann, 85
Ruenna, 103
Sus., 3
SNELL Na., 110
SNIDER Barb., 79
Cath., 57
Clarissa, 14
Eliza, 74, 87
Han., 15
Mahala, 29
Maria, 59
Mary, 25
Mary M., 25
Ruana A., 95
Sr., 106

Susan L., 90
SNIVELY Ann, 5
Ann Louisa, 41
Cath., 79
Eliz., 29, 56, 72,
105
Marg. A., 71
Marietta, 18
Molly, 4
Roz., 12
Sr. C., 113
SNORT Chna., 54
SNOWMAN Eliz., 7
SNYDER Adaline C., 9
Am., 18
Amanda E., 105
Ann Am., 32
Betsy, 32
Cath., 1, 15, 72,
85, 100, 114, 116
Cath. R., 71
Char., 59
Eliz., 5, 32, 49,
72, 77, 84, 96, 118
Eliz. A., 73
Eliz. Ann, 100
Emma, 106
Har., 3
Har. D., 45
Har. H., 56
Hetty Maria, 12
Jane, 21
Josephine, 42
Louisa, 88
Lydia Virginia, 45
Malinda, 77
Mar., 112
Marg., 80
Margaretta, 43
Mary, 24, 27, 71,
78, 92, 110, 119
Mary Ann, 6, 33, 45,
73
Mary Ellen, 30
Mary M., 9
Matilda, 43
Molly, 36
Na., 9, 30, 40
Pamelia Kate, 110
Peggy, 110
Polly, 75, 100
Reb., 12
Ros., 38
Ruann, 101
So. A., 111
Sr., 12, 63, 117,
118
Sr. N., 50
Sus., 16, 58, 78,
109

Susan, 65, 74, 92,
117
SOCKS, Eliz., 50
SOISTER Eliz., 72
SOMER Mary, 83
SONSALL Cath., 27
SOSEY Cath., 108
SOTTORY Mary, 77
SOUDER Marg., 95
SOUDERS Marg., 103
Mary Jane, 76
SOURBEER Marg., 94
SOUTH Am., 59, 115
Ann, 22
Eliz., 63
Eliza, 59
Har., 95
Mary, 35
Mary E., 7
Na., 114
So., 120
Sr., 17, 22, 34
Sr. Ann, 55
SOUTHWOOD Reb., 11
Sr. Jemina, 15
SPAHN Cath., 47
SPAHN (SPONG) Cath.,
29
SPANGLER Eliz., 93
Mag., 98
Maria, 116
Mary Susan, 81
SPAWLING Susan, 16
SPEAKER Chna., 83
Eliza Jane, 105
SPECART Cath., 119
SPECK Ann, 21
Cath., 26
Eliz., 49
Mary, 2
SPEELMAN Eve, 50
Sus., 114
SPEIGLER Eliz., 104
SPENCER Ann, 19
SPERR Barb., 47
SPESSARD Cath., 51
Chra., 103
Eliz., 27, 38
Lydia A., 80
Marg., 80
Maria, 10
Na., 23
Sr. E., 93
Sus., 62, 68
SPESSART Mary, 114
SPICKLER Ellenora, 114
Mary Ann, 83
SPIEGLER Barb., 120
Eliz., 52
SPIELER Na., 101

SPIELMAN Cath., 13,
93, 119
  Eliza Ann, 79
  Marg., 59
  Mary, 23
  Mary E., 108
  Sr., 25
  Susan, 50, 74, 109
SPIGLER Cath., 62
  Marg., 78
  Sus., 75
SPILLMAN Mary Ann, 22
SPITLER Ann C., 82
SPITNAGLE Barb., 20
SPITSNOGLE Na., 72
  Reb., 100
SPITTLER Har., 47
SPOHN Caroline, 17
SPONG Ann, 74
  Eleanor, 75
  Hen., 49
  Mary, 11, 43
  Rhuanna, 49
  Susan, 9
SPONSLER Chna., 110
  Eliz., 84
SPOTTS, Eliz., 39
  Susan, 113
SPRECHER Ann Eliz., 46
  Marg., 87
  Mary, 4
  Mary Ann, 74
SPRECKER Ann M., 55
  Eliz., 57
SPRIGG Maria, 87
SPRINGER Amanda, 119
  Cath., 13, 57
  Cath. A., 73
  Char., 29
  Eliz., 10, 32
  Eve, 3
  Mag., 93, 117
  Mar. Jane, 15
  Marg., 44, 68
  Mary, 76, 117
  Mary A., 54
  Na., 26
  Sus., 21, 95
SPRINKLE Matilda, 108
SQUIRES Ann, 15
STACK, Sus., 112
STAHL Ann, 103
  Eliz., 3
STAHLWORTH Eve, 108
STAIMEL Cath., 20
STAKE Am., 118
  Cath., 46
  Eliz., 17
  Eliza F., 28
  Marg., 76

Maria, 95
Mary, 61
Susan S., 93
STALE Mary, 13
STALEY, Jane, 99
  Louisa C., 110
  Marg., 60
  Marg. Eliz., 21
  Marg. S., 9
  Reb., 38
  Rosinda, 38
  Sr. Ann, 63
STALL Sr., 70
STAMM Eliz., 30
STANT Ann G., 81
STANTON Ann, 55
  Delila, 34
  Eliz., 45
STAPHEY Ann, 28
STARCH Cath., 70
STARE Mary, 90
STARLING Cath., 62
STARLIPER Cath., 70
STARR Ann Ferena, 94
  Marg. A., 65
START, Mary, 58
STARTMAN Eve, 74
STARTZMAN Am., 105
  Annie, 11
  Cath., 87
  Chna., 36
  Eva, 57
  Mary, 76
  Peggy, 45
  Ros., 113
  Sr., 26, 52
  Sus., 103
  Susan, 103
STATLER Cath., 119
STATTER Eliz., 51
STAUBS Ann, 41
  Eliz., 100
  So., 100
  Sr. Ann, 100
STAULE Mary, 109
STAUNTON Cath., 67
STAUP Eliz., 112
STAUPS Adelius, 75
STAYLEY Sr. Ann, 35
STEACE Eve, 87
STEECE Mary, 38
STEEL Mar., 12
  Mary, 4
  Rachel, 8
  Sus., 16
STEELE Rachel, 56
STEFFEY Barb., 3
  Caroline S., 102
  Cath., 51
  Eliz., 112

Emily E., 57
Han., 97
Mary, 6, 21
Sus., 24
Susan, 4
STEFFY Barb., 70
  Cath., 115
  Eliz., 44
  Mary, 114
  Sr., 3
STEFLER Eliz., 69
STEINER Eliz., 98
STEINMETZ Ann, 23
  Ann Cath., 25
STEMBAUGH, Eliz., 34
STEMPLE Cath., 102
  Mary, 107
STENGER Marg., 119
STEPHENS Eliz., 95
  Eliz. Jane, 30
  Har., 82
  Louisa, 14
  Na., 40, 115
  Na. I., 116
  Rachel, 35
  Reb., 97
  Wilimini, 79
STEPHENSON Ann, 42
  Marg. G., 27
STEPHEY Eliz., 51
STERLING Hen., 113
  Marg. E., 101
STERR Cath., 64
STERRETT Ann, 66, 92
  Maria, 29
STERROTT Josephine I.,
  6
STEVEBAUGH, Sr., 64
STEVEMATS Han., 67
STEVENSON Eliz. A., 88
  Lydia, 42
STEVESON Mary Ann, 13
STEWART Anna, 115
  Eliza, 111
  Grace, 87
  Mar., 76
  Marg., 6
  Mary, 51
  Mary Ann, 56
  Sr. W., 62
STICKLE, Margaretta,
  40
  Susan E., 86
STICKLER Eliza, 15
STICKLEY Rosina, 12
STIEWALT Hen., 74
STIFFLER Eliz., 49, 67
  Har. Ann, 77
  Louisa, 25
  Lydia, 39

Marg. Ann, 11
Mary, 12, 43, 49
Mary Ann, 27, 83
Sr., 54
STIFFY Marg., 80
STIFLER Lydia Ann, 90
STILLWELL Amanda, 94
STINE Ann Marg., 33
Ann Maria, 43
Cath., 21, 58, 79
Eliz., 24, 56, 99
Fanny, 87
Malinda, 21
Marg., 107
Maria, 39, 56, 87,
99
Mary, 86
Mary E., 10
Ros., 14
Sr. Ellen, 27
Susan, 28
Tracilla, 82
Tracy, 89
STINEMETZ, Eliz., 99,
100
Marg., 62
Mary, 100
Reb., 67
STIPP Mary, 74
STITE Cath., 94
STOCK Cath., 76
STOCKES Chna., 43
Sus., 45
STOCKSLAGER Caroline,
104
Eliz., 65
STOKER Barb., 5
STOKES Eliz., 117
STOLTZ Sus., 59
STONE Amanda Cath., 29
Mary Ann, 61, 68
STONEBRAKER Angelina,
60
Ann, 65
Ann Eliz., 92
Barb., 86
Caroline M., 18
Cath. E., 47
Eliz., 3, 71
Esther, 33
Hester Ann, 59
Kate A., 44
Lydia A., 56
Mag., 93
Maria, 7
Mary, 35, 60, 100
So., 7
Sus., 109
Susan, 4
Susan L., 33, 113

Urilla, 80
STONEBREAKER Savilla,
86
STONER, Barb., 7, 78
Cath., 54
Eliz., 50, 100
Louisa, 36
Maria, 96
Mary, 64
Na., 90
Rachel, 30
So., 7
STOOP Eliz., 18
STOOPS Reb., 50
STOPS Susan, 109
STORM Eliz., 35
STOTLER Ann, 56
Anna, 60
Cath., 60
Marg., 10
Maria, 51
Susan, 99
STOTTLEMEYER Eliz., 35
STOTTLEMYER Caroline,
11
Keziah, 88
Layann, 11
Mahala, 19
Mary, 63
Sabra A., 32
Sus., 45
Susan, 55
STOTTLER Eliz., 10
STOUFER, Mag., 50
STOUFFER Am., 116
Ann Am., 4
Cath., 65
Eliz., 53, 94, 100
Eliza, 77
Eliza A., 102
Emiline, 102
Eve, 86
Lydia, 27
Marg., 11
Marg. A., 111
Milly, 83
Na., 51, 60
Reb., 101
Sr., 30
Sr. Ann, 99
STOUGH Sus., 51
STOVER Ann Eliz., 110
Cath., 14, 25, 48,
101, 106
Eliz., 80, 90
Marg., 105
Marg. A., 73
Mary Ann, 11
Mary E., 119
Na., 90

Polly, 110
Reb., 65
Sr., 40, 105
STOY Dorothy, 11
STRAIN Har., 119
STRALEY Cath., 8
STRAUSE Eliza, 6
Marg. A., 25
Reb. A., 8
So., 94
STRIDER Marg., 52
Phillipe, 104
Sr. Ann, 30
STRIPE Ann M., 112
STRIPPY Cath., 53
STRIPTON (SHIPTON)
Mary, 61
STRITE Ann, 26
Na., 72
Sr., 68
STROCK Susan B., 15
STRODE, Na., 29
STROSNYDER Sr., 53
STUART Abigail, 63
STUCK Mina, 93
STUCKEY Marg., 30
STUDE Marg., 41
STULL Cath., 112
Ellen, 92
Holland, 45
Mary, 40
Matilda, 100
STULTZ Mary, 26
Polly, 26
Susan, 100
STUMP Am., 54
Han., 89
Mary, 111
Regena, 103
STURN Rhinhandle, 119
STURR (STURE) Eliz.,
113
STUTER Char., 106
SUDGICK Cath., 102
SULLENS Sr., 58
SULLIVAN Mary, 48
Mary Ann, 89
SULSER Susan, 102
SULTZER Anna, 63
Mary, 49
SUMAN Lydia, 85
SUMMER Marg., 40
SUMMERS Am., 78
Barb., 77
Cath., 45
Doleana, 54
Eliz., 106
Eliza, 17, 106
Lanah, 71
Mary, 16, 107

Mary Ann, 8, 77
Sr., 63
SUMMERVILLE Matilda, 40
SUTER Ann Maria, 5
Cath. M., 38
Eleanora, 11
Marion S., 45
Roz., 69
SUTTER Ann Maria, 116
SUTTON Mary, 5
SUVEN Cath., 65
SWADE Eliz., 52
SWAGELER Eliz., 63
SWAGELY Peggy, 119
SWAIN Sam., 107
SWANN Rachel, 36
SWARTZ Ann R., 70
Mary, 1
SWARTZWELDER Mary, 114
SWARTZWELLER Mary C., 84
SWEARINGER Cath., 18
Eliz. S., 86
Mar., 94
Mary, 37
SWEITZER Marg. A., 103
Na., 26
Sr., 77
SWENEY Eliz., 47
SWIFT Na., 18
SWINGER Mary Ann, 120
SWINGLEY Barb. E., 2
Eliz., 1
Sr., 2
Sus., 75
SWINGLY Eliz., 2
SWISHER Cath., 33
SWOOP Sr., 16
SWOPE Ann Cath., 30
Barb., 46
Barb. Ann, 34
Cath., 50, 92
Eliz., 5, 45, 74
Eliz. E., 40
Mar., 11
Mar. Ann, 19
Mary, 98
Mary Ann, 71, 107
Polly, 40
Sr., 41, 46
Sus., 119
SWORD Char., 51
SYANDS Rosa, 20
SYCAFOOS Virginia K., 84
SYDEL, Cath., 118
SYDERSTICK Am., 89
SYERS Reb., 58
SYESTER Eliz. K., 73

Reb., 57
SYLAR Marg., 33
SYPES Eliz., 110
SYSTER Mary, 109

-T-
TAGORE, Eliz., 31
TALBERT Abigail, 86
TALBOT Nelly, 55
TALBOTT Char., 53
TALEN Am., 109
TANEHILL Mary, 3
TANEY Cath. E., 5
Mary Ellen, 11
TANEYHILL Jane, 54
TANNER Mahetable, 86
TARE Peggy, 42
Sr., 72
TARLTON Barb., 6
Lucretia, 6
TAULHELLUM Eliz., 1
TAWNEY Amay, 4
TAYLOR Ann, 77, 100
Ann E., 34
Eddy, 73
Eliz., 66
Eliza, 6, 52
Frances, 26
Han., 17
Hen., 28
Mar., 118
Marg., 101
Maria, 49
Orphit, 84
Pheby, 94
Polly, 54
Rua, 81
Sidney R., 83
TEACH Mary, 43
TECUMSEH, Jane, 100
TEDRICK Matilda, 47
TEETERLY Chna., 119
TEIDERICK Mary, 116
TELLY Mary Ann, 87
TEMPLEMAN Jane, 32
TENANT Marg., 90
Mary, 76
Reb., 55
TERRY Frances, 29
THOMAS Amanda, 27
Ann Maria, 18
Anna, 99
Cath., 4, 65, 100, 110, 118
Clarissa, 31
Eliz., 12, 66, 89, 108, 111
Eliz. Jane, 96
Eliza, 69
Eliza A., 48

Han., 89
Julian, 38
Lavenia, 4
Leannah, 44
Lucinda, 64
Lucinda A., 7, 36
Lydia, 78
Mag., 18
Maria, 53
Maria Ann, 104
Mary, 29, 41, 100, 104
Mary Ann, 9, 49, 50, 53, 83
Polly, 4
Rachel, 63
Reb., 79, 116
Ros., 83, 105
Ruanna, 78
Sallie, 109
So., 63, 99
Sr., 8, 112
Sr. A.E., 99
Sr. Ann, 12, 38
Sus., 36, 50, 113
Susan, 62, 95
Susan Am., 105
THOMBSON Eliz., 31
THOMBURG Sr. Morgan, 29
THOMPSON Ann C., 90
Barb., 82
Cath., 71
Eliz., 44
Han., 67
Isa. Glass, 99
Marg. R., 8
Mary, 52
Mary L., 95
Na., 72
Polly, 107
Rachel, 96
Ruann, 74
Sr., 62
Sr. Ann, 111
Susan, 2, 93
THOMSON Elley, 13
THORNBOROUGH Sr., 102
THORNSBURG Hen. C., 109
Mary E., 118
THORNTON, Anna, 112
Ellen, 86
THORPER Ann, 101
THOUGHTS Darkey, 100
THRESHER Polly, 90
THROP Susan O., 26
THROPP Sr. Ann, 14
THUM, Anebel, 53
Ann, 79

THUMB Eliz., 112
  Mary Ann, 116
  Rachel, 11
  Sus., 92
THURSTON Elisa, 46
  Mary, 58
TICE Ann E., 62
  Barb., 50
  Cath., 108
  Eliz., 33
  Eliza, 3
  Esther, 48
  Eve, 118
  Frances, 96
  Lucy A., 32
  Lydia, 9
  Mary, 24, 75, 118
  Mary Jane, 8
  So., 11
  Sr., 23, 43
  Susan, 10
TICHES Na., 105
TILGHMAN Ann B., 50
  Louisa Lamar, 50
  Mary, 44
  Susan A., 24
TIMMERMAN Anne, 90
TINGARY, Ann, 37
TISHINGHAM Marg., 105
TITLOW Cath., 116
  Marg. Ann M., 16
TITUS Kate, 60
TOBY Barb., 5
  Elisa, 38
  Peggy, 8
TODD Eliz. C., 3
  So., 21
TOLAND Jane, 68
TOLBERT Ann, 68
  Eveline, 106
TOLEN Sus., 80
TOLHELM Eliz., 45
TOM Mary, 64
TOMS Cath., 84
  Elmira, 14
  Mary, 13
  Reb., 63
  Sr. Ann, 50
TONCRAY Eliz., 73
  Holday, 86
TONER Milley, 79
TOWNER Mary Virginia, 92
TOWSON Han., 83
  Mar. S., 99
  Sr., 98
TRACEY Eliz., 117
  Mary, 54
TRACY Malinda, 27
  Mary J., 42

Matilda, 101
  Na., 118
TRAINER Cath., 37
TRAVER Sr., 75
TRAVERSE Eveline, 2
TRAYER Mary, 71
TREIBER Chna., 36
TRENNER Eliz., 78
TRIDER, Sr. Ann, 106
TRIGGS Rachel, 16
TRIMBLES Marg., 24
TRITCH Cath., 69
  Sr., 39
  Sr. R., 14
TRITLE Marg., 92
  Susan, 117
TRITT Mary Ann, 61
TROLL Na., 23
TRONCE Marg. A.B., 112
TROUBTMAN Mrs. Ann M., 100
TROUP Ann, 10, 93
  Cath., 2
  Cath. A., 65
  Eliz., 116
  Lydia, 110
  Marg., 53
  Mary, 40
  Na., 55
  Polly, 109
  Rosa, 93
TROUT Sr., 81
TROVINGER Eliz., 58
  Mary, 56
  Reb., 119
TROXALL Eliz., 84
  Sr., 28
TROXELL Ann H., 2
TRUBEY Mary, 115
TRYTLE Cath., 104
TUCKER Eliz., 54
  Sus., 116
TURK, Cath., 83
TURNBECKER Marg., 82
TURNBOLT Sr. J., 20
TURNBULL Eliz., 69
TURNER Eliza Jane, 91
  Hen., 79
  Jane E., 92
  Mary, 31
  Mary A., 40
  Mary Jane, 116
  Reb., 54
  Sr., 67
  Susan, 52
TUTTEROW Eliz., 18
TUTWILER Fanny, 108
  Mary, 5
TWA Ann, 106
TWIG Cath., 54

TWIGG Sr., 97
TYLER Cath., 77
  Rachel, 6
TYSHER Dorothy, 93
  Eliz., 45
  Polly, 110
TYSON, Peggy, 47

-U-
ULHUM Jane, 73
UMBAUGH Kate E., 40
UNCLESBEE Belinda, 115
UNDERWOOD Susan, 100
UNGER Cath., 29
  Eliz., 34, 94
  Kate F., 9
  Sr., 20
  Susan, 87
UNKEL Marg., 48
UNKLESBEE Marg., 52
UNSELD Caroline, 87
UPDEGRAFF Leah, 118
  Mary E., 3
  Sr. A., 11
USHER Eleanor, 56

-V-
VAN HORN Matilda, 4
VAN LEAR Eliz., 22
  Eliz. England, 116
  Eliza, 33
  Maria, 17
  Mary, 33
  Mary I., 97
VAN METER Maria C., 111
  Na., 40
  Rachel, 48
VAN SWEARINGER
  Virginia T., 15
VANMETER Sr. Ann, 35
VANSANT Betsy, 24
VARNER Chna., 10
  Eliz., 102
  Mary, 7, 56
  Na., 105
VARVEL Marg. A., 29
VAS So., 1
VENRICK Eliz., 98
VERBLE Sr., 58
VERNON, Eliza, 99
VERROW, Eve, 89
VICARS Na., 66
VINCENHENNER Cath., 76

-W-
WACHTEL Ann Eliz., 44
  Emily V., 1
  Mag., 57
  Mary, 110

Mary Cath., 9
WACHTELL Sus., 39
WADE Eliz., 50, 91
  Jane, 9
  Mar. E., 33
  Mary, 106
  Ruhanmah, 15
  Sr. W., 106
  Susan, 69
WAGELLY Julianna, 109
WAGELY Barb., 113
WAGGONER Cath., 10
WAGNER Eliz., 81
  Marg., 57
WAGONER Ann S., 89
  Cath., 1, 29, 32
  Eliz., 14
  Marg., 8
  Maria L., 62
  Mary, 2, 46
  Mary L., 37
  Na., 38
  Sr., 22
WAKE Mary, 103
WAKENIGHT Caroline, 48
  Han., 15
WALDER Mary, 25
WALKER Marg., 21
  Sr., 52
WALLACE Cath., 46
  Eliza, 15
  Jane, 100
WALLER Caroline R.,
104
WALLICH Eliz., 32
  Ros., 32
WALLICK Mary, 62
  Sr., 54
WALLING Eliz., 118
  Mercy, 87
WALLINGFORD Ann, 17
WALLIS Mary, 65
WALPER Cath., 117
WALTERS Debora Ann, 95
  Sr., 98
WALTMERRY Sus., 26
WALTZ Mary, 108
  Na., 79
WAMB Barb., 1
WANTZ Ann E., 59
WARAFELTS Char., 19
WARBLE Cath., 3
  Lavinia, 46
  Mary C., 93
WARD Cath., 103, 117
  Cath. R., 66
  Eliz., 14, 105
  Mary, 55
  Patty, 113
  Rachel Ann, 39

Ruth, 2
WARDS Har. Ann, 14
WARE Louisa, 41
WARENFELS Mary, 65
WARFIELD Hen., 48
WARNER Cath., 94
  Chna., 20, 51
  Eliz., 10, 25, 81,
119
  Marg., 65
  Mary, 35, 43, 59
  Ros., 23
  Sr., 101
WARREL Mary C., 101
WARTH Eliz., 8
WARVEL Roanna, 51
  Sr., 30
WARWELL Eliz., 118
WATEMAN Susan, 77
WATERS Marg. F., 40
  Phebe, 114
WATKINS Eliz., 103
  Marg. A., 7
  Ros., 48
WATS, Cecilia, 62
WATSON Eliz., 63, 99
  Ellender, 73
  Lucinda, 99
  Lydia Ann, 41
  M.I., 103
  Mar. E., 27
  Marg., 99
  Marg. A., 90
  Mary C., 90
  Sr., 22, 58
WATTERS Mary S., 102
WATTS Eliz., 101
  Eliz. S., 104
  Har. Am., 62
  Mary, 72
  Mary Ann, 82
  Na., 36
  Pamela, 65
  Prucila Ann, 70
  Rachel, 66
  Sr., 86, 101
  Sr. Ann, 58
  Sus., 86
WAUGH Ann, 120
  Hen., 50
  Sally S., 74
WAUGHTELE Mary, 57
WAUGHTELL Marg., 109
WAYMAN Juliann, 35
WEADDLE Mary, 97
WEAGLEY Mary Cath., 20
  Matilda, 116
WEAGLY Isa., 51
WEALCK Eliz., 43
WEAST Cath., 54

Eliz., 14, 28
  Kate, 14
  Marg., 29
  Mary Ann, 2
  Mary C., 36
  Polly, 12
  Ruanna, 55
  Sr. Ann, 10
  Sr. J., 26
WEAVER Cath., 8, 52,
72, 101, 102, 110
  Eliz., 62, 82, 112
  Jane, 64
  Mary, 76
  Sus., 15
WEBB Ann, 4, 91
  Ann Maria, 45
  Cath. V., 39
  Eliz. Agnes, 49
  Leticia, 106
  Marg., 4, 34
  Mary, 4, 14, 35,
110, 114
  Mary Ann H., 20
  Mary Florence, 47
  Sr., 17
WEBSTER Sr., 30
WECK Marg., 83
WECKNIGHT Ann Maria, 9
WEDDLE Cath., 90
WEIS Eliz., 53
  Joanna, 90
  Susan, 57
WEISEL Marg., 87
  Sr., 116
WEISELL Eliz., 23
WEISMILLER Rosaly, 33
WEISNER Eliz., 72
WEITZELL Cath., 90
WELCH Cath., 62
  Marg., 80
  Mary, 118
WELCHHONCE Mahala
Cath., 111
WELCK Sr. A., 87
WELD Mag., 58
WELDY Eliz., 38
WELLER, 52
  Eliz., 104
WELLINGER, Ann, 14
WELLS Am., 55
  Cath. R., 16
  Ellender, 96
  Mary, 55
  Ros., 98
  So., 73
WELSH Barb., 64
  Eliz., 62
  Ellen, 96
  Har., 12

Kate, 92
Levina, 81
Marg., 16
Mary, 115
Mary E., 9
Na., 14
Sr., 19
Susan, 102
WELSHANCE Mary E., 107
WELSHANS Ruth, 107
Susan, 88
WELTY Amey, 32
Barb., 105
Cath., 32, 82
Cath. E., 53
Eliz., 9, 50, 51,
81, 106
Elizth, 114
Eve, 92
Lydia, 4
Mag., 30
Manscella, 59
Mary, 28, 37, 40,
96, 112
Na., 76, 112
WELTZHEIMER Mary, 61
WENDLING Han., 60
WENTLING Cath., 102
WENTLINGER Mary, 1
Mary A., 67
WERDEBECKER, Sus., 64
WERRICK Winney, 85
WERTEBECKER Eliz., 69
Mag., 55
WERTZ Sus., 65
WEST Elisa, 86
Eliz., 12
Eliza, 50
Isa., 69
Mary, 8
Mary Ann, 37
Matilda, 66
WESTEBERGER Mary, 66
Sus., 34
WESTENBERGER Cath., 1,
2
Eliz., 88
Sr., 91
WESTERBERGER Na., 58
Sus., 80
WESTONHAVER Cath., 47
WEVER Cath. W., 20
Char. D., 92
Eliz., 100
Emeline, 82
Louisa, 43
WHALEN Marg., 68
WHARTON Mary A.M., 2
WHEELER Na., 3
WHELING Mary, 28

WHERITT Ann C., 29
WHERRETT Cath., 34
Marg., 57
WHERROTT Lavina, 49
WHETSTONE, Eliz., 73
Marg., 10
Polly, 114
Sr., 98
WHETTIS Polly, 63
WHETZEL Susan, 97
WHIP Cath., 85
Ros., 3
WHITE Abigail, 27
Caroline E., 58
Cath., 60
Cynthia, 13
Marg., 38, 66, 84
Mary, 16
Na., 111
Ros. M., 16
Sus., 16
Susan, 20
WHITEKENNICK
(WITHENNECK)
Providence, 5
WHITINGTON Na. Ann, 47
WHITMIRE Cath., 51
WHITNEY Ann, 22
WHOY, Marg., 51
WIANT Cath., 30
Mary, 109
WICE Lay Ann, 28
WICKERS Rachel, 19
WICKERT Mary, 94
WICKHAM Mariah, 41
WIDDIS, Delilah, 60
WIEVEL Eliz., 97
WIGGINS Na., 64
Patty, 106
WIGGINTON Amanda, 25
WIKE Jane, 21
WILCOX Sr. Ann, 7
WILDERS Mary, 69
WILDS Barb., 28
WILDT Sr. C., 29
WILES Cath., 51
Mary C., 33
Reb. M., 86
WILHELM Ann Cath., 7
WILHIDE Mary Jane, 21
WILKENS Sr., 11
WILKES Eliz., 10
WILKINHOOD Julian, 116
WILKINS Ann, 23
Cath., 54
Lucinda Jane, 39
Moly, 96
Sr., 95
WILKINSON Na., 28
Rachel, 81

Sr., 67
Susan, 18
WILKS Cath., 34
Char., 5
WILL Eliz., 111
WILLCHANTZ Ruhannah,
116
WILLIAMS Cath. R., 37
Eleanor, 82
Eliz., 4, 5, 8
Eliz. B., 18
Ellen, 78, 103
Han., 17
Jane, 10, 72
Laura S., 50
Louisa Jane, 14
Mar., 8
Maria A., 6
Maria So., 14
Marietta, 42
Mary, 17, 43, 49
Na., 54, 81
Polly, 58
Prudence, 102
Rachel, 44, 51
Sr., 109
Sr. F., 114
Sr. S., 85
Virginia, 5
WILLIAMSON Jane, 80
Rachel, 35
WILLIARD Ann Jane, 22
Eliz., 87
Mary, 98
WILLIS Lucy Ann, 75
Sr., 27
WILLS Eliz., 60
WILLYARD Mary Ann, 60
WILSON, Cath., 67
Eliz., 3, 35, 54,
114, 119
Eliz. R., 68
Han., 13
Har., 10, 54
Lydia, 49
Maria, 108
Mary, 97, 99
Mary Ann, 23, 109
Na., 8
Reb., 32
Sr., 97
Sr. Ann, 41
WILT Sus., 2
WILTSHIRE, Ann M., 16
WIMMER Marg., 49
WINDEL Milkey, 57
WINDELL Eliz., 89
WINDER Cath., 62
Lavinia G., 13
Mary E., 53

Urilla, 30
WINDERS Ann Mary, 103
  Commella, 96
  Emily I., 31
  Lydia, 45
  Mary, 117
  Matilda, 100
  Matty, 40
  Na., 5
  Sr., 56, 60
  Sr. A., 73
  Susan, 5, 73
WINDLE Har., 119
  Na., 21
WINDSOR M.T.A., 68
WINEBRENNER Mary, 50
WINNELL Eliz., 84
WINSBOROW Marg., 47
WINSIGLER Mary Ann, 21
WINTERMYER Ann, 34
WINTERS Ann, 113
  Ann E., 50
  Anna, 110
  Annie M., 2
  Eliz., 1
  Marg., 61
  Mary, 35
  Mary Jane, 3
  Na. C., 37
  Sr. Ann, 55
  Sus., 60
  Susan, 6
WIREMAN Mary, 80
WISE Ann Mary, 11
  Ann. M., 15
  Eliz., 39
  Lucinda, 17
  Marg. Ann, 48
  Mary, 88, 119
WISENINGER So., 99
WISEWENKLE Na., 40
WISHARD Cath., 27
WISHART Sr., 39
WISINGER Eliz., 114
WISMAN Barb., 116
WISNER Barb., 94
WISSINGER Eliz., 114
WITHERS Susan, 69
WITHNAY Mary, 66
WITMER Barb., 117
  Cath. 12, 104
  Cornelia, 27
  Eliz., 25
  Eliza, 44
  Eliza H., 78
  Mary, 88
WITTER Maria, 48
  Na., 13
WOCHTEL Cath., 57
WOCHTELL Sr., 64

WOLAND Eliz., 19
WOLCOTT Eliz., 24
WOLDWINE Marg., 30
WOLESLAGER Cath., 98
WOLF Barb., 101
  Caroline, 35
  Cath., 65, 86, 118
  Eliz., 3, 20, 27,
  32, 35, 71, 86, 98
  Eve, 20, 23
  Frances, 62
  Julia Ann, 91
  Juliann, 77
  Lucretia, 51
  Mag., 45
  Malinda, 32
  Marg., 27, 29
  Marg. Ann, 62
  Maria, 53
  Mary, 30, 63, 98,
  100, 115
  Mary Ann, 110
  Mary C., 39
  Mary Susan, 34
  Peggy, 50
  Savilla, 70
  So., 102
  Sr., 33, 44, 79, 104
  Sus., 95, 105
  Susan, 113
  Susan Ann, 66
  Susan S., 54
  Tracy, 9
WOLFE Cath., 88
  Sus., 15
  Susan, 64
WOLFELSBURGER Cath.,
62
WOLFENBERGER Francis,
115
WOLFENSBERGER Eliz.,
49
  Na., 36
  Sus., 61
WOLFERSBERGER Cath.,
86
  Eleanora, 73
  Eliz., 58
  Mary, 40
  Mary Ann, 101
  Sr., 12, 71
WOLFERSBURGER Mary, 85
WOLFINGER Mary I., 19
WOLFKILL Eliza, 62
  Maria, 105
  Mary, 94
  Na., 77
WOLFORD Am., 119
  Eliz., 58
  Mary, 45, 66

Na., 10
  Polly, 51
  Saville, 65
  Sr., 21
  Susan, 15
WOLGAMOT Eliz., 106
WOLGAMOTT Mary, 5
WOLGOMOT Cath., 61
  Han., 48
WOLSLAGER Mary, 98
WOLTZ Angelica, 9
  Marg., 30
  Mary Eliza, 64
WOLVERTON Am. C., 105
  Char., 41
WOOD Eliz., 19
  Jane, 14
  Mary, 111
WOODBURY Eliz. B., 85
  Ellen M., 48
WOODEN Sr., 108
WOODWARD Jemimah, 50
WOOLFORD Sus., 59
WORLEY Amanda, 65
  Cath., 15
  Comfort Am., 84
  Mary, 30
WORNICK Barb., 32
WORSTER Elisha, 95
WOTTEN Mary, 12
WRIGHT Ann, 19
  Barb., 22
  Eliz., 70
  Jane, 54, 100
  Marg., 113
  Mary, 33
  Peggy, 111
  Sus., 13
WRITS Peggy, 94
WYAND Susan, 118
WYANT Eliz., 25
  Peggy, 72
  Polly, 30
  Sus., 28, 90
WYANTINE Cath., 100
WYLAND Ann, 89
WYLES Han., 32
WYNE Chra., 25
WYONFELTS Mag., 65

-Y-
YAKEL Eliz., 51, 104
YAKLE Sus., 34
YALER, Susan, 118
YARNALL Mary D., 6
YATES Sr., 104
  Susan, 80
YEAKEL Ann R., 90
  Caroline, 32
  Kate M., 43

Sr. A., 70
YEAKLE Chna., 59
  Mary Ann, 63
  Polly, 95
  Reb., 52
YEANEWEIRE Na., 9
YEARTY Sally, 49
YERK Peggy, 22
YERTY Amanda C., 59
  Ann, 54
  Eliz., 49, 78
  So., 49
YERTZ Abigail, 112
YESSLER Eliz., 29
YETNYRE Betsey, 119
YINGLING Cath., 8
YOE Mary E., 33
  Sr. Ann, 98
YONTZ Caroline, 109
  Eliz., 4
  Eliza Ann, 23
  Sr., 2
YOST, Lucinda H., 113
  Mary, 73
  Sus., 8
YOUNCE Polly, 57
YOUNG Ann, 1
  Ann Caroline, 70
  Cassandra, 10
  Cath., 2, 56, 58,
78, 97
  Chna., 46, 52
  Eliz., 7, 20, 37,
56, 91
  Eliza, 42
  Har. Ann, 71
  Jane, 40
  Lydia Ann, 112
  Malinda, 88
  Marg., 101, 120
  Maria, 72
  Mary, 8, 15, 48, 86,
107, 114
  Mary Ann, 114
  Mary Mag., 58
  Matilda, 101
  Reb., 60, 105
  Ruth, 11
  Sally, 44
  Sr., 20, 39, 60, 80
  Sr. Ann, 85
  Sr. J., 11
  Susan, 99
YOUNGERT Mary, 34
YOUNKINS A.C., 55
YOURCUS, Eliz., 19
YOUTZ Reb., 45, 52
  Willimina, 95
YOWLER Eliza, 1

-Z-
ZACHARIAS Cath., 12
  Eliz., 60, 64
ZEAKMAN Esther, 102
ZEIGLER Ann, 47, 63
  Barb., 14
  Cath., 15, 99
  Eliz., 70
  Han., 9
  Mag., 45
  Mary, 52
  Mary C., 42
  Molly, 93
ZEKEL Cath., 47
ZELLER Eliz. M., 57
  Marg., 22
  Mary, 22, 72
ZELLERS Helen, 33
  Marg., 117
  Mary, 73, 117
  Mary Matilda, 83
  Sr., 117
ZEMFT Chna., 52
ZENTMYER Eliz., 4
  Sr., 22
ZERBE Cath., 117
ZILHART Eliz., 58
  Sr., 120
ZIMMERMAN Amanda H.,
92
  Ann, 89
  Barb., 70
  Cath., 17
  Eliz., 13
  Lucretia A., 100
  Mar., 76
  Mary F., 49
  Na., 3
  Sr., 33, 90
  Susan, 112
ZIRK Phebe, 116
ZITTLE Ann Maria, 73
  Eliz., 46
  Mary Ann, 56
  Na., 73
  Susan, 83
ZOLLINGER Cath., 107
ZORR Eliz., 113
ZUCK Ann S., 115
  Lavina, 10
  Mary, 23, 24
  Na., 4, 71
ZWISHER Adeline M.L.,
26